CONTEMPORARY COMPOSERS ON CONTEMPORARY MUSIC

Expanded Edition

Contemporary
Composers

on Contemporary Music

Expanded Edition

Edited by
Elliott Schwartz and
Barney Childs
with Jim Fox

DA CAPO PRESS • NEW YORK

Library of Congress Cataloging-in-Publication Data

Contemporary composers on contemporary music / edited by Elliott
Schwartz and Barney Childs with Jim Fox.—Expanded ed.

  p.   cm.

  ISBN 0-306-80819-6 (alk. paper)

  1. Music—20th century—History and criticism. I. Schwartz, Elliott,
1936– . II. Childs, Barney. III. Fox, James, 1953– .

ML197.C7512 1998

780'.9'04—dc21   97-45587

                                                     CIP

                                                   MN

First Da Capo Press edition 1998

This Da Capo Press paperback edition of *Contemporary Composers
on Contemporary Music* is an expanded edition of the one first
published in New York in 1967, with minor textual emendations,
a new preface, and fifteen essays new to this edition.

Designer: Ernst Reichl

Published by Da Capo Press, Inc.
A Subsidiary of Plenum Publishing Corporation
233 Spring Street, New York, N.Y. 10013

Manufactured in the United States of America

ACKNOWLEDGMENTS   Grateful acknowledgment is made to the following publishers, authors, and agents who have so generously granted permission to reprint from their publications:

Aspen Institute for Humanistic Studies, Aspen, Colorado, for "Remarks on Receiving the Aspen Award," by Benjamin Britten; first printed in the *Saturday Review,* August 22, 1964.

Victor Bator for "The Influence of Peasant Music on Modern Music," by Béla Bartók; first printed in *Tempo,* Winter 1949-50; copyright by Victor Bator, Trustee of the Béla Bartók Estate.

John Cage for "An Interview with Roger Reynolds," first printed in *Generation;* copyright © 1962 by the University of Michigan.

The Chrysalis West Foundation for "What Concerns Me Is Music," by Charles Wuorinen; first printed in *Genesis West,* September, 1962; copyright © 1962 by The Chrysalis West Foundation.

Cornell University Press, Ithaca, New York, for excerpts from *The Making of Music,* by Ralph Vaughan Williams; copyright © 1955 by Cornell University.

Dobson Books, Ltd., London, England, for excerpts from *Erik Satie,* by Rollo H. Myers.

Doubleday & Company, Inc., Garden City, New York, for excerpts from *Dialogues and a Diary,* by Igor Stravinsky with Robert Craft; © 1961, 1962, 1963 by Igor Stravinsky.

Dover Publications, Inc., New York, New York, for excerpts from "Sketch of a New Esthetic of Music," by Ferruccio Busoni, reprinted 1962 in *Three Classics in the Aesthetic of Music,* by Debussy, Busoni, and Ives.

Harvard University Press, Cambridge, Massachusetts, for excerpts from *Music and Imagination,* by Aaron Copland; copyright 1952 by the President and Fellows of Harvard College; and for excerpts from *A Composer's World,* by Paul Hindemith, copyright 1952 by the President and Fellows of Harvard College.

High Fidelity, Great Barrington, Massachusetts, for "Who Cares If You Listen," by Milton Babbitt; copyright © 1958 by *High Fidelity.*

Journal of Music Theory, New Haven, Connecticut, for "Some Random Remarks on Electronic Music," by Otto Luening; copyright © 1964 by Yale School of Music.

Alfred A. Knopf, Inc., New York, New York, for excerpts from *Notes Without Music* by Darius Milhaud; copyright 1952, 1953 by Alfred A. Knopf, Inc.; and for excerpts from *New Musical Resources,* by Henry Cowell. Copyright 1930 by Alfred A. Knopf, Inc.; copyright renewed © 1958 by Henry Cowell.

Kulchur, New York, New York, for "An Interview with Morton Feldman," by Robert Ashley; copyright © 1965 by *Kulchur.*

Modern Music for "Folksong—American Big Business," by Roy Harris; copyright 1940 by the League of Composers—I.S.C.M.

Music Journal, New York, New York, for "Music and the Times," by Dimitri Shostakovitch; copyright © 1965 by *Music Journal.*

The Musical Quarterly, New York, for "Shop Talk by an American Composer," by Elliott Carter; copyright © 1960 by G. Schirmer, Inc.; and for "Man and Music," by Ernest Bloch; copyright 1933 by G. Schirmer, Inc.

v

The Music Review, Essex, England, for "Why is Schoenberg's Music so Hard to Understand?" by Alban Berg; copyright © 1956 by *The Music Review.*

W. W. Norton & Company, Inc., New York, New York, for excerpts from *Essays Before a Sonata and Other Writings,* by Charles Ives. Selected and edited by Howard Boatwright. Copyright © 1961, 1962 by W. W. Norton & Company, Inc.

Opera News, New York, New York, for "On Waiting for a Libretto," by Samuel Barber; copyright © 1958 by The Metropolitan Opera Guild, Inc.; and for "Grand and Not So Grand," by Jack Beeson; copyright © 1963 by The Metropolitan Opera Guild, Inc.

C. F. Peters Corporation for a portion of the score of John Cage's "Concert for Piano and Orchestra for Elaine de Kooning"; copyright © 1960 by Henmar Press Inc., New York, New York.

Princeton University Press, Princeton, New Jersey, for "The Changing Composer-Performer Relationship: A Monologue and a Dialogue," by Lukas Foss; copyright © 1963 by Princeton University; and for excerpts from *The Musical Experience of Composer, Performer, Listener,* by Roger Sessions; copyright © 1950 by Princeton University.

Random House, Inc., New York, New York, for excerpts from *Composers on Music,* edited by Sam Morgenstern; copyright © 1956 by Pantheon Books, Inc.; and for excerpts from *The State of Music;* Second Edition, Revised by Virgil Thomson; copyright © 1939, copyright © 1962 by Virgil Thomson.

The University of Wisconsin Press, Madison, Wisconsin, for excerpts from *Genesis of a Music,* by Harry Partch; copyright © 1949 by the Regents of the University of Wisconsin; copyright renewed © 1964 by Harry Partch.

The Viking Press, Inc., New York, New York, for excerpts from *Monsieur Croche the Dilettante Hater,* by Claude Debussy; copyright © 1928 by The Viking Press, Inc.; copyright © 1956 by The Viking Press, Inc.

La Monte Young for "Composers, Performance and Publication," and "Music, Electronic and Performed," by Richard Maxfield; originally printed in *An Anthology,* edited by La Monte Young; copyright © 1963 by La Monte Young and Jackson MacLow.

ACKNOWLEDGMENTS TO THE EXPANDED EDITION Grateful acknowledgment is made to the following publishers and authors who have so generously granted permission to reprint from their publications:

T. J. Anderson, for Elliott Schwartz's interview with the composer, undertaken in 1996 expressly for this volume.

Cornelius Cardew Estate, for "On Criticism" by Cornelius Cardew. For further information contact (UK) +44-181-299-1826.

European American Music Distributors Corporation, sole U.S. and Canadian agent for B. Schott's Soehne and Ernst Eulenberg, Ltd., London, for "György Ligeti—an interview with Josef Häusler"; originally published in German in *György Ligeti: eine Monographie,* by Ove Nordwall; copyright © 1971 by B. Schott's Soehne, Mainz; copyright © renewed. English translation by Sarah E. Soulsby published in *György Ligeti: in Conversation*; © 1983 by Ernst Eulenberg, Ltd., London. All rights reserved.

Brian Ferneyhough and James Boros, for "Composing a Viable (if Transitory Self): Brian Ferneyhough in Conversation with James Boros," first printed in *Perspectives of New Music*, Volume 32, Number 1 (Winter 1994).

Ben Johnston, for "Maximum Clarity," written in 1996 expressly for this volume.

Graham Lock for his interview with Anthony Braxton, excerpted from *Forces in Motion: Anthony Braxton and the Meta-reality of Creative Music* (Quartet Books, Ltd., London, 1988; U.S. edition by Da Capo Press).

Alvin Lucier for excerpts from *Chambers* (Wesleyan University Press, 1980).

New England Conservatory of Music, Boston, Massachusetts, for "Third Stream Revisited," by Gunther Schuller, first printed in an NEC brochure (1981); reprinted in *Musings*, by Gunther Schuller; copyright © 1986 by Oxford University Press.

Pauline Oliveros for "Some Sound Observations," first printed in *Source: Music of the Avant Garde* (1967); reprinted in *Software for People: Writings 1963-1980*, by Pauline Oliveros (Smith Publications/Printed Editions, 1982).

Oxford University Press, Oxford, England, for "Dreaming on Things to Come..." by Michael Tippett, reprinted from *Tippett on Music*, edited by Meirion Bowen; copyright © 1995 by Michael Tippett.

Pro/Am Music Resources, Inc., for William Bolcom's essay reprinted from *Something About the Music 2: Anthology of Critical Opinions*, edited by Thomas P. Lewis (1991).

Dorothea Redepenning for her interview with Sofia Gubaidulina, first printed as "Sofia Gubaidulina im Gespräch," in *Russische Avantgarde: Musikavantgarde im Osten Europas* (Heidelberg, 1992).

Steve Reich, for "Music as a Gradual Process (1968)," reprinted in *Writings About Music*, by Steve Reich (New York University Press, 1974).

George Rochberg for "On the Third String Quartet," first printed in *The Aesthetics of Survival: A Composer's View of Twentieth-Century Music*; copyright © 1984 by University of Michigan Press.

Gunther Schuller for "Third Stream," first printed in *The Saturday Review* (1961); reprinted in *Musings*, by Gunther Schuller; copyright © 1986 by Oxford University Press.

Karlheinz Stockhausen for "Five Revolutions Since 1950," originally "Fünf musikalische Revolutionen seit 1950," translated by Tim Nevill, reprinted in *Stockhausen, 60, Geburstag* (Kürten, 1988).

Preface to the Expanded Edition

During the thirty years that have elapsed since the first edition of this volume, there have been many dramatic changes in the musical landscape. When *Contemporary Composers on Contemporary Music* first appeared in 1967, certain musical values had acquired considerable weight, and were regarded by most musicians and listeners as solidly entrenched. We assumed that we knew the difference between "classical" concert music of the Western art tradition, and other brands of musical experience: jazz, popular and vernacular styles, and the musics of non-European cultures. These different strands rarely, if ever, mixed. And in the domain of classical concert music, atonality—whether articulated by rigorously serial means, or invoked through the employment of chance (in composition, performance, or both)—had seemingly triumphed over the extended tonality of Neoclassicism, not only at the "cutting edge" of new-music circles but in university and conservatory classrooms throughout the Western world. Other musical dimensions, apart from pitch, commanded our attention as well. Many composers, taking their cue from the models of Webern, Varèse, Cage, or Babbitt, had perfected an expressive language which delighted in sudden surprises, kaleidoscopic shifts in register, color and dynamic level, abrupt, aperiodic rhythms, and complex—or at least everchanging—textures.

Consistency was also considered a virtue, perhaps the greatest virtue. That is, most composers—no matter what their attitude to issues of pitch control or notational rigor—believed that one should "follow through" on the premises of a work, and that once a sound world and a grammar had been established it should be maintained. The fact that certain composers (such as Ives) refused to abide by this philosophy only confirmed their unique status as eccentrics or amateurs.

How values have changed! As early as the 1970s, the concern for stylistic consistency had begun to weaken, and soon gave way to a fresh look at eclecticism, collage and cultural cross-fertilization. Similarly, we began to see new approaches to tonality. Many of these musical changes were spurred on by even broader changes in the culture at large: the increasing influence of non-Eurocentric art and thought in our lives, the breakdown of distinctions between the "classical" and other styles of Western art, and the artistic (even multi-media) implications of the new digital technology. On another level, the influence of electronics upon our everyday musical environment has been all-pervasive. (Consider the increased use of amplification and electric instruments in live performance, the development of videotape and the compact disc, the esthetic of extreme discontinuity common to MTV and pop music radio, the eclectic juxtaposition of discs in record stores.) This electronic revolution has undoubtedly transformed our musical thinking and esthetic experience; composers have been quick to use those altered perceptions in creative ways.

Certainly in the late 1990s, there are as many prevailing styles and "trends" as there are composers. In some quarters, the "new romanticism" is ascendant: broad, sweeping gestures, *arioso* melody, and even a mystical, religious quality at times. Other composers may focus upon repetition and gradual process as primary structural and esthetic elements (the "new simplicity"); in contrast, another school of composers may delight in the "new complexity" which stresses simultaneous levels of intricate aperiodic rhythms and a textural fabric of dense overlays. In fact, it is fair to say, as our century comes to an end, that the state of contemporary music is richer, healthier and broader than ever before.

For this new edition of *Contemporary Composers on Contemporary Music* we have added a number of essays and interviews, by composers who have come to prominence since the 1960s or whose writings were not available when material for the earlier book was compiled. The new list extends from Braxton to Stockhausen, Gubaidulina to Bolcom, Oliveros to Ligeti. They represent a broad variety of viewpoints. If they were to agree on anything, it would probably be that the past thirty years have given rise to tumultuous changes and a host of new musical issues, and that (as always) these issues and concerns are best articulated by composers themselves.

There are many people who helped with the preparation of this volume, and to whom we offer our acknowledgment and appreciation. We reserve very special thanks to Jim Fox, who served as Barney Childs' right-hand man and alter ego; this volume could not have been completed without him. Thanks are due as well to Yuval Taylor, our editor at Da Capo Press for much of the manuscript's early life, and also to his successor Soo Mee Kwon. We are indebted to Laurel Fay, John Tilbury, Horace Cardew, Joan Tower, Michael Schelle, Brian Ferneyhough, Robert Hahn, Pamela Miller, and Dorothea Redepenning, for helping us with the daunting task of locating entries or securing permission to reprint. Scott Vaillancourt and Noel Verzosa of Bowdoin College performed important clerical duties without complaint, while Charlotta Janssen, Michael McDonnell and Jesse Shore assisted us with translations. Dorothy Schwartz wins Grand Prize for patience, encouragement and understanding, as always.

ELLIOTT SCHWARTZ   BARNEY CHILDS
South Freeport, Maine   Redlands, California
September 1997

Preface to the Original Edition

This collection of essays by composers of the twentieth century has been compiled on the basis of two important assumptions held by the editors. First, we believe that the study of contemporary music, like that of the music of earlier periods, must not be restricted to a mere survey of structural innovations and historical data. Valuable though such material may be, it can be properly evaluated only when considered in the context of a total musical philosophy encompassing the purposes and functions of music in society and the changing roles of its composers, performers, and audiences.

Similarly, an introductory study of techniques—serial organization, for example, or polytonality—is not enough, either for the layman or for the professional musician. Nor does even a thorough survey of the literature itself, of the major works and important composers, suffice to close the very real gap between the composer of new music and the musical public.

For these reasons, we believe that the music of our time is best understood as the product of a continuing esthetic revolution that involves a multiplicity of new ways of thinking about music, relating music to life and to society, relating composer and performer to music—and, to a great extent, reconsidering the postulates behind the definition of "music" itself. When twentieth-century music is studied in the context of this esthetic revolution, the rationale—in fact, the necessity—of structural innovation, as well as the significance of major figures, poses considerably fewer problems.

Second, we feel that these new attitudes and approaches have been best articulated by the composers themselves. Composers have always been able to satisfy the need to communicate, verbally as well as musically, with their colleagues and with an informed audience. In this century, composers have become prolific authors and persuasive speakers, and their comments and reflections, whether scholarly articles, popular books, lecture notes, or journals and autobiographies, are invaluable.

The essays in this volume have been assembled in order that the attitudes and musical philosophies of many contemporary composers might become more readily accessible to those interested in the music of this century. Admittedly, this material—with some notable exceptions—is available elsewhere, in a scattered variety of journals, books, and lecture texts, some of which are not easily obtainable or even out of print. There are many advantages in having this material collected in one volume, and we hope that the book will be of use to a great variety of readers. Concertgoers, amateur musicians, and all music lovers who are concerned with contemporary developments should find the essays highly provocative. We hope, furthermore, that this book will be valuable as a primary or supplementary text in contemporary music courses, and we trust that those involved in such other areas of study as esthetics, music history, introductory music, and humanities will find it useful as well. For this reason, most of the essays selected are relatively non-technical, requiring little or no knowledge of notation. The esthetic convictions and assertions set forth in this book are, therefore, equally accessible to the layman and the experienced musician.

The selection of specific composers and essays is, necessarily, an arbitrary procedure, determined in part by our own prejudices. We have attempted to include those composers who best represent the major musical trends of the century, including those of the immediate present. We wished to present a cross-section of generations, of cultural differences —notably European and American—and of widely divergent basic attitudes. The division of the volume into two large sections is equally arbitrary, but we feel that it represents a useful introductory long-range view of twentieth-century musical developments. Composers have been grouped according to their esthetic inclinations rather than their nationality or generation: first, those figures who worked within the mainstream of the European tradition, either by extending its premises or by consciously altering them; and second, the composers—many of them representing the immediate present—who have been more frankly "experimental," often working from premises alien to those of the mainstream. There has been no attempt, other than by this large division, to group composers into schools, influences, or other dubious pigeonholes. Each composer is, in one sense, "influenced" by the work of all other composers, and yet each man's approach is unique; any obvious relationships will be made apparent in the writings of the composers themselves.

For a number of reasons—in some cases because no writing was available or suitable for our purposes, in others because permission to reprint was denied us—several composers of importance are not represented. We particularly regret the omission of any writing by Anton Webern, Arnold Schoenberg, and such representatives of the European avant-garde as Boulez and Stockhausen. We have, nonetheless, a significant group of composers of stature and, hopefully, a consensus of all schools of thought and musical attitudes. A number of these contributions—those by Stefan Wolpe, Henry Brant, Morton Feldman, Chou Wen-Chung and Charles Wuorinen—have been written or rewritten specifically for this collection. These few essays alone demonstrate that the range and scope of composers' ideas about new music is varied and exciting; it is our hope that the ideas

Preface

in this book will enhance the understanding of contemporary music itself, thus making it more accessible to a larger audience.

We are indebted to many people for their advice, critical suggestions, and assistance with the preparation of the manuscript. Among those who have helped us the most in these respects are Vicki Lucas, Pat Schrock, John Landahl, Buryl Red, Milton Babbitt, Otto Luening, Dr. Benjamin Suchoff, Jeanette Ginn, John Rogers, Daphne Ehrlich, and Austin Clarkson. A Shell Grant from Bowdoin College partially financed the typing of the manuscript from our illegible notes and interview tapes.

Elliott Schwartz Barney Childs

Brunswick, Maine Deep Springs, California

February
1966

Introduction: The Revolution in Musical Esthetics

Any understanding of developments in twentieth-century music must inescapably begin with an awareness of the immediate nineteenth-century background. With Wagner and the other late German Romantics, certain musical tendencies had been developed to a point not previously reached. The vocabulary of tonal-functional harmony had been extended, by the use of extreme chromaticism, well into regions of ambiguity. Broadly coloristic techniques in the handling of orchestral masses had brought about the near-abandonment of rhythmic motion and motoric pulse, as well as the clearer textures of earlier years. With the expansion of the tonal vocabulary by means of increasingly complex chromaticism, harmonic motion — the maintenance of tension through the use of particular relationships of consonance and dissonance — became extreme.

As this approach to the materials of music evolved during the nineteenth century, parallel developments were taking place in the area of musical esthetics. The changes of emphasis in the musical language were being utilized to articulate new musical objectives. More than ever before, music came to stand for the expression of the individual composer's subjective will or self, and presented a moralistic picture through highly associational means. The earlier — and, by the nineteenth century, virtually unquestioned — doctrine of the "affections," which assumed that certain musical sounds, harmonies, and effects were inescapably linked to predictable and invariant emotional responses, was now combined with a new reliance upon the association of music with color, picture, the written word, and theatrical presentation. A highly programmatic and sensuous musical fabric resulted — in short, the stylistic approach that we inevitably associate with Romanticism. According to the adherents of this approach, music was "about" something; music "said" something to man's deepest emotions, and this operated not only on the immediate level of direct story-telling but beyond this into the realm of evocation and indirect association.

Twentieth-century music has dealt with these nineteenth-century heritages in many different ways, but the reactions can be best grouped to show, first, recognition and expansion, and second, opposition. The esthetic of late nineteenth-century music was extended by many composers, principally by the Austrian and German followers of Wagner. In the music of Mahler, Strauss, Schoenberg, Berg, and Webern, the ambiguity of Wagnerian tonal-functional harmony was taken to its logical conclusion, and resulted in the decay and final breakdown of the tonal system. It was replaced by the system of composing with twelve tones, introduced by Schoenberg. This concept resulted in the creation of a "serial" musical language, in which a composition is developed completely from an ordered set of the twelve tones of the chromatic scale, with vertical "harmonic" relationships replaced by intervallic and distributive aspects of this set.

With this also came what has been referred to as "the emancipation of the dissonance," in which dissonance became gradually independent of its previous tonal-harmony function and, finally, became a meaningless term. Although the shapes and structures of nineteenth-century music were often retained — the musical "forms" persist through Webern — the broader concept of "form" as such was freed of its dependence on the organizing implications of functional harmony, and thus became much more fluid in abstract and non-programmatic music.

Although these innovations may at first seem far removed from Romanticism, they have clearly come about as natural extrapolations from late nineteenth-century trends. Furthermore, these composers of the post-Wagnerian tradition retained the sense of gesture, the rhetoric, the approach to music as "expression," and the basic view of music as a moral and emotional force, of their predecessors.

On the other hand, there were those who turned away completely from this heritage, openly rejecting both its means and its ends; this reaction is principally apparent in twentieth-century French music. In the tradition of the French painters who were stimulated by new optical discoveries about the nature of color, Debussy's impressionism sought to present the essence of the moment, or the perceived, in music. Despite Debussy's innovations — a new treatment of tonal harmony, the use of exotic scales, the reduction of the coloristic palette to the nuanced, the delicate, and the transparent, and the limitation of musical gesture and rhetoric to an intimate scope — Impressionism remained basically Romantic in its esthetic assumption.

With Satie and Busoni, there came a much clearer break with the past. They effected a return to simpler textures, a heightened attention to musical objectivity in contrast to late Romantic expressivity, a strong basis in tonally-centered vocabulary, and a renewal of rhythmic drive as a structural force. Dissonance came to be used less in terms of harmonic function and more for its value in effects of shock, wit, and irony, more as "discord." These men were the first of a number of composers who made the conscious effort to return lightness, often in the form of humor, to music. All these tendencies are apparent in the early work of Stravinsky and Hindemith as well as in the music of Milhaud, Poulenc, and Prokofiev.

Much of this music composed in Europe from 1910 to 1930 is also important in that it represents the first attempt to utilize unusual musical material. Debussy's interest in Oriental music, the impact of that period's pseudo-African jazz on Stravinsky and others, the exotic elements absorbed by Milhaud during his years in South America are all examples of this departure from the Germanic tradition. At the same time nationalistic and ethnic materials provided another musical resource. Many composers incorporated unusual scales and modes, folk rhythmic and melodic material into their personal styles. Bartók and Vaughan Williams did research in the folk music of their countrymen; Bloch explored the heritage of Jewish music; Sibelius in Finland, and Copland and Harris in America drew not only from the actual material of the music but also from the spirit of the land and the people of their countries.

We can see, therefore, that the change from the music of the late nineteenth century to that of the twentieth is evident in the composers' approach to materials alone. The already existing musical language was being re-styled, and in many instances new resources were incorporated into the language. Equally strong, however, was the accompanying shift in musical philosophy. With few exceptions, composers turned away from the nineteenth-century concept of music as an expression of subjective will and moral force.

The twentieth-century composer views his function objectively: his aim is to "make" something, in the manner of the professional craftsman, as well as he can, and often, thus, to fill a social need. Typical is Hindemith's concept of *Gebrauchsmusik*, the view that music for specific uses and particular occasions—pageants, national events, civic presentations, even for teaching situations—is as valid as the Romantic approach to a composition as a "grand" work of art. This is a return to an earlier concept, present in music from the Middle Ages through Beethoven, which assumed the composer to be a useful member of his society contributing to all occasions, rather than an eccentric personality set apart from his fellow man.

Stravinsky, too, redefines the creative act in terms of problem-solving, treating a musical work not as a vehicle for "expression" but as a series of intelligible patterns to be developed, analytically and objectively, organizing sound in time. However, this concept differs from that of *Gebrauchsmusik*; for Stravinsky, the composer is always a free agent, working independently of society, even though the creation of a piece for specific social use is one legitimate kind of problem to be dealt with as the composer may choose.

In one sense, both these views are "neo-Classic," for they revive attitudes of previous generations. Stravinsky's approach is similar to that of the composers of the Middle Ages and the Renaissance; Hindemith's position is closely allied to the great post-Renaissance eras of patronage. Both men reject the major esthetic of the nineteenth-century German composers, and this "Romantic" ideal is pursued faithfully only by such twentieth-century Expressionists as Schoenberg, Berg and Webern.

At the beginning of the twentieth century, two major developments took place in America: first, the recognition and use of many elements alien to the common practices of Western music, such as Eastern material, newly created scales, and experiments with microtones; second, the development of a new concern for sonority, the invention of new instruments and unusual ways of dealing with ordinary instruments. Experiments such as these were perhaps more naturally suited to the American environment. In this hemisphere, alliance with the Western musical tradition was artificial — imposed from Europe by importation, rather than indigenous to the land; for this reason, the alliance was easier to dissolve.

Similar experimental ideas had been tentatively advanced in Europe by Debussy, Busoni, and others, but had not been developed. Nor did the Americans who chose to follow these exploratory paths immediately influence their countrymen; the more experimental composers were for many years isolated creative talents not recognized by the imported European conservatory tradition which had long dominated American music. We have only recently begun to appreciate the significance of the work advanced by Ives, Ruggles and Brant in the east, Partch and Becker in the midwest, Cowell, Cage and Harrison in the west.

Further, in America, the "melting pot" encouraged a unique synthesis of the major European tendencies. Many American composers after World War I studied in Paris with Nadia Boulanger, either absorbing the Stravinsky-oriented discipline she propounded or, like Virgil Thomson, turning from it to the simplicity of such French composers as Satie. In the 'thirties, major European composers such as Bartók, Bloch, Hindemith, Schoenberg, and Stravinsky settled in America. Many of them influenced American composers directly, through their teaching at major universities. The "middle generation" of American twentieth-century composers therefore synthesized whatever they found valid in contemporary European trends with the growing individuality of "American" music as exemplified in the work of such men as Copland, Harris, Piston, and Sessions. They infused into their music a vitality and spacious tunefulness, a direct folk influence or, more indirectly, an evocation of national and regional atmosphere and the rhythms of jazz. The men of this generation were still fundamentally "conservative" in that they retained the shape and gesture, and often the emotional context, of the tradition of Western music.

The period after World War II produced several challenging new developments. Of these, the three most important were the expansion of serial technique, the evolution of electronic music, and the admission of chance, choice, and improvisation. Serial procedures, originally applied by Schoenberg and his disciples solely to pitch, were expanded to include strict mathematical organization of all the parameters of musical expression, such as rhythm, dynamics, timbre and duration. Similarly, the use of electronic media may demand considerable technical and mathematical knowledge on the part of the composer; utilizing the raw resources of electronically generated sound, traditional "musical" sound, or natural sound from the world about us, music is created on magnetic tape. The composer works directly with his sonic material rather than through the medium of performers and instruments.

Finally, many composers are working with music in which the performer's role is enlarged. The performer is allowed choices of what to play, when to play it, perhaps the possibility for improvisation and a role in the direct production, structuring, and ordering of material — all within larger limits set beforehand by the composer. Some composers use random or chance techniques in composing the music, in addition to allowing the performer freedom.

It is interesting to note the changes here in composer-performer relationships. In serial music and electronic music, the composer takes over many of the traditional functions of the performer, sometimes eliminating him altogether; in chance music, the performer is allowed to assume many of the standard obligations of the composer.

Of course, not every contemporary composer is working in these new directions. Many still write music, some of it excellent, in styles that derive directly from the "mainstream" of twentieth-century music. Today, however, there is a much wider range of musical and esthetic possibilities available to the composer, including total organization at one margin and total spontaneity at the other; these extremes, together with the ever-expanding middle ground, present a vast gamut of technique and esthetic for further development. However, since the "fringes" and more experimental developments possibly foreshadow a new musical synthesis to come, the remarks in the next few paragraphs will be directed to these.

The new rhetoric, defined by the three new styles, springs most directly from the work of Webern and Varèse, Ives and the other American experimentalists. It is marked by jagged melodic contours; tonality that is concealed if it is present at all; an interest in the potential of textures and sonorities; an objective and depersonalized use of musical instruments, involving extreme ranges and previously unorthodox sounds; and the fragmentation and dissolution of the melodic line. Most significant, however, is the breakdown in the concepts of continuity, structure, and form that constitute the last stronghold of earlier music.

The doctrine of the "affections" was given its first severe blow by Webern; post-1945 "experimentalists" finished the job. They asserted that music no longer need depend on what one writer has termed the "linguistic" flow, and refuted the assumption that the narrative progression, the development in time, of a musical composition should maintain itself, for formal and extra-musical reasons, in a continuity comparable to that of human speech or, more accurately, human thought. Furthermore, the more experimental composers have argued that this music is "about" nothing at all; its sole concern is with sound newly and freshly heard *as sound,* and silence as silence. Nevertheless, if the composer wishes, it is still possible for him to find the gamut of the entire expressive range in the new rhetoric.

Stravinsky's analytic approach to the process of composition has found general acceptance, at least to the degree that the *process* of composition often assumes great importance; in fact, according to this view, the piece *is* the working-out of a process. The process may be totally controlled, or may constitute an environment that is developed to allow choice and improvisation, or may occupy any of the variety of middle positions between these extremes. Despite the potential of this approach, there are composers who feel that the attention to process as pre-eminent is a crippling residuum of the past, and that music as such needs no such explication or justification.

Among the experimentalists, there is no longer any allegiance to *Gebrauchsmusik,* since this is highly specialized in its appeal to a specific audience and since the composer of such music may be forced to burden himself with limitations he finds technically and esthetically irksome. Nor is there today any specific nationalism in music; with the advent of serialism we are perhaps closer in the 1960's to an international style than at any time since the Renaissance.

It is too easy to say that the time-worn dichotomy of Classic vs Romantic is still with us. One factor to be considered, now more than ever, is the degree of control of means and process that the composer exerts in his composition. The chance composers, in their quest for unfettered expression, echo Romanticism; the serialists, in their insistence upon rational principles, would seem to be the heirs of Classicism. But in 1966 it is generally accepted that this dichotomy is the result of superficial classification. The difference between either previous Romanticism or previous

Introduction

Classicism and today's new music is in the conception of the function and nature of music.

We have seen, and will observe further in the essays collected here, the gradual transformation during this century of the composer's aims and ideals. The older music, "representational" and geared to our conditioned emotional responses through time-honored associations, has led composers into new avenues of expression, unusual relationships of pitch, timbre, and duration, and perhaps a new kind of abstraction — concerned with sound and structure for their own sake. Despite particular theoretical devices and approaches, it is in this esthetic distinction that we discover the true twentieth-century revolution in musical composition.

Contents

Contents

II. EXPERIMENTAL MUSIC AND AMERICAN DEVELOPMENTS

Contents

III. POSTMODERNISM AND RECENT CONCERNS

Contents

EUROPEAN
MUSIC
BEFORE
1945

1

Ferruccio Busoni

[1866 - 1924]

Although he was most famous in his lifetime—and is best remembered today—as a pianist rather than as a composer, Busoni's influence upon the course of music history has been considerable. Born in Italy and educated in Germany, he understood the musical traditions of both nations well, and attempted to reconcile them in his own music. Perhaps because of his objectivity, he was one of the first musicians in Germany to react negatively to the Romantic esthetic prevalent there. His position in the history of German music, therefore, is similar to that of Satie in France; like Satie, too, he saw years pass before his theories gained acceptance.

Much of Busoni's reaction to Wagnerianism took the form of a conscious espousal of earlier practices: the lyricism and lighter textures of Mozart, the Baroque fondness for counterpoint, and the use of small chamber ensembles and less pretentious forms. Indeed, the movement later known as neo-Classicism had its roots in the ideas first proposed by Busoni.

Many of his theories were far in advance of his time; his constructions of artificial scales (resulting from his refusal to accept the limitations of major and minor modes), his experiments with quarter-tones, and his interest in mechanical means of sound production are all prophetic of very recent practices. A number of such ideas are set forth in the following excerpts from his influential "Sketch of a New Esthetic of Music."

Busoni's influence may be observed in the music of Stravinsky, Bartok, and later German composers such as Hindemith, as well as his American pupil Otto Luening, whose work with electronic sound-producing media represents an uncanny fulfillment of one of Busoni's visions.

"Sketch of a new Esthetic of Music," translated by Dr. Theodore Baker, from *Three Classics in the Aesthetic of Music* (New York, Dover Publications, 1962), pp. 76-83, 88-97. This translation first published c. 1911.

From
"Sketch of a
New Esthetic of Music"

Music as art, our so-called occidental music, is hardly four hundred years old; its state is one of development, perhaps the very first stage of a development beyond present conception, and we—we talk of "classics" and "hallowed traditions"! And we have talked of them for a long time![1]

We have formulated rules, stated principles, laid down laws;—we apply laws made for maturity to a child that knows nothing of responsibility!

Young as it is, this child, we already recognize that it possesses one radiant attribute which signalizes it beyond all its elder sisters. And the lawgivers will not see this marvelous attribute, lest their laws should be thrown to the winds. This child—*it floats on air!* It touches not the earth with its feet. It knows no law of gravitation. It is wellnigh incorporeal. Its material is transparent. It is sonorous air. It is almost Nature herself. It is—free.

But freedom is something that mankind have never wholly comprehended, never realized to the full. They can neither recognize nor acknowledge it.

They disavow the mission of this child; they hang weights upon it. This buoyant creature must walk decently, like anybody else. It may scarcely be allowed to leap—when it were its joy to follow the line of the rainbow, and to break sunbeams with the clouds.

Music was born free; and to win freedom is its destiny. It will become the most complete of all reflexes of Nature by reason of its untrammeled immateriality. Even the poetic word ranks lower in point of incorporealness. It can gather together and disperse, can be motionless repose or wildest tempestuosity; it has the extremest heights perceptible to man —what other art has these?—and its emotion seizes the human heart with that intensity which is independent of the "idea."

It realizes a temperament, *without* describing it, with the mobility of the

[1] Tradition is a plaster mask taken from life, which, in the course of many years, and after passing through the hands of innumerable artisans, leaves its resemblance to the original largely a matter of imagination.

4

soul, with the swiftness of consecutive moments; and this, where painter or sculptor can represent only one side or one moment, and the poet tardily *communicates* a temperament and its manifestations by words.

Therefore, representation and description are not the nature of music; herewith we declare the invalidity of program-music, and arrive at the question: What are the aims of music?

Absolute Music! What the lawgivers mean by this, is perhaps remotest of all from the Absolute in music. "Absolute music" is a form-play without poetic program, in which the form is intended to have the leading part. But Form, in itself, is the opposite pole of absolute music, on which was bestowed the divine prerogative of buoyancy, of freedom from the limitations of matter. In a picture, the illustration of a sunset ends with the frame; the limitless natural phenomenon is enclosed in quadrilateral bounds; the cloud-form chosen for depiction remains unchanging for ever. Music can grow brighter or darker, shift hither or yon, and finally fade away like the sunset glow itself; and instinct leads the creative musician to employ the tones that press the same key within the human breast, and awaken the same response, as the processes in Nature.

Per contra, "absolute music" is something very sober, which reminds one of music-desks in orderly rows, of the relation of Tonic to Dominant, of Developments and Codas.

Methinks I hear the second violin struggling, a fourth below, to emulate the more dexterous first, and contending in needless contest merely to arrive at the starting-point. This sort of music ought rather to be called the "architectonic," or "symmetric," or "sectional," and derives from the circumstance that certain composers poured *their* spirit and *their* emotion into just this mould as lying nearest them or their time. Our lawgivers have identified the spirit and emotion, the individuality of these composers and their time, with "symmetric" music, and finally, being powerless to re-create either the spirit, or the emotion, or the time, have retained the Form as a symbol, and made it into a fetish, a religion. The composers sought and found this form as the aptest vehicle for communicating *their* ideas; their souls took flight—and the lawgivers discover and cherish the garments Euphorion left behind on earth.

> A lucky find! 'Twas now or never;
> The flame is gone, it's true—however,
>   No need to pity mankind now.
> Enough is left for many a poet's tiring,
>   Or to breed envy high and low;
> And though I have no talents here for hiring,
>   I'll hire the robe out, anyhow.

5

Ferruccio Busoni

Is it not singular, to demand of a composer originality in all things, and to forbid it as regards form? No wonder that, once he becomes original, he is accused of "formlessness." Mozart! the seeker and the finder, the great man with the childlike heart—it is he we marvel at, to whom we are devoted; but not his Tonic and Dominant, his Developments and Codas.

Such lust of liberation filled Beethoven, the romantic revolutionary, that he ascended one short step on the way leading music back to its loftier self:—a short step in the great task, a wide step in his own path. He did not quite reach absolute music, but in certain moments he devined it, as in the introduction to the fugue of the Sonata for Hammerclavier. Indeed, all composers have drawn nearest the true nature of music in preparatory and intermediary passages (preludes and transitions), where they felt at liberty to disregard symmetrical proportions, and unconsciously drew free breath. Even a Schumann (of so much lower stature) is seized, in such passages, by some feeling of the boundlessness of this pan-art (recall the transition to the last movement of the D-minor Symphony); and the same may be asserted of Brahms in the introduction to the Finale of his First Symphony.

But, the moment they cross the threshold of the *Principal Subject*, their attitude becomes stiff and conventional, like that of a man entering some bureau of high officialdom.

Next to Beethoven, Bach bears closest affinity to "infinite music."[2] His Organ Fantasias (but not the Fugues) have indubitably a strong dash of what might be overwritten "Man and Nature."[3] In him it appears most ingenuous because he had no reverence for his predecessors (although he esteemed and made use of them), and because the still novel acquisition of equal temperament opened a vista of—for the time being—endless new possibilities.

Therefore, Bach and Beethoven[4] are to be conceived as a *beginning*, and not as unsurpassable finalities. In spite and emotion they will probably remain unexcelled; and this, again, confirms the remark at the beginning of these lines: That spirit and emotion remain unchanged in value through changing years, and that he who mounts to their uttermost heights will always tower above the crowd.

---

[2] "Die Ur-Musik," is the author's happy phrase. But as this music *never has been*, our English terms like "primitive," "original," etc., would involve a *non sequitur* which is avoided, at least, by "infinite." [Translator's Note.]

[3] In the recitatives of his Passions we hear "human speech"; *not* "correct declamation."

[4] As characteristic traits of Beethoven's individuality I would mention the poetic fire, the strong human feeling (whence springs his revolutionary temper), and a portent of modern nervousness. These traits are certainly opposed to those of a "classic." Moreover, Beethoven is no "master," as the term applies to Mozart or the late Wagner, just because his art foreshadows a greater, as yet incomplete. (Compare the section next-following.)

What still remains to be surpassed, is their form of expression and their freedom. Wagner, a Germanic Titan, who touched our earthly horizon in orchestral tone-effect, who intensified the form of expression, but fashioned it into a *system* (music-drama, declamation, leading-motive), is on this account incapable of further intensification. His category begins and ends with himself; first, because he carried it to the highest perfection and finish; secondly, because his self-imposed task was of such a nature, that it could be achieved by one man alone.[5] The paths opened by Beethoven can be followed to their end only through generations. They—like all things in creation—may form only a circle; but a circle of such dimensions, that the portion visible to us seems like a straight line. Wagner's circle we can view in its entirety—a circle within the great circle.

The name of Wagner leads to program-music. This has been set up as a contrast to so-called "absolute" music, and these concepts have become so petrified that even persons of intelligence hold one or the other dogma, without recognition for a third possibility beyond and above the other two. In reality, program-music is precisely as one-sided and limited as that which is called absolute. In place of architectonic and symmetric formulas, instead of the relation of Tonic to Dominant, it has bound itself in the stays of a connecting poetic—sometimes even philosophic—program.

Every motive—so it seems to me—contains, like a seed its life-germ within itself. From the different plant-seeds grow different families or plants, dissimilar in form, foliage, blossom, fruit, growth and color.[6]

Even each individual plant belonging to one and the same species assumes, in size, form and strength, a growth peculiar to itself. And so, in each motive, there lies the embryo of its fully developed form; each one must unfold itself differently, yet each obediently follows the law of eternal harmony. *This form is imperishable, though each be unlike every other.*

The motive in a composition with program bears within itself the same natural necessity; but it must, even in its earliest phase of development renounce *its own proper mode of growth* to mould—or, rather, twist—itself to fit the needs of the program. Thus turned aside, at the outset, from the path traced by nature, it finally arrives at a wholly unexpected climax, whither it has been led, not by its own organization, but by the way laid down in the program, or the action, or the philosophical idea.

And how primitive must this art remain! True, there are unequivocal descriptive effects of tone-painting (from these the entire principle took its

---

[5] "Together with the problem, it gives us the solution," as I once said of Mozart.
[6] ". . . Beethoven, dont les esquisses *thématiques ou élémentaires* sont innombrables, mais qui, sitòt les thémes trouvés, semble par cela même en avoir établi tout le développement. . ." [Vincent d'Indy, in "César Franck."]

rise), but these means of expression are few and trivial, covering but a very small section of musical art. Begin with the most self-evident of all, the debasement of Tone to Noise in imitating the sounds of Nature—the rolling of thunder, the roar of forests, the cries of animals; then those somewhat less evident, symbolic—imitations of visual impressions, like the lightning-flash, springing movement, the flight of birds; again, those intelligible only through the mediation of the reflective brain, such as the trumpet-call as a warlike symbol, the shawm to betoken ruralism, march-rhythm to signify measured strides, the chorale as vehicle for religious feeling. Add to the above the characterization of nationalities—national instruments and airs—and we have a complete inventory of the arsenal of program-music. Movement and repose, minor and major, high and low, in their customary significance, round out the list.—These are auxiliaries, of which good use can be made upon a broad canvas, but which, taken by themselves, are no more to be called music than wax figures may pass for monuments.

And, after all, what can the presentation of a little happening upon this earth, the report concerning an annoying neighbor—no matter whether in the next room or in an adjoining quarter of the globe—have in common with that music which pervades the universe?

To music, indeed, it is given to set in vibration our human moods: Dread (*Leporello*), oppression of soul, invigoration, lassitude (Beethoven's last Quartets), decision (*Wotan*), hesitation, despondency, encouragement, harshness, tenderness, excitement, tranquillization, the feeling of surprise or expectancy, and still others; likewise the inner echo of external occurrences which is bound up in these moods of the soul. But not the moving cause itself of these spiritual affections;—not the joy over an avoided danger, not the danger itself, or the kind of danger which caused the dread; an emotional state, yes, but not the psychic species of this emotion, such as envy, or jealousy; and it is equally futile to attempt the expression, through music, of moral characteristics (vanity, cleverness), or abstract ideas like truth and justice. Is it possible to imagine how a poor, but contented man could be represented by music? The contentment, the soul-state, can be interpreted by music; but where does the poverty appear, or the important ethic problem stated in the words "poor, but contented"? This is due to the fact that "poor" connotes a phase of terrestrial and social conditions not to be found in the eternal harmony. And Music is a part of the vibrating universe.

I may be allowed to subjoin a few subsidiary reflections:—The greater part of modern theatre music suffers from the mistake of seeking to repeat the scenes passing on the stage, instead of fulfilling its own proper mission of interpreting the soul-states of the persons represented. When the scene presents the illusion of a thunderstorm, this is exhaustively apprehended by the eye. Nevertheless, nearly all composers strive to depict the storm in tones — which is not only a needless and feebler repetition, but likewise a failure to perform their true function. The person on the stage is either psychically influenced by the thunderstorm, or his mood, being absorbed in a train of thought of stronger influence, remains unaffected. The storm is visible and audible without aid from music; it is the invisible and inaudible, the spiritual processes of the personages portrayed, which music should render intelligible.

Again, there are "obvious" psychic conditions on the stage, whereof music need take no account. Suppose a theatrical situation in which a convivial company is passing at night and disappears from view, while in the foreground a silent, envenomed duel is in progress. Here the music, by means of continuing song, should keep in mind the jovial company now lost to sight; the acts and feelings of the pair in the foreground may be understood without further commentary, and the music — dramatically speaking — ought not to participate in their action and break the tragic silence.

Measurably justified, in my opinion, is the plan of the old opera, which concentrated and musically rounded out the passions aroused by a moving dramatic scene in a piece of set form (the aria). *Word* and stage-play conveyed the dramatic progress of the action, followed more or less meagrely by musical recitative; arrived at the point of rest, music resumed the reins. This is less extrinsic than some would now have us believe. On the other hand, it was the ossified form of the "aria" itself which led to inveracity of expression and decadence.

The creator should take over no traditional law in blind belief, which would make him view his own creative endeavor, from the outset, as an exception contrasting with that law. For his individual case he should seek out and formulate a fitting individual law, which, after the first complete realization, he should annul, that he himself may not be drawn into repetitions when his next work shall be in the making.

The function of the creative artist consists in making laws, not in following laws ready made. He who follows such laws, ceases to be a creator.

Creative power may be the more readily recognized, the more it shakes itself loose from tradition. But an intentional avoidance of the rules cannot masquerade as creative power, and still less engender it.

The true creator strives, in reality, after *perfection* only. And through bringing this into harmony with *his own* individuality, a new law arises without premeditation.

So narrow has our tonal range become, so stereotyped its form of expression, that nowadays there is not one familiar motive that cannot be fitted with some other familiar motive so that the two may be played simultaneously. Not to lose my way in trifling,[7] I shall refrain from giving examples.

That which, within our present-day music, most nearly approaches the essential nature of the art, is the Rest and the Hold (Pause). Consummate players, improvisers, know how to employ these instruments of expression in loftier and ampler measure. The tense silence between two movements — *in itself music*, in this environment — leaves wider scope for divination than the more determinate, but therefore less elastic sound.

What we now call our Tonal System is nothing more than a set of "signs"; an ingenious device to grasp somewhat of that eternal harmony; a meagre pocket-edition of that encyclopedic work; artificial light instead of the sun. — Have you ever noticed how people gaze open-mouthed at the brilliant illumination of a hall? They never do so at the millionfold brighter sunshine of noonday. —

And so, in music, the signs have assumed greater consequence than that which they ought to stand for, and can only suggest.

How important, indeed, are "Third," "Fifth," and "Octave"! How strictly we divide "consonances" from "dissonances" — *in a sphere where no dissonances can possibly exist!*

We have divided the octave into twelve equidistant degrees, because we had to manage somehow, and have constructed our instruments in such a way that we can never get in above or below or between them. Keyboard instruments, in particular, have so thoroughly schooled our ears that we are no longer capable of hearing anything else — incapable of hearing except through this impure medium. Yet Nature created an *infinite gradation — infinite!* who still knows it nowadays?[8]

[7] With a friend I once indulged in such trifling in order to ascertain how many commonly known compositions were written according to the scheme of the second theme in the Adagio of the Ninth Symphony. In a few moments we had collected some fifteen analogues of the most different kinds, among them specimens of the lowest type of art. And Beethoven himself: — Is the theme of the Finale in the "Fifth" any other than the one wherewith the "Second" introduces its Allegro? — or than the principal theme of the Third Piano Concerto, only in minor?

[8] The equal temperament of 12 degrees, which was discussed theoretically as early as about 1500, but not established as as a principle until shortly before 1700 (by Andreas Werkmeister), divides the octave into twelve equal portions (semitones, hence 'twelve-semitone system') through which mean values are obtained; no interval is perfectly pure, but all are fairly serviceable." (Reimann, "Musik-Lexikon.") Thus, through Andreas Werkmeister, this master-workman in art, we have gained the "twelve-semitone" system with intervals which are all impure, but fairly serviceable. But what is "pure," and what "impure"? We hear a piano "gone out of tune," and whose intervals may thus have become "pure, but unserviceable," and it sounds *impure* to us. The diplomatic "Twelve-semitone system" is an invention mothered by necessity; yet none the less do we sedulously guard its imperfections.

And within this duodecimal octave we have marked out a series of fixed intervals, seven in number, and founded thereon our entire art of music. What do I say—*one* series? Two such series, one for each leg: The Major and Minor Scales. When we start this series of intervals on some other degree of our semitonic ladder, we obtain a *new key*, and a "foreign" one, at that! How violently contracted a system arose from this initial confusion,[9] may be read in the law-books; we will not repeat it here.

We teach four-and-twenty keys, twelve times the two Series of Seven; but, in point of fact, we have at our command only two, the major key and the minor key. *The rest are merely transpositions.* By means of the several transpositions we are supposed to get different shades of harmony; but this is an illusion. In England, under the reign of the high "concert pitch," the most familiar works may be played a semitone higher than they are written, without changing their effect. Singers transpose an aria to suit their convenience, leaving untransposed what precedes and follows. Songwriters not infrequently publish their own compositions in three different pitches; in all three editions the pieces are precisely alike.

When a well-known face looks out of a window, it matters not whether it gazes down from the first story or the third.

Were it feasible to elevate or depress a landscape, far as eye can reach, by several hundred yards, the pictorial impression would neither gain nor lose by it.

Upon the two Series of Seven, the major key and the minor key, the whole art of music has been established; one limitation brings on the other.

To each of these a definite character has been attributed; we have learned and have taught that they should be heard as contrasts, and they have gradually acquired the significance of symbols:—Major and Minor—Maggiore e Minore—Contentment and Discontent—Joy and Sorrow—Light and Shade. The harmonic symbols have fenced in the expression of music, from Bach to Wagner, and yet further on until today and the day after to-morrow. *Minor* is employed with the same intention, and has the same effect upon us now, as two hundred years ago. Nowadays it is no longer possible to "compose" a funeral march, for it already exists, once for all. Even the least informed non-professional knows what to expect when a funeral march—whichever you please—is to be played. Even such an one can anticipate the difference between a symphony in major and one in minor. We are tyrannized by Major and Minor—by the bifurcated garment.

Strange, that one should feel major and minor as opposites. They both present the same face, now more joyous, now more serious; and a mere

---

[9] It is termed "The Science of Harmony."

touch of the brush suffices to turn the one into the other. The passage from either to the other is easy and imperceptible; when it occurs frequently and swfitly, the two begin to shimmer and coalesce indistinguishably. — But when we recognize that major and minor form one Whole with a double meaning, and that the "four-and-twenty keys" are simply an elevenfold transposition of the original twain, we arrive unconstrainedly at a perception of the UNITY *of our system of keys* [tonality]. The conceptions of "related" and "foreign" keys vanish, and with them the entire intricate theory of degrees and relations. *We possess one single key.* But it is of most meagre sort.

"Unity of the key-system."

— "I suppose you mean that 'key' and 'key-system' are the sunbeam and its diffraction into colors?"

No; that I can not mean. For our whole system of tone, key, and tonality, taken in its entirety, is only a part of a fraction of one diffracted ray from that Sun, "Music," in the empyrean of the "eternal harmony."

However deeply rooted the attachment to the habitual, and inertia, may be in the ways and nature of humankind, in equal measure are energy, and opposition to the existing order, characteristic of all that has life. Nature has her wiles, and persuades man, obstinately opposed through he be to progress and change; Nature progresses continually and changes unremittingly, but with so even and unnoticeable movement that men perceive only quiescence. Only on looking backward from a distance do they note with astonishment that they have been deceived.

The Reformer of any given period excites irritation for the reason that his changes find men unprepared, and, above all, because these changes are appreciable. The Reformer, in comparison with Nature, is undiplomatic; and, as a wholly logical consequence, his changes do not win general acceptance until Time, with subtle, imperceptible advance, has bridged over the leap of the self-assured leader. Yet we find cases in which the reformer marched abreast of the times, while the rest fell behind. And then they have to be forced and lashed to take the leap across the passage they have missed. I believe that the major-and minor key with its transpositional relations, our "twelve-semitone system," exhibits such a case of falling behind.

That some few have already felt how the intervals of the Series of Seven might be differently arranged (graduated) is manifested in isolated passages by Liszt, and recently by Debussy and his following, and even by Richard Strauss. Strong impulse, longing, gifted instinct, all speak from these strains. Yet it does not appear to me that a conscious and orderly conception of this intensified means of expression had been formed by these composers.

I have made an attempt to exhaust the possibilities of the arrangement of degrees within the seven-tone scale; and succeeded, by raising and lowering the intervals, in establishing *one hundred and thirteen different scales*. These 113 scales (within the octave C-C) comprise the greater part of our familiar twenty-four keys, and, furthermore, a series of new keys of peculiar character. But with these the mine is not exhausted, for we are at liberty to *transpose* each one of these 113, besides the blending of two such keys in harmony and melody.

There is a significant difference between the sound of the scale c-db-eb-fb-gb-ab-bb-c when c is taken as tonic, and the scale of db minor. By giving it the customary C-major triad as a fundamental harmony, a novel harmonic sensation is obtained. But now listen to this same scale supported alternately by the A-minor, Eb-major, and C-major triads, and you cannot avoid a feeling of delightful surprise at the strangely unfamiliar euphony.

But how would a lawgiver classify the tone-series c-db-eb-fb-g-a-b-c, c-db-eb-f-gb-a-b-c, c-d-eb-fb-gb-a-b-c, c-db-e-f-gb-a-bb-c? — or these, forsooth: c-d-eb-fb-g-a#-b-c, c-d-eb-fb-g#-a-b-c, c-db-eb-f#-g#-a-bb-c?

One cannot estimate at a glance what wealth of melodic and harmonic expression would thus be opened up to the hearing; but a great many novel possibilities may be accepted as certain, and are perceptible at a glance.

With this presentation, the unity of all keys may be considered as finally pronounced and justified. A kaleidoscopic blending and interchanging of twelve semitones within the three-mirror tube of Taste, Emotion, and Intention—the essential feature of the harmony of to-day.

The harmony of *to-day*, and not for long; for all signs presage a revolution, and a next step toward that "eternal harmony." Let us once again call to mind, that in this latter the gradation of the octave is *infinite*, and let us strive to draw a little nearer to infinitude. The tripartite tone (third of a tone) has for some time been demanding admittance, and we have left the call unheeded. Whoever has experimented, like myself (in a modest way), with this interval, and introduced (either with voice or with violin) two equidistant intermediate tones between the extremes of a whole tone, schooling his ear and his precision of attack, will not have failed to discern that tripartite tones are wholly independent intervals with a pronounced character, and not to be confounded with ill-tuned semitones. They form a refinement in chromatics based, as at present appears, on the whole-tone scale. Were we to adopt them without further preparation, we should have to give up the semi-tones and lose our "minor third" and "perfect fifth;" and this loss would be felt more keenly than the relative gain of a system of eighteen one-third tones.

But there is no apparent reason for giving up the semitones for the sake of this new system. By retaining, for each whole tone, a semitone, we obtain a second series of whole tones lying a semitone higher than the original series. Then, by dividing this second series of whole tones into third-tones, each third-tone in the lower series will be matched by a semitone in the higher series.

Thus we have really arrived at a system of whole tones divided into sixths of a tone; and we may be sure that even sixth-tones will sometime be adopted into musical speech. But the tonal system above sketched must first of all train the hearing to thirds of a tone, without giving up the semitones.

To summarize: We may set up either two series of third-tones, with an interval of a semitone between the series; or, the usual semitonic series *thrice repeated* at the interval of one-third of a tone.

Merely for the sake of distinction, let us call the first tone C, and the next third-tones C#, and D ; the first semitone (small) c, and its following thirds-c# and d ; the result is fully explained by the table below:

c	c#	db	d	d#	eb	e	e#	fb	f	f#	gb	g	g#	ab	a	a#	bb	
C	C#	Db	D	D#	Eb	E		Fb	F	F#	Gb	G	G#	Ab	A	A#	Bb	etc.

A preliminary expedient for notation might be, to draw six lines for the staff, using the lines for the whole tones and the spaces for the semitones:

then indicating the third-tones by sharps and flats:

etc.

The question of notation seems to me subordinate. On the other hand, the question is important and imperious, how and on what these tones are to be produced. Fortunately, while busied with this essay, I received from America direct and authentic intelligence which solves the problem in a

simple manner. I refer to an invention by Dr. Thaddeus Cahill.[10] He has
constructed a comprehensive apparatus which makes it possible to transform an electric current into a fixed and mathematically exact number of
vibrations. As pitch depends on the number of vibrations, and the apparatus may be "set" on any number desired, the infinite gradation of the
octave may be accomplished by merely moving a lever corresponding to
the pointer of a quadrant.

Only a long and careful series of experiments, and a continued training
of the ear, can render this unfamiliar material approachable and plastic for
the coming generation, and for Art.

And what a vista of fair hopes and dreamlike fancies is thus opened for
them both! Who has not dreamt that he could float on air? and firmly
believed his dream to be reality?—Let us take thought, how music may be
restored to its primitive, natural essence; let us free it from architectonic,
acoustic and esthetic dogmas; let it be pure invention and sentiment, in
harmonies, in forms, in tone-colors (for invention and sentiment are not the
prerogative of melody alone); let it follow the line of the rainbow and vie
with the clouds in breaking sunbeams; *let Music be naught else than
Nature mirrored by and reflected from the human breast;* for it is sounding
air and floats above and beyond the air; within Man himself as universally
and absolutely as in Creation entire; for it can gather together and disperse
without losing in intensity.

In his book "Beyond the Good and the Bad" (*Jenseits von Gut and
Böse*) Nietzsche says: "With regard to German music I consider precaution
necessary in various ways. Assuming that a person loves the South (as I
love it) as a great training-school for health of soul and sense in their
highest potency, as an uncontrollable flood and glamour of sunshine
spreading over a race of independent and self-reliant beings;—well, such
an one will learn to be more or less on his guard against German music,
because while spoiling his taste anew, it undermines his health.

"Such a Southlander (not by descent, but by belief) must, should he
dream of the future of music, likewise dream of a redemption of music
from the North, while in his ears there rings the prelude to a deeper,
mightier, perchance a more evil and more mysterious music, a super-
German music, which does not fade, wither and die away in view of the
blue, sensuous sea and the splendor of Mediterranean skies, as all German

[10] "New Music for an Old World." Dr. Thaddeus Cahill's Dynamophone, an extraordinary
electrical invention for producing scientifically perfect music. Article in McClure's Magazine
for July, 1906, by Ray Stannard Baker. Readers interested in the details of this invention are
referred to the above-mentioned magazine article.

music does; — a super-European music, that asserts itself even amid the tawny sunsets of the desert, whose soul is allied with the palm-tree, and can consort and prowl with great, beautiful, lonely beasts of prey.

"I could imagine a music whose rarest charm should consist in its complete divorce from the Good and the Bad; — only that its surface might be ruffled, as it were, by a longing as of a sailor for home, by variable golden shadows and tender frailties: — an Art which should see fleeing toward it, from afar off, the hues of a perishing moral world become wellnigh incomprehensible, and which should be hospitable and profound enough to harbor such belated fugitives."

And Tolstoi transmutes a landscape-impression into a musical impression when he writes, in "Lucerne": "Neither on the lake, nor on the mountains, nor in the skies, a single straight line, a single unmixed color, a single point of repose; — everywhere movement, irregularity, caprice, variety, and incessant interplay of shades and lines, and in it all the reposefulness, softness, harmony and inevitableness of Beauty."

Will this music ever be attained?

"Not all reach Nirvana; but he who, gifted from the beginning, learns everything that one ought to learn, experiences all that one should experience, renounces what one should renounce, develops what one should develop, realizes what one should realize — he shall reach Nirvana."[11] (Kern, *Geschichte des Buddhismus in Indien.*)

If Nirvana be the realm "beyond the Good and the Bad," *one* way leading thither is here pointed out. A way to the very portal. To the bars that divide Man from Eternity — or that open to admit that which was temporal. Beyond that portal sounds *music.* Not the strains of "musical art."[12] — It may be, that we must leave Earth to find that music. But only to the pilgrim who has succeeded on the way in freeing himself from earthly shackles, shall the bars open.

---

[11] As if anticipating my thoughts, M. Vincent d'Indy has just written me: ". . . laissant de côte les contingences et les petitesses de la vie pour regarder constamment vers un idéal qu'on ne pourra jamais atteindre, mais dont il est permis de se rapprocher."
[12] I think I have read, somewhere, that Liszt confined his Dante Symphony to the two movements, *Inferno* and *Purgatorio*, "because our tone-speech is inadequate to express the felicities of Paradise."

Claude Debussy
[1862 - 1918]

The stylistic innovations of Debussy and the other Impressionists, French and English, represent the first significant break with the nineteenth-century German tradition. Although no less Romantic in nature, and equally atmospheric and programmatic, Impressionism differs from the earlier tradition in many respects — particularly with reference to new concepts of harmony, form, and instrumentation. It provides an important transition between the Wagnerian esthetic and the more radical changes to come during the First World War.

The innovations most prominent in Debussy's work include a new concept of harmony, less functional and less subject to the scheme of consonant-dissonant relationships; brief, fragmented melodic lines, which are proliferated and extended, rather than "developed" in the traditional manner; the use of ancient and exotic scales; a less architectural, more flexible and spontaneous approach to forms and rhythm. By such means, Debussy arrived at an esthetic ideal far removed from the Wagnerian. He was concerned to achieve, above all, a clarity of line, an uncluttered and unlabored texture, and a rhetoric of implication rather than overstatement. As the following essays reveal, these aims are frequently stated with great precision and wit in his writings.

"Monsieur Croche the Dilettante Hater," translated by B. N. Langdon Davies (New York, 1928), reprinted in Three Classics in the Aesthetics of Music (New York, Dover Publications, 1962), pp. 16-19, 38-40, 44-49, 61-65.

From "Monsieur Croche the Dilettante Hater"

The Symphony

A fog of verbiage and criticism surrounds the *Choral Symphony*.[1] It is amazing that it has not been finally buried under the mass of prose which it has provoked. Wagner intended to complete the orchestration. Others fancied that they could explain and illustrate the theme by means of pictures. If we admit to a mystery in this Symphony we might clear it up; but is it worth while? There was not an ounce of literature in Beethoven, not at any rate in the accepted sense of the word. He had a great love of music, representing to him, as it did, the joy and passion piteously absent from his private life. Perhaps we ought in the *Choral Symphony* to look for nothing more than a magnificent gesture of musical pride. A little notebook with over two hundred different renderings of the dominant theme in the *Finale* of this Symphony shows how persistently Beethoven pursued his search and how entirely musical his guiding motive was; Schiller's lines can have only been used for their appeal to the ear. Beethoven determined that his leading idea should be essentially self-developing and, while it is of extraordinary beauty in itself, it becomes sublime because of its perfect response to his purpose. It is the most triumphant example of the moulding of an idea to the pre-conceived form; at each leap forward there is a new delight, without either effort or appearance of repetition; the magical blossoming, so to speak, of a tree whose leaves burst forth simultaneously. Nothing is superfluous in this stupendous work, not even the *Andante,* declared by modern aestheticism to be over long; is it not a subtly con-ceived pause between the persistent rhythm of the *Scherzo* and the instru-mental Flood that rolls the voices irresistibly onward to the glory of the *Finale*? Beethoven had already written eight symphonies and the figure nine seems to have had for him an almost mystic significance. He deter-mined to surpass himself. I can scarcely see how his success can be ques-tioned. The flood of human feeling which overflows the ordinary bounds of the symphony sprang from a soul drunk with liberty, which, by an ironical

[1] Beethoven's 9th Symphony in D minor, op. 125. The last movement is nominally a setting of Schiller's *Hymn to Joy*, with full orchestra, full choir and four solo singers.

18

decree of fate, beat itself against the gilded bars within which the misdi-
rected charity of the great had confined him. Beethoven must have suffered
cruelly in his ardent longing that humanity should find utterance through
him; hence the call of his thousand-voiced genius to the humblest and
poorest of his brethren. Did they hear it? That is the question. Recently the
Choral Symphony was performed together with several of Richard Wagner's highly-spiced masterpieces. Once again Tannhauser, Siegmund and
Lohengrin voiced the claims of the *leit-motif!* The stern and loyal mastery
of our great Beethoven easily triumphed over this vague and high-flown
charlatanism.

It seems to me that the proof of the futility of the symphony has been
established since Beethoven. Indeed, Schumann and Mendelssohn did no
more than respectfully repeat the same forms with less power. The Ninth
Symphony none the less was a demonstration of genius, a sublime desire
to augment and to liberate the usual forms by giving them the harmonious
proportions of a fresco.

Beethoven's real teaching then was not to preserve the old forms, still
less to follow in his early steps. We must throw wide the windows to the
open sky; they seem to me to have only just escaped being closed for ever.
The fact that here and there a genius succeeds in this form is but a poor
excuse for the laborious and stilted compositions which we are accustomed to call symphonies.

The young Russian school has endeavoured to give new life to the
symphony by borrowing ideas from popular melodies; it has succeeded in
cutting brilliant gems; but are not the themes entirely disproportionate to
the developments into which they have been forced? Yet the fashion for
popular airs has spread quickly throughout the musical world—from east
to west the tiniest villages have been ransacked and simple tunes, plucked
from the mouths of hoary peasants, find themselves, to their consternation,
trimmed with harmonic frills. This gives them an appearance of pathetic
discomfort, but a lordly counterpoint ordains that they shall forget their
peaceful origin.

Must we conclude that the symphony, in spite of so many attempted
transformations, belongs to the past by virtue of its studied elegance, its
formal elaboration and the philosophical and artificial attitude of its audience? Has it not in truth merely replaced its old tarnished frame of gold
with the stubborn brass of modern instrumentation?

A symphony is usually built up on a chant heard by the composer as a
child. The first section is the customary presentation of a theme on which
the composer proposes to work; then begins the necessary dismemberment; the second section seems to take place in an experimental labora-

tory; the third section cheers up a little in a quite childish way interspersed with deeply sentimental phrases during which the chant withdraws as is more seemly; but it reappears and the dismemberment goes on; the professional gentlemen, obviously interested, mop their brows and the audience calls for the composer. But the composer does not appear. He is engaged in listening modestly to the voice of tradition which prevents him, it seems to me, from hearing the voice that speaks within him.

Beethoven

Last Sunday was an irresistibly beautiful day. The first sunshine of spring seemed to preclude all idea of listening to music; it was weather to bring the swallows back again.

Weingartner[2] seized the opportunity to conduct the orchestra of the *Concerts Lamoureux*.[3] No one is perfect!

He first conducted the *Pastoral Symphony*[4] with the care of a conscientious gardener. He tidied it so neatly as to produce the illusion of a meticulously finished landscape in which the gently undulating hills are made of plush at ten francs the yard and the foliage is crimped with curling-tongs.

The popularity of the *Pastoral Symphony* is due to the widespread misunderstanding that exists between Man and Nature. Consider the scene on the banks of the stream: a stream to which it appears the oxen come to drink, so at least the bassoons would have us suppose; to say nothing of the wooden nightingale and the Swiss cuckoo-clock, more respresentative of the artistry of M. de Vaucanson[5] than of genuine Nature. It is unnecessarily imitative and the interpretation is entirely arbitrary.

How much more profound an interpretation of the beauty of a landscape do we find in other passages in the great Master, because, instead of an exact imitation, there is an emotional interpretation of what is invisible in Nature. Can the mystery of a forest be expressed by measuring the height of the trees? Is it not rather its fathomless depths that stir the imagination?

[2] The celebrated conductor and composer, Paul Felix Weingartner, was born in Zara, Dalmatia, in 1863.

[3] Charles Lamoureux, the founder of the celebrated Paris concerts bearing his name, born Bordeaux, 1834; died Paris, 1899. His son-in-law, Camille Chevillard, became his assistant and continued the concerts after Lamoureux's death.

[4] Beethoven's 6th Symphony in F major, op. 68.

[5] Jacques de Vaucanson, 1709-1782, a mechanician of Grenoble; his automata *The Duck* and *The Flute Player* are famous.

In this symphony Beethoven inaugurates an epoch when Nature was seen only through the pages of books. This is proved by the storm, a part of this same symphony, where the terror of man and Nature is draped in the folds of the cloak of romanticism amid the rumblings of rather disarming thunder.

It would be absurd to imagine that I am wanting in respect for Beethoven; yet a musician of his genius may be deceived more completely than another. No man is bound to write nothing but masterpieces; and, if the *Pastoral Symphony* is so regarded, the expression must be weakened as a description of the other symphonies. That is all I mean.

Then Weingartner conducted an orchestral fantasy by Chevillard[6]; in which the most extraordinary orchestration lends itself to a highly personal method of developing his ideas. A gentleman who was extremely fond of music furiously expressed his dislike of the fantasy by whistling on a key. This was excessively stupid. Could anyone tell whether the said gentleman was criticising Weingartner's manner of conducting or the composer's music? One reason is that the key is not an instrument of warfare, but a domestic article. Monsieur Croche always preferred the butcher-boys' elegant method of whistling with their fingers: it is louder. Perhaps the gentleman is still young enough to learn this art!

Weingartner recovered ground by conducting Liszt's *Mazeppa* magnificently. This symphonic poem is full of the worst faults, occasionally descending even to the commonplace; yet the stormy passion that rages throughout captures us at last so completely that we are content to accept it without further reasoning. We may affect an air of contempt on leaving, because that is pleasant—though it is sheer hypocrisy. The undeniable beauty of Liszt's works arises, I believe, from the fact that his love of music excluded every other kind of emotion. If sometimes he gets on easy terms with it and frankly takes it on his knee, this surely is no worse than the stilted manner of those who behave as though they were being introduced to it for the first time; very polite, but rather dull. Liszt's genius is often disordered and feverish, but that is better than rigid perfection, even in white gloves.

Weingartner's personal appearance suggests at the first glance a new knife. His gestures have a kind of angular grace; then suddenly the imperious movement of his arms seems to compel the trombones to bellow and to drive the cymbals to frenzy. It is most impressive and verges on the miraculous; the enthusiasm of the audience knows no bounds.

[6] See Note 3 above.

Richard Strauss

Richard Strauss,[7] who recently conducted the orchestra at the *Concerts Lamoureux*, is no relation to *The Blue Danube*:[8] he was born at Munich in 1864, where his father was a musician in the Royal Household. He is practically the only original composer in modern Germany; his remarkable technique in the art of handling an orchestra allies him to Liszt, while his desire to found his music on literature allies him to Berlioz; witness the titles of his symphonic poems, *Don Quixote, Thus Spake Zarathustra, The Merry Pranks of Till Eulenspiegel*. As a matter of fact the art of Richard Strauss is not invariably so exclusively interpretative; but he undoubtedly thinks in colour-pictures and he seems to draw the line of his ideas by means of the orchestra. This is no commonplace method and few people have adopted it. Richard Strauss, moreover, develops it along peculiarly personal lines; it is no longer the rigid and architectural method of Bach or Beethoven, but the working out of a scheme of rhythmic colours; he combines with the utmost assurance the most wildly discordant notes, quite regardless of their possibly painful effect as long as they satisfy his demand that they should live.

All these characteristics reach a pitch of frenzy in the *Heldenleben*, the symphonic poem of which Richard Strauss here gave the second performance in Paris. One may not care for certain experiments which border on the commonplace or for a kind of tortured Italianism; but after a minute or two one is captured first by the tremendous versatility of his orchestration, then by the frenzied energy which carries one with him for as long as he chooses; the hearer is no longer master of his emotions, he does not even notice that this symphonic poem exceeds the limits that our patience usually allows to such compositions.

Once again, it is a book of pictures, or even a cinematograph. But one must admit that the man who composed such a work at so continuously high a pressure is very nearly a genius.

He began by giving *Italy*, a symphonic fantasy in four parts—an early work, I believe—where the future originality of Strauss is already discernible. The elaboration seemed to me a trifle long and stereotyped. But the third part, *In the Bay of Sorrento*, is very beautiful in colour. Then came a love scene from *Feuersnot*, his last opera. This suffered considerably through being detached from its context; and, since the programme gave

[7] Richard Strauss, the famous conductor and composer of *Salome, Elektra, Der Rosenkavalier*, etc., was born in Munich, 1864.
[8] The famous waltz *An der schönen blauen Donau*, writtten by the famous composer and conductor of dance music, Johann Strauss, born Vienna, 1825; died 1899.

22

no explanation, its relation to the rest was wholly incomprehensible. An episode which evoked such orchestral torrents seemed somewhat formidable for a love scene! It is probable that in the opera the torrent is justified. Perhaps it may afford an opportunity for the opera houses to produce something new; for I do not think they can pretend to teach us anything at all by producing the modern operas of Young Italy.

Richard Strauss has no wild lock of hair, no epileptic gestures. He is tall and has the free and determined bearing of those great explorers who journey among savage tribes with a smile on their lips. Perhaps this sort of bearing is necessary to shake the conventionality of the public. He has, however, the head of a musician; but his eyes and gestures are those of a Superman, to quote Nietzsche, from whose teaching he must have imbibed his energy. From Nietzsche too he must have learned his lofty scorn of feeble sentimentalities and his desire that music should not go on for ever providing a more or less satisfactory illumination for our nights, but that it should shine like the sun. I can assure you that there is sunshine in the music of Strauss. Unquestionably the majority of the audience did not like sunshine of this kind, for quite famous musical enthusiasts showed unmistakable signs of impatience. But that did not prevent Strauss from being greeted with rapturous applause. I say again that it is not possible to withstand his irresistible domination.

Richard Wagner

The *Société des Grandes Auditions de France*[9] did not honour me with an invitation to listen to the recent performance of *Parsifal* at the *Nouveau Théâtre* under the director, Alfred Cortot.[10] Alfred Cortot is the French conductor who has used to the best advantage the pantomime customary to German conductors. Like Nikisch[11] — who, however, is Hungarian — he

---

[9] The *Société des Grandes Auditions Musicales de la France* was founded about twenty-five years ago by the Countess Greffulhe. The moving spirit was Raoul Gunsbourg (see note 13). Its activities were erratic and ceased to all intents and purposes about 1911.

[10] Alfred Denis Cortot, born Nyon, Switzerland, 1877; educated at the Paris Conservatoire, studied under Decambes, Rouquon and Diemer, winning the piano prize in 1896, and in that year made his debut at the Colonne concerts. He arranged and produced the first performance in Paris of *The Götterdämmerung* in 1902. From 1902 to 1911 he was director of the Chorus at Bayreuth. His first performance in England was at the Queen's Hall Orchestra Symphony Concert on February 14th, 1914.

[11] Arthur Nikisch, one of the foremost of the world's conductors, born 1855, on Baron Sina's estate in Hungary; died 1922.

has a lock of hair, and that lock is in the highest degree arresting owing to the quivers of passion which agitate it on the slightest provocation. Sometimes it droops sadly and wearily in the tender passages, interposing a complete screen between Cortot and the orchestra. Then again it rears itself proudly in the martial passages. At such moments Cortot advances on the orchestra and aims a threatening baton, like a banderillero when he wants to irritate the bull. The members of the orchestra are as cool as Icelanders: they have been there before. Cortot, like Weingartner, leans affectionately over the first violins, murmuring intimate secrets; he swoops round to the trombones, adjuring them with an eloquent gesture, that might be translated: "Now my lads! Put some go into it! Try to be supertrombones!" and the obedient trombones conscientiously do their best to swallow the brass tubes.

It is only fair to add that Cortot understands the innermost secrets of Wagner and is himself a perfect musician. He is young, his love of music is quite disinterested; and these are good reasons enough for not being too hard on him for gestures that are more decorative than useful.

To return to the *Société des Grandes Auditions,* did it intend to punish me for my Wagnerian iconoclasm by depriving me of *Parsifal?* Did it fear a subversive attitude or a bombshell? I do not know, but I should prefer to think that these private performances are designed for people whose nobility or position in high society entitles them to attend such little entertainments with a well-bred indifference to what is played. The unimpeachable distinction of the name on the programme frees them from the need of any other illumination and makes it possible to listen attentively to the latest scandal or to watch those pretty movements of the heads of women who are not listening to music. But let the *Société des Grandes Auditions* beware! They will turn Wagner's music into a fashionable at home. After all, that phase of Wagnerian art which originally imposed on his votaries costly pilgrimages and mysterious rites is irritating. I am well aware that this Religion of Art was one of Wagner's favourite ideas; and he was right, for such a formula is excellent for capturing and holding the imagination of an audience; but it has miscarried by becoming a kind of Religion of Luxury, excluding perforce many people who are richer in enthusiasm than in cash. The *Société des Grandes Auditions,* by carrying on these traditions of exclusiveness, seems to me doomed to end in that most detestable thing, the art of fashionable society. When Wagner was in a good humour he liked to maintain that he would never be so well understood as in France. Was he referring to aristocratic performances only? I do not think so. King Louis II of Bavaria[12] was already annoying him

[12] King Louis of Bavaria became Wagner's patron in 1864. It was due to him that Wagner became a naturalised Bavarian; and for him that Wagner wrote the *Huldigungsmarsch.*

enough with questions of arbitrary etiquette; and Wagner's proud sensitiveness was too acute to miss the fact that true fame comes solely from the masses and not from a more or less gilded and exclusive public. It is to be feared that these performances, directed avowedly at the diffusion of Wagnerian art, may serve only to alienate the sympathy of the masses: a cunning trick to make it unpopular. I do not mean that the performances will hasten a final eclipse; for Wagner's art can never completely die. It will suffer that inevitable decay, the cruel brand of time on all beautiful things; yet noble ruins must remain, in the shadow of which our grandchildren will brood over the past splendour of this man who, had he been a little more human, would have been altogether great.

In *Parsifal,* the final effort of a genius which compels our homage, Wagner tried to drive his music on a looser rein and let it breathe more freely. We have no longer the distraught breathlessness that characterises Tristan's morbid passion or Isolde's wild screams of frenzy; nor yet the grandiloquent commentary on the inhumanity of Wotan. Nowhere in Wagner's music is a more serene beauty attained than in the prelude to the third act of *Parsifal* and in the entire Good Friday episode; although, it must be admitted that Wagner's peculiar conception of human nature is also shown in the attitude of certain characters in this drama. Look at Amfortas, that melancholy Knight of the Grail, who whines like a shop girl and whimpers like a baby. Good heavens! A Knight of the Grail, a king's son, would plunge his spear into his own body rather than parade a guilty wound in doleful melodies for three acts! As for Kundry, that ancient rose of hell, she has furnished much copy for Wagnerian literature; and I confess I have but little affection for such a sentimental draggle-tail. Klingsor is the finest character in Parsifal: a quondam Knight of the Grail, sent packing from the Holy Place because of his too pronounced views on chastity. His bitter hatred is amazing; he knows the worth of men and scornfully weighs the strength of their vows of chastity in the balance. From this it is quite obvious that this crafty magician, this old gaol-bird, is not merely the only human character but the only moral character in this drama, in which the falsest moral and religious ideas are set forth, ideas of which the youthful Parsifal is the heroic and insipid champion.

Here in short is a Christian drama in which nobody is willing to sacrifice himself, though sacrifice is one of the highest of the Christian virtues! If Parsifal recovers his miraculous spear, it is thanks to old Kundry, the only creature actually sacrificed in the story: a victim twice over, once to the diabolical intrigues of Klingsor and again to the sacred spleen of a Knight of the Grail. The atmosphere is certainly religious, but why have the incidental children's voices such sinister harmonies? Think for a moment of the childlike candour that would have been conveyed if the spirit of Palestrina had been able to dictate its expression.

The above remarks only apply to the poet whom we are accustomed to admire in Wagner and have nothing to do with the musical beauty of the opera, which is supreme. It is incomparable and bewildering, splendid and strong. *Parsifal* is one of the loveliest monuments of sound ever raised to the serene glory of music.

Berlioz

Berlioz never had any luck. He suffered from the inadequacy of the orchestras and the intellects of his time. To-day, however, the inventive genius of M. Gunsbourg,[13] supported by the *Société des Grandes Auditions Musicales de France*, has undertaken to revive and to augment Berlioz's posthumous glory by adapting *The Damnation of Faust* to the stage.

Without condemning the policy of such an adaptation we may at least urge the undeniable fact that, since Berlioz died without leaving any precise views on its suitability, it is aesthetically debatable. Besides this, to step into a dead man's shoes without a specific invitation seems to me a deliberate flouting of the respect which we usually show to the dead. But here again M. Gunsbourg's unwavering confidence in his own genius gives him a natural right to treat Berlioz as a brother, and to carry out instructions which have probably come to him from beyond the grave.

In doing this M. Gunsbourg carries on the unfortunate tradition which requires masterpieces to breed a teeming horde of commentators, adapters and manipulators, whose representatives spring into existence without any further definite function than that of befogging with pompous words and epithets the said unhappy masterpieces.

Berlioz, alas, is not the only victim! There is the smile of the famous *Gioconda,* which a strange perversity has labelled for all time mysterious. There is Beethoven's *Choral Symphony* which has been subjected to such transcendental interpretations, that even such a powerful and straightforward work as this has become a universal nightmare. There is the whole work of Wagner, which needed all its solidity to withstand the industrious enthusiasm of its editors.

Such practices result in a kind of special literature and even in a recognised profession in which success is certain provided the beaten track is

[13] Raoul Gunsbourg, born at Bukarest, 1859; is a literary man, a composer and Director of the Opera at Monte Carlo. He organised a series of performances of *La Damnation de Faust* adapted for the stage. See note 9 on *La Société des Grandes Auditions Musicales de la France.*

never left, since its members being engaged in criticising others are bound to be immune from the danger of mutual criticism. In some respects it is a laudable profession; in others it seems to have a certain futility, though a greater or less degree of cleverness may win fame for its members.

So far, Berlioz had escaped any such intrusion; only Jullien,[14] in an admirably documented book, had piously recorded the calvary of his fame and Fantin-Latour had interpreted his music in lithographic dreams. Incidentally, the work of Berlioz, through his pre-occupation with colour and incident, became at once a subject for artists; one might even say without irony that Berlioz has always been the favourite musician of those who do not know much about music. Other musicians are alarmed at the liberties he takes with harmony — they even call them blunders — and his "Go-to-the-devil!" style. Are these the reasons which make his influence on modern music negligible and leave his own, in a way, unique? In France, with the exception of Gustave Charpentier,[15] I can hardly find a trace of his influence, and even there only in a superficial sense, since Charpentier's art is undoubtedly individual as far as concerns anything that is fundamental in his music.

This brings me to the fact that Berlioz was never, properly speaking, a stage-musician. Despite the real beauties of *Les Troyens,* a lyrical tragedy in two parts, faulty proportions make its performance difficult and produce an almost monotonous, not to say wearisome, effect. For the rest, Berlioz has nothing new to offer in this work. He echoes Gluck, whom he passionately admired, and Meyerbeer, whom he religiously hated. We must not seek Berlioz here. We must seek him in his pure symphonic music or in his *Enfance du Christ,* which is perhaps his masterpiece; nor must we forget the *Symphonie Fantastique* and the music of his *Romeo and Juliet.*

But M. Gunsbourg was on the watch and said: "My dear Berlioz, you know nothing about it! If you have never succeeded on the stage, it is because, unfortunately, I was not at hand to help you with my experience. Now you are dead, and we can put everything to rights. Listen! You composed a dramatic legend, *The Damnation of Faust.* It is not bad, but it is not alive! And what interest can you expect people to take in your *Marche Hongroise* if they do not see soldiers exercising at the back of the stage? As for your *Ballet des Sylphes,* it is most charming music. But you will never make me believe that a mere symphony orchestra can ever take the place

[14] Adolphe Jullien, the author of Hector Berlioz, *sa vie et ses œuvres,* illustrated with fourteen original lithogravures by Fantin-Latour, Paris, 1888.

[15] Gustave Charpentier, born Dieuze, 1860; best known as the composer of the opera *Louise.* In 1900 he founded the *Conservatoire populaire de Mimi Pinson* to give free courses in popular music and classical dancing.

of an attractive ballet dancer! Your *Course à l'Abîme* is terrifying, my dear fellow! But you wait and see; I will make it poignant and ghastly. I will turn aside the course of rivers in order to make natural waterfalls; I will make a rain of real blood supplied by the slaughter-houses; the horses of Faust and Mephistopheles shall trample upon real corpses. Fortunately, too, you won't be able to interfere! You were so eccentric when you were alive that your presence could only spoil the whole thing."

So saying, M. Gunsbourg set to work and adapted frantically. As he made his way through *Faust* he was even more convinced that this "confounded Berlioz" knew nothing whatever about it. "Too much music," he grumbled, and "what facility!" but "it is disconnected, I must have recitatives. It is a pity that he is really dead, but it can't be helped! We must get along without him." And M. Gunsbourg got along without him; he added recitatives and altered the order of the scenes. Everything, or nearly everything, gave him an excuse for ballets and supers, resulting in a performance in which the tricks of the pantomime were combined with the attractions of the *Folies-Bergère*.

At Monte Carlo it might have succeeded. People do not go there just to listen to beautiful music, which has about as much importance for them as a fine afternoon. The delightful adventurers who adorn that resort are not very particular, and the charming cosmopolitan young ladies only regard music as an unobtrusive and useful accompaniment to their smiles.

Something better was essential for Paris; so the *Société des Grandes Auditions*, for whose well-known eclecticism no sacrifice is too great, intervened. In this case, it seems to me, they sacrificed everything, even the most elementary good taste. Their desire to give France lessons in the best music has, I fear, carried them beyond all bounds; but the fashionable set, owing to a lack of interest, may be more easily deceived than others. Besides that, there were admirable singers such as M. Renaud, perhaps the only artist who, by his tact and good taste, could make the Mephistopheles, conceived by the fancy of M. Gunsbourg, tolerable. M. Alvarez and Mme. Calvé are too celebrated not to be perfect, even in *Faust*. But, good Heavens! what marionettes they had to be!

Finally, there are two beings who would have been amazed at the performance. In the first place Faust, though he did meet his old friend M. Colonne, would have been astonished at finding himself filling the passages in which he had been accustomed to keep still with a patomime which he would be at a loss to understand. In the second place the Spirit of Music would have recoiled from the consciousness of often being *de trop* or even utterly unnecessary. She is so little at home on the stage, poor thing, that she blushes at the sound of her own voice and at the awkward figure she cuts in the staging imposed on her by M. Gunsbourg.

**From "Monsieur Croche
the Dilettante Hater"**

For the future, M. Gunsbourg may sleep in peace. His bust will face that of Berlioz in the gardens at Monte Carlo; he will be much more at home there, and Berlioz will certainly have no reason to complain of his proximity.

Erik
Satie

[1866 - 1925]

It was Satie, even more than Debussy, who broke with the traditions of nineteenth-century Romanticism, and presented an entirely new system of esthetic values. When Satie's work first attracted widespread attention in the years immediately following World War I, these new values — simplicity, humor and satire, understatement rather than melodramatic rhetoric, and the use of jazz elements — were growing fashionable. Satie's music is particularly interesting, and in a sense prophetic, because he pursued these aims many years before his name became known to the musical world. Until that time — and, in some circles, for many years thereafter — he was regarded as no more than an amateurish dilettante.

There are many elements in Satie's work deserving of study, including his highly original approach to texture and harmony, but the aspect that most often continues to command attention is his wit. He used his great talent for satire as a weapon of propaganda, initially to combat the Wagnerianism that was stifling French music, and, later in his career, to denounce Impressionism as equally decadent and affected. Through his words and by the example of his music, Satie presented an alternative to the precious, atmospheric idiom that had superseded Wagnerian rhetoric but had not challenged its Romantic premises. Satie's work, in short, is aggressively anti-Romantic, and it was this quality above all that brought his name to the attention of Cocteau, Picasso, and such young French composers as Poulenc and Milhaud. His ideas about music, as evidenced by the following epigrammatic essays, remain as irreverent and biting as the music itself.

"Intelligence and Musicality Among the Animals," from Sam Morgenstern, *Composers on Music* (New York, Pantheon Books, 1956), pp. 357-58. First published in *La Revue S.I.M.*, X (1914), p. 69. Later translated by Rollo H. Myers, "The Orchestra in Opera" and "Debussy," *Erik Satie* (London, 1948), p. 32.

Three
Brief
Epigrams

Intelligence and Musicality
among the Animals

The intelligence of animals cannot be questioned. But what does man do to improve the mental level of those long-suffering co-citizens? He offers them a mediocre education, full of holes, incomplete, such as no human child would wish on himself, and he would be right, the little dear. This education aims above all at developing the instincts of cruelty and vice atavistically resident in the individual. In this curriculum questions of art, literature, natural and moral sciences or other matters do not appear. Carrier pigeons are in no way prepared for their mission by the study of geography; fishes are kept innocent of the study of oceanography; cattle, sheep and lambs are kept totally unaware of the scientific arrangements of a modern slaughterhouse, know nothing of the nutritive rôle they play in man-made society.

Few animals benefit from human instruction. The dog, the mule, the horse, the donkey, the parrot and a few others are the only animals to receive a semblance of education. And yet, can you call it education? Compare this instruction if you please, to that given the young human undergraduate by the universities, and you will see it is worthless, it can neither broaden the knowledge nor facilitate the learning which the animal might have acquired through his own labors, by his own devotion. But musically? Horses have learned to dance; spiders have remained under a piano throughout an entire concert—a long concert organized for them by a respected master. So what? So nothing. Now and then we are told about the musicality of the starling, the melodic memory of the crow, the harmonic ingenuity of the owl who accompanies himself by tapping his stomach—a purely artificial contrivance and polyphonically meagre.

As for the perennially cited nightingale, his musical knowledge makes his most ignorant auditors shrug. Not only is his voice not placed, but he absolutely no knowledge of clefs, tonality, modality or measure. Perhaps he is gifted? Possibly, almost certainly. But it can be stated flatly that his artistic culture does not equal his natural gifts, and that the voice of which he is so inordinately proud, is nothing but an inferior useless instrument.

The Orchestra
in Opera

There is no need for the orchestra to grimace when a character comes onstage. Do the trees in the scenery grimace? What we must do is create a musical scenery, a musical atmosphere in which the characters move and talk. No "couplets,"—no "leitmotiv," but aim at creating an atmosphere that suggests Puvis de Chavannes.

Debussy

When I first met Debussy, he was full of Moussorgsky and was very deliberately seeking a way that wasn't very easy for him to find. In this problem I was well in advance of him. I was not weighed down with the *Prix de Rome*, nor any other prize, for I am a man like Adam (of Paradise) who never won any prizes—a lazy fellow, no doubt.

At that time I was writing *Le Fils des etoiles* to a libretto by Joseph Péladan, and I explained to Debussy that a Frenchman had to free himself from the Wagnerian adventure, which wasn't the answer to our national aspirations. I also pointed out that I was in no way anti-Wagnerian, but that we should have a music of our own—if possible without any *Sauerkraut*.

Why could we not use the means that Claude Monet, Cezanne, Toulouse-Lautrec and others had made known? Why could we not transpose these means into music? Nothing simpler.

Darius
Milhaud

[1892 - 1974]

As a young man, Milhaud became seriously involved in the growing French reaction to both Impressionism and German Romanticism—a reaction that often took the form of satire, inspired by the music of Parisian music halls, circuses, and American jazz. Led informally by Erik Satie, and with Jean Cocteau as their literary spokesman, a small group of young composers began to impress this new esthetic upon musical Paris. The group became known simply as Les Six, and three of the six—Milhaud, Poulenc, and Honegger—rose to prominence as individual composers of importance.

Milhaud's music, both early and recent, demonstrates this reaction to the grand rhetoric of the nineteenth century. His style is fluently melodic, yet rhythmically driving, harmonically complex and often polytonal in texture. While always maintaining an objectivity opposed to the expressionistic German manner, the music nonetheless expresses a variety of moods, from the savage and barbaric to the gayly colorful. Milhaud is an important figure in the early development of contemporary techniques and musical philosophy, and has influenced many younger composers through his constant teaching and by his own creative work.

The following excerpts from Milhaud's autobiography recount a number of the significant influences upon his musical development, the early turning points in his career.

Notes without Music, translated by Donald Evans, edited by Rollo H. Myers (New York, A. A. Knopf, 1953), pp. 116-24.

From "Notes without Music"

My First Encounter
With Jazz

In June 1920 Claudel, who was then Minister to Denmark and High Commissioner for the Schleswig-Holstein plebiscite, came to Paris for a few days, and invited me to motor back with him to Copenhagen. I gladly accepted. We waited just long enough for me to get the necessary papers and then set out. We had with us Copeau's daughter, little Marie-Hélène, who was going to spend her vacation with her grandmother in Denmark. We were favored by the weather and had a very pleasant journey despite the fact that it was rather hurried because Claudel had to attend an official dinner on the occasion of the plebiscite that had just been held. So we sped across Belgium and Holland and through the empty harbors of a Germany in the deadly grip of inflation, across the Great Belt and the Little Belt, and over the plains of Denmark. One hour after our arrival at the Legation, Claudel, hatless and wearing the Grand Cordon of the Order of Danbrog, chewing leaves he idly plucked from the bushes as we went by, set out on foot for the Royal Palace.

I loved Copenhagen, with its sixteenth-century quays, its beautifully laid-out ancient palaces rubbing elbows with huge colorful modern brick buildings reddened by the sun. The museum amazed me by its important collection of sculptures by Carpeaux of the famous personalities of the Second Empire. Claudel took me to Elsinore. As we gazed at the portrait of the royal family, whose members had wedded so many sovereigns, Claudel confided in me that he would like to see a performance of Hamlet in a décor like that in the picture, with its padded furniture and satin cushions. As we went back to Copenhagen, the car seemed to be floating through a sea of cyclists lured out into the countryside by the long bright evenings. I took advantage of my free time to make a start on my first two Etudes for piano and orchestra and a dance suite for the piano, inspired by South American rhythms and not based on folk music, entitled Saudades do Brasil. Each piece bore the name of one of the districts of Rio.

I was to join Cocteau in London for some performances of Le Bœuf sur le *toit.* I went by way of Esbjerg. We soon realized that the charming young man who acted as our manager had only the vaguest ideas of how our show should be organized; instead of acrobatic dancers, he had engaged some weird-looking youths who looked as if they had come straight out of Whitechapel. The rehearsals were held at the Baroness d'Erlanger's house, Lord Byron's former town house in Piccadilly. Our dubious-looking actors came every day to study their dance movements among the priceless furniture of a richly appointed drawing-room. The bar was represented by a splendid Coromandel screen laid across two chairs. *Le Bœuf* was to hold the bill for two weeks at the Coliseum, London's biggest music hall. This seemed rather risky to us, but its audiences were apparently used to the most heterogenous programs; the Ballets Russes had played there with great success. The rehearsals were difficult, with musicians unaccustomed to playing music like mine, and I often had to berate the lady horn-players. To mollify me, they would show me photos of their babies during the intermissions. I conducted the first performance, and all went well. *Le Bœuf* was sandwiched in between a number by Japanese acrobats and Ruth Draper's highly original sketches. In any case, this was not the last time *Le Bœuf* was given in a music hall. Mme Rasimi, the manager of the Ba-ta-clan, put it in one of her revues, famous for their displays of nudity and their comedians' broad humor. One night Cocteau heard one of the audience—a workman wearing a cloth cap—say to his wife: "It ain't that it makes you laugh; but it's different, see, so it makes you laugh!"

It was during this visit to London that I first began to take an interest in jazz. Billy Arnold and his band, straight from New York, were playing in a Hammersmith dance hall, where the system of taxi-girls and taxi-boys had been introduced. A dozen young men in evening dress and girls in blue dresses with lace collars sat around in a box, and for sixpence any timid young man or neurotic old maid could have one of them to dance with. For the same fee they could have another dance with the same or any other partner.

In his *Coq et l'arlequin* Cocteau had described the jazz accompaniment to the number by Gaby Deslys at the Casino de Paris in 1918 as a "cataclysm in sound." In the course of frequent visits to Hammersmith, where I sat close to the musicians, I tried to analyze and assimilate what I heard. What a long way we had traveled from the gypsies who before the war used to pour their insipid, mawkish strains intimately into one's ears, or the singers whose glides, in the most dubious taste, were upborne by the wobbling notes of the cimbalom, or the crudity of our bals-musette, with the unsubtle forthrightness of cornet, accordion, and clarinet! The new music was extremely subtle in its use of timbre; the saxophone breaking in, squeezing out the juice of dreams, or the trumpet, dramatic or languorous by turns, the clarinet, frequently played in its upper register, the lyrical use of the trombone, glancing with its slide over quarter-tones in crescendos of volume and pitch, thus intensifying the feeling; and the whole, so various yet not disparate, held together by the piano and subtly punctuated by the complex rhythms of the percussion, a kind of inner beat, the vital pulse of the rhythmic life of the music. The constant use of syncopation in the melody was of such contrapuntal freedom that it gave the impression of unregulated improvisation, whereas in actual fact it was elaborately rehearsed daily, down to the last detail. I had the idea of using these timbres and rhythms in a work of chamber music, but first I had to penetrate more deeply into the arcana of this new musical form, whose technique still baffled me. The musicians who had already made use of jazz had confined themselves to what were more or less interpretations of dance music. Satie in the *Rag-Time du Paquebot* of *Parade* and Auric in the fox-trot *Adieu New York* had made use of an ordinary symphony orchestra, and Stravinsky had written his *Ragtime* for eleven solo instruments, including a cimbalom.

I had lost sight of Jean Wiéner since the war. Life had not been easy for him, and he was married and had a little daughter. Putting a bold face on things, he now earned his living by playing the piano in a night club. He came to me and suggested that we should transfer our Saturday evening meetings to the place where he worked. I was attracted by this idea and hurried off to see Cocteau, whom I greeted with the words: "I've got a bar for you!" The very next Saturday my apartment was abandoned in favor of the Bar Gaya in the rue Duphot. We were given a warm welcome by the owner, Moyses, who had even adorned the walls with little many-colored posters, each bearing one of our names. As the bar's customers invariably arrived later than we did, and left before us, there was always one part of the evening when we were all alone and free to make music to our hearts' content. Jean Wiéner played syncopated music with aerial grace and sensitivity, with an especially light rhythm. We loved to listen to his playing, and to that of his partner, Vance, the Negro, who was an admirable saxophonist and banjo-player. Without any transition these two would pass from fashionable ragtime and fox-trots to the most celebrated works of Bach. Besides, syncopated music calls for a rhythm as inexorably regular as that of Bach himself, which has the same basis.

In May 1921 Pierre Bertin put on an *avant-garde* show. The program included a play by Max Jacob, imbued with the spirit of chivalry, and Radiguet's charming one-act play *Le Pélican*, with music by Auric. I remember one very amusing scene in which Monsieur Pélican points out to his son that he ought to think of taking a pen name if he wanted to be a poet, to which the young man retorts that: "Pélican is no sillier than Corneille (crow) or Racine (root)." Together with these plays, a play by

Cocteau called *Le Gendarme incompris* was given; it rather audaciously introduces a whole passage from Mallarmé. This is so apt in the new context that, as it was pronounced with the traditional comic accent of the stage policeman, no one ever suspected its origin. Poulenc had composed music so witty and pungent that I have always felt sorry he would not allow it to be played again. Gratton, the Negro, danced a shimmy composed by me and entitled *Caramel mou*. (Cocteau had written some words for it; it was scored for clarinet, saxophone, trumpet, trombone, and percussion.) But the chief event of the evening was undoubtedly Satie's extraordinary play *La Piège de Méduse,* whose dialogue was full of his own inimitable wit. The unbridled fantasy of this play bordered on the absurd. In the role of Baron Méduse, Bertin wore a make-up that made him look like Satie himself; it was as if he had assumed the latter's actual bodily presence. The action was interrupted from time to time by a stuffed monkey, which came down from its pedestral to execute a little dance. Satie had written very short dance tunes scored for a small group of instruments; this was to be conducted by Golschmann, who, however, withdrew at the last minute as a result of a tiff.

Shows of this kind, so variegated in character, were excellent training for us, enabling us to experiment in all sorts of techniques and to strive constantly after new forms of expression.

"Musique d'ameublement"
and Catalogue Music

Just as one's field of vision embraces objects and forms, such as the pattern on the wallpaper, the cornice of the ceiling, or the frame of the mirror, which the eye sees but to which it pays no attention, though they are undoubtedly there, Satie thought that it would be amusing to have music that would not be listened to, *"musique d'ameublement,"* or background music that would vary like the furniture of the rooms in which it was played. Auric and Poulenc disapproved of this suggestion, but it tickled my fancy so much that I experimented with it, in cooperation with Satie, at a concert given in the Galerie Barbazange. During the program, Marcelle Meyer played music by Les Six, and Bertin presented a play by Max Jacob called *Un Figurant au théâtre de Nantes,* which required the services of a trombone. He also sang Stravinsky's *Berceuses du chat* to the accompaniment of three clarinets, so Satie and I scored our music for the instruments used in the course of these various items on the program. In order that the music might seem to come from all sides at once, we posted the clarinets in three different corners of the theater, the pianist in the fourth, and the trombone in a box on the balcony floor. A program note warned the audience that it was not to pay any more attention to the ritornellos that would be played during the intermissions than to the candelabra, the seats, or the balcony. Contrary to our expectations, however, as soon as the music started up, the audience began to stream back to their seats. It was no use for Satie to shout: "Go on talking! Walk about! Don't listen!" They listened without speaking. The whole effect was spoiled. Satie had not counted on the charm of his own music. This was our one and only public experiment with this sort of music. Nevertheless Satie wrote another *"ritournelle d'ameublement"* for Mrs. Eugene Meyer, of Washington, when she asked him, through me, to give her an autograph. But for this *Musique pour un cabinet préfectoral* to have its full meaning, she should have had it recorded and played over and over again, thus forming part of the furniture of her beautiful library in Crescent Place, adorning it for the ear in the same way as the still life by Manet adorned it for the eye. In any case, the future was to prove that Satie was right: nowadays, children and housewives fill their homes with unheeded music, reading and working to the sound of the radio. And in all public places, large stores and restaurants the customers are drenched in an unending flood of music. In America cafeterias are equipped with a sufficient number of machines for each client to be able, for the modest sum of five cents, to furnish his own solitude with music or supply a background for his conversation with his guest. Is this not *"musique d'ameublement,"* heard, but not listened to?

We frequently gave concerts in picture galleries. At Poiret's, Auric and I gave the first performance of Debussy's *Épigraphes antiques* for piano duet. At the Galerie la Boétie, Honegger played his violin sonatas with Vaurabourg, and the pianist André Salomon pieces by his friend Satie. Delgrange conducted my *Machines agricoles.*

I had written musical settings for descriptions of machinery taken from a catalogue that I had brought back from an exhibition of agricultural machinery which I had visited in company with Mme de B. and Mlle de S., who wanted to choose a reaper for their estate in the Bordeaux area. I had been so impressed by the beauty of these great multicolored metal insects, magnificent modern brothers to the plow and the scythe, that the idea came to me of celebrating them in music. I had put away in a drawer a number of catalogues, that I came across in 1919. I then composed a little suite for singer and seven solo instruments in the style of my little symphonies; the titles were *"La Faucheuse"* (reaper), *"La Lieuse"* (binder), *"La Déchaumeuse-Semeuse-Enfouisseuse"* (harrow, seeder, and burier), *"La Moissonneuse Espigadora"* (harvester), *"La Fouilleuse-Draineuse"* (subsoil and draining plow), "*La Faneuse*" (tedder). A few months later I used the same group of instruments for settings to some delightful poems by Lucien Daudet inspired by a florist's catalogue: *Catalogue de fleurs.*

Not a single critic understood what had impelled me to compose these works, or that they had been written in the same spirit as had in the past led composers to sing the praises of harvest-time, the grape harvest, or the "happy plowman," or Honegger to glorify a locomotive, and Fernand Leger to exalt machinery. Every time anyone wanted to prove my predilection for leg-pulling and eccentricity he cited *Les Machines agricoles.* I have never been able to fathom why sensible beings should imagine that any artist would spend his time working, with all the agonizing passion that goes into the process of creation, with the sole purpose of making fools of a few of them.

Ernest Bloch

[1880 - 1959]

Swiss by birth, widely traveled in his youth, and a resident of the United States for much of his life, Ernest Bloch revealed in his music the cosmopolitan mingling of many diverse elements. These are not so much successfully fused as they are opposed — Romantic influences alternate with neo-Classic, German with French. The single strongly personal strain in his work, unifying the eclectic elements, is the conscious evocation of the Jewish spirit and Jewish ritual found in much of his music. Nationalism of the most inspired degree emerges in these works, none the less nationalism because it springs from liturgy rather than from the folk music of a particular place.

Bloch was not only a successful composer, with the ability to communicate readily with listeners, but a dedicated teacher (numbering Roger Sessions and Douglas Moore among his pupils) and an often eloquent writer on musical subjects. As can be seen in the following essay, Bloch's thoughts about music, intense and moralistic, are as impassioned as his music itself.

"Man and Music," translated by Waldo Frank, from *The Musical Quarterly*, XIX 4 (October 1933), pp. 374 – 81. In a prefatory note, Bloch explains that the article was first written in 1916, but that "since then my ideas have not greatly changed."

Man
and Music

Thus far the war does not seem to have had any great effect on music and musicians. I am not speaking from the practical standpoint, nor do I refer to the musicians who are at the front or to those who, from a safe distance in the rear, discuss with such violence the need of boycotting the music of the enemy. I am not thinking of the occasional music the war has called forth: music in sentimental colored covers, military marches, songs for "charity bazaars," the inevitable current merchandise elaborated by smug gentlemen in the seclusion of their sitting-rooms. I do not believe in this "music from afar." And I am convinced that if anything permanent remains of all this, it will be some obscure plaint, some racy soldier-song sprung from the suffering or the ecstacy of action.

At the beginning of the war, when it was the common belief that the struggle would be short, a fond hope prevailed that art and music would rise from it refreshed. But as the conflict drags on, and the end recedes, speculation about art has dropped away. All forces strain toward a single goal for which everything is sacrificed, and the social organism, at bay, has rallied all its energies for the narrow struggle of existence. During this vast and tragic upheaval in which almost the entire world is caught and which cannot fail to transform the entire aspect of things, what has music become? Has it also passed through the tempest, has it grown to be the voice of the people in their new sufferings and hopes? Can we find in it the impress of what is actually taking place? It seems not. Before all this overwhelming trouble, music remains indifferent. This, the most direct of all arts, the art that is best qualified to express life and human passions in their entirety, seems to have remained alien to the great drama.

There is something tragic in the degree to which music has gradually divorced itself from life and become an ego-centric and an artificial thing. Already before the war, it had wandered from the source where all art must find its strength and its continual rebirth; it was no longer the expression of our soul and of our mind, of our epoch with its struggles, its agonies and its aspirations. It lacked emotive life; it lacked humanity. In all its branch-creation, interpretation, modes of instruction and critique — it had become a cold and calculated thing, lifeless and unspirited. Music was no longer the emanation of a race and a people, spontaneous birth out of life. It was a music of musicians. . . .

This, one vaguely apprehended, was the situation before the war. And this has scarcely changed. The public loves the same type of sterile work; the exploiters continue to provide it. And "serious" composers persist in their obsession with technique and procedure. They discuss and argue. They laboriously create their arbitrary and brain-begotten works, while the emotional element—the soul of art—is lost in the passion for mechanical perfection. Everywhere, virtuosity of means; everywhere, intellectualism exalted as the standard. This is the plague of our times, and the reason of its inevitable dearth.

But this is not the first time that such perverse conditions have obtained in the history of art. Virtuosity of means, exalted as the end-and-all of art, the substitution of automatism for life are nothing new in music. There were the early excesses of the contrapuntalists in the first days of vocal polyphony. Later, "bel-canto" was reduced to a vice, and more recently still instrumental virtuosity was carried to excess, just as today we have harmonic, contrapuntal, and orchestral acrobatics. But wherever this parisitism has prevailed, it has done so to the detriment of music. And it has been encouraged when the inventive and creative force was low: when the art's true nourishment was meager. At such times, the artist, creative and interpretive, is driven to a substitute for real emotion and real life. The artifice of form is a last resource with which he holds the languishing attention of a weary public.

Only that art can live which is an active manifestation of the life of the people. It must be a necessary, an essential portion of that life, and not a luxury. It must have its roots deep within the soil that brings it forth. Needless to say, it cannot be the direct output of crowds; but, however indirectly, they must have contributed to its substance. A work of art is the soul of a race speaking through the voice of the prophet in whom it has become incarnate. Art is the outlet of the mystical, emotional needs of the human spirit, it is created rather by instinct than by intelligence, rather by intuition than by will. Primitive and elemental races have had marvelous arts; and there have been periods of superior civilization, sterile in this form of expression: particularly those in which the practical and intellectual elements have been dominant. Indeed, it would seem as if certain social states like certain individual conditions give forth an atmosphere that is hostile to art and exclude it. And it is a proper question whether a society, primarily utilitarian like our own, is of a sort to foster art. For art is a completely disinterested function; it is free of all practical compromise and deaf to the law of supply and demand.

Still, the nutritive elements of art are not wanting among us. Throughout its many avatars, humanity remains the same; the conflicts that spring from human passion change only in outer semblance, and scarcely in that!

42

Man
and Music

The struggle of the man with nature and the struggle of man with man are as tragic as ever. There is little distinction between the ancient war of primordial tribes and the modern war of the trenches. Despite the development of machinery and of the technique of living, no gulf separates the toiling of millions in the choking furnaces of Pittsburgh from the passionate and painful struggle of the first men at the dawn of history for food and shelter. The picture is one; its light alone is different. It is the eternal wrestling of man with matter.

There was a time, however, when men drew inspiration from their daily life and their daily conflicts. Everything had its deep aspect of poetry. But today the artist turns away and avoids what ought to command him. Where he should plunge into life, feel himself impregnate with it, draw forth its essence magnified and ennobled, he prefers to devote his powers to the inventing of an artificial work.

This schism between life and art is a dangerous one indeed. It may well make of art what it has already made of religion: a dogmatic and dessicated form, remote from nature, morbid, lifeless, a fairy-tale that has lost all its meaning. Why has this break between life and art occurred?

It is a vast and complex problem; for the factors linking an art to a culture are numerous and subtle, especially in music. Moreover, the experience of history is not always commandingly helpful. An equation that was once true may today be false, since the terms have altered with the evolving facts. Still, among the impulses that have driven art into its present perverted state there are two which appear to me to be essential: the industrial development which art has undergone and the acute intellectualism of our times. These two elements have enslaved the artist; they have taken from him, little by little, and in many subtle ways, his freshness of sensation, his complete sincerity and his freedom.

Art is becoming an industry. It is in the hand of exploiters of all stamps, men who wring great profits from it, who presume to "direct" it and to regulate its "market," which, like all markets, is subject to the law of supply and demand. Unhappy is the fate of the independent and original artist, if he is not rich and lacks a second nature, that of the merchant!

Either he is crushed, annihilated by the vast and terrible machine of art; or, if he prefers not to starve to death, he is forced to conform to the laws and the conditions of these art-traffickers! Let him rush to a place under their yoke, if he wants to eat!

This is one of the shames of our social system: of all art, it favors most the meretricious and the degraded. It encourages the production of those sweetened, cloying works, of all those lies that today poison the public; it supports those "arrangements" — derangements rather — that mutilate our masterpieces for the sake of profit. It produces that surfeit of facile medio-

Ernest
Bloch

crity whose false contagion ruins the taste of the masses. And, on the other hand, it pushes aside the true artist whose sincerity is useless, since it lacks a market-value.

This commercialism is universal in the world of art. What does one usually learn from the concert-programs? Does one find there a love of art, or a fad for artists? Is there any end to the concessions that are made from commercial motives? Always and again, the law of supply and demand. Conductors and virtuosi repeat *ad nauseam* the drummed-out, antiquated works that flatter their patrons. Our concerts have been dead museums; and what they have to offer has no real relation with the life about us. Moreover, the dissatisfaction is widespread; great is the hunger for release. But it is vague and undirected. Inertia has its way.

This shameful state of affairs has of course infected the press. In Europe, doubtless in America as well, place and attention are not always accorded to the true work of art, to the true man of art. Public opinion has become vitiated; and those whose mission it is to enlighten the masses are most active in perverting them.

This, however, is only one side of the question. It explains but one aspect, the "nether regions" of art. There is a whole category of artists whose material ease and conscience as well enable them to hold far aloof from all this promiscuous evil. But are they, for all this, freer than the others? Are they free to live, to see, to feel, to think first and then to proclaim what they have received, without constraint and without concession? I think not. Another tyranny, equally dangerous, holds them down. They are not the slaves of merchant-editors and directors, of an easy and degraded public taste; but they are the slaves of the conventions of our time, of fashion, of the attenuated pleasures of a special set. Above all, they are subject to the intellectualism which by its constraint withers and renders false the true conception of art. Most of our artists today do not live an ample, integrated life. Their life is rarified, cerebral, artificial: largely a seeking of technique.

In certain epochs of history, broad truths, social, political or religious, have set up wide currents of thought and feeling that have swept man along in a unity of action and of faith. In such times, art has been one with life and its expression has stood for humanity. Egypt, Greece, the Middle Ages, the Renaissance knew such an art. It seems to me that the lastest example of one of these collective states of soul in music was Richard Wagner; for in him we find incarnate the future dream and development of his race. But since Wagner's time no great conception, no great conviction has fertilized mankind. On the other hand, the critical instinct has developed, the positive sciences have reigned; industrialism and the vulgarization of art, heightened communication and interchange of ideas have foisted on our consciousness a febrile mixture of thought and feeling. We find the most hostile theories living side by side. The old convictions are shattered, and new ideas are not strong enough to become convictions. Everywhere there is chaos. And art indeed has been the mirror of our uncertainties. It is significant to find, in a single epoch, the flourishing of works and styles so varied and so opposed: Reger to Strauss, Mahler to Schoenberg; Saint-Saens to d'Indy or Debussy; Puccini to Dukas. Our arts tend more and more toward an individualistic, non-representative and non-racial expression. Nor is the factitious renaissance of national arts which manifested itself before the war to be taken seriously. The ardor of these prophets was an affair of the will, of the intellect. Their influence on the real domain of art is negligible.

There can be no doubt, for instance, that a great artist like Claude Debussy stands for the best and purest traditions of the French. But he is representative chiefly aesthetically and in form. The essence of his inspiration has little in common with the present state of France. He stands far less for France than a Rabelais, a Montaigne, a Voltaire, a Balzac, a Flaubert. He represents in reality only a small part of his country.[1]

Debussy represents the goal of the pre-Raphaelite doctrines propounded by the symbolist poets and painters of France. Above all, he represents Claude Debussy. And it is precisely in this fact that his immense value lies — his personality, his special individuality.

Unfortunately, this is not what musicians have sought in him. Quite on the contrary, they appreciate and emulate the exterior part of his work which is of importance only because of what it expresses; so that the fate of Debussy has been the usual one. First he was ignored. Now, he is understood and admired only through his superficial and trivial qualities. An army of imitators, of second-hand manufacturers, pounced on the technique of Claude Debussy. And through their ironical activities that which was the peculiar accent of a peculiar personality becomes a debased tongue: musicians who have nothing in common with Debussy now think that they must use his words. And criticism which seems perennially unable to distinguish the true work from the pastiche exalts with the same adjectives the authentic expression and the sickening imitation.

Of course, the language of Debussy has become vulgarized and denatured; false usage has emptied it of its native color. It has become a mechanical procedure, without power and without soul. And the consequence, as with Wagner, has been a constant musical depreciation. For the ears of these moderns Debussy is already "vieux jeu." Debussy has had to

[1] Perhaps it is unjust to seek this manifestation of France in her music. Her poets and novelists, painters and sculptors are certainly more typical. Each race has its arts of predilection.

be outbidden. From one tonal exaggeration to another, we have been hurried along until our ears have become actually perverse and incapable of savoring the clean and fresh beauty of old masterpieces. Our appetite increases for still hotter spices, for still wilder complexities.[2]

First, the Wagnerians created "Wagnerism" — a narrow doctrine that declared itself the absolute truth; then the admirers of Debussy forged their "Debussyism," a doctrine equally narrow and equally intolerant of the past. And now comes a new aesthetic — that of the *bored ones!* It is based exclusively upon technical considerations. With the charge of rhetoric it denies most of the superb eras of musical history — as if its own rhetoric were better! — and it succeeds utterly in confounding the means of art with its end. Its cry is for novelty, and still more novelty. This frenzied search for originality has led to cubism, futurism, all those tendencies which above everything are creations of reason and not of feeling.

Here is a new criterion; and all our musicians, artists, critics are touched by it in some degree. When I say that they are not free, I mean that an intellectual barrier exists between their emotion and their work — a sort of sensory perversion that twists their thoughts, inhibits their inspiration, and warps their taste. They are forever thinking of the development of their art — not as the corollary of a logical growth of thought, not as a spontaneous expression of life, but as a thing-in-itself, apart from life. And the truth is that they neither understand nor are interested in anything so much as the elaboration of their technique.

In conclusion, I should say that at the present time the world of art is divided into two great currents. The lower one is that of the masses: their facile taste is sinking with the love of platitude and the weight of mechanical inventions — phonograph, radio, cinematograph.[3] The other current is that of the "high-brow." With perverted taste, it looks on art as a luxury, as a purveyor of rare senations, as a matter of intellectual acrobatics.

Both on its higher and lower levels art has broken with life. And this, doubtless, explains why the fearful events now transfiguring mankind have had so little effect upon it.

The two worlds gravitate upon different orbits. But what must be the result? Are we at a period of transition; or are we virtually on the decline? Like all things, art is born, lives, dies. Is its story told? Are we definitively approaching a world of materialism, of egotism, of sensual satisfaction? Is the soul to atrophy in the dry-dust atmosphere of industrialism which now swirls about us and whose chaotic noises overwhelm and submerge us,

[2] The same external evolution has taken place in the domains of counterpoint and orchestration.
[3] Witness the slow but sure degradation of opera.

day by day? Or is a rebirth coming? Perhaps. I, for one, do not believe that Humanity has finished its march. Humanity has merely turned a corner. We are not ready to deny the best within ourselves. But, to be sure, it will not be formulas, procedures, new theories that will create the art of to-morrow! Form is all important, since by means of it the artist materializes his vision; and for new thoughts there must indeed spring up new manners and modes of expression. In this sense, all experiment is better than mere stagnation and the effort of the *tasters* of art will not have been in vain. However false their direction, they at least work upon the soil in which must stir the harvest of tomorrow. They set their stakes. But the harvest cannot rise until a new seed has been planted.

Will the war bring forth that seed? I am rather of the opinion that this will be a distant consequence. I believe that some day we shall be weary of this daily miserable struggle, that a little true love will be reborn in the withered hearts of men. Perhaps, after our hatred, kindled only by a few, there will come one of those cleansing revolutions that will shake the world on its foundations and sweep away the poisonous vapors. Perhaps, then, a new life will rise up and with it something of youth and verdure and joy; while the old limping religions, the gods in whom no one be-lieves, will be swept away with the ruins. A new dawn will shine, and in their hearts men will feel once more the eternal flame that they believed extinct. A little fraternity, a little love, a little gladness will gleam on the face of the world and catch up the hearts of all men in one impulse, in one rhythm. And for these new hearts there will need to be new songs!

I am certain, then, that art, like a thirsty and withered plant which finds once more its native soil, will replunge its yearning roots into the old, good earth; it will hold fast; it will drain the pith of life, and, quite naturally, without effort, having found its home, its truth, it will blossom afresh.

Igor Stravinsky

[1882 - 1971]

Igor Stravinsky and Arnold Schoenberg, perhaps the two most powerful musical figures of the past fifty years, have differed widely in their esthetic theories and approaches to composition. Whereas Schoenberg extended the scope and technique of German Romanticism, evolving from it a new approach to dissonance and tonality, Stravinsky preferred to break with the Wagnerian tradition entirely. In place of its chromatic restlessness, he substituted a strongly tonal, often polytonal, casting of melody and harmony. In place of the Romantic sense of spaciousness and lyricism, he substituted a more urgent, driving sense of rhythm, pulse, and accent. Stravinsky's reaction to Wagnerianism, in these respects at least, was akin to that of the French Six, Satie, and the early Hindemith. Like them, he was strongly attracted to American jazz.

But Stravinsky's greatest contribution to the musical esthetic of our time is uniquely his own. It not only helps to explain his varied—and often mystifying —changes of style, including his recent adoption of the serial technique, but may account for his undiminished influence over even the youngest generation of composers. This contribution has been his position with respect to the Romantic concept of the composer's attitude toward his work. Stravinsky views a composition not as the outward manifestation of the creator's inner drives—that is, the "expressions"of extramusical ideas or emotions—but as a purely objective arrangement of pitches in time, a thing that one makes to satisfy no other urge than the desire to create an object. In composing, Stravinsky believes that he is solving problems, making choices, creating patterns, and ordering his materials. As the problems differ, so do the individual pieces—the solutions.

Thus, while Stravinsky has altered his methods on many occasions, he has never contradicted his fundamentally "objective" approach to his craft. Some aspects of this approach are indicated in the following essay, a retrospective view of his long career, along with some surprisingly impassioned statements about the state of music, audiences, performers, and recordings.

Igor Stravinsky and Robert Craft, Dialogues and A Diary (Garden City, N.Y., Doubleday & Co., Inc., 1963), pp. 23-36.

48

From
"Dialogues and
A Diary"

Thoughts of
an Octogenarian

"And in his old age the wisdom of his song shall exceed even the beauties of his youth; and it shall be much loved" (Psellus Akritas of Alexandria, *De Ceremonies*, XIV, 7). I am not so sure.

I was born out of time in the sense that by temperament and talent I would have been more suited for the life of a small Bach, living in anonymity and composing regularly for an established service and for God. I did weather the world I was born to, weathered it well, you will say, and I have survived—though not uncorrupted—the hucksterism of publishers, music festivals, recording companies, publicity, including my own ("Self-love is unquestionably the chief motive which leads anyone to speak, and more especially to write respecting himself."—Alfieri, *Memoirs*), conductors, critics (with whom my real argument is that the person who practices the vocation of music should not be judged by the person who has no vocation and does not understand musical practice, and to whom music must therefore be of infinitely less fundamental consequence), and all of the misunderstandings about performance the word concerts has come to mean. But the small Bach might have composed three times as much music.

At eighty I have found new joy in Beethoven, and the Great Fugue now seems to me—it was not always so—a perfect miracle. How right Beethoven's friends were when they convinced him to detach it from opus 130, for it must stand by itself, this absolutely contemporary piece of music that will be contemporary forever. (I wonder, do these statements surprise students of my own later work, the Great Fugue being all variation and development whereas my later music is all canonic and therefore static and objective—in fact, the antithesis of Beethoven's fugue? Do students of my music expect me to cite something like Josquin's *Hic me sidereo* as my "favorite" piece?) Hardly birthmarked by its age, the Great Fugue is as rhythm alone more subtle than any music composed in my own century —I mean, for example, the consequences implied by the notation ♫ as

Herr Webern knew. It is pure interval music, this fugue, and I love it beyond any other.

An example of a musical antithesis to me in my own time is *Wozzeck,* though it is a masterpiece of an entirely different sort than the Great Fugue. What disturbs me about *Wozzeck,* a work I love, is the level of its appeal to "ignorant" audiences, with whom one may attribute its success to: 1) the story; 2) Bible, child sentiment; 3)sex; 4)brevity; 5) dynamics, pppp to ffff^a; 6) muted brass, ▲ ■ *col legno,* etc.; 7) the idea that the vocal line ♪↘♪ = emotion; 8) the orchestral flagellation in the interludes; 9) the audience's feeling that is being frightfully modern.

But "passionate emotion" can be conveyed by very different means than these, and within the most "limiting conventions." The Timurid miniaturists, for example, were forbidden to portray facial expression, and in one of my favorite scenes, from the life of an early Zoroastrian king, the artist shows a group of totally blank faces. The dramatic tension is in the way the ladies of the court are shown eavesdropping, and in the slightly discordant gesture of one of the principal figures. In another favorite miniature, two lovers confront each other with stony looks, but the man unconsciously touches his finger to his lips and this packs the picture with, for me, as much passion as the *crescendo molto* in *Wozzeck.*

The dualism of the self and the body-container widens, as though I had become the demonstration instrument in a platonic form-argument, and the container is more foreign each day, and more of a penance. I wish to walk faster, but my unwilling partner will not execute the wish, and one imminent tomorrow it will refuse to move at all, at which time I shall insist upon an even sharper distinction between the alien form instrument and myself. At four-score, the alienation of the body image is a necessary psychological safety device, and those Lourdeses of glandular and cellular rejuvenation are indispensable articles of belief.

The brain cells are unique in that they cannot be renewed. May I adduce from this that we are born with our talents, that we may "think" or "will" ourselves into command of them, but the thinking and willing potentiality, or call it the cerebral biochemistry, is given? That I was born with the possibility of becoming a composer, and the circumstances of my formation have made me this composer?

I regard my talents as God-given, and I have always prayed to Him for strength to use them. When in early childhood I discovered that I had been made the custodian of musical aptitudes, I pledged myself to God to be worthy of their development, though, of course, I have broken the pledge and received uncovenanted mercies all my life, and though the custodian has too often kept faith on his own all-too-worldly terms.

Creation is its own image and thought is its own mirror. As I think about this metaphor language — it gives me claustrophobia — the word mirror frightens me. Seventy-five years ago as a child alone in my room, I once saw my father instead of myself in the looking glass, and my already strong case of father-fears became mirror-fears as well. I expect Purgatory to be full of many-dimensional mirrors.

What about the much publicized "infinity of possibilities" in connection with the new art material of electronically produced sound? With few exceptions "infinite possibilities" has meant collages of organ burbling, rubber suction (indecent, this), machine-gunning, and other — this is curious — representational and associative noises more appropriate to Mr. Disney's musical mimicries. Not the fact of possibilities, of course, but choice is the beginning of art. The sound lab is already a part of the musical supermarket, however. (Especially in the field of publicity. The structure of a new piece by Xenakis is advertised as having been "worked out on the IBM 7090 electronic computer" as though that were a guarantee of quality.) I know of a composer who wanted "something electronic, kind of middle range, bassoon-trombone like" — these were his only instructions to the sound engineer, who nevertheless flipped a toggle switch, made a few connections, and handed the composer an envelope containing a tape of the desired noise. The composition, I am told, sounds like "electronic Brahms."

Sounds by themselves may be aesthetic, or, at least, painful or pleasurable, but to me they are only a putative material of music. They have another use, too, and a fascinating one, in the new field of audio-analgesics. But a composer is not, by intention, a musical therapist.

An electronic machine cannot dehumanize (whatever that may be); indeed, it can only do what it has been directed to do. It may extend memory functions, for example, when a man has established its memory locations and devised the means to signal and connect them. But the most nearly perfect musical machine, a Stradivarius as well as an electronic synthesizer, is useless until joined to a man with musical skill and imagination. The stained-glass artists of Chartres had few colors, and the stained-glass artists of today have hundreds of colors but no Chartres. Organs, too, have more stops now than ever before, but no Bach. Not enlarged resources, then, but men and what they "believe."

What is the "human measure" in music? And is this a possible question? Isn't the wish to prescribe merely another instance of the fear of becoming other, of changing the past? And, in any case, won't the "human measure" *be* whatever we agree it ought to *be*? As for myself, I am no more concerned with a definition Man than I am with subjective grunts like "good" and "bad." My "human measure" is not only possible, but also exact. It is, first of all, absolutely physical, and it is immediate. I am made bodily ill, for example, by sounds electronically spayed for overtone removal. To me they are a castration threat.

Time, too, is a physical measure to me, and in music I must feel a physical here and there and not only a now, which is to say, movement from and toward. I do not always feel this sense of movement or location in, say, Boulez's *Structures* or those fascinating score-plans by Stockhausen (I have not yet heard his *Momente* for voices and thirteen instruments, but the title augurs well), and though every element in those pieces may be organized to engender motion, the result often seems to me like the essence of the static. A time series may very well postulate a new parable about time, but that is not the same thing as a time experience, which for me is the dynamic passage through time. Nor, of course, are these composers concerned about "dynamic passage through," which betrays an essentially dramatic concept, Greek in origin, like all of my ideas of musical form. The very phrase exposes the gulf between myself and the Teddy Boys of music, and between me and the Zen generation as a whole, and so does their favorite word, vector, which for me is a metaphor in no way analogous to a musical experience, vector being a spatial concept to me, music a purely temporal art.

Anyone who survives a sixty-year span of creative activity in our century must sometimes feel a satisfaction merely in being able to metabolize new experience, to "stay with it"; or, at any rate, this appears to be a greater feat now, where the "ins" are in for a shorter term than in the time of such octogenarians (so far as one can judge other times and generalize about octogenarians) as Sophocles, Voltaire, and Goethe, and where no one can be *primus inter pares,* or hold not only the historical center but even the redoubts for more than two or three years.

I was born to causality and determinism, and I have survived to probability theory and chance. I was born to a world that explained itself largely in dogmatic terms and I have lived, through several changes of management, to a world that rationalizes itself almost entirely in psychoanalytic terms. Educated by simple fact—the trigger one squeezed was what shot the gun—I have had to learn that, in fact, the universe of anterior contributing possibilities was responsible. But I was also born to a nonprogressivist notion of the practice of my art, and on this point, though I have survived into a musical society that pursues the opposite idea, I have not been able to change. I do not understand the composer who says we must analyze and determine the evolutionary tendency of the whole musical situation and proceed from there. I have never consciously analyzed any musical situation, and I can follow only where my musical appetites lead me.

From "Dialogues and A Diary"

And how are we to know "the whole musical situation"? I am something of an aldermanic figure in music today and a composer still considered to be capable of development in some departments of musical practice, yet recently, trying to read an essay on current techniques by a formost scholiast of supraserial music, I discovered that I understood hardly a word — or, rather, hardly a diagram, for the essay looked like an IBM punch card. Whether I am a forefront or rear-guard or road-hog composer is beside the point, which is the disparity between the doer and the explainer. I as a doer have not been able to "keep up" even in my own specialized and ever-narrowing preserves. And because anything one writes is already out of date on publication (reread the first page of these *pensées* and you will see that they have become quite moldy), the professional literature of the future (which is now) can consist only of summaries and supplements — developments in the field during the previous week. Dr. Toynbee's last book was called "Volume Twelve: Reconsiderations." And Volume Thirteen? Further Reconsiderations? And so on.

"Mortify the past." The past as a wish that creates the probability pattern of the future? Did John of the Cross mean that, and the fear of changing the past which is fear of the present? I mortify *my* past every time I sit at the piano to compose, in any case, though I have no wish to go back or to relive a day of my life. But I have relived much in recent years, perhaps because four cerebral thromboses have unshuttered the remotest reaches of memory or spilled a restorative chemical over the palimpsest of my baby book. I have been able to roam in the Phoenix Park of childhood as I could not a decade ago, but I tug at my memory as a mountain-climber tugs at his rope: to see how and where it is tied; I do not go back, in the threat of time, because of a wish to return. And even though my subconscious may be trying to close the circle, I want to go on rectilinearly as always: the dualism again. The archaeologist's dream — Renan's — of the past recaptured, is another of my visions of Purgatory, and the poet's dream — Coleridge's — of restoring the collective experience of a mind's whole past existence is, to me, an insanity threat.

My agenbite of inwit is that I do not know while composing, am not aware of, the value question. I love whatever I am now doing, and with each new work I feel that I have at last found the way, have just begun to compose. I love all of my children, of course, and like any father, I am inclined to favor the backward and imperfectly formed ones. But I am actually excited only by the newest (Don Juanism?) and the youngest (nymphetism?). I hope, too, that my best work is still to be written (I want to write a string quartet and a symphony), but "best" means nothing to me while I am composing, and comparisons of the sort that other people make about my music are to me invidious or simply absurd.

Were Eliot and myself merely trying to refit old ships while the other side—Joyce, Schoenberg—sought new forms of travel? I believe that this distinction, much traded on a generation ago, has disappeared. (An era is shaped only by hindsight, of course, and hindsight reduces to convenient unities, but all artists know that they are part of the same thing.) Of course we seemed, Eliot and myself, to have exploited an apparent discontinuity, to have made art out of the *disjecta membra,* the quotations from other poets and composers, the references to earlier styles ("hints of earlier and other creation"), the detritus that betokened a wreck. But we used it, and anything that came to hand, to rebuild, and we did not pretend to have invented new conveyors or new means of travel. But the true business of the artist *is* to refit old ships. He can say again, in his way, only what has already been said.

Contemporary Music and Recording

Con-tempo: "with the times." Con-tempo music is the most interesting music that ever has been written, and the present moment is the most exciting in music history. It always has been. Nearly all con-tempo music is bad, too, and so it was ever. The "lament of present days," as Byron called it, is as old as the first antiquarian.

Modern: *modernus, modo:* "just now." But, also, *modus,* "manner," whence "up-to-date" and "fashionable." A more complex word, and evidently of urban origin, though I shall have to look this up in Latin and French poets. (Rimbaud: *"Il faut être absolument moderne."*)

And "new music"? But surely that misplaces the emphasis. What is most new in new music dies quickest, and that which makes it live is all that is oldest and most tried. To contrast the new and the old is a *reductio ad absurdum,* and sectarian "new music" is the blight of contemporaneity. Let us use con-tempo, then, not technically, in the sense that Schoenberg and Chaminade lived at the same time, but in my meaning: "with the times."

To the performer, a recording is valuable chiefly as a mirror. He is able to reflect himself in it, to walk away from his subjective experience and look at it. A recording session is a shuttling from subjective to objective, and the performer is like the muralist who has to back away from his work to see it in perspective. In my case the perspective of the object, the play-back, dwindles to a point of identity when I conduct, and the located object, myself conducting the music, is replaced by, simply, the music—or, rather, as it is my music, myself in the music, for I am always aware of my being in my music. This mirroring is the main point, I think, and not whether a recording extends the range of peripheral hearing or canalizes hearing selectively (dangers as well as advantages): a record is a lever that can lift one outside of one's performance involvement, or "far out" enough, at least, to establish the illusion.

Mirrors are also mnemonic devices. One sees what one was rather than what one is; the immediate has too many shadings. One looks into one's mirrors and is aware only of the subtraction; one listens to oneself to compare. The recognition of a time seam and its point of view is evident to me in other people's recordings of other composers, too, of course, though there my reaction is more passive. But I imagine that any still-growing performer must be similarly disturbed.

By definition, contemporary music is unfamiliar, and, by deduction, it is more difficult than other types of music to record. (I do not say that it is more difficult to perform; it is and it isn't, in different ways.) The fifty recordings of the Beethoven symphony are fifty different angles of distortion, but these distortions actually protect the scope of the work: the larger the variorum, the greater the guarantee that Beethoven himself will remain intact. The recording of the contemporary, on the other hand, lacking comparison, fixes the music at a single angle, and the gravest danger of this fixed angle, which is that the truly contemporary exists on the precarious edge of the comprehensible, is not obvious. What is wrong with the Beethoven performance is evident and cannot damage the work, but what is wrong in the performance of the unfamiliar work is not at all evident, and the line between sense and nonsense in it may, and often does, depend upon its performance. The difference between a Kandinsky and a doodler, a Schoenberg and a lunatic, was apparent to only a few imaginative and highly trained perceivers in 1912. We know that even such a close disciple as Alban Berg could not at that time readily follow *Pierrot lunaire.* I state as axiomatic, then, that performance of the unfamiliar is a greater responsibility and must seek higher standards than performance of the familiar. Every first recording is a risk.

The question of value in repertory versus non-repertory: I see no artistic reason to proliferate recordings of music that is widely performed live. I mean the concertos in B-flat Minor, the tone poems in E-flat Major, the symphonies in E Minor. A recording is, or should be, a performance, and who can suffer exactly the same set of performance limitations more than once—at least with familiar music? I do suffer them when the music is unfamiliar, but with less pain because they do not distract unduly from the learning process, the becoming familiar. The recording of non-repertory, of what is not generally available live, should be the *raison d'être* of the industry.

How many people in the United States have heard live performances of Schoenberg's larger dramatic works? The answer—in full figures for per capita comparison—is 000,000,000, and the conclusion is obvious: recordings, rather than isolated and sporadic concerts, are the chief means of communication between the contemporary composer and his audience.

A footnote on non-repertory with another meaning of that term: non-existent. An advertisement for a new disc from the current catalogue says something about "Stokowski's Bach." But no such Bach ever existed. "Bach's Stokowski" would make far more sense historically. And I have just received an album with a blurb about "The great conductor" von K.'s "Mozart." But what does von K.'s conducting really do to Mozart? It opens his bier, unclasps his hands from his bosom, and folds them behind his head.

I have just received some programs of a concert series in Leningrad dedicated to my later music. Every musician—composer, conductor, music educator—to whom I have shown them has pronounced the same comment: "I wonder what the performances sounded like, as no one there has heard the music." In other words, the printed page is no longer self-sufficient, but should be supplemented by a recorded guide.

What are my attitudes to my own recorded performances? I have already said that I only listen to them critically and that I could not do any of them the same way again. But even the poorest are valid readings to guide other performers, and the best, like the new *Zvezdoliki* and *Symphony in C*, are very good indeed. What are the poorest? Those pieces which were too new to me, and for which I had no settled ideas and technical habits of performance. The recordings of *The Rake's Progress*, *Lulu*, and *Moses und Aron* have very effectively helped to kill those operas in America, where—the latter two, anyway—they are known only by records.

What, to a composer, is most important about a recorded performance? The spirit, of course, the same as in any performance. The spirit of the London recordings of my music has fallen arches, for instance, the spirit of the Mercury recordings has been propped up in Adler elevator shoes, and the spirit of the L'Oiseau-Lyre *Dumbarton Oaks* is that of a very slow choochoo. Next to the spirit come the two chief questions of the flesh: tempo and balance. I am annoyed by the violin solo in my *Agon* recording. It seems to emanate from the bedroom, while the trombone accompaniment sounds as though it is in my lap. But imbalances of this sort were common in early stereo recordings, and whereas a monaural was a closet, an early stereo was three closets. We also heard things we had never heard before, but we didn't always want to. Now we have learned to let backgrounds be backgrounds, like bygones, and we know that acoustics pretends to be, but is not yet, a science. But I am even more irritated by an impossible tempo. If the speeds of everything in the world and in ourselves have changed, our tempo feelings cannot remain unaffected. The metronome marks one wrote forty years ago were contemporary forty years ago. Time is not alone in affecting tempo—circumstances do too, and every performance is a different equation of them. I would be surprised if any of my own recordings follow the metronome markings.

"Live music is at least a performance"—which is meant to imply that recordings are not. In fact, though, performers can be inspired even in recording studios and concentration there is at least as great as it is in concerts. But with technically complex contemporary music, true performance on records, though it should always be the goal, is difficult to attain. The published version usually, in fact, is a pastiche of excerpts from the best of several forays. I can make this clear only be a description of such a session.

It lasts three hours. The music has not been rehearsed, of course, and the first two hours are therefore used in spot-rehearsing it. During this time, microphones are adjusted, balance tests are made, positions of instruments are changed, and sometimes the whole orchestra is reseated. The conductor's faculties are entirely concentrated on the problem of when to stop and explain or correct—on deciding what a player or an orchestra is likely to resolve the next time around on its own and what it will never understand without prompting and explanation. This is a matter of the conductor's and the orchestra's experience, but not entirely of that, and some part of the decision will always be a gamble. When this perfunctory contact with the music is over and the actual recording has begun, the attention of the conductor is turned to the clock. From then on he becomes a machine for making decisions. Can this section be improved if it is played once more, and how much time remains, and how much music has still to be recorded? The recording director will advise him to go on, of course, telling him that the section may be repeated "if time is left at the end" (quotation from the standard A-&-R recording director's manual), but every recording session is a photo finish, and even if one could return to something recorded earlier, the sound levels would not match.

(Editing and preparing the master record from such a session is an equally interesting non-musical exercise, largely because such a charming vocabulary has developed: scrub the tuba, dip the room noise, dig for the cellos, echo the splice. But if I were to expose the realities of editing, I would bury the bluff about performance and kill the sale of records.)

If the conductor is the surgeon in this three-hour operation, his anesthetist is the A-&-R supervisor. This accomplice must be a virtuoso listener and score-reader, a child psychologist, and a liar ("Marvelous take, everybody"). He also must know his artist to such an extent that he can keep him directed toward a performance that the artist himself may have lost sight of. And he must hide his boredom, too, for he spends most of his time recording the Liberaces of classical music, and the contemporary music he does do (in this case not contemporary, but modern) is likely to be the gimmick pieces for vibraphones, *Sprechstimme,* and *ponticello*—in other words, sound effects rather than music. Qualified recording supervisors are rare, and the opportunity to collaborate with them is rarer still. I have such a collaboration at present—Mr. John McClure of Columbia—and I hope to make many more records.

Alban Berg

[1885 - 1935]

Of the many pupils of Arnold Schoenberg, two in particular have become to be regarded as composers of major importance: Anton Webern and Alban Berg. Of the two, Berg is the more traditional in orientation, and his works are, correspondingly, more accessible. He was strongly influenced by Schoenberg and, like Schoenberg, by post-Wagnerian chromaticism, expansive, lyric and "expressionistic" in mood.

In Berg's music the twelve-tone system is used with great dramatic effect, at times within the context of tonality. Although Berg, as one of the three great Viennese twelve-tone masters, is certainly a major contemporary figure, he can also be considered — at least for the reasons already cited — the last important exponent of nineteenth-century German Romanticism, the link between one esthetic and another.

During the last ten years of his life, when his name had become known to the musical public, Berg wrote a number of essays defending and championing the twelve-tone technique and the music of his teacher. The essay reprinted here communicates the spirit of Berg's impassioned pleas.

"Why is Schoenberg's Music So Hard to Understand?," translated by Anton Swarowsky and Joseph H. Lederer, from *The Music Review*, XIII/2 (May 1952), 187–96. First published in the special issue of *Musikblatter des Ambruch* honoring Schoenberg's fiftieth birthday, September 13, 1924.

Why is
Schoenberg's music
so hard to understand?

In answering this question one might be inclined to ferret out the ideas behind Schoenberg's music, to examine the music in terms of intellectual content: to do, in other words, what is done so frequently: approach music with philosophic, literary, and other considerations. This is not my intention! I am concerned only with what takes place musically in Schoenberg's work, with the compositional means of expression. This, like the specific language of any work of art (one presupposes its acceptance as such) is the only meaningful one. Generally speaking, to understand this language in its entirety and details means recognizing the entrance, duration, and end of all melodies, hearing the simultaneous sounding (*Zusammenklang*) of the voices not as random occurrences, but as harmonies, and experiencing the small and large concatenations and contrasts as such. It means following a piece of music as a person with full command of the language follows the working of a piece of poetry. For one who is able to think musically, this is equivalent to understanding the work itself. Therefore, the question at the head of our investigation seems already answered if we can only succeed in examining Schoenberg's musical ways of expression for their intelligibility, and in determining the extent of their lucidity.

Why is Schoenberg's music so hard to understand?

Knowing how much can be accomplished through detailed examination, I want to do this on the basis of a single example chosen at random, there being few passages in Schoenberg's music which would not serve equally well.

It may be that today, ten years after their composition, the ten measures of Ex. 1 (the first of the D minor Quartet) are not considered unintelligible or even difficult. Still, one who wishes to recognize only the main voice and follow it, on first hearing, to the end of these ten measures will encounter difficulties as early as the third bar, especially if he would like to experience the main voice as a single melody, which, since it is precisely that, should be as singable as the beginning of one of Beethoven's quartets. Accustomed to a melodic structure the main feature of which is the symmetry of its periods, and a thematic structure limited to even numbered measure groups (rules governing all music of the last 150 years with few exceptions), an ear so restrictively pre-conditioned begins to doubt the correctness of the first bars of the melody, which, contrary to expectations, consists of two and a half bar phrases.

Avoidance of thematic structure built on two or four measures is, after all, nothing new. On the contrary, Bussler[1] says quite correctly that "the

---

[1] Ludwig Bussler, 1839-1900, German writer and theoretician.

61

greatest masters of form (he means Mozart and Beethoven) cherish free and bold constructions and rebel against being squeezed into the confines of even numbered measure groups." But how seldom does one find such a thing in the classics or among classical composers (with the possible exception of Schubert). And how is it that this faculty, so natural to the eighteenth century and before, got lost in the period of romantic music (Brahms' folk melodies excepted), the music of Wagner, and the whole New German school that ensued! Even the theme of Strauss' *Heldenleben*, which once seemed so audacious, is conspicuous for being built entirely on two to four bar phrases leading to a repetition of the first after the usual sixteen measures. In the music of Mahler and—to mention a master of a completely different style—Debussy, we find melodic structures with even numbers of bars almost exclusively. And when Reger (the only post-romantic exception besides Schoenberg) prefers rather free constructions, reminiscent of prose, as he himself says,[2] then this is the reason for the relative formidability of his music. I would go so far as to say the only reason—since none of its other qualities: the motivic development of the multi-toned phrases, the harmonic structure, certainly not the contrapuntal mode of writing, would render his musical language incomprehensible.

Understandably, when free and asymmetrical construction of themes is considered to be just as natural as the two, four, and eight bar kind—and that is perhaps the most important element in Schoenberg's way of writing—such music is likely to be followed with difficulty or, as in his later works, not at all.

During its rapid growth and surging restlessness, the theme, in our example, utilizes the right of variation in the second repetition of this rhythmically almost incomprehensible phrase. If, then, such a theme should receive the following shortened form

the listener loses the thread before the first melodic climax is reached two measures later:

[2] An expression used by Schoenberg, independently of Reger, to refer to the language of his own music.

the sixteenth note motive of this climax may strike the listener as having dropped out of thin air, though, again, it is only the natural continuation of the principal theme secured also through variation. Indeed, just this succession of chromatic jumps of a seventh, as may be observed even today at performances of the Quartet, presents an insuperable obstacle for one who is used to a gradual unfolding of the theme, or possibly only one development, through sequences and unvaried repetitions. Moreover, the listener is generally unable to fit the motive of the sixteenth note figures into a harmonic scheme. It is present, of course; but the notes speed by too quickly. Thus he loses the last means of orientation to appreciate this portion for its cadential value, let alone experience it as a *caesura* or climax. He hears it rather as an arbitrary grouping of "cacophonies" produced by the zigzag of the first violin part, which seems senseless to him. Of course he loses the continuity and with it, the new, though connected theme constructions which contain the richest motivic detail, and lead, nineteen measures later, to a repetition of the principal theme in E flat.

How much easier for the listener if the beginning of the Quartet—forgive my irreverence—were to take the following form, deliberately avoiding the rich rhythmic construction, motivic variation, and thematic detail, and retaining only the number of measures and the organic melodic invention.

Here the asymmetry of the original is actually made to disappear, being replaced by a two bar construction capable of pleasing even the most obdurate listener. The motivic and rhythmic growth unfolds slowly, eschewing every possibility of variation; an *alla breve* of sixteenth notes, over which a listener might stumble, is completely avoided, and with it, the final obstacle: the difficulty of hearing as melody these chromatic jumps of a seventh, accomplished by continuing harmonization on the half bar and by not speeding up beyond the value of an eighth note. Should a theme, so mutilated, still stand in danger of not being understood, then an exact repetition in the principal key entering immediately after the first statement is finished will guarantee a general understandability, verging on popularity.

How different with Schoenberg! "To penetrate into the psychology of his creative process, the sketchbooks, used exclusively in the epoch of this Quartet, are of supreme importance. No one who has skimmed through them could brand his music as contrived, cerebral, or any of the other catchwords used by those who want to protect themselves from Schoenberg's over-rich imagination". Also, "each thematic idea is invented along with its countersubject."[3]

And all this needs to be heard! One might receive a general impression of the beginning of the Quartet, and still miss the persuasive melody of the middle voice. The voice, an exception, is built on one or two bar phrases, set contrapuntally against the first five measure groups of the violin theme.

If the listener misses the expressive singing of the bass part, likely because of its dissolution into two—now three bar phrases, then he cannot grasp correctly even the principal theme.

One who does not react spontaneously to the beauty of such themes (and this type of music in general) requires at least the ability to keep separate such characteristically distinct voices. He must also be able to recognize melodic segments of varied lengths, continually beginning and ending anew at different points in these first six bars. This means following their various paths, in addition to coming sympathetically to rest when they sound simultaneously, as well as coping with Schoenberg's infinitely

[3] *Arnold Schoenberg* by Egon Wellesz.

varied and differentiated rhythms—all of which constitutes a formidable task.

In the face of the aforementioned, consider the above quoted cello part in which a hopping, syncopated eighth note scale develops out of the long drawn *legato* phrases[4] as early as in the seventh measure. Two bars later a seven-tone theme of weighty quarter notes, rushing upward, alternately in fourths and thirds (E flat, A flat, C, F) is added in contrast, thus revealing two integral motivic parts of the Quartet. Observe how these rhythmic figures are made to relate contrapuntally to the other parts, whose note value-relations develop along entirely different lines.

When music contains rhythms in such abundance and in so concentrated a form, vertically as well as horizontally, one really has to be completely deaf or malicious to call it "arhythmical"! Of course if this word is made to mean all note and metric combinations not directly derivable from mechanical movement (e.g. millwheel and railway) or body movement (march, dance, etc.) I cannot object to its application to Schoenberg's music. But then I must insist on the same treatment for the music of Mozart and the other classical masters, where they have not sought to produce regular, and hence easily understandable rhythms (as in scherzo and rondo movements, or others borrowed from the old dance forms).

Or is it possible that this word "arhythmical" is not really a musical term at all, but—like "ethos", "cosmos", "dynamics", "mentality" and other catchwords of our time—a word which applies where there is any motion at all, whether it be in art or sport, philosophy or industry, world history or finance! Such a term, stemming as it does from other than the motion of music, is not exclusively definable in the context of music. Rather, it is vague, permitting one to talk of the rhythm of music in the same tone of voice one might use to mention a drop in the stock market. Such looseness of nomenclature is out of the question for anyone who can discern the rhythmic occurrences in a piece of music, where they originate from musical detail and expand over the whole work. Unfortunately, the blame for this adulteration of terms lies where, for professional reasons, we might least expect it: that is, with a good many composers themselves. This only proves how hard it is to understand a music which demands critical judgment in terms of its own art—not some extraneous "point of view".

Thus we return to the domain of our investigation: why it is so hard to understand Schoenberg's music. As we have seen, its riches—the thematic, contrapuntal, and rhythmic beauties—have created these very difficulties. There remains only to discuss the harmonic richness, the unending supply

---

[4] If the sixth measure is recognized as a variation of the third, and the seventh as nothing else but a variation of the preceding one, then the feeling of musical coherence (without which music would be meaningless) is immediately achieved.

of chords and chord combinations, which, after all, are nothing but the result of a polyphony quite unique in contemporary music: a juxtaposition of voices, the melodic lines of which possess a flexibility heretofore unknown. Their superabundance of harmony was, therefore, just as misunderstood as everything else, and with as little justification.

This strict chorale-like four part writing is by no means the nucleus of an *adagio,* extending in a wide sweep, as one might easily imagine. It is the harmonic skeleton of the beginning of this much discussed Quartet.

Incredible that anything so simple could ever have missed being understood, that, moreover, audiences, in search of sensation, regarded it as an orgy of dissonances. With striking logic, various and sundry chords are here assembled in the confines of ten rapidly moving *alla breve* bars. This alone can explain why a listener accustomed to the poverty of harmonic degrees in other contemporary composers, is not equal to the task of comprehending fifty or more chords in a few seconds. He therefore charges "decadence" (another deadly *cliché*) where only wealth and abundance reign. The structure of the chords and their different combinations cannot be the reason why this music is so hard to understand. The last example was meant to demonstrate this. Not even in the least accented sixteenth note of these ten measures can one find a harmonic sound that might give pause to an ear conditioned by the harmonic conventions of the last century. Nor will the two whole tone chords at*, with their harmonic preparation and resolution, be the cause of moral indignation in anyone who prefers not to appear ridiculous in the eyes of the whole musical world.

One can see from this how inappropriate it is, and always was, to say that "modern" voice leading lacked consideration for the resulting vertical sounds, since everything I have shown in these ten bars could be proven for any part of this work. Even the boldest harmonic developments are far from a confluence of accidental sounds. Neither here nor anywhere else does anything happen by accident. Anyone who, in spite of all this, cannot follow the music should consider it his own fault and, without embarrassment, trust the ear of a master who conceives all these seemingly difficult matters as easily as he dashes off the most complicated counterpoint exercises for his students, and who, when asked if a particularly difficult passage of his had ever been realized, replied jocularly and profoundly, "Yes, when I composed it".

A mode of composing that results from such unerring musicianship embraces all compositional possibilities and is, therefore, never totally comprehensible. This analysis, complete though I have tried to make it, has by no means exhausted the possibilities of these few measures. One could say, for instance, that the voices, initially invented in double counterpoint—thus polyphonic in this respect also—permit a many-sidedness, which, of course, appears in the various recapitulations of the principal theme. Even in this early work of Schoenberg he lets the violin and cello change places, avoiding all mechanical repetitions. Illustrating it graphically, what stands (in the first measures of the Quartet) in vertical order

1   3
2 is now brought into the sequence of 2 (in octaves)
3   1

Alban Berg

At the third appearance (p. 8)* the secondary voices, while retaining the same melodic tones, are radically varied. The sequence is then

2 (variant in sixteenths)
1 (in octaves)
3 (embellished by eighth note triplets)

Finally, the principal and secondary parts—not to mention their combinations with other themes—appear in the last exposition of the last principal section (p. 53)* in the sequence of

3 (variant in eighth note triplets, but different from the preceding one)
1 (in octaves)
3 (inversion in eighths with diminution).

But these opening ten measures and their varied repetitions constitute a very small fraction of this work which lasts nearly an hour, and can only give an idea of the profusion of polyphonic and harmonic detail released in thousands of measures and unknown since Bach. It may be said without exaggeration that the minutest part—each accompanying figure—is important for the development and changing rhythm of these four voices, that it is, in other words, thematic. And all this in one big symphonic movement, the colossal architecture of which we cannot even begin to discuss in the framework of this article. It is hardly surprising that with such things going on, an ear accustomed to the music of the last century cannot take it all in. The music of that period is homophonic almost throughout: the themes are built on two or four measure phrases, the growth and development of which would be unthinkable without sequences, copious repetitions—mostly of the mechanical type—and the relative simplicity of harmonic and rhythmic events thereby conditioned. Imbued with such things for decades, the listener of today is incapable of understanding music of a different kind. Deviation from even one of these familiar musical features—though the rules may well permit it—is irritating to him. How much more so when, as in Schoenberg's music, there exists a simultaneous combination of all these qualities, usually regarded as attributes of good music, but generally found isolated and diffused throughout various epochs.

Think of the polyphony of Bach, of the theme structure of the classics and their antecedents, often quite free in rhythm and construction, exhibiting a mastery of the variation form; of the Romantics with their juxtaposition of keys, only distantly related, bold, even today; of Wagner's new chord structures, achieved through chromatic alteration and enharmonic change, and his effortless way of incorporating them into the tonality;

*Omitted in the present selection (Editors: E.S./B.C.).

68

finally of Brahms' thematic and motivic work, often encompassing the finest detail of art. Obviously, music that combines all the possibilities handed down to it by the classics must differ from a contemporary music, which—as I will show—is not a synthesis of this kind. It is in spite of these qualities, recognizable as attributes of every good music, and in spite of the richness with which they are employed in all musical fields—or actually because of them—that Schoenberg's music seems as recondite as it does.

I shall be reproached for having proved something that did not need proving: the difficulty of the D minor Quartet, a tonal piece which long ago ceased to be a problem and has even been generally accepted and understood! This may be somewhat exaggerated, and I admit that the question at the head of this article would appear answered only if everything here, based on a few measures in the minor mode, had been shown on the basis of at least one example of the so-called "atonal" music. But, after all, this article does not deal exclusively with the question of difficulty, but also with the proof that every event in this music is completely above-board and fashioned only along the lines of highest art. Of course this was easier to show using an example still based on major and minor tonality. But it is nonetheless appropriate for our study, since in earlier times it prompted as much agitation as his "atonal" music today. Now, however, when I view them both as accomplished facts—which they surely are—I need only apply everything I have said about these ten measures to any passage of his later or very latest works. This is possible not only because of the creativeness of Schoenberg, the "father of atonal thought", as he is generally called, but also because of the music's acceptance by a large part of the musical world. This would appear to have solved the riddle of our title and established that both kinds of music encompass the same high standards of art—and therefore employ legitimate means of expression. Thus it will be clear that the music's abstruseness lies not so much in its so-called "atonality", which by now is the means of expression for so many contemporaries, but in that structure of Schoenberg's earlier music, the inexhaustible artistic techniques—applied also in this later harmonic style—the use of all compositional possibilities of the music of centuries: in short, its boundless opulence. Here we find the same variety of harmonic treatment, with various degrees of cadence; also melodies suitable to such harmonic treatment, making boldest use of the possibilities of the twelve tones; the unsymmetrical, free thematic construction of themes, with its motivic work never ebbing; the art of variation, projecting itself thematically as well as in the harmonization, contrapuntally as well as in the rhythm; also the polyphony that expands over the whole work and the unequalled technique of contrapuntal part-writing; and finally the variety of rhythms, subject both to their own laws and those of variation, so that in this respect also, Schoenberg aims at an art of construction entirely remote from the "dissolved rhythm" so foolishly attributed to him.

Viewed from such a universal standpoint, how different in every respect is the position of other contemporary composers, even if in their harmonic language they have broken with the predominance of the triad. In their music, too, we can find the artistic techniques just enumerated, but never — as with Schoenberg — combined in the work of a single personality. Rather, they are always distributed among various groups, schools, years, nations and their respective representatives. One type likes the polyphonic way of writing which reduces thematic development and the art of variation to a bare minimum. The other prefers bold harmonic structure which does not shrink from any chord, though its melodic construction scarcely goes beyond homophony and may even be characterized by the use of only two and four measure phrases. The "atonality" of the one consists in putting wrong basses to primitively harmonized periods; others simultaneously provide two or more (respectively major and minor) keys, whereby the other musical features of each attest to a frightful poverty of invention. A music characterized by frequently changing melody and free thematic constructions suffers from an inertia of harmony, as shown by its dearth of harmonic degrees, sustained chords, endless pedal points and continually recurring chord clusters. I would almost go so far as to assert that a music so constructed cannot exist without mechanical repetitions and the most primitive sequences. This is shown especially in the rhythm, which reaches the very limit of monotony, often only simulating a richness of form, through changing time signatures and rhythmic displacement, where everything else is poverty. More often than one would think, this rhythm — sometimes rigid, sometimes hammering, sometimes dancelike and similarly animated — is the only thing keeping such otherwise unsubstantial music from falling apart. The practitioners of this technique of composition are the ones sure to be called "strong rhythmic talents".

The orientation toward these more or less rigid principles, often degenerating into one-sidedness — this satisfaction with being (as the beautiful saying goes) "modern, but not extreme" — helps such "atonal" or "progressively oriented" music to be understood and moderately liked. After all, it may confront the listener with one or more difficult problems, but in all other respects it does not deviate from the usual, often not even from the deliberately primitive. Thanks to these negative qualities it can also please the ears of the musically less gifted: in other words, it makes "easy listening." Even more so, since composers of such music can conform to style by being aware only of their special brand of modernity, without also accepting responsibility for a combination of all these possibilities. That inescapable necessity of accepting even the most extended consequences of musical universality is found only once; namely in the music of Schoenberg. Having said this I believe the last and perhaps strongest reason for its abstruseness has been stated. However, the fact that this noble compulsion is being fulfilled with a sovereignty bestowed, I would say, only upon a genius, allows for the assumption, or, rather, the assertion, that when the "classics of our time" belong to the past, Schoenberg will be among the very few remembered as a classic for all time. For not only has he, as Adolf Weissmann so aptly says, "drawn the last bold conclusions from musical culture",[5] but he has also progressed further than those, who, lacking definite direction, looked for new paths, and—consciously or unconsciously—negated the art of this musical culture. Thus, without being a prophet one can say even today on Schoenberg's fiftieth birthday that the work he has already given the world seems to have secured not only the pre-eminence of his personal art, but, more important, that of German music for the next fifty years.

[5] *Music in World Crisis* by Adolf Weissmann.

Béla
Bartók

[1881 - 1945]

Combining talents as pianist, composer, musicologist, and teacher, Bartók was one of the major musical figures of his time in Europe. Vigorously outspoken against the Nazi regime, he left Hungary for America in 1940, there to live out his last years in relative obscurity. After his death his music enjoyed a remarkable resurgence in popularity as one of the significant, original musical styles of our time.

Vitally concerned with the folk music of his native Hungary, Bartók spent years in the field, collecting, recording, and analyzing this music. Unlike composers such as Liszt who had previously used Hungarian musical material, Bartók had no interest in "civilized" café presentations. His compositions and compositional thinking reveal an absorption in the actual music itself. His concerns with ethnomusicology and composition, therefore, are not mutually exclusive, but demonstrate two facets of a single musical personality. This dual relationship is clarified in the article that follows.

One should not suppose, however, that Bartók's creative work was merely the "arrangement" of folk material. His music reveals not only the rhythms, melodies, and harmonic ingenuity of Slavic folk music, but also a deft handling of the formal structures of the past and a keenly creative ear for sound. Such major works as his six string quartets open up new worlds of instrumental color and technical effects unparalleled in the literature.

"The Influence of Peasant Music on Modern Music," translated by Eva Hajnal-Konyi, from *Tempo*, 14 (Winter, 1949–50), pp. 19–23. Originally published in *Uj Idok* (1931).

The Influence of
Peasant Music
on Modern Music

At the beginning of the twentieth century there was a turning point in the history of modern music.

The excesses of the romanticists began to be unbearable for many. There were composers who felt: "this road does not lead us anywhere; there is no other solution but a complete break with the nineteenth century."

Invaluable help was given to this change (or let us rather call it rejuvenation) by a kind of peasant music unknown up till then.

The right type of peasant music is most varied and perfect in its forms. Its expressive power is amazing, and at the same time it is void of all sentimentality and superfluous ornaments. It is simple, sometimes primitive but never silly. It is the ideal starting point for a musical renaissance, and a composer in search of new ways cannot be led by a better master. What is the best way for a composer to reap the full benefits of his studies in peasant music? It is to assimilate the idiom of peasant music so completely that he is able to forget all about it and use it as his musical mother-tongue.

In order to achieve this, Hungarian composers went into the country and made their collections there. It may be that the Russian Strawinsky and the Spaniard Falla did not go on journeys of collection, and mainly drew their material from the collections of others, but they too, I feel sure, must have studied not only books and museums but the living music of their countries.

In my opinion, the effects of peasant music cannot be deep and permanent unless this music is studied in the country as part of a life shared with the peasants. It is not enough to study it as it is stored up in museums. It is the character of peasant music, indescribable in words, that must find its way into our music. It must be pervaded by the very atmosphere of peasant culture. Peasant motifs (or imitations of such motifs) will only lend our music some new ornaments: nothing more.

Some twenty to twenty-five years ago well disposed people often marvelled at our enthusiasm. How was it possible, they asked, that trained musicians, fit to give concerts, took upon themselves the "subaltern" task of going into the country and studying the music of the people on the spot. What a pity, they said, that this task was not carried out by people unsuita-

Béla
Bartók

ble for a higher type of musical work. Many thought our perseverance in our work was due to some crazy idea that had got hold of us.

Little did they know how much this work meant to us. We went into the country and obtained first-hand knowledge of a music that opened up new ways to us.

The question is, what are the ways in which peasant music is taken over and becomes transmuted into modern music?

We may, for instance, take over a peasant melody unchanged or only slightly varied, write an accompaniment to it and possibly some opening and concluding phrases. This kind of work would show a certain analogy with Bach's treatment of chorales.

Two main types can be distinguished among works of this character.

In the one case accompaniment, introductory and concluding phrases, are of secondary-importance, they only serve as an ornamental setting for the precious stone: the peasant melody.

It is the other way round in the second case: the melody only serves as a "motto" while that which is built round it is of real importance.

All shades of transition are possible between these two extremes and some times it is not even possible to decide which of the elements is predominant in any given case. But in every case it is of the greatest importance that the musical qualities of the setting should be derived from the musical qualities of the melody, from such characteristics as are contained in it openly or convertly, so that melody and all additions create the impression of complete unity.

At this point I have to mention a strange notion wide-spread some thirty or forty years ago. Most trained and good musicians then believed that only simple harmonizations were well suited to folk-tunes. And even worse, by simple harmonies they meant a succession of triads of tonic, dominant and possibly subdominant.

How can we account for this strange belief? What kind of folk-songs did these musicians know? Mostly new German and Western songs and so-called folk-songs made up by popular composers. The melody of such songs usually moves along the triad of tonic and dominant; the main melody consists of a breaking up of these chords into single notes ("Oh Du lieber Augustin"). It is obvious that melodies of this description do not go well with a more complex harmonization.

But our musicians wanted to apply the theory derived from this type of songs to an entirely different type of Hungarian songs built up on "pentatonic" scales.

It may sound odd, but I do not hesitate to say: the simpler the melody the more complex and strange may be the harmonization and accompaniment that go well with it. Let us for instance take a melody that moves on two successive notes only (there are many such melodies in Arab peasant music). It is obvious that we are much freer in the invention of an accompaniment than in the case of a melody of a more complex character. These primitive melodies moreover, show no trace of the stereotyped joining of triads. That again means greater freedom for us in the treatment of the melody. It allows us to bring out the melody most clearly by building round it harmonies of the widest range varying along different keynotes. I might almost say that the traces of polytonality in modern Hungarian music and in Strawinsky's music are to be explained by this possibility.

Similarly, the strange turnings of melodies in our eastern European peasant music showed us new ways of harmonization. For instance the new chord of the seventh which we use as a concord may be traced back to the fact that in our folk melodies of a pentatonic character the seventh appears as an interval of equal importance with the third and the fifth. We so often heard these intervals as of equal value in the succession, that what was more natural than that we should try to make them sound of equal importance when used simultaneously. We sounded the four notes together in a setting which made us feel it not necessary to break them up. In other words: the four notes were made to form a concord.

The frequent use of quart intervals in our old melodies suggested to us the use of quart chords. Here again what we heard in succession we tried to build up in a simultaneous chord.

Another method by which peasant music becomes transmuted into modern music is the following: The composer does not make use of a real peasant melody but invents his own imitation of such melodies. There is no true difference between this method and the one described above.

Strawinsky never mentions the sources of his themes. Neither in his titles nor in footnotes does he ever allude to it, whether a theme of his is his own invention or whether it is taken over from folk-music. In the same way the old composers never gave any data: let me simply mention the beginning of the *Pastoral Symphony*. Strawinsky apparently takes this course deliberately. He wants to demonstrate that it does not matter a jot whether a composer invents his own themes or uses themes from elsewhere. He has a right to use musical material taken from all sources. What he has judged suitable for his purpose has become through this very use his mental property. In the same manner Molière is reported to have replied to a charge of plagiarism: "Je prends mon bien où je le trouve." In maintaining that the question of the origin of a theme is completely unimportant from the artist's point of view, Strawinsky is right. The question of origins can only be interesting from the point of view of musical documentation.

Lacking any data I am unable to tell which themes of Strawinsky's at his so-called "Russian period" are his own inventions and which are borrowed from folk-music. This much is certain, that if among the thematic material of Strawinsky's there are some of his own invention (and who can doubt that there are) these are the most faithful and clever imitations of folk-songs. It is also notable that during his "Russian" period, from *Le Sacre du Printemps* onward, he seldom uses melodies of a closed form consisting of three or four lines, but short motives of two or three bars and repeats them "à la ostinato". These short recurring primitive motifs are very characteristic of Russian music of a certain category. This type of construction occurs in some of our old music for wind instruments and also in Arab peasant dances.

This primitive construction of the thematic material may partly account for the strange mosaic-like character of Strawinsky's work during his early period.

The steady repetition of primitive motifs creates an air of strange feverish excitement even in the sort of folk-music where it occurs. The effect is increased a hundredfold if a master of Strawinsky's supreme skill and his precise knowledge of dynamic effects employs these rapidly chasing sets of motifs.

There is yet a third way in which the influence of peasant music can be traced in a composer's work. Neither peasant melodies nor imitations of peasant melodies can be found in his music, but it is pervaded by the atmosphere of peasant music. In this case we may say, he has completely absorbed the idiom of peasant music which has become his musical mother tongue. He masters it as completely as a poet masters his mother tongue.

In Hungarian music the best example of this kind can be found in Kodály's work. It is enough to mention "Psalmus Hungaricus", which would not have been written without Hungarian peasant music. (Neither, of course, would it have been written without Kodály.)

On the Significance
of Folk Music

Many people think it a comparatively easy task to write a composition round folk-tunes. A lesser achievement at least than a composition on "original" themes. Because, they think, the composer is dispensed of part of the work: the invention of themes.

This way of thought is completely erroneous. To handle folk-tunes is one of the most difficult tasks; equally difficult if not more so than to write a major original composition. If we keep in mind that borrowing a tune means being bound by its individual peculiarity we shall understand one part of the difficulty. Another is created by the special character of a folk-tune. We must penetrate into it, feel it, and bring it out in sharp contours by the appropriate setting. The composition round a folk-tune must be done in a "propitious hour" or—as is generally said—it must be a work of inspiration just as much as any other composition.

There are many who think the basing of modern music on folk-music harmful and not suited to our time.

Before arguing with that school of thought let us consider how is it possible to reconcile music based on folk-music with the modern movement into atonality, or music on twelve tones.

Let us say frankly that this is not possible. Why not? Because folk-tunes are always tonal. Folk-music of atonality is completely inconceivable. Consequently, music on twelve tones cannot be based on folk-music.

The fact that some twentieth century composers went back for inspiration to old folk-music acted as an impediment to the development of twelve tone music.

Far be it from me to maintain that to base his music on folk-music is the only way to salvation for a composer in our days. But I wish that our opponents had an equally liberal opinion of the significance of folk-music.

It is only recently that one of our reputable musicians held forth like this: "The ulterior motive behind the movement of collecting folk-songs that has spread all over the world, is love of comfort. There is a desire to become rejuvenated in this spring of freshness; a wish to revitalize the barren brain. This desire tries to hide an inner incompetence and to evade the struggle by comfortable and soul-killing devices."

This regrettable opinion is based on erroneous assumptions. These people must have a strange idea of the practice of composing. They seem to think the composer addicted to collecting folk-songs will sit down at his writing desk with the intention of composing a symphony. He racks and racks his brain but cannot think of a suitable melody. He takes up his collection of folk-songs, picks out one or two melodies and the composition of his symphony is done without further labour.

Well, it is not as simple as all that. It is a fatal error to attribute so much importance to the subject, the theme of a composition. We know that Shakespeare borrowed the stories of his plays from all sources. Does that prove that his brain was barren and he had to go to his neighbours begging for themes? Did he hide his incompetence? Molière's case is even worse. He not only borrowed the themes for his plays, but also part of the construction, and sometimes took over from his source expressions and whole lines unchanged.

Béla
Bartók

We know that Handel adapted a work by Stradella in one of his oratorios. His adaptation is so masterly, so much surpassing the original in beauty, that we forget all about Stradella. Is there any sense in talking of plagiarism, of barrenness of brain, of incompetence in these cases?

In music it is the thematic material that corresponds to the story of a drama. And in music too, as in poetry and in painting, it does not signify what themes we use. It is the form into which we mould it that makes the essence of our work. This form reveals the knowledge, the creative power, the individuality of the artist.

The work of Bach is a summing up of the music of some hundred and odd years before him. His musical material is themes and motives used by his predecessors. We can trace in Bach's music motifs, phrases which were also used by Frescobaldi and many others among Bach's predecessors. Is this plagiarism? By no means. For an artist it is not only right to have his roots in the art of some former times, it is a necessity.

Well, in our case it is peasant music which holds our roots.

The conception that attributes all that importance to the invention of a theme originated in the nineteenth century. It is a romantic conception which values originality above all.

From what has been said above, it must have become clear that it is no sign of "barrenness" or "incompetence" if a composer bases his music on folk-music instead of taking Brahms and Schumann as his models.

There exists another conception of modern music which seems exactly the opposite of the former one.

There are people who believe that nothing more is needed to bring about the full bloom in a nation's music than to steep oneself in folk-music and to transplant its motives into established musical forms.

This opinion is founded on the same mistaken conception as the one discussed above. It stresses the all-importance of themes and forgets about the art of formation that alone can make something out of these themes. This process of moulding is the part of the composer's work which proves his creative talent.

And thus we may say: folk-music will become a source of inspiration for a country's music only if the transplantation of its motifs is the work of a great creative talent. In the hands of incompetent composers neither folk-music nor any other musical material will ever attain significance. If a composer has no talent it will be of no use to him to base his music on folk-music or any other music. The result will in every case be nothing.

Folk-music will have an immense transforming influence on music in countries·with little or no musical tradition. Most countries of southern and eastern Europe; Hungary, too, are in this position.

The Influence of Peasant
Music on Modern Music

May I, to conclude my thoughts, [finish] by quoting what Kodály once said in this context about the importance of folk-music.

"So little of written old Hungarian music has survived that the history of Hungarian music cannot be built up without a thorough knowledge of folk-music. It is known that folk language has many similarities with the ancient language of a people. In the same way folk-music must for us replace the remains of our old music. Thus, from a musical point of view, it means more to us than to those peoples that developed their own musical style centuries ago. Folk-music for these peoples become assimilated into their music, and a German musician will be able to find in Bach and Beethoven what we had to search for in our villages; the continuity of a national musical tradition."

Paul
Hindemith

[1895 - 1963]

*Although Hindemith's music has often been referred to as neo-Classic,
its roots are more complex than this simple term would indicate. The
spirit of eighteenth-century music is often evoked in Hindemith's work,
particularly in its insistence upon strong metric drive, its feeling for tonal
center, and its heavy reliance upon contrapuntal technique. On the
other hand, his stand on the ethical obligations of the composer toward
society is reminiscent of the nineteenth century, and would be considered Romantic when compared with the more objective approaches of
Stravinsky and Babbitt. Moreover, he was a great innovator in the early
years of his career, and was among the first to explore the uses of jazz,
chords built in fourths rather than the traditional thirds, and dissonant
counterpoint.*

*The essays reprinted here illustrate important tenets in Hindemith's
philosophy. He believed that music has a social role to play, and that all
music must be composed—and judged—with a specific social purpose
in mind. Much of his own music was written with such a purpose; his
Gebrauchsmusik ,"music for use" or "workaday music". includes works
composed for neglected instruments, for performance by children or
amateurs, for occasions of state. These are only a few of the circumstances that—in Hindemith's view—demand music of the contemporary
composer.*

*This view of the composer's role assumes that the creation of new
music is only one of many ways—including performing, conducting,
writing and teaching—in which the composer must function as a complete musician, enriching the cultural life of his community.*

Reprinted from Paul Hindemith, *A Composer's World, Horizons and
Limitations* (Cambridge, Mass., Harvard University Press, 1952), pp.
104-12, 121-25, 177-87.

From
"A Composer's
World"

Technique and Style

There is a widespread opinion that questions of technique are irrelevant: that the creator of music, in particular, need not bother with the worldly problem of how to assemble tones, since he, the gods' favorite, cannot help simply and involuntarily fulfilling his superhuman mission. This opinion promptly leads to the often-heard statement that in music the question is merely one of quality: that there is only good or bad music. This is a statement you hear equally from the initiated, namely the composer, and from the layman, be he a plain music-lover or a well-trained philosopher. What the composer's attitude towards this statement ought to be we shall see later on. Here and now, in our quest to clarify the role of technique in the process of musical production and reproduction, we must resort to the experience of the performer, the man who, as we have found, is by his very actions necessarily closest to such decisions.

If all music ever written could only be classified as "good" or "bad" with some pieces perhaps occasionally falling short of either extreme, what would a singer or player do with a composition of the highest quality, viewed objectively, but not serving his personal purposes? Take one of the more florid Gregorian melodies, such as those sung at Easter time or on Whitsunday, which will doubtless be considered by every musician of some taste the most perfect, the most convincing one-line compositions ever conceived. Of course, in order to fully understand their overwhelming linear power, you cannot restrict yourself to just reading or hearing them. You must participate in singing these melodic miracles if you want to feel how they weld the singing group into a spiritual unit, independent of the individualistic prompting of a conductor, and guided only by the lofty spirit and the technical excellence of the structure. Now imagine that you are forced to sing them by yourself—solo, that is—transplanting those immaculate creations into another environment. Don't you feel as if you were expelled from a community of worthy friends? Has the music not lost its savor and assumed a taste of bitterness instead? And then play these same melodies, which were the precious vessels of highest linear revelations, on a wind instrument, then on a fiddle, and finally on the piano. The quality of the melodic line seems to disappear gradually, greatness turns into inexpressive melismatism, then becomes insipid passage-work, and finally ends in ridicule. If, as our aforementioned light-hearted philosophers believed, perfection remained perfection under all circumstances, how could such a disintegration of values take place merely by altering the means of performance?

Let us once more illustrate our point, this time with an example in which the change of the means of expression is not quite as drastic as in the gradual metamorphosis of a chorus into a piano, but which, due to its closeness to our everyday musical experience, is perhaps even more convincing. We all agree that in a fugue the linear arrangement of the musical material must be strongly emphasized, and this is often carried to the highest degree of contrapuntal rigidity. Consequently, any group of instruments that allows this contrapuntal fabric to appear in transparent lucidity should in principle be preferable to all others. Since linear writing for pianos or other keyboard instruments can only be an artificial projection of several independent melodic planes into one single plane, a keyboard fugue played on nonkeyed melodic instruments should reveal its linear spirit in a more appropriate and therefore more convincing manner than the original form could ever do. Now play some of the undisputed masterpieces of this species, namely fugues from Bach's *Wohltemperiertes Klavier*, as string trio or string quartet pieces. You will have a queer and rather disagreeable sensation: compositions which you knew as being great, heavy, and as emanating an impressive spiritual strength, have turned into pleasant miniatures. With the increase in contrapuntal clarity we have had to accept a deplorable loss of majesty and gravity. Although the supremacy of the piece has remained the same, the pieces have shrunk, despite the improved reproduction, and their structural and spiritual relation to the original keyboard form has become that of a miniature mummified Incan head to its previous animate form. In our fugues we have reduced to almost nothing the heavy technical resistance that a player of polyphonic keyboard music has to overcome, since the string players have produced their isolated lines without noticeable effort.

This example shows clearly that with the artless classification of good and bad, nothing is said about the real technical quality of a composition so long as no further criteria are introduced. One of these criteria is, as our experiments in the transformation of Gregorian and Bach pieces have demonstrated, the degree of resistance that the particular technical form of a composition offers to the players' or singers' technique of performance, a factor which the performer has to cope with before either the listener or the producer need be aware of it.

A composer may remain totally ignorant of the wider world of musical thought, musical creation, and musical reception shown in these pages; he may never outgrow his oxlike devotion to the moment's technical demands; but may we not hope that after he is told of the performer's keenness in respect to a composition's technique he, for his part, will comprehend that his own technique of assembling musical material should likewise be applied with utmost dicrimination — a discrimination not arising out of his own preoccupation with the peculiarities of sounds and their application, but determined by factors more important than his individualistic speculations?

What are these factors?

There is, first of all, the prosaic decision concerning the space in which a piece is to be performed. In a very small hall, in a living room, we can readily discern the most involved melodic lines, the most complex harmonies, and the most intricate rhythmical patterns, because we are in closest spatial connection with the source of the sound. And besides, the instruments and singers can make use of the most refined subtleties of technique, because nothing will get lost, and the performers themselves can transmit their production as directly as in intimate talk. The composer, writing for such conditions, enjoys the greatest possible freedom to develop his technique into the most esoteric realms. Almost everything he writes will have a chance to be lucidly presented and clearly understood. No wonder, therefore, that chamber music has always, so far as application of the musical elements is concerned, been the preferred medium for technical audacity.

A composer writing for a larger hall loses a good deal of the freedom afforded by the small one. Melodies, in order to be understood, must be written so that the physical and mental distance between the performers and listeners cannot distort them. In rhythm, metrical structures will push themselves into the foreground, due to their greater intelligibility. Thus rhythmic patterns which, in order to be grasped intelligently, require a keen analytic mind on the part of the listener, ought to be avoided. Rapidly moving harmonies or harmonies of too great a complexity are not advisable, for the same reason. It is striking to see how sensitive our classical masters were in this respect. The technique of their symphonic works is essentially different from that of their chamber music, although all the basic material is identical. Nowadays we find many writers who neglect these necessities. Oftentimes we hear orchestra pieces written in a technique of complete linear independence, of great harmonic and tonal detail, and of rhythmic obscurity, all of which lose about fifty per cent of their substance before they reach the listener's ears. On the other hand, some chamber music pieces are presented in the rudest orchestral technique, which in small places of performance gives merely an impression of boorish awkwardness. What would an expert in steel production say, if a simple-minded waitress suggested the use of paper drinking cups as the most suitable molds for whitehot steel? Or what sense would there be in serving a milk shake in a Bessemer converter? In music we find many works the musical contents of which are no less incongruous with their containers — the places of performances — than milk shakes and steel in our metaphor. The larger such places are, the more the complexity of technique has to be reduced. So far no music has been written that would fit our gigantic stadiums and bowls. We are using them for the performance of classical music, music that depends on the closest physical and mental proximity of not more than a few hundred listeners, and now this music is blown up to fill spaces in which the listener in the last row of the third balcony hears the fiddles' tones about a second after he has seen the players' bows executing them (a second equaling one half measure in 4/4 time at ordinary walking tempo!). Here again we could learn from the past — from Perotin, for instance, who about 1200 wrote his Organa for the then overwhelmingly new spatial conception of the Gothic cathedrals. These pieces, by no means primitive, provided in their technical planning even for the echo within those columned and vaulted halls, so that retarded echoing harmonies, intermingling with the straight progress of the normal harmonies could not disturb the over-all impression.

Once I heard a performance of Beethoven's Ninth Symphony in one of those tremendous stadiums which seat thirty thousand or more people. The piece was performed by a chorus of about one thousand singers with a five-hundred piece orchestra. The group of performers, although of a high quality, and the dimensions of the place were so utterly disproportionate to the shape and character of the piece, that it sounded ghastly. One could not make head or tail of it. After this symphony a dance was performed by thousands of school children to the accompaniment of some specially manufactured music of no significance. It was written for a couple of recorders, two or three lower-ranged instruments, and some soft percussion. This music, transmitted by loud-speakers, made a masterpiece appear like an amateurish attempt at composition by some nincompoop. Had Beethoven, while writing the symphony in its familiar technique, conceived it for the spatial conditions just mentioned, we would have to accuse him of the grossest technical miscalculation. Fortunately, he had the finest feeling for the proportional relationship between space and compositional technique and he cannot be blamed for the sins of his interpreters. Our performers may, for their own ephemeral glory, adhere to such barbarisms as playing a Brandenburg concerto, written for not more than fifteen players and an audience of fifty to one hundred, with eighty or more players before an assembled audience of forty thousand, but the living composer should at least try to prevent his own pieces from being performed under adverse conditions. Alas, he usually is only too elated if his compositions are played at all, no matter what the conditions of performance are.

There are other factors besides places of performance that influence — or, let us say, ought to influence — the composer's technical considerations. There is the intellectual capacity of his listeners. If he writes for an audience well acquainted with symphonic music and its performance, he can apply a technique more involved than the one he would use for unaccustomed listeners. For instance, an orchestral piece that is good for New York or Boston is not necessarily good for Musselshell, Mo.; and chamber music, enjoyed in a salon by a sophisticated, overcritical bunch of highbrow intellectuals, may be boring to people with plain musical intelligence or those with a desire for uninhibited directness in musical communications. Of course, there is always the haughty point of view of the composer who does not want to step down to the populace, "My music is as it is. I am not influenced by all these considerations. If people want to understand my music, they will have to grow up to my standards." It is one thing to write down to the bad instincts of the unrefined listener, and another to satisfy by technical means the just demands of a cultured customer. The attitude of the arrogant composer is similar to that of the millionaire who cannot understand that other people are in want of money. Even the loftiest musical spirit grew from a state of simple-mindedness to its superior position; thus, it is acting the parvenu to look with contempt upon those left far behind on the road to success. Moreover, there are many people who never will be and never want to be millionaires, financially or musically. Are we to lose them and their propensity towards music merely because we are unable or unwilling to write music that satisfies their demands?

Another important factor in technical decisions is the performer's degree of skill in playing and singing. For the Boston Symphony you can write anything from open strings to complicated arrangements approximating those that only Harvard's "mechanical brain" could be expected to handle with a formidable consumption of electric current; they will play it. But what about orchestras in small towns, amateur groups, and school orchestras? What about amateurs who have perhaps one hundred times the good will of the professional musician but only one hundredth of his technical skill? If the nature of our pieces is such that they can master them only after fifty rehearsals and even then never to their own satisfaction, they will gladly consign their fiddles and voices to cold storage and become one hundred per cent listeners, driven away from practical music by the very musician who usually complains bitterly of the public's ever-growing aversion to practical participation in music.

Finally, do we want to drive away all those who have all the culture and education that make them perfect listeners; and those excellent players or singers, professionals or amateurs, who simply are not always in the mood to solve intricate musical problems? Shall we leave them to tin-pan alley and the juke boxes? There is a great choice of technical possibilities that can take care of their needs.

Once, in the Rocky Mountains, I had a strange musical experience. In a gorge famous for its waterfalls and filled with aerial railways, summer guests, cars, and ice-cream vendors, a well-coordinated loud-speaker system screamed Isolde's *Liebestod* all over the place, as part of the gorge's daily routine. I am sure the managers of the establishment wanted to please their customers, true to the rule which seems to be one of the leading theses of the American way of life: enjoyment plus enjoyment gives you more enjoyment.

We cannot blame them for the idea that the accumulation of single enjoyments results in an accumulated sensation: that *Liebestod* plus waterfalls plus ice cream give us more pleasure than *Liebestod* or waterfalls or ice-cream solo. After all, it was the composer of the *Liebestod* himself who concocted the idea of the *Gesamtkunstwerk,* in which singing voices, orchestra, stage, light effects, horses, rivers, cardboard mountains, artificial beards, et cetera, et cetera, were part of the over-all enjoyment. The catch in this conception is that our over-all enjoyment cannot be more than one hundred per cent. Hence, three factors of enjoyment, which each by itself would provide one hundred per cent enjoyment, do not add up to three hundred per cent; they are, rather, compressed into the one hundred per cent, so that each of them, if participation is equal, has but thirty-three and a third per cent of its original effect. I personally even believe that too much of an accumulation of artistic or presumedly artistic enjoyments not only reduces the percentage of the single constituent enjoyment, but also reduces the over-all effect from its one hundred per cent to a much lower degree. Thus the effect of the aforementioned *Gesamtkunstwerk* in the mountains will most likely be that you will take your car, cursing waterfalls, *Liebestods,* and ice cream in equal percentage and drive to a place where there is nothing but a hundred per cent view.

This time the disproportion between the composition and its performance was not, as it was in the case of the Ninth Symphony, of a musical-technical nature. Although the operatic piece was originally not written for gorges and waterfalls, the many loud-speakers provided an even distribution of sound, so that acoustically the conditions of a big opera house were reproduced not too inaptly, and thus the technical shape of the piece was not in disturbing disagreement with the space in which it was performed.

The disturbing effects in this case originated in a discrepancy between styles. The piece with all its technical, intellectual, historical, and aesthetical implications belonged to one certain sphere of style, from which the style of the pleasure-voracious crowd with their dull, indeterminate, and resistless surrender to anything sensuous is far removed—if ever such brutishness can be honored with the name style—a term that usually indicates at least a faint tendency toward a cultured life!

It is obvious that the gorge's managerial benefactors of the vacationing crowd thought "If *Liebestod* is good in the Metropolitan, it will be equally good in our gorge." They forgot that the composition deals with the most refined feelings of two sublime lovers, expressed in exalted music for those who come especially prepared for its reception, and that it should not be projected into an environment which, although gigantic, has become nothing but a tremendous prop for the proverbial having-a-good-time of thousands of daily vacationists. The discrepancy between the vacationists' good time and Isolde's unfortunate experience is more than disgusting.

Let us investigate briefly some allegedly "modern" achievements. The best known and most frequently mentioned is the so-called twelve-tone technique, or composition in preëstablished tone series. The idea is to take the twelve tones of our chromatic scale, select one of its some four hundred million permutations, and use it as the basis for the harmonic (and possibly melodic) structure of a piece. This rule of construction is established arbitrarily and without any reference to basic musical facts. It ignores the validity of harmonic and melodic values derived from mathematical, physical, or psychological experience; it does not take into account the differences in intervallic tensions, the physical relationship of tones, the degree of ease in vocal production, and many other facts of either natural permanence or proven usefulness. Its main "law" is supplemented by other rules of equal arbitrariness, such as: tones must not be repeated; your selected tone series may skip from one stratum of the texture to any other one; you have to use the inversion and other distortions of this series; and so on—all of which can be reduced to the general advice: avoid so far as possible anything that has been written before.

The only segment of our conventional body of theoretical musical knowledge which the dodecaphonists have deigned to admit and which, in fact, alone makes their speculations possible, is the twelve-tone tempered scale. We have already been told of this scale's weakness: because of its basic impurity it can be used only as a supplementary regulative to a tone system containing natural intervals—at least, so long as we want to save our music from total instrumental mechanization and have human voices participate in its execution. True, some kind of a restricted technique of composition can be developed on a foundation of compromise scales and arbitrary working rules, but doubtless the general result will always be one similar to the kind of poetry that is created by pouring written words out of a tumbler without calling in grammar and syntax. A higher tonal organization is not attempted and cannot be achieved, especially if one permits the technical working rules to slip off into the aforementioned set of supplementary statutes which are nothing but stylistic whims and, as such, not subject to any controlling power of general validity. Of course, there are those superrefined prophets who proudly claim that they can, by the rules of this stylistic method, write pieces in C major, which seems to be a procedure as direct as leaving one's house in New England through the front door and entering the back door by a little detour via Chicago.

Twelve-tone operations are not the only nightmares that haunt the composing zealot who wants to be up to date. Are there not city sky lines whose ragged contours demand to be reproduced in melodic lines? Some other composers invent, with the aid of addition, subtraction, and other numerical operations, ways of combining tones mechanically; and finally, there are always colors as organizing agents. It is easy to recognize the underlying principle in all these and similar methods: it is a simple equation between a given number of tones and anything else that consists of an equal number of constituent parts. We could go on counting such methods of tonal equations, but only to enter a sphere in which there is almost nothing that could not be brought into direct equational relationship with harmony and melody: fever curves, cooking recipes, railroad timetables (the music resulting from them may be rather monotonous, though), catalogues of country fairs, the depth of the ocean between Halifax and Ireland, and so on.

If the inventors of such systems had looked into music history, they would have found that their methods are by no means as modern as they think. Moreover, their predecessors' lack of lasting success should have made them suspicious. The earliest attempts at composing by a method of this kind can be found in several treatises of the eleventh and twelfth centuries, in which an equation of the five vowels of the Latin language and five successive tones of a church mode is used. The melodies thus constructed must, even to the inventor of this system, have sounded trivial enough, because we see an additional, transposed equation recommended to heighten the poor melodic effect somewhat. (I was never quite sure that this invention was not contrived with tongue in cheek.) Obviously this method did not appeal to contemporary composers, since in spite of the medieval theorists' fondness for plagiarizing each other, it did not reappear in later treatises.

Other equations were devised with the spots of dice, a pastime very popular in Mozart's time—in fact, some of the methods of composing with this recipe are published under Mozart's or Haydn's name, one even in Boston, Massachusetts.

The method which in my opinion showed the greatest subtlety is one suggested in a little book published in 1751 by the English musician William Hayes. Its title is *The Art of Composing Music by a Method Entirely New, Suited to the Meanest Capacity*. It is a satire on the wave of Italian music, with its composers of frequently inferior quality, which at that time swept over London. His advice is, to take a brush with stiff bristles (like a toothbrush), dip it into an inkwell, and, by scraping the bristles with the finger, spatter with one sweep a whole composition onto the staff paper. You have only to add stems, bar lines, slurs, et cetera, to make the opus ready for immediate performance. Whole and half notes are entirely absent, but who cares for sustained tones anyway! (What a striking forecast of one of the ulgiest modern musical diseases!)

Despite the intentional humor of these directions, the similarity with our twelve-tone technique cannot be overlooked. The characteristic difference seems to be that Hayes's method gives the composer, or whatever you want to call the fellow who uses the brush—the "spruzzarino," as he calls it—a greater freedom in artistic enterprises than does the rather rigorous twelve-tone technique. Moreover, it prevents the once accepted technique from degenerating into stylistic irrelevancies.

Movements of this kind spring up like epidemics of measles, and they disappear just as enigmatically. We have already once seen a twelve-tone movement die, due to lack of interest on the part of musicians who liked music more than operations on music. That was shortly after World War I. At that time the germ was introduced to this country and caused minor disturbances, which by now have all but disappeared, with a few scars remaining. After World War II, Europe was again infected, but already the patients are feeling better and there is hope that after some minor relapses only a few diehards will survive to be the prophets who, in quiet solitude, will prepare the next big outburst. This, if we can trust past experience, will probably occur after World War III, provided any people are left over to be interested in tone combinations. One little sign of reconvalescence may perhaps be seen in the following fact, which could not remain hidden even to the most stalwart dodecaphonists (or is it dodecacophonists, as many people have it?): with this method no pieces can be produced which could fill big spaces with broad symphonic colors, or which could satisfy many people's demands for simplicity, directness, and personal sympathy.

A strange feature of all these movements is their sectarian character. It is almost as in the Nazi state or in a Red dictatorship: the supreme condition for your participation is that you have no disbelief whatsoever in the perfection of the system. You will have to fight against the adherents of other "systems," against the writers of program music, and against those who use sky lines and numerical equivalents other than the permutations of the numbers one to twelve, although your "meanest capacity" would tell you, that their activities are of the same kind as those you adore. The parallelism to religious sects goes so far, that an idol is felt to be necessary, to whom everything of importance ever created or uttered in music is ascribed, although for his glory some real instigators and inventors may have to be obscured and rendered innocuous. It is all so reminiscent of some kind of voodoo cult, and the idolizers of the superstition seem to bear a painful similarity to the haruspices in ancient Greece and Rome. The entrails of sacrificial animals by means of which the haruspex predicted the future have just as little to do with world events as have numerical permutations with musical creation.

I would not have dwelt so long on these strange peripheral endeavors, were it not for the fact that such a discussion shows how far one can be led astray by the emphasis upon a musical factor of secondary importance —namely, style. The ethical power of music is entirely neglected; the composer's obligations towards his fellow men are degraded to a game of double-crostics, which certainly gives enough stimulus to one's self-content but leaves the other fellow like the doleful child outside the house in which the Christmas tree is shining. If music written on this basis has any message for others, it is the crassest order "you have to obey, you have to believe in my constructions," in a time when we all are so terribly in need of some shiny little reflection of that other message, the one that Schiller and Beethoven gave to mankind: *Seid umschlungen, Millionen*—be embraced, ye millions.

Education

In earlier times composition was hardly taught at all. If a boy was found to be gifted for music, he was given as an apprentice into the care of a practical musician. With him he had to get acquainted with many branches of music. Singing was the foundation of all musical work. Thus singing, mostly in the form of group singing, was one of the most important fields of instruction. The practical knowledge of more or less all instruments was a *sine qua non*. Specialization was almost unknown. Frequently a musician may have been better on the keyboard than with the bow and with woodwinds or brass, but that would not have absolved him from playing as many other instruments as possible. And all this playing was done with one aim in mind: to prepare the musician for collective work; it was always the community that came first. Soloistic training was nothing but a preliminary and preparatory exercise for this purpose. Hand in hand with this daily all-round routine in instrumental training went a solid instruction in the theory of music—not only what we call theory in our modern curricula, namely harmony, counterpoint, and other branches of practical instruction, but true theory, or if you prefer another name, the scientific background of music.

This vast stock of general musical knowledge was the hotbed in which the germs of composing grew. If a musician had any talent for composition, he could always draw on this tremendous accumulation of practical experience, once he wanted to convert his ideas into audible structures. Composing was not a special branch of knowledge that had to be taught to those gifted or interested enough. It simply was the logical outgrowth of a healthy and stable system of education, the ideal of which was not an instrumental, vocal, or tone-arranging specialist, but a musician with a universal musical knowledge—a knowledge which, if necessary, could easily be used as a basis for a more specialized development of peculiar talents. This system, although it provided for the composer the best preparation possible, did not guarantee him any success. Only posterity decided whether he was to be counted among the few extraordinary creative musical figures each country had produced throughout the world, or among the many preparers and pioneers who had to blast the way for those great fulfillers, or finally among those who generalize, smooth out, and popularize the more original work of the genius.

Today the situation is quite different.

First of all, it is almost never the gift of composing that sends young people into this field of musical activity. Musical creative gift cannot, in my opinion, be recognized until after a rather well developed general knowledge of practical music has been acquired. If there is no such knowledge, the sole evidence of that gift can be afforded by written-down attempts at building musical structures. Usually such attempts are not at all a sign of creative talent. The minimum requirements for entering the creative field, such as a good ear for musical facts and perhaps even a feeling for absolute pitch, are too common among all people, musical or nonmusical, to be taken for the foundation upon which to build a composer's career. Their presence acknowledged, the further creative inclination of a youth inexperienced in practical music normally is the desire to express himself in some way or another. The ordinary urge to put something on paper is most readily attracted by notation symbols. Their being distinctly remote from the banalities of written language symbols, the widespread talismanic

91

belief that by some power of their own they may turn from a vague conception into a work of art, and finally the pictorial satisfaction they give to people otherwise lacking the gift of drawing or painting — all these factors make the writing of notation symbols, following some self-imposed rules of combination, the ideal medium for minds who in their youthful innocence try to compensate for confusion and immaturity by means of exorcistic mysteriousness.

Another familiar starting point for presumptive composers is the ambition to imitate somebody whose name is known, to become a famous man, which in the opinion of most candidates can be accomplished in the field of musical creation with less effort and with a greater expectation of success than in other activities. In all these cases the driving factor is the inclination towards release of some tension — frequently but not necessarily of a general artistic nature — and not primarily a musical gift that decides in favor of composition.

True, all these factors must not be underrated. Once a workable knowledge of practical music is acquired, they can aid the assiduous mind considerably. Alone, however, unbacked by solid experience, they are of no greater value than an infant's determination to become a streetcar driver or a garbage man.

Although genuine musical knowledge is lacking, some experience with music is usually evident with those intending to enter musical composition. The main fact in their favor is that they listened most frequently and eagerly to music, predominantly in the form of records or radio transmissions, and that their actual musical activity consisted in turning the radio dial, or putting the records on the Victrola, which latter effort grew obsolete with the introduction of automatic record turners and long-playing disks and was reduced simply to an admiring and utterly unproductive attitude. The fellow who comes as a fiddler or a wind instrument player from a high-school orchestra or band and sees in the study of composition a complementary discipline of his general musical education that eventually may or may not lead him into specialization is already a rather rare bird. And the case in which people come from the place that ought to be the normal breeding ground of future composers — namely, the family that has made singing and playing a part of their daily cultural life — is almost nonexistent.

The situation we described shortly before as the ideal seems to be reversed. In former times one had to be a good musician before he could take up composing, and it was up to history to decide whether or not he was to be regarded a great creative genius. Nowadays we can be sure to find in most applicants' souls, openly shown or bashfully hidden, the conviction "I feel that I am a great creative genius, therefore people have to take me for an excellent musician"; and the equally meaningless and boastful addition "I am feeling an irrepressible urge to compose" can be taken for granted. Frequently ominous amendments follow these basic statements, such as: "I do not play any instrument, and I never had any regular instruction in theory and composition, since several attempts in this direction failed due to the fussiness of the teachers who wanted me to go through years of boring technicalities instead of promoting my creative gift; I have written many pieces, some of which have been performed and won awards; in a recent nationwide competition I won the first prize over a number of trained composers and theory teachers." We may count ourselves lucky if the courageous ignoramus does not end up with "My compositions are written in an atonal vein."

If you are a good-natured person and want to give this fellow a chance, you may ask him to submit his compositions for an examination, although you know from hundreds of preceding experiences that there is no hope of discovering a creative musician this way. Nature doubtless has her whims and sometimes permits him to appear, meteorlike, among hundreds of thousands of regular cases, unprepared, uninhibited and full of talent, energy, and fervor, and you want to assist this prodigy in coming to the fore. But despite all well-meaning midwifery, untrained natural talent has not the same chances in music that it has in poetry or painting. In the latter arts the material is much more easily accessible, since language is everybody's property anyway, and there is nobody who does not, from his earliest childoood, have access to pencils, colors, and drawing paper and with them the possibility of acquiring some rudimentary artistic knowledge. In music, however, as in architecture and in sculpture, the materialistic obstacles that rise between the first mental conception of a creation, no matter how naïve, and its final form are stupendous and cannot remain cloaked. Thus our applicant turns to the gratifying mysterious symbolism of musical notation, gets doped by writing down his uncontrolled inventions, and uses notation's imperfection as the mask that deceives not only his amazed family, but first and permanently himself—and frequently the teacher and, later on, possible audiences.

Who would ever expect a young man without any experience concerning the carrying capacity of beams, pillars, and walls, or the rules of organizing living spaces three-dimensionally, to enter an architect's office with the words, "I never did anything in this field, but I am a great architectural genius"? In music, this is quite common. How common, is shown by the answer a student gave me when he was told about the years he had to spend in acquiring a decent technique, provided he showed some talent. He said, "But Mr. H., there must be some short cut." This typical remark did not properly assess the situation. Do we not know how long an extraordinary musician like Mozart had to struggle till he was able to bend, press, and mold the tonal material into the shape he wanted it? As a boy of five he wrote little compositions, at nine he was as qualified a composer as many others of that period, at twelve he had thoroughly mastered the technique of his time; yet it took him about twenty more years of his short life to write himself free from all restraints, so as to reach that superior technique—not to mention the uninhibited power to reveal his visions in musical forms—which for us is one of the intrinsic qualities of his works. No short cuts for the Mozarts! And none for other great masters. Even such an apparently easygoing composer as Schubert—what a colossal arc of technical and mental development he had to traverse from "Hagars Klage" to the "Taubenpost."

The most conspicuous misconception in our educational method is that composers can be fabricated by training. If you go through two years of Harmony, one of Counterpoint, fulfill your requirements in Composition I and Composition II, have some courses in Orchestration and Form, throw in some minor courses for credits, and do some so-called "free" work in a post-graduate course, you are inevitably a composer, because you paid for your courses—or somebody else did—and you can expect to get something for your good money. We produce composers the democratic way, as we produce congressmen. The citizen is by provision of the law entitled to the career of a congressman, and with elbow power and persistence he merely has to convince the majority of about three hundred thousand people of his superiority in order to gain a seat in Washington. Why cannot the man who writes music have the same kind of a career? If a method of production is good for one class of people, why should it not be applied to others?

It cannot be done. Elbow power and persistence are in this field no proof of your superiority, and seats in highest assemblies signify neither quality nor knowledge on the part of a composer. We have never heard of a natural gift peculiar to and indispensable for congressmen, but music cannot be invented without a specific creative talent. This talent cannot be implanted in people, like good manners or smallpox bacilli, and composing cannot be taught the democratic way. If there is anything remaining in this world that is on the one side basically aristocratic and individualistic and on the other as brutal as the fights of wild animals, it is artistic creation. It is aristocratic, because it is the privilege of a very restricted number of people. If it could be democratized, it would lose its quality as an art, become reduced to a craft, and end as an industry. In many branches of our musical life we already have reached this lowest, industrial phase, as we let musical democracy have its unbridled way. Artistic creation is individualistic, because it is as private as your dreams; nobody can interfere with your artistic phantasms, and although physical powers may prevent a work of art from coming into structural existence, the individualistic act of creation in the artist's mind can never be touched. And finally, artistic creation is excessively brutal, because works that have no strength are eliminated and forgotten like living beings that cannot survive the struggle of life, and no reasoning, no excuse can prolong their life or protect them against the crude power of the stronger work.

Although artistic creation cannot be governed and rationalized by democratic methods, although democratic methods of teaching cannot produce a creative talent, nothing is to be said against a spirit of true democracy in the admission to creative instruction, provided we develop an equally well-functioning weeding system that removes the weaklings, the unfoundedly presumptuous, and the untalented. Nowadays many are admitted to an artistic education who in former times had no chance, and with this broad accessibility we have at least reduced the possibility that a supreme artist could be overlooked or lost. But with the influx of the masses the percentage of geniuses in a population will not be increased. A fair estimate is that in our time and in countries adhering to our way of producing and consuming music, about fifty million inhabitants are needed to produce a composer of classical rank. Of course, we know that all these terms, "composer," "classic," "rank," have no accurate meaning; each of them would have to be explained and fixed in its significance before it could be used in a scientific way. But we are now talking about art, art in a very general sense at that, not art in its clearly definable technical aspects; and artistic statements in spite of their inevitable vagueness convey a rather clear meaning to those who agree to a common basis of understanding, namely to the sum total of our individual experiences with music and our knowledge of musical development at least during the last three hundred years with all its social, political, economic, in short, human implications. Fifty millions, producing one significant composer, can only mean, that after years, decades, and perhaps a century this one composer will finally be recognized as the musical apex of his epoch, but that tens of close runners, hundreds of camp followers and competitors, and thousands of miniature contributors had to do their share to make the great creator possible. However, the tragic destination of the individual will hardly ever permit him to understand his role in this gambling for future glory. In no case can he foresee the fate of his production. The creator of the surviving and significant works may not be recognized in his own time, he may feel himself to be the lowliest, the most insignificant musician; and simultaneously some minor writer may think of himself as the master mind of his time, may even see all the glory and admiration of the present bestowed on him, and yet may be forgotten before his last note is written.

If we believe in the truth of these statements, it will be hard to understand how support can be given to a system of musical education which hides this reality from the students' eyes, deceives them with each exercise they are given. It is extremely dishonest to give every student the education that is meant to turn out a Beethoven, while we know that he will never be more than a medium-sized commonplace composer. Would it not be better, more honest, and even more economical, to provide him with an all-round technique of general validity, on which his talents may thrive. In other words, don't feed people with caviar and champagne which in the long run they cannot digest, but bring them up with a solid fare and teach them to appreciate the extraordinary as a unique donation of heaven. Tell the student: "The gift of composing is nothing that exists by itself, nor can it be nursed and trained separately. It is the fruit of a plant, this plant being the entity of musical experience and talent of a musician. We cannot have healthy and sturdy fruits, if the plant is weak and under-developed. Consequently we must first of all raise a healthy plant. It will bear its fruits in time, and we may even have the chance to produce an extraordinary prize-winning fruit. If our labor is not to be blessed with the production of a fruit, we at least have the satisfaction of having done our utmost to raise a healthy plant."

And, for heaven's sake, have the courage to discourage his ambitions as a composer, if his productions are worthless as an artistic communication.

Once this conviction has become our pedagogic credo, we will have to change our education of composers entirely. In fact, we will have to reconvert it into the old, solid, and reasonable system of teaching described above — the system that was, by a wave of general megalomania, distorted into our production line, the result of which can only be battalions of composing mediocrity. This means that practical music would again be the backbone of instruction, composing would not be taught as an end in itself, no illusions would be implanted in the minds of students. Fewer composers would be produced, but the few who grew out of the fertile field of general musicianship would have better prospects of surviving and representing our time than hundreds of half-gifted or ungifted writers. One figure who is nowadays the most deplorable product of our system of education would disappear entirely: the composer who is unable either to sing or to play his own composition, who has to rely entirely on the ability and the good will of other performers. Our era is unique in having produced this pseudomusician, and for this sin alone our educational system deserves every punishment possible.

Trained in this old and renewed system — if the most natural musical activity can be called a system — composers would again be musicians, who could be used in many fields of music equally well; who are useful

players, not of one instrument, but of several; who sing acceptably, who
know how to handle classes, choirs, and orchestras; who have a decent
knowledge of theory, and beyond all, who certainly know how to compose. For them the idea of extreme specialization is abhorrent. They must
be good performers, but never at the expense of their comprehensive
musicianship. If amidst this wealth the gift of composing shows up, it will
be fostered by all possible means, but even then always with the understanding that composing is never a profession, that it can hardly be regarded as a job which nourishes its proprietor, and that the talent may one
day cease to yield further fruits, or may disappear altogether, just as mysteri-
ously as it appeared. There will be little similarity to those frequent products of our average instruction: the fellow full of vanity and empty of real
erudition; and the other fellow, who caught, along with some wisdom, all
the frustrations a never-fulfilled aspiration creates.

Teaching according to these maxims, I never found vanity or frustration
as a result. How can you be conceited if the overwhelming number of
musical facts you can learn makes you conscious of your smallness every
moment of your musical existence? And how can you be frustrated, if you
know composing is not necessary unless the creative talent shows up
unexpectedly? Musicians brought up this way will by the very nature of
this instruction see their initial enthusiasm preserved throughout their
musical career; disappointment in their vocation will most likely remain
unknown to them.

Once I had a discussion on this subject with a well-known composer.
He said: "I think your system of teaching composers is all wrong. It dis-
courages young people, to face an almost unsurmountable heap of
knowledge and technique. When I studied with a famous teacher in
Europe, every student in the class had the feeling that he was the elected
genius of the future, that the piece he was writing right now was superb,
and that it was merely a question of time and practice before his fate as a
successful composer was confirmed." The response to this reproval is: If
one cannot face the obstacles lying before a composer's career he should
not be permitted to embark upon it at all. Why must an apprentice composer be wrapped in cotton, when instrumentalist students come in touch
with those obstacles from the very first day in obvious and mostly discouraging forms? Certainly it it not necessary to emphasize obstacles, but an
honest teacher can never hide them. And what else is the result of a constantly flattering instruction but a pampered egotist who to the end of his
life will be the only one convinced of his greatness, when everyone else
ceased to share this opinion shortly after the performance of his first composition? There is but one conclusion that can be drawn from these statements: Don't teach composition the way it is usually done. Teach musi-

cians. If once in a long while one of your students shows creative talent, let nature have its course. A fellow educated in the way here described will use all his manifold experiences to the right purpose, and what you can teach him beyond all this is more valuable than the teacher's instructing a pupil: it is the united effort of two equals in the search of perfection, in which the one participant is mostly but not always leading, for his is the greater experience.

Serge Prokofiev

[1891 - 1953]

Prokofiev, like many of the composers of his generation, began his career as a musical rebel, strongly opposed to the excesses of Romanticism. Belonging, as well, to the last generation of Russians before the 1917 Revolution, he reacted less overtly to Wagnerianism than to the introspective, mystical qualities of Scriabin and Rachmaninov, the sentimentality of Tchaikovsky, and the academicism of his teacher Rimsky-Korsakov. His early music, tonal yet strongly dissonant, harsh in texture, and intentionally "shocking" in its grotesque effects, stems from the same spirit of revolt that marks of work of Stravinsky, Milhaud, and Hindemith in a similar vein.

A brilliant pianist, Prokofiev spent many years in Europe and the United States as a touring virtuoso, acquiring fame as a performer but suffering comparative neglect as a composer. As his music became more respected in the 1930's, Prokofiev devoted his energies more exclusively to composition, and returned to Russia—now the Soviet Union—as a major figure. Permanently residing there, despite occasional trips. Prokoliev produced many of his major works in the last few decades of his life. In these later works, the tendencies that had once brought him great notoriety are tempered by a strong melodic lyricism and a neo-Classic sense of form.

Prokofiev was a prolific author of articles on musical matters, which presented a concise statement of his philosophy as a Soviet composer. Several of these writings are presented here.

Autobiography, Articles, Reminiscences, translated by Rose Prokofieva and edited by S. Shlifstein (Moscow, c. 1960), pp. 99-100, 106-07, 133-36. The original sources of the selections are as follows: The Path of Soviet Music, from Izvestia, November 16, 1934; The Masses Want Great Music, from Prokofiev's notebooks, 1937; Flourishing of Art, from Pravda, 1937; Music and Life, from News, 1951.

"Autobiography, Articles, Reminiscences"

The Path of Soviet Music

The question as to what kind of music should be written at the present time is one of great concern to many Soviet composers. I have given considerable thought to the problem in the past two years and I believe that the correct solution would be the following.

What is needed above all is *great* music, i.e., music that would correspond both in form and in content to the grandeur of the epoch. Such music would be a stimulus to our own musical development, and abroad too it would reveal our true selves. The danger of becoming provincial is unfortunately a very real one for modern Soviet composers.

At the same time, in turning his attention to serious, significant music, the composer must bear in mind that in the Soviet Union music is addressed to millions of people who formerly had little or no contact with music. It is this new mass audience that the modern Soviet composer must strive to reach.

I believe the type of music needed is what one might call "light-serious" or "serious-light music." It is by no means easy to find the right idiom for such music. It should be primarily melodious, and the melody should be clear and simple without, however, becoming repetitive or trivial. Many composers find it difficult enough to compose any sort of melody, let alone a melody having some definite function to perform. The same applies to the technique, the form—it too must be clear and simple, but not stereotyped. It is not the old simplicity that is needed but a new kind of simplicity. And this can be achieved only after the composer has mastered the art of composing serious, significant music, thereby acquiring the technique of expressing himself in simple, yet original terms.

If I were to be asked how I would classify my own music, I would place in the first group my symphonies, the *Symphonic Song, On the Dnieper,* and a few other compositions which in form represent a definite break with the past and might present certain difficulties even to some leading musicians.

In the second group I would place *Lieutenant Kijé* and *Egyptian Nights* (I have made symphonic suites of them) and also the collective-farm songs I am now writing for the Moscow Radio Committee.

The Masses Want
Great Music

The time is past when music was written for a handful of aesthetes. Today vast crowds of people have come face to face with serious music and are waiting with eager impatience. Composers, take heed of this: if you repel these crowds they will turn away from you to jazz or vulgar music. But if you can hold them you will win an audience such as the world has never before seen. But this does not mean that you must pander to this audience. Pandering always has an element of insincerity about it and nothing good ever came of that. The masses want great music, the music of great events, great love, lively dances. They understand far more than some composers think and they want to deepen their understanding.[1]

Flourishing of Art

The search for a musical idiom in keeping with the epoch of socialism is a worthy, but difficult task for the composer. Music in our country has become the heritage of vast masses of people. Their artistic taste and demands are growing with amazing speed. And this is something the Soviet composer must take into account in each new work.

It is something like shooting at a moving target: only by aiming ahead, at tomorrow, will you avoid being left behind at the level of yesterday's needs. That is why I consider it a mistake for a composer to strive for simplification. Any attempt to "play down" to the listener is a subconscious underestimation of his cultural maturity and the development of his tastes; such an attempt has an element of insincerity. And music that is insincere cannot be enduring.

In my own work written in this fruitful year, I have striven for clarity and melodiousness. At the same time I have scrupulously avoided palming off familiar harmonies and tunes.

That is where the difficulty of composing clear, straightforward music lies: the clarity must be new, not old.

My main work this year has been a large cantata dedicated to the 20th anniversary of October. Its principal themes are the Great October Socialist Revolution, victory, industrialization and the Constitution.

The cantata is written for two choruses, professional and amateur, and

---

[1] This item taken from Prokofiev's notebook is evidently an outline of the main points for an article or speech. This is born out by the marginal note: "Conclusions."

four orchestras—symphony, military, percussion and accordion bands. No less than 500 people are required for its performance.

It gave me great pleasure to write this cantata. The complex events reflected in it demanded a complex musical idiom. But I trust that the passion and sincerity of the music will make it accessible to our audiences.[2]

Another large work just completed is a suite for chorus, soloists and orchestra which I intend to entitle *Songs of Our Days*. It will be performed for the first time on January 5 in the Large Hall of the Moscow Conservatory. It is written to words by Lebedev-Kumach, Marshak and other texts translated from Ukrainian and Byelorussian folk-lore and published in *Pravda*.. My melodies here are written in the style of the given nationality. I hope they will be easily understood and remembered.

I have also composed several marches for military band, some mass songs and romances to Pushkin's verse on the occasion of the centenary of his death. Unfortunately, the theatres have not made use of the incidental music I wrote for a number of Pushkin productions.[3]

Not long ago my Second Concerto for violin and the 2nd suite from *Romeo and Juliet* were performed for the first time and were very warmly received. It was pleasant to learn that the celebrated American violinist Heifetz is playing this concerto everywhere with signal success. A no less welcome event for me was the publication of two splendid symphonies by Miaskovsky[4] and a piano concerto by the talented young composer Khachaturian.

Music and Life

I have never lived in Salt Lake City, Utah, nor have I given any concerts there. Even when I visited the United States in 1938 at the invitation of my American friends, I did not have an opportunity to see that city—an omission I rather regret, for I have no doubt that music has quite as many devotees there as anywhere else in the world.

A short while ago a rather curious sidelight on musical life in Salt Lake City came to my attention, in the shape of an Associated Press dispatch

[2] The cantata was never performed. Part of the musical material was used for the *Ode on the End of the War*.

[3] Reference to music for the projected productions of *Boris Godunov* and *Eugene Onegin* and for the film *The Queen of Spades*. Part of this music was used in other compositions; some of it went into the opera *War and Peace* (scene in Hélenè's house), and the Fifth Symphony (*Adagio*).

[4] In 1937 Miaskovsky wrote his 17th Symphony in G-sharp minor, Op. 41, and his 18th Symphony in C major, Op. 42.

from that city stating that the conductor of the Utah Symphony Orchestra, Maurice Abravanel, had been warned by an anonymous telephone caller that he would be killed or injured if he conducted Prokofiev's Fifth Symphony as scheduled on the programme of his concert. The programme, however, was not revised, and the concert took place as scheduled, the dispatch stated.

This incident might perhaps have not been worth mentioning but for one rather important aspect that concerns me personally. Why should Prokofiev's Fifth Symphony have evoked such a violent reaction? As far as I know the symphony has always been well received by American concert-goers. It has been successfully performed on more than one occasion by the Boston Symphony Orchestra, by the New York Philharmonic Orchestra conducted by Artur Rodzinski, and by several other orchestras. I happen to own recordings of these performances. Why should a conductor be threatened with death for including the symphony in his programme? Could it be because the music is a hymn to the freedom of the human spirit?

My Fifth Symphony was intended as a hymn to free and happy Man, to his mighty powers, his pure and noble spirit. I cannot say that I deliberately chose this theme. It was born in me and clamoured for expression. The music had matured within me, it filled my soul. This is the music — or perhaps the idea — that is so distasteful to some people in Utah. Doubtless they prefer music that debases man, blunts his perceptions and warps his finer feelings.

The other day as I was looking over some old copies of my music published in various countries, I came across the Seventh Piano Sonata with annotations by Olin Downes, published in New York. (Incidentally, I have an excellent recording of this work made by American musicians who have performed it any number of times.) I also found my symphony fairy-tale *Peter and the Wolf* with annotations by Harold Sheldon (I conducted a performance of this work in Boston in 1938); a sonata for violin and piano, the *Alexander Nevsky* Cantata of which I have a recording by the Philadelphia Orchestra conducted by Eugene Ormandy, and several other compositions.

All these works are extremely varied in genre, theme and technique. Yet they are linked by one and the same idea — they all treat of Man, and are created for him. I am convinced that it is this quality that has endeared them to music lovers in many countries of the world, including the United States.

Not long ago I composed a new oratorio. It is entitled *On Guard for Peace*. I did not seek this theme either, nor did I select it from a number of others. It sprang from life itself, my life and the life of my people.

. . . The road from Moscow to my country home where I usually spend the summer months runs from the heart of the city through the outskirts and into the country, past forests old and new, across rivers and through grain-fields. As I drive to town from the country, past a field of tall rye, I see a new machine, a self-propelled harvester combine working on the field. A few dozen kilometres farther on I see a group of rosy-cheeked children from a Moscow factory kindergarten playing on a meadow under the watchful eye of their teachers. A short distance away cranes are at work planting venerable lime-trees along either side of the road. Another few kilometres and I see some new apartment houses which have just emerged from the scaffolding. And finally, at the very approaches to Moscow, the majestic contours of the new, splendid Moscow University building soar up amid a shimmering golden haze. All these are scenes from every-day Soviet life.

I know that what I observe on my brief journey from the country to Moscow is typical of the life of my country as a whole. I know some celebrated scientists who have left their Moscow laboratories for a time and gone off to Central Asia to help build the Main Turkmenian Canal. I know some young engineers who went straight from University in Moscow to the banks of the Volga, the Don and the Dnieper to lend a hand with the huge power developments under construction there. I have many friends and acquaintances who are writing books, planting gardens and building houses. Their whole lives are filled with the poetry of peaceful labour. And that is how the theme of my new oratorio came into being.

It tells of the grim days of World War II, of the tears of mothers and orphans, of towns swept by fire, of the terrible trials that fell to the lot of our people; of Stalingrad and the victory over the enemy; of the radiant joy of creative labour, of the happy childhood of our children. In this composition I have sought to express my ideas about peace and war, and my firm belief that there will be no more wars, that the nations of the world will safeguard the peace, save civilization, our children, our future.

Perhaps all this sounds somewhat too ambitious for such a modest work, but I think the oratorio expresses the principles I mentioned before.

I am now working on a large symphonic poem dedicated to the joining of the two Russian rivers, the Volga and the Don. *The Volga Meets the Don* I have called it. The theme for this composition, too, was suggested by reality. There are many old Russian folk songs about the Volga and the Don, and to these, new songs have now been added, those that sing of the exploits of man, the remaker of Nature.

A great deal has been said in America and Western Europe about the artist's mission and his freedom to create. But can the true artist stand aloof from life and confine his art within the narrow limits of subjective emotions, or should he be where he is needed most, where his art can help people to live a better, finer life?

Recall the lives of Beethoven and Shakespeare, Mozart and Tolstoy, Tchaikovsky and Dickens, those titans of the human mind and spirit. Were they not great precisely because they followed the dictates of their conscience and devoted their talents to the service of man? Is it not this that has made them immortal?

When I was in the United States and England I heard much talk about music and whom it was intended for, whom a composer ought to write for and to whom his music ought to be addressed. In my view the composer, just as the poet, the sculptor or the painter, is in duty bound to serve Man, the people. He must beautify human life and defend it. He must be a citizen first and foremost, so that his art might consciously extol human life and lead man to a radiant future. Such is the immutable code of art as I see it.

I may be accused of voicing platitudes. It may be said that my arguments have only the remotest bearing on what happened in Salt Lake City. Yet I feel sure that there is an inner connection.

Before sitting down to write this article I asked my colleagues what they are doing at the present time. Dmitri Shostakovich told me he is planning a composition dedicated to our great new construction projects. Tikhon Khrennikov has begun a composition on the triumph of peace throughout the world. Yuri Shaporin, who has been engaged for the past few years on his opera *The Decembrists,* is also writing a cantata based on Russian classical and modern poetry. Nikolai Peiko, a gifted young composer, a pupil of the late Miaskovsky, is writing a symphonic poem for soloists, chorus and orchestra entitled *Morning of Our Homeland.*

Soviet composers are creating music for the people; the peaceful life of the people is its theme.

The incident in Salt Lake City is for me additional confirmation of the correctness of the path we have chosen. Our music strives to imbue the people with confidence in their strength and in their future. That is why it is so abhorrent to those who scheme to destroy that future and thrust humanity into new sanguinary wars. But they are powerless to drown out our music, our symphonies of peace and labour—of this I am certain. The Fifth Symphony *was* performed in Salt Lake City after all.

Dmitri Shostakovitch

[1906 - 1975]

It is difficult to discuss the music of Shostakovitch without taking into account the society from which it springs and, in turn, to which it is directed. Shostakovitch, therefore, is often regarded primarily as a Soviet composer, and less as an individual creator, although the former is not a designation that would offend him. On the contrary, he has come to regard his creative role as a social rather than personal one; he is the composer of Gebrauchsmusik in which the state is directly involved. Shostakovitch's views in this regard are worth noting, as he may be considered representative of the Soviet composer in a way that Prokofiev was not. Whereas Prokofiev was of an earlier generation, Shostakovitch reached maturity and received his musical training after the 1917 Revolution. He has also traveled less widely than his older colleague had.

A comparison of the two composers reveals many similarities: a fondness for open textures, biting dissonances, and striking wit that often borders on the bizarre. Shostakovitch's use of instruments is perhaps more virtuosic, exploiting various attacks, registers, and idiomatic possibilities; in general, he may be less inclined toward sustained lyricism than his predecessor. Although Shostakovitch's rhythms are angular and often syncopated, he rarely strays from a strong sense of regular pulse; his harmonic idiom, likewise, is firmly rooted in tonality. Accessibility to a large listening public is a paramount consideration for him, as he is committed to a philosophy of art that mistrusts the exclusive and the erudite. Part of this philosophy is set forth in the essay reprinted here.

"Music and the Times," from Music Journal (January, 1965), pp. 33, 85, 86.

Music and the Times

Art, if we can put it this way, has its own standard for measuring time—its own hours, days, years and centuries which do not always fall in with the usual course of time in life, now lagging behind it, now getting well ahead of it. And profoundly as it is correlated with life, art moves ahead and develops in accordance with its own laws. It takes time for the qualitative changes and advances in it to assert themselves and for us to divine them.

I mention all this because it is so difficult for me to reveal the outward expression of the changes that have taken place in Soviet art in recent years. The changes are there, but their character and impact are profoundly intrinsic. A statement to the effect that our writers and composers have attained greater distinction in their art in the current year and have produced more works than in the previous year would be naïve to say the least. On the other hand we can say with every assurance that we work now differently.

I should say that musical life in our country has entered upon a new creative stage. *Music today is literally inundating the entire land.* Festivals of Russian Soviet music, for example, have been held with the greatest success in Moldavia, Kirghizia, Uzbekistan and Buryatia. Some time ago an interesting festival devoted to Lenin took place in cities on the Volga banks—Ulyanovsk, Kuibyshev and Kazan. A visit paid by Leningrad composers to Saratov proved a fruitful undertaking. We all, participants of these meetings, receive a charge of energy on such meetings. Our music can be heard everywhere. By living contact with our public, through broad discussions and debates, we know what our listeners think of the music we compose.

Nevertheless, well-organized concerts and the cordiality of personal meetings with the public cannot, of course, take the place of that which is all-important—*the creative results of our work.* Here is where we come in for criticism. A review of the works of Rostov composers held in May at Rostov-on-Don revealed the standard of most of the pieces played to us not to be high. This is all the more painful since in the same city we listened to splendid amateur music groups.

The question of quality, of artistic skill, is a question of the life of art. How can we talk of artistic gains when the composer does not have full command of his medium? While attaching immense importance to the content of our art, we must bear in mind that no idea will ever reach the listener nor be grasped by him if it is expressed crudely and incompetently. Having good intentions and hitting upon a good theme do not yet make for art.

Apropos of this I wish to say a few words about light music. The situation in this sphere of music cannot but give us cause for anxiety Light music, including jazz, continues to this day to be cut off from the great tasks of our art. And yet this music is of tremendous impact, able to reach out to millions of people. We want it to be striking and invigorating, a music of good taste and high standard of skill. *We are in favor of good jazz, good popular songs and good dance music.* But we do not need poor substitutes and cheap imitation.

Among the many problems of the musical life of our times that of so-called vanguardism troubles me greatly. I do not know how this term originated but its application to certain phenomena in the art of our days seems to me a fraud of the worst kind. Dodecaphony, serial, pointillist and other kinds of music are one of the greatest evils of 20th century art. The few composers in our land who endeavor to follow these fads are gravely deluding themselves. They are misled both in essence and historically. The so-called vanguardist movement in music is far past its youth. It has come into existence fifty years ago and yet I cannot name a *single* work in this vein which lives and has an influence on the public to this day.

Any movement in art is first and foremost important because of its positive contribution to art. For all their contradictions, this is true of impressionism in painting and verism in music. What, however, will "vanguardism" leave to posterity? Nothing but smouldering cinders which its propagandists, shouting from the housetops, are trying to make us believe are a living forest.

For all the publicity which the "vanguardist" composers give themselves, for all the exposure they receive from musical journals, societies, radio and television abroad, what we witness in reality is an appalling picture. The listeners turn a deaf ear to this music. I have had occasion to visit many countries where so-called vanguardism is officially recognized and is encouraged in every way. And each time I saw how few people attended concerts at which such music was played. This shows how absurd are the efforts to create this kind of music. Surely a composer writing for the public wishes his ideas and thoughts to be grasped by it.

Unfortunately those who grow infatuated with such art are oblivious to the fact that "vanguardist" music is not new music. Moreover, it obliterates individuality, standardizes music and drains it of the least suggestion of content. Often enough as I have listened to the spurious works of the "vanguardists" to this day I cannot tell the difference between the music say of Boulez and that of Stockhausen, Henze and that of Stuckenschmidt. I am convinced that "vanguardism" is a screen for many composers to hide their lack of talent. There have been several instances (in West Germany and France) when composers having decided to break with "vanguardism" and write realistic music failed to do so because they possessed neither gifts nor skill—nothing but a pitiable void, reminding one of the emperor's new clothes in Andersen's story.

Take the career of the composer Arnold Schoenberg, one of the founders of "vanguardism." He made his enormous talent serve false ideas of his own invention. He claimed that music does not express anything and is incapable of expressing anything, that it is merely an empty play of sounds. However, even Schoenberg was sufficiently moved by the tragedy of World War II to cast aside his former declarations and to attempt to translate into music its ghastly horrors. He wrote a considerable oratorio entitled *Witness from Warsaw* in the "vanguardist" medium. The idea of this piece which was directed against fascism and the disasters of war was praiseworthy. But on listening to the music I realized how utterly incompatible its humanist ideas were with the form in which they were clothed. The result was a confused and unintelligible work.

This and many other works of music, often written by quite progressive-minded composers, make it clear ·that the intricate "vanguardist" artistic system falls short of expressing even the most humanistic content.

Once I happened to speak to an Italian composer who was not without talent but was blindly devoted to "vanguardism." His work which was progressive in idea proved a complete flop when played to the audience. He told me this did not worry him as he was certain that fifty years hence he would be understood by the public. I felt sorry for him. He was deriving comfort from the same thought which had been cherished by the disciples of "vanguardism" forty or fifty years ago. But the years go by and no interest is shown in their pretentious works.

It is most regrettable that a great musician like Stravinsky, who has so much beautiful music to his credit, has in recent years identified himself with these old-fashioned trends, and, alas, has failed to produce anything significant.

There exists an opinion that the value of "vanguardism," as it were, lies in its experiments in the sphere of the musical idiom. "This is questing," the defenders of "vanguardism" declare. I heartily disagree with this. To strike out for the new is the sacred duty of all artists. Without new ideas and forms art will die. But what do we mean when we speak of the new —creation which has at all times inspired progressive artists or destruction alone which we can observe among the "vanguardists"? The answer is clear enough: *Pioneering for the new must proceed within the cur-*

109

*rent of realism if that new is to be progressive and comprehensible to the
people for whom art is in effect being created.*

In the West, many progressive musicians, such as Benjamin Britten,
Darius Milhaud, Paul Hindemith, Carl Orff, Samuel Barber, Gian-Carlo
Menotti, Aaron Copland and many others, who are vehemently opposed to
"vanguardism" have been producing splendid realistic works of music.

In conclusion a few words about what I would like to call the regime of
a composer's work. All of us who constitute the leadership both of the
Composers' Union of the Russian Federation and the Composers' Union of
the USSR are already in an advanced age. But we started work at a time
when the Union of Soviet Composers was formed, at a time when we were
thirty years younger. I am all for our talented, interesting youth to be drawn
into public activities, into the leadership of composers' unions, into active
work all over the country; I want them to follow our example in this
respect.

At present the most cherished thought of Soviet composers is to create
big works worthy of the great dates in the history of our country: the 50th
anniversary of Soviet power and the 100th anniversary of Lenin's birth.

About myself I can say that my principal task for the present is to
complete the opera I am now writing which is *And Quiet Flows the Don*,
based on Mikhail Sholokhov's novel.

Ralph Vaughan Williams

[1872 - 1958]

England's musical stature has risen sharply during the twentieth century, and now approaches the position of respect and influence it once held during the Renaissance and early Baroque periods. This resurgence was chiefly due to the work of Ralph Vaughan Williams, who as a young man led the movement to rediscover the traditions of England's musical past. Like Sibelius in Finland and Bartók in Hungary, Vaughan Williams studied his native folk music, and assimilated its stylistic features into his own idiom. He was also led to a study of such early English masters as Dowland and Purcell, and absorbed many of their characteristics as well.

As his unique style evolved, Vaughan Williams produced many important works — symphonies, concertos, operas — that successfully combine the English manner with the broad European symphonic tradition. He also composed many works of a more functional nature: music for national festivals, holidays, and pageants, teaching pieces, film background music. The selections reprinted here demonstrate his great belief in the value of functional music, in many respects akin to Paul Hindemith's concept of Gebrauchsmusik. Vaughan Williams's ideas on the subject, however, are particularly related to the role music may play in the life of one's country, and thus offer the reader a provocative view of nationalistic music.

Reprinted from Ralph Vaughan Williams, *The Making of Music* (Ithaca, N.Y., Cornell University Press, 1955), pp. 45-52.

From
"The Making
of Music"

What are the
Social Foundations of Music?

We must not suppose that composers invent their music out of the blue, without forerunners or surroundings. The innovators are the small men who set the ball rolling. The big men come at the end of a period and sum it up. Thus it was with Bach. The period of Haydn and Mozart, not to speak of the smaller people like Cherubini and Hummel, led the way to the supreme master, Beethoven. We can trace the art of Wagner through the early *Singspiele* of Adam Hiller and his contemporaries in the eighteenth century, through Weber and Marschner, to find its culmination in *Die Meistersinger* and *Tristan*. These were the right men coming at the right time and under the right circumstances; that is what enabled them to be great. Sometimes the potentially right man comes at the wrong time. Purcell, for example, was a bit too early for his flower to bloom fully; Sullivan, who in other circumstances might have written a *Figaro*, was thwarted by mid-Victorian inhibitions: the public thought that great music must be portentous and solemn, an oratorio, or a sacred cantata at the least, and that comic opera was beneath notice as a work of art.

The great example of the right man, at the right time, in the right place, is John Sebastian Bach. He was not a biological sport: he came from a long line of musical ancestors. And what is more, the musical gift did not die out with him, for he had several sons who would have shone brightly in the musical firmament if they had not been partly eclipsed by their great father. John Sebastian's first musical ancestor appears to have been Veit Bach, by profession a baker and miller, who used to spend his spare time playing on his beloved zither. Veit had a son who became a *Spielmann*, or professional musician; and from that time onward the tribe of family musicians grew until nearly every town in Thuringia had a Bach as its "town piper," as the official musicians were called. They held a humble enough position; their duty was to provide music for all civic occasions as well as for weddings, banquets, and funerals. Doubtless some little thing of their own was often played on these occasions. Then came 1685: the

time was ready, the place was ready, and the circumstances were ready for
the man who, to my mind, is the greatest musician of all time. J. S. Bach's
position was, nominally, not much more important than that of his numerous cousins and uncles. True, Leipzig is a comparatively large town, and
he was dignified by the name of "cantor," but his duties included teaching, not only music, but also Latin, to the boys at the public school. He had
to play the organ, either himself or by deputy, in two churches and to
conduct the services. Every week he had to provide a little thing of his own
for performance on Sunday. It happened that these compositions included
the *St. Matthew Passion* and the B-Minor Mass.

The Folk-Song Movement

Hubert Parry, in his great book *The Evolution of the Art of Music,* has
shown that a Beethoven symphony, for instance, is not a unique phenomenon but that its whole structure can be traced back, stage by stage, to the
art of the primitive folk singer.

The early nineteenth century started a movement among composers to
short-circuit all the intervening evolutionary process and cut straight back
to the origin of things. These nationalist composers tried to found their style
on the folk songs of their own countries. I think the movement started in
Russia when Glinka began using street songs in his operas; the idea was
taken up, *con amore,* by his successors, Moussorgsky and Borodin, who
not only used traditional melodies in their compositions, but built up their
original work on the same basis. Even Tchaikovsky and Rachmaninoff,
though they were frowned on by the ultranationalists as not being
true Russians, often showed the influence of Russian folk songs in their
compositions.

Members of the fashionable Russian world were shocked at anything
national, as we know from Tolstoi's and Turgenev's novels, and habitually
talked French to each other, reserving their native Russian for peasants and
droshky drivers; therefore it is not surprising that they labelled this nationalist style as "coachman's music." But the coachman's music has survived,
while the sham classical style of Rubinstein has almost disappeared.

I have just used the word "classical"; antinational musical critics are in
the habit of declaring that the so-called classical style is the only true path,
and that the nationalist music of the Russians, of Dvorak, and of Grieg is
mere affectation or cliquishness. But what is the classical style? It is nothing
more or less than the Teutonic style. It so happened that for nearly a
hundred years, in the eighteenth and early nineteenth centuries, the great

composers, with the possible exception of Haydn, were all German or Austrian. So the Teutonic style became accepted as the classical model. But what is the Teutonic style? When people hear a German or Austrian folk song, they say, "This is just like Mozart or Beethoven in their simpler moods; it is not a folk song at all, but was probably composed by Michael Haydn or Leopold Mozart." It never occurs to these good people that Mozart, Beethoven, and Schubert came from the humbler classes and were doubtless imbued from childhood with the popular music of their country. The truth, I believe, is not that Teutonic folk songs are like the melodies of classical composers but that the simpler melodies of classical composers are like Teutonic folk songs, and that we can claim Mozart and Beethoven as nationalists as much as Dvorak and Grieg.

Music, like language, derives ultimately from its basic beginnings. May I give an instance from my own country? About fifty years ago Cecil Sharp made his epoch-making discovery of English folk song. We young musicians were intoxicated by these tunes. We said to ourselves, "Here are beautiful melodies of which, until lately, we knew nothing. We must emulate Grieg and Smetana, and build up, on the basis of these tunes, a corpus of compositions arising out of our own country and character." And we proceeded to pour out Overtures and Rhapsodies and Ballad Operas to show the world that we were no longer a land without music. We had our critics, who took the curious line that, though it was perfectly right and proper for a Russian or a Norwegian to build up his style on his own national melodies, if an Englishman tried to do so, he was being what they described by that appalling, invented word "folky."

Of course the movement has had its camp followers: composers have thought that if they pitchforked one or two of Sharp's discoveries into a ready-made mixture imported from Russia or France they were inventing a national style. This was the bad side of the movement, and none of the more level headed of us imagined that because Beethoven quoted a Russian tune in one of his Razumovsky quartets he thereby became a Russian composer; or that because Delius used an English folk song in one of his compositions it made him into an Englishman. Those who claim England as the birthplace of Delius' art must base their argument on more valid premises than this. The movement is now fifty years old, the tunes are again common property, and every English child must know them as well as he knows his own language, whether he likes it or not. Composers of the younger generation emphatically do not like it, but they cannot help being influenced by these beautiful tunes. As Gilbert Murray says, "The original genius is at once the child of tradition and a rebel against it."

Benjamin Britten

[1913 - 1976]

Britten has continued the renascence of English music in this century begun by Vaughan Williams, and carried it even further. His total output of works reveals a strong interest in all media, from simple teaching pieces to full-scale stage works; vocal music predominates, and all of Britten's compositions project a broad sense of the lyric. They are thus accessible to a large public, and Britten is one of the most widely performed of living composers.

His musical style may best be termed an eclectic one that utilises all available techniques from the most contemporary to those of many centuries past; in this regard, Britten seeks the best musical means for his expressive ends. He tends to compose as a man of the theater, experienced in vocal music and incidental music. Even his purely instrumental works imply a dramatic situation; they are never "abstract" in the neo-Classic sense. Although Britten's music, therefore, may range from an astringent atonality to a Wagnerian richness to a simple harmonic progression, an underlying sense of dramatic continuity unifies the whole. Britten is, in this sense, very much the Romantic, believing deeply in the composer's obligation to communicate and relate his work to the human condition.

The following essay was written in response to the citation and award bestowed upon Britten in 1964 by the Aspen Institute for Humanistic Studies.

"On Winning the First Aspen Award" from Saturday Review (August 22, 1964), pp. 37-39, 51.

On Winning
the First
Aspen Award

When last May President Alvin C. Eurich and Chairman Robert O. Anderson told me they wished to travel the 5,000 miles from Aspen to Aldeburgh to have a talk with me, they hinted that it had something to do with an Aspen Award for Services to the Humanities—an award of very considerable importance and size. I imagined that they felt I might advise them on a suitable recipient, and I began to consider what I should say. Who would be suitable for such an honor? What kind of person? Doctor, priest, social worker, politician? An artist? Yes, possibly (that, I imagined, could be the reason that Mr. Anderson and Professor Eurich thought I might be the person to help them). So I ran through the names of the great figures working in the arts among us today. It was a fascinating problem, rather like one's schooltime game of ideal cricket elevens or, slightly more recently, ideal casts for operas—but I certainly won't tell which of our great poets, painters, or composers came to the top of my list.

Mr. Anderson and Professor Eurich paid their visit to my home in Aldeburgh. It was a charming and courteous visit, but it was also a knockout. It had not occurred to me, frankly, that it was I who was to be the recipient of this magnificent award, and I was stunned. I am afraid my friends must have felt I was a tongue-tied host. But I simply could not imagine why *I* had been chosen for this very great honor. I read again the simple and moving citation. The key word seemed to be "humanities." I went to the dictionary to look up its meaning. I found *humanity:* "the quality of being human" (well, that applied to me all right). But I found that the plural had a special meaning: "Learning or literature concerned with human culture, as grammar, rhetoric, poetry, and especially the ancient Latin and Greek classics." (Here I really had no claims since I cannot properly spell even in my own language, and when I set Latin I have terrible trouble over the quantities.) *Humanitarian* was an entry close beside these, and I supposed I might have some claim here, but I was daunted by the definition: "One who goes to excess in his human principles (in 1855 often contemptuous or hostile)." I read on, quickly, *Humanist:* "One versed in humanities," and I was back where I started. But perhaps, after all, the clue was in the word "human," and I began to feel that I might have a small claim.

I certainly write music for human beings—directly and deliberately. I consider their voices, the range, the power, the subtlety, and the color potentialities of them. I consider the instruments they play—their most expressive and suitable individual sonorities, and where I may be said to have invented an instrument (such as the Slung Mugs of "Noye's Fludde") I have borne in mind the pleasure the young performers will have in playing it. I also take note of the *human* circumstances of music, of its environment and conventions; for instance, I try to write dramatically effective music for the theater—I certainly don't think opera is better for not being effective on the stage. I fear some people think that effectiveness must be superficial. And then, the best music to listen to in a great Gothic church is the polyphony that was written for it and took account of the great resonance: this was my approach in *War Requiem*—I calculated it for a big reverberant acoustic, and that is where it sounds best. I believe therefore in *occasional* music, although I admit there are some occasions that can intimidate one—I do not envy Purcell writing his "Ode to Celebrate King James's Return to London from Newmarket." On the other hand, almost every piece I have ever written has been composed with a certain occasion in mind, and usually for definite performers, and certainly always *human* ones.

You may ask perhaps: how far can a composer go in thus considering the demands of people, of humanity? At many times in history the artist has made a conscious effort to speak with the voice of the people. Beethoven certainly tried, in works as different as the Battle of Vittoria and the Ninth Symphony, to utter the sentiments of a whole community. From the beginning of Christianity there have been musicians who have wanted and tried to be the servants of the church to express the devotion and convictions of Christians as such. Recently we have had the example of Shostakovich, who set out in his Leningrad Symphony to present a monument to his fellow citizens, an explicit expression for them of their own endurance and heroism. At a very different level, one finds composers such as Johann Strauss and George Gershwin aiming at providing the people with the best dance music and songs that they were capable of making. And I can find nothing wrong with the objectives—declared or implicit—of these men, nothing wrong with offering to my fellowmen music that may inspire them or comfort them, touch them or entertain them, even educate them, directly and with intention. On the contrary, it is the composer's duty, as a member of society, to speak to or for his fellow human beings.

When I am asked to compose a work for an occasion, great or small, I want to know in some detail the conditions of the place where it will be performed, the size and acoustics, what instruments or singers will be available and suitable, the kind of people who will hear it, and that language they will understand—and even sometimes the age of the listeners and performers. For it is futile to offer children music by which they are bored, or which makes them feel inadequate or frustrated, which may set them against music forever; and it is insulting to address anyone in a language that he does not understand. The text of my *War Requiem* was perfectly in place in Coventry Cathedral—the Owen poems in the vernacular, and the words of the Requiem Mass familiar to everyone—but it would have been pointless in Cairo or Peking.

During the act of composition one is continually referring back to the conditions of performance—as I have said, the acoustics and the forces available, the techniques of the instruments and the voices—such questions occupy one's attention continuously and certainly affect the stuff of the music. In my experience they are not only a restriction but a challenge, an inspiration. Music does not exist in a vacuum. It does not exist until it is performed, and performance imposes conditions. It is the easiest thing in the world to write a piece virtually or totally impossible to perform—but oddly enough that is not what I prefer to do; I prefer to study the conditions of performance and shape my music to them.

Where does one stop, then? In answering people's demands? It seems that there is no clearly defined "Halt" sign on this road. The only brake that one can apply is that of one's own private and personal conscience; when that speaks clearly, one must halt; and it can speak for musical or non-musical reasons.

In the last six months I have been several times asked to write a work as a memorial to the late President Kennedy. On each occasion I have refused—not because in any way I was out of sympathy with such an idea; on the contrary, I was horrified and deeply moved by the tragic death of a very remarkable man. But for me I do not feel the time is ripe; I cannot yet stand back and see it clearly. I should have to wait very much longer to do anything like justice to this great theme. But had I, in fact, agreed to undertake a limited commission, my artistic conscience would certainly have told me in what direction I could go, and when I should have to stop.

There are many dangers that hedge round the unfortunate composer: pressure groups that demand true proletarian music, snobs who demand the latest avant-garde tricks; critics who are already trying to document today for tomorrow, to be the first to find the correct pigeonhole definition. These people are dangerous—not because they are necessarily of any importance in themselves, but because they may make the composer, above all the young composer, self-conscious, and instead of writing his own music, music that springs naturally from his gift and personality, he may be frightened into writing pretentious nonsense, or deliberate obscurity. He may find himself writing more and more for machines, in conditions dictated by machines, and not by humanity; or, of course, he may end by creating grandiose claptrap when his real talent is for dance tunes or children's piano pieces. Finding one's place in society as a composer is not a straightforward job. It is not helped by the attitude toward the composer of some societies.

My own, for instance, semi-socialist Britain, and conservative Britain before it, has for years treated the musician as a curiosity to be barely tolerated. At a tennis party in my youth I was asked what I was going to do when I grew up — what job I was aiming at. "I am going to be a composer," I said. "Yes, but what else?" was the answer. The average Briton thought, and still thinks, of the arts as suspect and expensive luxuries. The Manchester counselor who boasted he had never been to a concert and didn't intend to go is no very rare bird in England. By Act of Parliament, each local authority in England is empowered to spend a 6d. rate on the arts. In fact, it seems that few of them spend more than one twentieth of this — a sign of no very great enthusiasm! Until such a condition is changed, musicians will continue to feel out of step in our semi-welfare state.

But if we in England have to face a considerable indifference, in other countries conditions can have other, equally awkward effects. In totalitarian regimes, we know that great official pressure is brought to bring the artist into line and make him conform to the state's ideology. In the richer capitalist countries, money and snobbishness combine to demand the latest, newest manifestations, which I am told go by the name in this country of Foundation Music.

The *ideal* conditions for an artist or musician will never be found outside the *ideal* society, and when shall we see that? But I think I can tell you some of the things that any artist demands from any society. He demands that his art shall be accepted as an essential part of human activity and human expression; and that he shall be accepted as a genuine practitioner of that art and consequently of value to the community; reasonably, he demands a secure living from society, and a pension when he has worked long enough; this is a basis for society to offer a musician, a modest basis. In actual fact there are very few musicians in my country who will get a pension after forty years' work in an orchestra or in an opera house. This must be changed; we must at least be treated as civil servants. Once we have a material status, we can accept the responsibility of answering society's demands on us. And society should and will demand from us the utmost of our skill and gift in the full range of music-making. (Here we come back to occasional music.) There should be special music made and played for all sorts of occasions: football matches, receptions, elections (why not?), and even presentations of awards. I would have been delighted to have been greeted with a special piece composed for today. It might have turned out to be another piece as good as the cantata Bach wrote for the municipal election at Muhlhausen, or the Galliard that

Dowland wrote as a compliment to the Earl of Essex. Some of the greatest pieces of music in our possession were written for special occasions, grave or gay. But we shouldn't worry too much about the so-called permanent value of our occasional music. A lot of it cannot make much sense after its first performance, and it is quite a good thing to please people even if only for today.

That is what we should aim at—pleasing people today as seriously as we can, and letting the future look after itself. Bach wrote his *St. Matthew Passion* for performance on one day of the year only—the day which in the Christian church was the culmination of the year, to which the year's worship was leading. It is one of the unhappiest results of the march of science and commerce that this unique work, at the turn of a switch, is at the mercy of any loud roomful of cocktail drinkers—to be listened to or switched off at will, without ceremony or occasion.

The wording of your institute's constitution implies an effort to present the arts as a counterbalance to science in today's life. And though I am sure you do not imagine that there is not a lot of science, knowledge, and skill in the art of making music (in the calculation of sound qualities and colors, the knowledge of the technique of instruments and voices, the balance of forms, the creation of moods and the development of ideas), I would like to think you are suggesting that what is important in the arts is not the scientific part, the analyzable part of music, but the something that emerges from it but transcends it, which cannot be analyzed because it is not in it, but of it. It is the quality which cannot be acquired by simply the exercise of a technique or a system: It is something to do with personality, with gift, with spirit. I simply call it magic—quality which would appear to be by no means unacknowledged by scientists, and which I value more than any other part of music.

It is arguable that the richest and most productive eighteen months in our music history is the time when Beethoven had just died, when the other nineteenth-century giants, Wagner, Verdi, and Brahms, had not begun; I mean the period in which Franz Schubert wrote the *Winterreise*, the C-Major Symphony, his last three Piano Sonatas, the C-Major String Quintet, as well as a dozen other glorious pieces. The very creation of these works in that space of time seems hardly credible; but the standard of inspiration, of magic, is miraculous and past all explanation. Though I have worked very hard at the *Winterreise* the last five years, every time I come back to it I am amazed not only by the extraordinary mastery of it—for Schubert knew exactly what he was doing (make no mistake about that) and he had thought profoundly about it. But each time the magic is renewed, and the mystery remains. This magic comes only with the sounding of the music, with the turning of the written note into sound—and it only comes (or comes most intensely) when the listener is one with the composer, either as performer himself or as a listener in active sympathy. Simply to read a score in one's armchair is not enough for evoking this quality. Indeed, this magic can be said to consist of just the music that is not in the score. Sometimes one can be quite daunted when one opens the *Winterreise* — there seems to be nothing on the page. One must not exaggerate; the shape of the music and its substance is perfectly clear — sometimes, as in his last great B Flat Sonata, elaborately so. What cannot be indicated on the printed page are the innumerable small variants of rhythm and phrasing which make up the performer's contribution. In the *Winterreise,* it was not possible for Schubert to indicate exactly the length of rests and pauses, or the color of the singer's voice or the clarity or smoothness of consonants. This is the responsibility of each individual performer, and at each performance he will make modifications. The composer expects him to; he would be foolish if he did not. For a musical experience needs three human beings at least. It requires a composer, a performer, and a listener; and unless these three take part together there is no musical experience.

The experience will be that much more intense and rewarding if the circumstances correspond to what the composer intended: if the *St. Matthew Passion* is performed on Good Friday in a church, to a congregation of Christians; if the *Winterreise* is performed in a room, or in a small hall of truly intimate character to a circle of friends: if *Don Giovanni* is played to an audience which understands the text and appreciates the musical allusions. The further one departs from these circumstances, the less true and more diluted is the experience likely to be. One must face the fact today that the vast majority of musical performances takes place as far away from the original as it is possible to imagine. I do not mean simply *Falstaff* being given in Tokyo, or the Mozart Requiem in Madras. I mean, of course, that such works can be audible in any corner of the globe, at any moment of the day or night — through a loudspeaker, without question of suitability or comprehensibility. Anyone, anywhere, at any time, can listen to the B-Minor Mass upon one condition only: that they possess a machine. No qualification is required of any sort — faith, virtue, education, experience, age. Music is now free for all. If I say the loudspeaker is principal enemy of music, I don't mean that I am not grateful to it as a means of education or study, or as an envoker of memories. But it is not part of true musical experience. Regarded as such, it is simply a substitute, and dangerous because deluding. Music demands more from a listener than simply the possession of a tape machine or a transistor radio. It demands some preparation, some effort — a journey to a special place, saving up for a ticket, some homework on the program perhaps, some clarification of the ears and sharpening of the instincts. It demands as much effort on the listener's part as the other two corners of the triangle, this holy triangle of composer, performer, and listener.

This award is the latest of the kindnesses for which I am indebted to your country. I first came to the United States twenty-five years ago, at the time when I was a discouraged young composer—muddled, fed up and looking for work, looking to be used. I was most generously treated here, by old and new friends, and to all of these I can never be sufficiently grateful. Their kindness was past description; I shall never forget it. But the thing I am most grateful to your country for is this: It was in California, in the unhappy summer of 1941, that, coming across a copy of the poetical works of George Crabbe in a Los Angeles bookshop, I first read his poem of *Peter Grimes;* and, at this same time reading a most perceptive and revealing article about it by E. M. Forster, I suddenly realized where I belonged and what I lacked. I had become without roots, and when I got back to England six months later I was ready to put them down. I have lived since then in the same small corner of East Anglia, near where I was born. And I find as I get older that working becomes more and more difficult away from that home. I plot and plan my music when I am away on tour, and I get great stimulus and excitement from visiting other countries. With a congenial partner, I like giving concerts, and in the last years we have traveled as far as Vancouver and Tokyo, Moscow and Java. I like making new friends, meeting new audiences, hearing new music. But I belong at home—there—in Aldeburgh. I have tried to bring music to it in the shape of our local festival; and all the music I write comes from it. I believe in roots, in associations, in backgrounds, in personal relationships. I want my music to be of use to people, to please them, to "enhance their lives" (to use Berenson's phrase). I do not write for posterity; in any case, the outlook for that is somewhat uncertain. I write music, now, in Aldeburgh, for people living there, and further afield, indeed for anyone who cares to play it or listen to it. But my music now has its roots in where I live and work. And I only came to realize that in California in 1941.

People have already asked me what I am going to do with your money; I have even been told in the post and press exactly how I ought to dispose of it. I shall of course pay no attention to these suggestions, however well or ill-intentioned.

The last prize I was given went straight away to the Aldeburgh Festival, the musical project I have most at heart. It would not surprise me if a considerable part of the Aspen award went in that direction; I have not really decided. But one thing I know I want to do; I should like to give an annual Aspen prize for a British composition. The conditions would change each year. One year it might be for a work for young voices and a school orchestra, another year for the celebration of a national event or centenary, another time a work for an instrument whose repertory is small—but in any case for specific or general usefulness. And the jury would be instructed to choose only that work which was a pleasure to perform and inspiriting to listen to. In this way I would try to express my interpretation of the intention behind the Aspen Institute, and to express my warmest thanks, my most humble thanks, for the unbelievable honor which you have awarded me today.

EXPERIMENTAL MUSIC AND AMERICAN DEVELOPMENTS

II

Charles Ives

[1874 - 1954]

The many musical innovations found in Ives's music are sufficiently well known not to require repeating here. It is worth noting, briefly, that in his experiments Ives anticipated atonality, polytonality, polyrhythms, and other such advances—that is, he explored these areas years before they were made famous by Stravinsky, Milhaud, Schoenberg, and others. Ives, ironically, remained an unknown musical figure throughout most of his long life. Fame came to him some fifty years after the composition of his best works.

Although Ives's influence on his European contemporaries is at best negligible, his contribution .to the development of American music is of crucial importance. This influence can be observed in the music of Cowell, Riegger, Copland, Carter, and Brant, to name but a few. The eclecticism of Ives's style fascinates many—his use of ideas both simple and complex, highly original and obviously derivative, in the context of the same work or even the same passage. Others are stimulated by his imaginative use of American folk elements, expressed in a manner often opposed to traditional European practices. Still other composers have been most influenced by Ives's radically new approach to musical textures, demonstrated by his fondness for the unsynchronized, the simultaneous occurrence of unrelated events (to be heard as unrelated and not as "counterpoint"), and for the charm of the "accidental"·as he heard it in the environment and captured it in his own work.

Paradoxically, though forward-looking in so many respects, Ives was in others very much a nineteenth-century Romanticist. His writings, in particular, reveal a deep concern for the relation between art and life, an almost moralistic view of music's expressive power. And his sharp, often brusque, defense of his artistic stand belies a deeper desire to communicate.

Postface to 114 Songs, from Essays before a Sonata, and Other Writings, edited by Howard Boatwright (New York, Norton, 1961), pp. 120-31.

Postface
to 114 Songs

Greek philosophers, ward-politicians, unmasked laymen, and others, have a saying that bad habits and bad gardens grow to the "unintendedables"; whether these are a kind of "daucus carota," "men," "jails," or "mechanistic theories of life" is not known—but the statement is probably or probably not true. The printing of this collection was undertaken primarily in order to have a few clear copies that could be sent to friends who from time to time have been interested enough to ask for copies of some of the songs, but the job has grown into something different; it contains plenty of songs which have not been and will not be asked for. It stands now, if it stands for anything, as a kind of "buffer state"—an opportunity for evading a question somewhat embarrassing to answer: "Why do you write so much —————— which no one ever sees?" There are several good reasons, none of which are worth recording.

Another, but unconvincing, reason for not asking publishers to risk their capital or singers their reputation may be charged to a theory (perhaps it is little more than a notion, for many do not agree with it—to be more exact, a man did agree with it once; he had something to sell—a book, as I remember, called, "The Truth about Something," or "How to write Music while Shaving!") Be that as it may, our theory has a name: it is, "the balance of values," or "the circle of sources" (in these days of chameleon-like efficiency every whim must be classified under a scientific-sounding name to save it from investigation). It stands something like this: that an interest in any art-activity from poetry to baseball is better, broadly speaking, if held as a part of life, or of a life, than if it sets itself up as a whole—a condition verging, perhaps, toward a monopoly or, possibly, a kind of atrophy of the other important values, and hence reacting unfavorably upon itself. In the former condition, this interest, this instinctive impulse, this desire to pass from "minor to major," this artistic intuition, or whatever you call it, may have a better chance to be more natural, more comprehensive, perhaps, freeer, and so more tolerant—it may develop more muscle in the hind legs and so find a broader vantage ground for jumping to the top of a fence, and more interest in looking around, if it happens to get there.

Now all this may not be so; the writer certainly cannot and does not try to prove it so by his own experience, but he likes to think the theory works out somewhat in this way. To illustrate further (and to become more involved): if this interest, and everyone has it, is a component of the ordinary life, if it is free primarily to play the part of the, or a, reflex, subconscious-expression, or something of that sort, in relation to some fundamental share in the common work of the world, as things go, is it nearer to what nature intended it should be, than if, as suggested above, it sets itself up as a whole — not a dominant value only, but a complete one? If a fiddler or poet does nothing all day long but enjoy the luxury and drudgery of fiddling or dreaming, with or without meals, does he or does he not, for this reason, have anything valuable to express? — or is whatever he thinks he has to express less valuable than he thinks?

This is a question which each man must answer for himself. It depends, to a great extent, on what a man nails up on his dashboard as "valuable." Does not the sinking back into the soft state of mind (or possibly a non-state of mind) that may accept "art for art's sake" tend to shrink rather than toughen up the hitting muscles — and incidentally those of the umpire or the grandstand, if there be one? To quote from a book that is not read, "Is not beauty in music too often confused with something which lets the ears lie back in an easy-chair? Many sounds that we are used to do not bother us, and for that reason are we not too easily inclined to call them beautiful? . . . Possibly the fondness for personal expression — the kind in which self-indulgence dresses up and miscalls itself freedom — may throw out a skin-deep arrangement, which is readily accepted at first as beautiful — formulae that weaken rather than toughen the musical-muscles. If a composer's conception of his art, its functions and ideals, even if sincere, coincides to such an extent with these groove-colored permutations of tried-out progressions in expediency so that he can arrange them over and over again to his delight — has he or has he not been drugged with an overdose of habit-forming sounds? And as a result do not the muscles of his clientele become flabbier and flabbier until they give way altogether and find refuge only in exciting platitudes — even the sensual outbursts of an emasculated rubber-stamp, a 'Zaza,' a 'Salome' or some other money-getting costume of effeminate manhood? In many cases probably not, but there is this tendency."

If the interest under discussion is the whole, and the owner is willing to let it rest as the whole, will it not produce something less vital than the ideal which underlies, or which did underlie it? And is the resultant work from this interest as free as it should be from a certain influence of reaction which is brought on by, or at least is closely related to, the artist's over-anxiety about its effect upon others?

And to this, also, no general answer must be given — each man will answer it for himself, if he feels like answering questions. The whole matter is but one of the personal conviction. For, as Mr. Sedgwick says in his helpful and inspiring little book about Dante, "in judging human conduct" — and the manner in which an interest in art is used has to do with human conduct — "we are dealing with subtle mysteries of motives, impulses, feelings, thoughts that shift, meet, combine and separate like clouds."

Every normal man — that is, every uncivilized or civilized human being not of defective mentality, moral sense, etc. — has, in some degree, creative insight (an unpopular statement) and an interest, desire and ability to express it (another unpopular statement). There are many, too many who think they have none of it, and stop with the thought, or before the thought. There are a few who think (and encourage others to think) that they and they only have this insight, interest, etc., and that (as a kind of collateral security) they and they only know how to give true expression to it, etc. But in every human soul there is a ray of celestial beauty (Plotinus admits that), and a spark of genius (nobody admits that).

If this is so, and if one of the greatest sources of strength, one of the greatest joys and deepest pleasures of men is giving rein to it in some way, why should not everyone instead of a few be encouraged and feel justified in encouraging everyone, including himself, to make this a part of every one's life, and his life — a value that will supplement the other values and help round out the substance of the soul?

Condorcet, in his attitude towards history; Dryden, perhaps, when he sings, ". . . from heavenly harmony, This universal frame began. . . . The diapason closing full in man"; more certainly Emerson in the "Over-soul" and [in the idea of the] "common-heart" seem to lend strength to the thought that this germ-plasm of creative art interest and work is universal, and that its selection theory is based on any condition that has to do with universal encouragement. Encouragement here is taken in the broad sense of something akin to unprejudiced and intelligent examination, to sympathy and unconscious influence — a thing felt rather than seen. The problem of direct encouragement is more complex and exciting but not as fundamental or important. It seems to the writer that the attempts to stimulate interest by elaborate systems of contests, prizes, etc., are a little overdone nowadays. Something of real benefit to art may be accomplished in this way, but perhaps the prizes may do the donors more good than the donatees. Possibly the pleasure and satisfaction of the former in having done what they consider a good deed may be far greater than the improvement in the quality of the latter's work. In fact, the process may have an enervating effect upon the latter — it may produce more Roderick Hudsons than Beethovens. Perhaps something of greater value could be caught without this kind of bait. Perhaps the chief value of the plan to establish a "course at Rome" to raise the standard of American music (or the standard of American composers — which is it?) may be in finding a man strong enough to survive it. To see the sunrise a man has but to get up early, and he can always have Bach in his pocket. For the amount of a month's wages, a grocery clerk can receive "personal instruction" from Beethoven and other *living* "conservatories." Possibly, the more our composer accepts from his patrons, "*et al.,*" the less he will accept *from himself.* It may be possible that a month in a "Kansas wheat field" will do more for him than three years in Rome. It may be that many men — perhaps some of genius (if you won't admit that all are geniuses) — have been started on the downward path of subsidy by trying to write a thousand-dollar prize poem or a ten-thousand-dollar prize opera. How many masterpieces have been prevented from blossoming in this way? A cocktail will make a man eat more but will not give him a healthy, normal appetite (if he had not that already). If a bishop should offer a "prize living" to the curate who will love God the hardest for fifteen days, whoever gets the prize would love God the least — probably. Such stimulants, it strikes us, tend to industrialize art rather than develop a spiritual sturdiness — a sturdiness which Mr. Sedgwick says shows itself in a close union between spiritual life and the ordinary business of life, against spiritual feebleness, which shows itself in the separation of the two. And for the most of us, we believe, this sturdiness would be encouraged by anything that will keep or help us keep a normal balance between the spiritual life and the ordinary life. If for every thousand dollar prize a potato field be substituted, so that these candidates of Clio can dig a little in real life, perchance dig up a natural inspiration, art's air might be a little clearer — a little freer from certain traditional delusions: for instance, that free thought and free love always go to the same café — that atmosphere and diligence are synonymous. To quote Thoreau incorrectly: "When half-Gods talk, the Gods walk!" Everyone should have the opportunity of not being over-influenced. But these unpopular convictions should stop — "On ne donne rien si liberalement que ses conseils."

A necessary *part* of this *part* of progressive evolution (for they tell us now that evolution is not always progressive) is that every one should be as free as possible to encourage every one, including himself, to work and to be willing to work where this interest directs, "to stand and be willing to stand unprotected from all the showers of the absolute which may beat upon him, to use or learn to use, or at least to be unafraid of trying to use, whatever he can of any and all lessons of the infinite which humanity has received and thrown to him, that nature has exposed and sacrificed for him, that life and death have translated for him," *until* the products of his labor shall beat around and through his ordinary work — shall strengthen, widen, and deepen all his senses, aspirations, or whatever the innate power and impulses may be called, which God has given man.

Charles
Ives

Everything from a mule to an oak which nature has given life has a right to that life, and a right to throw into that life all the values it can. Whether they be approved by a human mind or seen with a human eye is no concern of that right. The right of a tree, wherever it stands, is to grow as strong and as beautiful as it can whether seen or unseen, whether made immortal by a Turner, or translated into a part of Seraphic architecture or a kitchen table. The instinctive and progressive interest of every man in art, we are willing to affirm with no qualification, will go on and on, ever fulfilling hopes, ever building new ones, ever opening new horizons, until the day will come when every man while digging his potatoes will breathe his own epics, his own symphonies (operas, if he likes it); and as he sits of an evening in his backyard and shirt sleeves smoking his pipe and watching his brave children in *their* fun of building *their* themes for *their* sonatas of *their* life, he will look up over the mountains and see his visions in their reality, will hear the transcendental strains of the day's symphony resounding in their many choirs, and in all their perfection, through the west wind and the tree tops!

It was not Mark Twain but the "Danbury News Man" who became convinced that a man never knows his vices and virtues until that great and solemn event, that first sunny day in spring when he wants to go fishing, but stays home and *helps* his wife clean house. As he lies on his back under the bed—under all the beds—with nothing beneath him but tacks and his past life, with his soul (to say nothing of his vision) full of that glorious dust of mortals and carpets, with his fingertips rosy with the caresses of his mother-in-law's hammer (her annual argument)— as he lies there taking orders from the hired girl, a sudden and tremendous vocabulary comes to him. Its power is omnipotent, it consumes everything—but the rubbish heap. Before it his virtues quail, hesitate, and crawl carefully out of the cellar window; his vices—even they go back on him, even they can't stand this—he sees them march with stately grace (and others) out of the front door. At this moment there comes a whisper, the still small voice of a "parent on his father's side"—"Vices and Virtues! Vices and Virtues! they ain't no sech things—but there's a tarnal lot of 'em." Wedged in between the sewing machine and the future, he examines himself, as every man in his position should do: "What has brought me to this? Where am I? Why do I do this?" "These are natural inquiries. They have assailed thousands before our day; they will afflict thousands in years to come. And probably there is no form of interrogation so loaded with subtle torture —unless it is to be asked for a light in a strange depot by a man you've just selected out of seventeen thousand as the one man the most likely to have a match. Various authors have various reasons for bringing out a book, and this reason may or may not be the reason they give to the world; I know not, and care not. It is not for me to judge the world unless I am elected. It is a matter which lies between the composer and his own conscience, and I know of no place where it is less likely to be crowded. . . . Some have written a book for money; I have not. Some for fame; I have not. Some for love; I have not. Some for kindlings; I have not. I have not written a book for any of these reasons or for all of them together. In fact, gentle borrower, I have not written a book at all" —I have merely cleaned house. All that is left is out on the clothes line; but it's good for a man's vanity to have the neighbors see *him*—on the clothes line.

For some such or different reason, through some such or different process, this volume, this package of paper, uncollectable notes, marks of respect and expression, is now thrown, so to speak, at the music fraternity, who for this reason will feel free to dodge it on its way—perhaps to the waste basket. It is submitted as much or more in the chance that some points for the better education of the composer may be thrown back at him than that any of the points the music may contain may be valuable to the recipient.

Some of the songs in this book, particularly among the later ones, cannot be sung, and if they could, perhaps might prefer, if they had a say, to remain as they are; that is, "in the leaf" —and that they will remain in this peaceful state is more than presumable. An excuse (if none of the above are good enough) for their existence which suggests itself at this point is that a song has a *few* rights, the same as other ordinary citizens. If it feels like walking along the left-hand side of the street, passing the door of physiology or sitting on the curb, why not let it? If it feels like kicking over an ash can, a poet's castle, or the prosodic law, will you stop it? Must it always be a polite triad, a "breve gaudium," a ribbon to match the voice? Should it not be free at times from the dominion of the thorax, the diaphragm, the ear, and other points of interest? If it wants to beat around in the valley, to throw stones up the pyramids, or to sleep in the park, should it not have some immunity from a Nemesis, a Rameses, or a policeman? Should it not have a chance to sing to itself, if it can sing?—to enjoy itself without making a bow, if it can't make a bow?—to swim around in any ocean, if it can swim, without having to swallow "hook and bait," or being sunk by an operatic greyhound? If it happens to feel like trying to fly where humans cannot fly, to sing what cannot be sung, to walk in a cave on all fours, or to tighten up its girth in blind hope and faith and try to scale mountains that are not, who shall stop it?

> —In short, must a song
> always be a song!

Henry
Cowell

[1897 - 1965]

The work of Henry Cowell has been of crucial significance in the development of American music in this century. Cowell's music, like that of Charles Ives, departs from the earlier American practice of imitating European models. Moreover, and again like the music of Ives, it combines and juxtaposes highly complex and curiously simple elements. It may be significant to note here that Cowell and his wife Sidney are the co-authors of the most comprehensive book on the subject of Ives yet produced. Certainly the relationship between the two composers is an important one.

   Yet Cowell's aims and musical style are uniquely his own. He was one of the first composers of our time seriously concerned with the study of primitive music, folkloristic music of all peoples, and particularly with non-Western musical elements. His many experiments with new means of sound production—the best known of which involved the use of the fist, palm and forearm on the piano keyboard, producing "tone clusters"—inspired composers of later generations to investigate this area still further.

   Cowell's inquisitive and imaginative approach to all musical questions is demonstrated in his early book, New Musical Resources, a volume decades ahead of its time in such areas as notation, rhythms and harmonic possibilities. Selected passages from that book are reprinted here.

New Musical Resources (New York, A. A. Knopf, 1930), pp. 49-56, 111-122.

From
"New Musical
Resources"

Rhythm

Time

The accepted fundamental unit with which to measure musical time (or duration) is a whole note. Melody, harmony, and counterpoint might conceivably be made up without departing from this simple time-unit. In practice, of course, variety is introduced, and this by well-known methods. One step is to vary the length of the time-unit by subdividing it into half, quarter, eighth, sixteenth notes, etc. The other step is to combine these longer and shorter units into so-called "figures," which, recurring in a given composition, give it a certain distinctive rhythmical quality.

However great a variety in time effect is made possible by this existing system, certain limitations at once suggest themselves. We are always at liberty to divide a whole note into two halves, a half-note into two quarters, a quarter into two eighth-notes, and so on. And any combination of these lesser time-units is acceptable so long as their sum is the equivalent of the single whole note that we have taken as our base. Rests, subdivided on the same principle as notes, are treated in the same way as their rhythmic equivalents in sounded notes. But if we wish to introduce into a composition a whole measure of normal length divided into three notes of equal length, there is no way of doing so except by the clumsy expedient of writing the figure 3 over three successive half-notes filling a measure. In other words the notes as written down have a certain time-value impossible under the circumstances, and the discrepancy is reconciled by explaining that in reality notes of a different time-value are intended. Were the use of such notes of rare occurrence, this method might be justifiable; since, however, these notes and others having a similar discrepancy in time are very often used, should not an independent method of notation be found for them?

That question may stand for a moment, however, while the subject of time in music is approached from another angle. Assume that we have two melodies moving parallel to each other, the first written in whole notes, and the second in half-notes. If the time for each note were to be indicated by the tapping of a stick, the taps for the second melody would recur with double the rapidity of those for the first. If now the taps were to be increased greatly in rapidity without changing the relative speed, it will be seen that when the taps for the first melody reach sixteen to the second,

135

those for the second melody will be thirty-two to the second. In other words, the vibrations from the taps of one melody will give the musical tone C, while those of the other will give the tone C one octave higher. Time has been translated, as it were, into musical tone. Or, as has been shown above, a parallel can be drawn between the ratio of rhythmical beats and the ratio of musical tones by virtue of the common mathematical basis of both musical time and musical tone. The two times, in this view, might be said to be "in harmony," the simplest possible.

There is a well-known acoustical instrument which produces a sound broken by silences. When the silences between the sound occur not too rapidly, the result is a rhythm. When the breaks between the sound are speeded, however, they produce a new pitch in themselves, which is regulated by the rapidity of the successive silences between the sounds.

There is, of course, nothing radical in what is thus far suggested. It is only the interpretation that is new; but when we extend this principle more widely we begin to open up new fields of rhythmical expression in music.

Referring back to our chart, we find that the familiar interval of a fifth represents a vibration ratio of 2:3. Translating this into time, we might have a measure of three equal notes set over another in two. A slight complication is now added. Corresponding to the tone interval of a major third would be a time-ratio of five against four notes; the minor third would be represented by a ratio of six against five notes, and so on. If we were to combine melodies in two (or four) beats, three beats, and five beats to the measure, we should then have three parallel time-systems corresponding to the vibration speeds of a simple consonant harmony. [(See Example 1.)] The conductor of such a trio, by giving one beat to a measure, could lead all the voices together; for the measure, no matter what time divisions it included, would begin and end at the same instant.

Vibration ratio

Into the fundamental variety of such a system incidental variety could be introduced in two ways.

First, the result of all this could be a single continuous rhythmic harmony in which the units of the time-scheme could shift from one voice to another. [(See Example 2.)] Or, as would usually be the case, if greater variety were desired, the complete rhythmic harmony could be changed at will, so that the effect would correspond to a succession of different chords, in the selection of which the principles of tonal harmony might be observed. [(See Example 3.)]

The second method of securing variety would be to divide and subdivide the notes of any given time-value, just as in present-day music whole notes are divided into halves, quarters, etc. Obviously, if the measure is to be divided on the principle of three beats, the note that would take up one-half of the measure would be one and a half beats long. The measure would be completed, then, in another half-beat and a whole. A convenient mathematical representation would be: 3/6 + 1/6 + 2/6=6/6=1. The half-beat required in subdividing measures of an uneven number of beats (five, seven, etc.) is nothing but another application of the principle of the dotted note: 2/8 + 3/8 + 1/8 + 2/8=8/8=1.

In order to speak accurately of notes of new time-values, they might be given distinctive names. At present a note occupying one-fourth the time of a whole note is called a quarter-note. Consequently, instead of calling a note occupying a third the time of a whole note a "half-note triplet," why not refer to it as a third-note? Hereafter in this work a note will be designated by a fractional number indicating what portion of a whole note it occupies.

It would be found in practice that in order to establish certain ratios groups might have to be used which include fractions; for example, if the lower octave of a note the ratio of which is eleven were to be used, the proper ratio would be five and one-half notes in a single measure. The kind of notes used to express such a ratio would be the equivalent of two eleventh-notes tied together, and might be termed two-elevenths notes. By accepting the smallest fraction as one count, the proportionate time of any fractional or other notes can be counted easily. Thus, in the previous example five two-elevenths notes and one eleventh-note would be used in a measure, and if one count were given to the eleventh-note, and two counts each to the two-elevenths notes, a total of eleven counts would be obtained for the measure as a whole.

It will be seen that while there has been some use of such time-values as eleven in the time of a whole note, the conception of a two-elevenths note is new; and by treating other rhythmic ratios in the same way, many other time-values are obtained which are unfamiliar in music; also by dotting a two-elevenths note, a three-elevenths note is obtained; by doubling it, a four-elevenths note, etc. These finer rhythmical distinctions open up a new field for investigation. Not only do nearly all Oriental and primitive peoples use such shades of rhythm, but also our own virtuosi, who, instead of playing the notes just as written, often add subtle deviations of their own.

Professor Hornbusel, of Berlin, has made the experiment of recording the time-values of a passage, as actually played by a capable musician, notated as in Example 4.

He found that the lengths of notes as played were quite irregular; for example, the first of the first two eighth-notes was almost twice as short as the second, while the quarter-note following was not twice as long as either of the eighth-notes.

Our system of notation is incapable of representing any except the most primary divisions of the whole note. It becomes evident that if we are to have rhythmical progress, or even cope with some rhythms already in use, and particularly if we are to continue with our scheme of related rhythms and harmonies, new ways of writing must be devised to indicate instantly the actual time-value of each note. We are dealing, of course, not with three-fourths metre, five-fourths metre, etc., but with a whole note divided into three or five equal parts.

There is readily suggested, however, a modification of the notation system based upon familiar musical practice. In our present notation the shape of notes is the same; their time-value, whether whole notes, half-notes, quarter-notes, etc., is designated by printing the note as open or solid and by adding stems and hooks. All that need be done, then, is to provide new shapes for notes of a different time-value-triangular, diamond-shaped, etc. The use of open and solid notes, of stems, and of hooks is equally applicable to these notes of varied shape. A few adjustments in regard to designating rests would make the system complete.

Chord-Formation

Building Chords from Different Intervals

In the conventional study of harmony the process of explaining the method of building up chords is to point out that they are formed, in their original positions, by the addition of intervals of a third, one on top of another. Thus, a "common chord" or major triad is found to contain a major third underneath, on which has been superimposed a minor third. A minor chord is formed in reverse manner, by adding a major third on top of a minor third. A diminished triad is formed by the use of two minor thirds together, while an augmented triad is built from two major thirds. When additional material is desired, another major or minor third is added to either of the four triads, making what is called a seventh chord, as the outside interval so formed will always be a seventh. Certain seventh chords have been preferred for frequent use, such as the "dominant" seventh chord, formed by two minor thirds above a major one. The reason for this is doubtless that such a chord is actually formed by the overtone series (fourth to seventh partials, inclusive). The use of all other forms of seventh chords, however, as well as ninth chords, which are formed by adding still another third to a seventh chord, is general in contemporary music. No particular reason for building chords in thirds rather than other intervals is customarily given; but the reason becomes evident in the light of the interpretation of the history of chord usage, given in the first chapter.* In early times the first few overtone intervals, fifths, fourths, and octaves, were regarded as the foundation of intervals, and the musical theory of those times permitted only fifths and octaves as points of rest, while thirds and sixths, or any other intervals, were resolved to the "perfect" intervals. Thus it can be seen that the harmony of that time, which was considered incidental to the counterpoint, was built on fifths and their inversion, fourths. Later, when thirds and their inversion, sixths, came to be considered concordant, they were made the basis of chords, and this is the system still taught. The overtones represented are the next removed from those forming fifths and fourths — namely, from the fourth partial to the seventh, the overtones there being spaced as thirds, first a major third, then two minor thirds. It is only by leaving out the eighth partial that the ninth, necessary for the formation of a ninth chord, may be said to fall among the possibilities of chords built in thirds. The simplest theoretical explanation of seventh chords other than the dominant, and ninth chords other than the dominant, seems to be to regard them as polychords, with tones in common, formed by closely related harmonies. Thus, the tonic major seventh chord (such as C, E, G, B) can be considered a combination of the tonic triad (C, E, G) with the mediant triad (E, G, B).

Since we have seen the development of the use of chords from the simplest ones in ancient times, through somewhat more complex ones later, and still more complex ones in present-day music, all following the overtone series on upwards, it seems inevitable that the system of building up chords must eventually include the next overtones after those related in thirds — namely, from the seventh overtone upwards. There seems to be need of such a system to further the understanding of contemporary material, which has had no adequate theoretical co-ordination, in spite of being in everyday use in composition. It is impossible to explain all modern materials as being further complications of chords built in thirds.

If we are to have a better understanding of the materials possible within the limits of a scale of twelve tones to an octave, we must have three systems, rather than one; and these three systems, being entirely similar in their working-out, can be readily co-ordinated. The first system is of chords built in fifths and their inversions, fourths, and diminished fifths. This was suggested as a beginning by the ancients, was left during the classical

*Omitted in the present selection (Editors: E.S./B.C.).

140

period, and now is being investigated by composers such as Schönberg and Rudhyar. This discovery on their part of the possibilities of a system in fifths seems to fill in a historical gap, bringing an ancient idea forward to its final use, rather than a step forward in the line of progress, as the perfect intervals are the most primary of the overtone series. It is interesting to observe that the triad or common chord of a system of fifths (such as C, G, D) is in many ways more concordant than the familiar triad in thirds (such as C, E, G), as it is a more open sound, and the resultant sound-complex contains fewer beats. The second system of the three necessary to cover the entire field is the familiar one based on thirds, and their inversions, sixths.

The third system would be based on the next higher overtones after thirds — namely, seconds, both major and minor. Through inversion, sevenths would be included in this system as well. From the seventh partial onwards, a series of major seconds is formed by the overtones; very large seconds at first, then smaller and smaller until between the fifteenth and sixteenth partials a minor second is reached. The overtones from the seventh to the fourteenth partials (if the twelfth, which occurs in a lower octave, is omitted) form a whole-tone scale, which is thus seen to have a sound acoustical foundation. Many of the chords employed by Debussy and others in whole-tone music give the suggestion of being built on major seconds. These chords, however, are rarely bunched together in groups of seconds, but are more often spaced more widely apart.

The use of chords based on clusters of seconds, built as they are on the next reaches of the overtones after thirds, would seem inevitable in the development of music. There is no reason to suppose that the progress along the overtones which has been made from early musical times to the present will suddenly stop. Also, it may be pointed out that the natural spacing of so-called dissonances is as seconds grouped together, as in the overtone series, rather than as sevenths or ninths; since from the time of the entrance of the seventh partial, the first dissonance according to the text-books, the partials travel in ever-narrowing seconds. Groups spaced in seconds may be made to sound very euphonious, particularly if played in conjunction with fundamental chord notes taken from lower in the same overtone series. This blends them together and explains them to the ear. The wider spacing in sevenths and ninths is often desirable, of course, particularly in counterpoint, as it gives the inner parts more space in which to move about. It has probably been from a feeling (perhaps without much investigation) that the parts would be cramped in groups of tones spaced in seconds that more attention has not been given to the possibilities lying in such groups, in which the parts need not be cramped if a study is made of how to proceed with them.

There has been sporadic use of the device of adding a second of some sort to a common chord, with the excuse of "adding colour." This, of course, is not a tenable explanation of why the particular second should be used, and is a confusion of the theory and purpose of music. The purpose of every note in a large chord may be to add colour to the composition as a whole, yet from the standpoint of theory there must be some reason why the chord used was one which, in the way it was handled, would produce colour. To say that in such a group as C, D, E played together the D is a colour-note does not explain why it should be there, nor why another note would not be just as good as a colour-note; it merely gives a name. The same is true when an attempt is made to explain the D as a passing-note played at the same time as the other notes. This also is only a name and is no explanation of why a passing-note, which is distinctly a melodic device, should suddenly without further reason be acceptable in harmony. All attempts which would relegate the D to a secondary position to the C and E beg the question and are a result of trying to explain everything from the standpoint of the axiomatic supremacy of thirds, which standpoint has no tenable foundation. It is far simpler to consider all the notes in any chord as equal and independent, accepting the chord C, D, E as one built on a system of seconds, not as part of the triad of C, unexplainably filled in with an extra note which does not belong to it.

In order to distinguish groups built on seconds from groups built on thirds or fifths, they will hereafter be called tone-clusters.

Tone-clusters

Tone-clusters, then, are chords built from major and minor seconds, which in turn may be derived from the upper reaches of the overtone series and have, therefore, a sound foundation. In building up clusters from seconds, it will be seen that since both major and minor seconds are used, just as major and minor thirds are used in the familiar systems in thirds, there is an exact resemblance between the two systems, and the same amount of potential variety in each. Thus we have the following formula for common triads: major, a major third with a minor third on top; minor, a minor third with a major on top; diminished, two minor thirds; augmented, two major thirds. This formula can be transplanted to the system in seconds, and we arrive at exact equivalents: (1)

a major second with a minor on top gives us, building from C, the cluster C, D, E flat; (2) a minor second with a major on top—C, D flat, E flat; (3) two minor seconds—C, D flat, E double-flat; (4) two major seconds—C, D, E. These four triads are the basis of all larger clusters, which can have great variety, owing to the many different possible juxtapositions of the triads within larger clusters. (See Example 5.)

When clusters are used alone, large ones often prove less cramped than small ones, as in very small clusters

used alone there may not be enough room in which to move the parts. (See Example 6.) A running part in clusters may be effective in connexion with chords in other systems. (See Example 7.)

Small clusters used only occasionally between chords of other systems may be desirable if handled cautiously, particularly in dissonant counterpoint. (See Example 8.)

etc.

In harmony it is often better for the sake of consistency to maintain a whole succession of clusters, once they are begun; since one alone, or even two, may be heard as a mere effect, rather than as an independent and significant procedure, carried with musical logic to its inevitable conclusion.

One reason that a large cluster is a natural reinforcement when played at the same time as a simple chord is that whenever a simple triad is played, the higher overtones of all three tones, which are plainly audible to a sensitive ear, form such a cluster. It would seem that only listeners with very crude hearing can be shocked at the sound of either a cluster or any natural dissonance, since a musical ear would already be familiar with the sound through hearing it as overtones of familiar chords.

On the piano smaller clusters of any sort are playable, but larger ones are more easily played if they are either chromatic, including all the keys between specific outer limits, or all on black keys, or all on white keys. This forms pentatonic clusters on the black keys, five different cluster chords of the same length being possible. On the white keys seven different cluster chords of the same length may be formed, and major, minor, or various modal scales may be used. There is less possible variety on the piano than with the orchestra, where clusters are at their best; nevertheless, there is more variety than would appear at first, made possible by changing the length of the clusters, as well as by their innumerable relationships to chords in other systems. A sense of monotony which may be felt by a listener through first hearing successions of clusters soon vanishes when the ear begins hearing the subtle distinctions between the different placements of major and minor seconds in the inner parts, just as it does now with thirds. (See Example 5.) In orchestral use we have all the possible variety of large clusters which are neither all chromatic nor all diatonic, but constructed from a consistent building up of diversified smaller cluster triads. (See Example 5.)

In familiar theory there are certain well-known ways of building with

musical material, such as by use of chord-connexions, contrapuntal melodic relationship, canonic imitation, retrograde, thematic structure, etc. All
of these methods may be applied to clusters, which also bring with them,
however, some new processes of their own.

A characteristic quality of harmony is the possibility of movement
within outside tones; that is, in changes of harmony the inner voices
usually move to tones which were contained within the outer limits of the
tones of the previous chord. But so long as our scale is limited to half-tone
intervals, it is obviously impossible to shift tones within the outer limits of a
chromatic cluster, except through interchanging the parts. The cluster must
be treated like a single unit, as a single tone is treated. All movement must
be up or down the scale, as in melody.

Owing to the difficulty of reading such clusters, it is suggested that they
be rotated by means of a single note running through from the highest to
the lowest note of the cluster. The above cluster would then be presented
thus:

A cluster, obviously, must be measured to show its size, and this may
easily be done as intervals are measured, using the distance between the
outside members of the clusters. Thus, a cluster of three consecutive
chromatic tones may be called a cluster major second, a cluster of four
consecutive tones may be called a cluster minor third, etc. (See Example 9.)
The important tones, the ones that are most plainly heard, are those of the
outer edges of a given cluster, just as we hear best the soprano and bass of
a four-part chord. Given a series of clusters of the same interval, we can
conveniently designate them by the names of their lowest tones.

Aaron Copland

[1900 - 1990]

Of all American composers, Aaron Copland has probably done the most, and in the greatest variety of ways, to further the cause of contemporary music. He has worked hard to advance the status of the serious American composer, and to bridge the notorious "gap" between composer and audience. In pursuit of these goals, Copland has written books about music for the layman, lectured, taught numerous courses, organized many concerts and festivals of American music, and has helped to improve the serious composer's economic situation as well, through the founding of the American Composers' Alliance.

Copland's career as a composer further illustrates his genuine concern for communicating with the music-loving public. As a young man, he became the first of many American composers to study in France with Nadia Boulanger, and for a number of years thereafter composed in a sharply dissonant, dispassionate Stravinskian style. His musical language gradually changed, however, as he became more interested in American music and the diversity of American musical culture—folk music of various regions, popular music, jazz, and the musical theatre. As many of these elements were absorbed into Copland's own style, his music became more accessible to the larger listening public. He emerged as one of the leaders of a group of American composers, including Roy Harris and William Schuman, seriously concerned with the expression of the national character—distinctively American—in symphonic music.

In recent years Copland's style has again become more abstract, influenced in part by the twelve-tone technique. His music still retains its power to communicate easily, and he remains a lyricist, primarily concerned with the expressive powers of music. The essay reprinted here demonstrates the wide scope of this concern.

Music and Imagination (Cambridge, Mass., Harvard University Press, 1952), pp. 40-57.

The Creative Mind
and the
Interpretative Mind

In the art of Music, creation and interpretation are indissolubly linked, more so than in any of the other arts, with the possible exception of dancing. Both these activities — creation and interpretation — demand an imaginative mind — that is self-evident. Both bring into play creative energies that are sometimes alike, sometimes dissimilar. By coupling them together it may be possible to illuminate their relationship and their interaction, one upon the other.

Like most creative artists, I have from time to time cogitated on the mysterious nature of creativity. Is there anything new to be said about the creative act — anything really new, I mean? I rather doubt it. The idea of creative man goes back so far in time, so many cogent things have been written and said — acute observations, poetic reflections, and philosophic ponderings, that one despairs of bringing to the subject anything more than a private view of an immense terrain.

Still, the serious composer who thinks about his art will sooner or later have occasion to ask himself: why is it so important to my own psyche that I compose music? What makes it seem so absolutely necessary, so that every other daily activity, by comparison, is of lesser significance? And why is the creative impulse never satisfied; why must one always begin anew? To the first question — the need to create — the answer is always the same — self-expression; the basic need to make evident one's deepest feelings about life. But why is the job never done? Why must one always begin again? The reason for the compulsion to renewed creativity, it seems to me, is that each added work brings with it an element of self-discovery. I must create in order to know myself, and since self-knowledge is a never-ending search, each new work is only a part answer to the question "Who am I?" and brings with it the need to go on to other and different part-answers. Because of this, each artist's work is supremely important — at least to himself. But why does the artist presume to think, and why do other men encourage him to think, that the creation of one more work of art is of more than merely private import? That is because each new and significant work of art is a unique formulation of experience; an experience that would be utterly lost if it were not captured and set down by the artist. No other artist will ever make that particular formulation in exactly that way.

**Aaron
Copland**

And just as the individual creator discovers himself through his creation, so the world at large knows itself through its artists, discovers the very nature of its Being through the creations of its artists.

Jacques Maritain has summarized this idea of the necessity and uniqueness of the work of art in these terms: it is the artist's condition, he says, "to seize obscurely his own being with a knowledge that will not come to anything, save in being creative, and which will not be conceptualized save in a work made by his own hands." Thus the creator finds himself in a precarious position because, first, the involuntary nature of creation makes the moment of engendering an art work uncertain, and then, once conceived, there comes the fear that the conception may not be brought to fruition. This gives a dramatic aspect to the composer's situation. On the one hand the need for self-expression is ever-present, but on the other hand, he cannot, by an act of will, produce the work of art. It must either be entirely spontaneous, or if not spontaneous, then cajoled, induced, gradually perceived — so that each day's work may spell failure or triumph. No wonder many creative artists have been reputed to have had unstable characters.

Up to this point, the situation of the musical interpreter is not so very different from that of the creator. He is simply the intermediary that brings the composer's work to life — a kind of midwife to the composition. He partakes of the same dedication of purpose, the same sense of self-discovery through each performance, the same conviction that something unique is lost, possibly, when his own understanding of a work of art is lost. He even partakes of the involuntary nature of creation, for we know that he cannot at will turn on the wellsprings of his creativity so that each performance may be of equal value. Quite the contrary, each time he steps out upon the concert platform we wish him luck, for he shares something of the creator's uncertain powers of projection. Thus we see that interpretation, even though it may rightfully be thought of as an auxiliary art, does share elements of creativity with the mind that forms the work of art.

But now let us consider the essential way in which creation and interpretation are radically different. The interpretative mind can exercise itself on a given object; it cannot itself supply that object. The making of something out of nothing is the special province of the creative mind. The composer is a kind of magician; out of the recesses of his thought he produces, or finds himself in possession of, the generative idea. Although I say "the recesses of his thought," in actuality the source of the germinal idea is the one phase in creation that resists rational explanation. All we know is that the moment of possession is the moment of inspiration; or to use Coleridge's phrase, the moment when the creator is in "a more than usual state of emotion." Whence it comes, or in what manner it comes, or how long its duration one can never foretell. Inspiration may be a form of superconsciousness, or perhaps of subconsciousness—I wouldn't know; but I am sure that it is the antithesis of self-consciousness. The inspired moment may sometimes be described as a kind of hallucinatory state of mind: one half of the personality emotes and dictates while the other half listens and notates. The half that listens had better look the other way, had better simulate a half attention only, for the half that dictates is easily disgruntled and avenges itself for too close inspection by fading entirely away.

That describes, of course, only one kind of inspiration. Another kind involves the personality as a whole, or rather, loses sight of it completely, in a spontaneous expression of emotional release. By that I mean the creative impulse takes possession in a way that blots out in greater or lesser degree consciousness of the familiar sort. Both these types of inspiration—if one can call them types—are generally of brief duration and of exhausting effect. They are the rarer kind, the kind we wait for every day. The less divine afflatus that makes it possible for us to compose each day—to induce inspiration, as it were—is a species of creative intuition in which the critical faculty is much more involved. But I shall come to that in a moment. Long works need intuitiveness of that sort, for it is generally the shorter ones that are entirely the result of spontaneous creativity.

Mere length in music is central to the composer's problem. To write a three-minute piece is not difficult; a main section, a contrasting section, and a return to the first part is the usual solution. But anything that lasts beyond three minutes may cause trouble. In treating so amorphous a material as music the composer is confronted with this principal problem: how to extend successfully the seminal ideas and how to shape the whole so that it adds up to a rounded experience. Here, too, inspiration of a kind is needed. No textbook rules can be applied, for the simple reason that these generative ideas are themselves live things and demand their individual treatment. I have sometimes wondered whether this problem of the successful shaping of musical form was not connected in some way with the strange fact that musical history names no women in its roster of great composers. There have been great women musical interpreters, but thus far—I emphasize, *thus far*—no examples of women composers of the first rank. This is a touchy subject, no doubt, but leaving aside the obscure and various reasons for the historical fact, it appears to indicate that the conception and shaping of abstract ideas in extended forms marks a clear boundary between the creative mind and the interpretative mind.

In all that I have been saying about creative thinking there is implied the strongly imaginative quality of the artist's mentality. I stress this now because there has been a tendency in recent times to put the emphasis rather on the artist as craftsman, with much talk of the composer's technique. The artist-craftsman of the past is held up to us as the model to be emulated. There is a possible source of confusion here: amidst all the talk of the craftsmanlike approach we must always remember that a work of art is not a pair of shoes. It may very well be useful like a pair of shoes, but it takes its source from a quite different sphere of mental activity. Roger Sessions understood this when he wrote recently: "The composer's technique is, on the lowest level, his mastery of the musical language . . . On a somewhat higher level . . . it becomes identical with his musical thought, and it is problematical in terms of substance rather than merely of execution. On this level it is no longer accurate to speak of craftsmanship. The composer is no longer simply a craftsman; he has become a musical thinker, a creator of values—values which are primarily aesthetic, hence psychological, but hence, as an inevitable consequence, ultimately of the deepest human importance."

It is curious that this concern with craftsmanship should have affected an art that has developed no successful large-scale primitive practitioners, in the sense that there are accepted primitive painters. Music boasts no Henri Rousseau, no Grandma Moses. Naiveté doesn't work in music. To write any sort of a usable piece presumes a minimum kind of professionalism. Moussorgsky and Satie are the closest we have come in recent times to a primitive composer, and the mere mention of their names makes the idea rather absurd.

No, I suspect that the stress placed upon the composer as craftsman, especially in teacher-pupil relationships, comes from a basic mistrust of making private aesthetic judgments. There is the fear of being wrong, plus the insecurity of not being able to *prove* that one is right, even to oneself. As a result an attitude is encouraged of avoiding the whole messy business of aesthetic evaluation, putting one's attention on workmanship and craft instead, for there we deal in solid values. But that attitude, to my mind, side-steps the whole question of the composer's own need for critical awareness and for making aesthetic judgments at the moment of creation. As I see it, this ability is part of his craft, and the lack of it has weakened, when it hasn't entirely eliminated, many potentially fine works.

The creative mind, in its day-to-day functioning, must be a critical mind. The ideal would be not merely to be aware, but to be "aware of our awareness," as Professor I. A. Richards has put it. In music this self-critical appraisal of the composer's own mind guiding the composition to its inevitable termination is particularly difficult of application, for music is an emotional and comparatively intangible substance. Composers, especially young composers, are not always clear as to the role criticism plays at the instant of creation. They don't seem to be fully aware that each time one note is followed by another note, or one chord by another chord, a decision has been made. They seem even less aware of the psychological and emotional connotations of their music. Instead they appear to be mainly concerned with the purely formal rightness of a general scheme, with a particular care for the note-for-note logic of thematic relationships. In other words, they are partially aware but not fully aware, and not sufficiently cognizant of those factors which have a controlling influence on the success or failure of the composition as a whole. A full and equal appraisal of every smallest contributing factor with an understanding of the controlling and most essential elements in the piece, without allowing this to cramp one's freedom of creative inventiveness—being, as it were, inside and outside the work at the same time; that is how I envisage the "awareness of one's awareness." Beethoven's genius was once attributed by Schubert to what he termed his "superb coolness under the fire of creative fantasy." What a wonderful way to describe the creative mind functioning at its highest potential!

It is one of the curiosities of the critical creative mind that although it is very much alive to the component parts of the finished work it cannot know everything that the work may mean to others. There is an unconscious part in each work—an element that André Gide called *la part de Dieu*. I have often felt familiar, and yet again unfamiliar, with a new work of mine as it was being rehearsed for the first time—as if both the players and I myself had to accustom ourselves to its strangeness. The late Paul Rosenfeld once wrote that he saw the steel frames of skyscrapers in my Piano Variations. I like to think that the characterization was apt, but I must confess that the notion of skyscrapers was not at all in my mind when I was composing the Variations. In similar fashion an English critic, Wilfrid Mellers, has found in the final movement of my Piano Sonata "a quintessential musical expression of the idea of immobility." "The music runs down like a clock," Mellers writes, "and dissolves away into eternity." That is probably a very apt description also, although I would hardly have thought of it myself. Composers often tell you that they don't read criticisms of their works. As you see, I am an exception. I admit to a curiosity about the slightest cue as to the meaning of a piece of mine—a meaning, that is, other than the one I know I have put there.

Quite apart from my own curiosity, there is always the question of how successfully one is communicating with an audience. A composer who cannot in advance calculate to some extent the effect of his piece on the listening public is in for some rude awakenings. Whether or not he ought to take this effect upon an audience into account at the time of composing is another matter. Here again composers vary widely in their attitude. But whatever they tell you, I think it is safe to assume that although a conscious desire for communication may not be in the forefront of their minds, every move toward logic and coherence in composing is in fact a move toward communication. It is only a slight step when a composer tries for coherence in terms of a particular audience. This idea of music directed to a particular public is usually a bit shocking to the music-lover. It doesn't matter how many times we tell the familiar story of Bach writing each week for the honest burghers of Leipzig, or Mozart's relations with the courtly musical patrons of his day; audiences still prefer to think of the musical creator as a man closeted with his idea, unsullied by the rough and tumble of the world around him. Whether or not contemporary composers think about this matter of communication with their audience, they haven't been signally successful at it. . . .

The subject of communication with an audience brings us quite naturally to a consideration of the performer's role, and the interaction of the creative and the interpretative mind which is crucial to the whole musical experience. These two functions — creation and interpretation — were usually performed, in pre-Beethoven days, by a single individual. The composer was his own interpreter; or, as frequently happened, interpreters wrote music for their own instrument. But nowadays, as we all know, these functions are more usually separated, and the composer is in the position of a man who has lost his power of speech and consigns his thoughts by letter to an audience that cannot read words. Consequently they both have need of a middleman, a talented reader who can arouse response in an audience by the public reading of the composer's message.

A prime question immediately presents itself: what does the composer expect of his reader, or interpreter? I think I know what one of the main preoccupations of the interpreter is: elocutionary eloquence, or, to put it in musical terms, the making of beautiful sounds. All his life long he has trained himself to overcome all technical hurdles and to produce the most admirable tone obtainable on his instrument. But there's the rub; the composer is thinking about something quite different. He is concerned not so much with technical adequacy or quality of tonal perfection as with the character and specific expressive nature of the interpretation. Whatever else happens he doesn't want his basic conception to be falsified. At any moment he is ready to sacrifice beauty of tone for the sake of a more meaningful reading. Every performing artist has something of the elocutionist in him; he wants the words to shine, and the sound of them to be full and right. Every composer, on the other hand, has something of a playwright in him; he wants above all to have his "actors" intent upon the significance of a scene or its import within a particular context, for if that is lost, all elocutionary eloquence becomes meaningless — irritating even, since it hinders the creative mind from getting across to the auditor the whole point and purpose of the work of art.

152

Further analogies with playacting exist. The notion of the actress who has been hopelessly miscast in a play is familiar to all of us. But musical actors, so to speak, often miscast themselves, and with less justification. The woman violinist who has the robust, healthy tone of a washerwoman will never successfully invoke from her instrument the sweet innocence of a *jeune fille*. The singer who is a nice person, and who possesses an excellent voice, may have no inner comprehension for the tragic sense of life, and hence will never successfully communicate that sentiment. One might almost maintain that musical interpretation demands of the performer an even wider range than that of the actor, because the musician must play every role in the piece.

At this point I can hear the querulous performer asking: But is there only *one* way of reading a piece of music? Aren't divergent readings of the same music possible? Most certainly they are. As a composer I should like to think that any one of my works is capable of being read in several ways. Otherwise a work might be said to lack richness of meaning. But each different reading must in itself be convincing, musically and psychologically — it must be within the limits of one of the possible ways of interpreting the work. It must have stylistic truth, which is to say it must be read within the frame of reference that is true for the composer's period and individual personality.

This question of the proper style in playing or singing is one of the thornier problems of music. There have been instances when I have listened to performances of my work and thought: this is all very fine, but I don't think I recognize myself. It may be that the performer misses the folklike simplicity I had intended, or that he underplays the monumental tone at the conclusion of a piece, or that he overemphasizes the grotesque element in a scherzo section. Personally I have always found the finest interpreters most ready to accept a composer's suggestions. And similarly, it is from the finest interpreters that the composer can learn most about the character of his work; aspects of it that he did not realize were there, tempi that are slower or faster than he had himself imagined were the correct ones, phrasings that better express the natural curve of a melody. Here is where the interaction of composer and interpreter can be most fruitful.

All questions of interpretation sooner or later resolve themselves into a discussion of how faithful the performer ought to be to the notes themselves. No sooner do we ask this than a counterquestion suggests itself: how faithful are composers to the notes they themselves put down? Some performers take an almost religious attitude to the printed page: every comma, every slurred staccato, every metronomic marking is taken as sacrosanct. I always hesitate, at least inwardly, before breaking down that fond illusion. I wish our notation and our indications of tempi and dynamics were that exact, but honesty compels me to admit that the written page is only an approximation; it's only an indication of how close the composer was able to come in transcribing his exact thoughts on paper. Beyond that point the interpreter is on his own. I know that there are some contemporary composers who have been exasperated by the extreme liberties taken with the notes by romantic artists. As a result they have gone to the other extreme and said: "Stop concerning yourselves with interpretation, just play the notes." That attitude blithely ignores the insufficiencies of musical notation, and thus refuses to take into account the realities of the situation. The only sensible advice one can give a performing artist is to ask that a happy balance be found between slavish adherence to inadequate signs and a too liberal straying from the clear intentions of the composer.

In order to get insight into the interpreter's mentality it is necessary to be able to bring judgment to bear on the performance. The interpretation itself must be interpreted if we are to evaluate what the executant is contributing to a performance. This is not easy for the layman. Observation has convinced me that even the truly musical layman often has difficulty in making subtle distinctions in the judging of musical performance. He seems to lack the criteria necessary for such critical judgment. The difficulty arises from the fact that the listener, in order to exercise such criteria, is expected to know in advance what the performance *ought* to sound like before he hears what it *does* sound like. In other words, he must have an ideal performance in his mind's ear alongside which he can place the actual performance heard for purposes of comparison. To do this he must understand, first, the style appropriate to the historical period of the composition and to the composer's development up to that time; and secondly, he must be able to describe precisely the nature of the given execution so that he can particularize the qualities special to that performer and none other. To do this well presupposes wide historical knowledge, a great deal of experience in listening, with the admixture of an instinctive musicality of one's own.

In interpreting the interpretation, as I put it, we must never lose sight of the preponderant role of the individual personality of the performer. I like to think that if I were to hear successively three unidentified pianists behind a screen I could give you a brief personality sketch of each one of them, and come somewhere near the truth. This may of course be merely an illusion of mine, but no matter; it indicates what I mean by the thought that a performance is both an exposition of the piece and an exposition of the personality traits of the performer. This is particularly true for singers. Like actors on the stage, they must be impressive in themselves, even before they utter a sound. Singers are really "on the spot"; unlike the

154

conductor they cannot turn their backs to us; they face us, and the song and the personality are inextricably mixed. You can't get at the one except through the other. The same is true of instrumentalists, except that in their case our sight of the instrument and their busy fingers make less obvious the role played by personality. But it is there nonetheless. When a performer lacks personality we call the performance dull; when he has too much personality we complain that he obscures the piece from view. A just appreciation of the exact part played by the performer's personality in any given execution is therefore essential for precise judgment.

Now let us get down to cases. Let us observe the interpreter in action, for the purpose of describing certain basic psychological types that are met with most frequently.

Great interpretation, as the "big" public understands it, is generally of the fiery and romantic type. Since so much of the music we hear publicly performed comes from the romantic period, many performers are forced to adopt the manner, even though they may not be born to it. But the true romantic—the interpreter who creates an impression of giving himself in an uninhibited way—has great power over audiences everywhere. I am now thinking in terms of the real thing, not merely of the unfortunate individual making a public spectacle of himself. By only a slim margin a tasteless exhibitionism is separated from an experience that can be deeply moving. When this kind of performance doesn't come off, we want to laugh—if we are charitably inclined; in less charitable moments it can be infuriating, for the simulation of strong feelings on the part of an interpreter who is really feeling nothing at all strikes us as a public lie; we want to rise up and denounce it. On the other hand, the performer who is deeply moved, and who without a shadow of embarrassment can openly appeal to what is warmest and most human in man's psyche, and who in a sense exhibits himself in this state of vibrant sympathy before the glazed stare of a large and heterogeneous crowd—that is the performer who really communicates with an audience and who usually wins the loudest plaudits.

Another of the truly potent ways of engendering legitimate excitement in an audience is for the player or singer to give the impression that chances are being taken. To create this kind of excitement there must really be a precarious element present. There must be danger: danger that the performance will get out of hand; that the performer, no matter how phenomenal his natural gift may be, has set himself a task that is possibly beyond even his capability of realizing it.

Nothing is so boring as a merely well-rehearsed performance, well-rehearsed in the sense that nothing can be expected to happen except what was studiously prepared in advance. This has vitiated more than one tasteful and careful performance. It is as if the musician, during the execution, had stopped listening to himself, and was simply performing a duty rather than a piece. It is axiomatic that unless the hearing of the music first stirs the executant it is unlikely to move an audience. A live performance should be just that—live to all the incidents that happen along the way, colored by the subtle nuances of momentary emotion, inspired by the sudden insights of public communication. Wonderful performances can be of many different kinds, but the virtuoso performance that is breathlessly exciting, to my mind, always implies this almost-but-not-quite out-of-control quality, the antithesis of the well-rehearsed execution.

Still another type of performer, whose sphere of action is somewhere in the neighborhood of the romantic, is the musician who gives a personalized reading of a work. Every performance that has been logically conceived represents a reading in some sense, but in this case the reading is more particularized and personalized, so that the composition is not just the composition, but the composition as our performer on that one occasion understands its meaning and tries to communicate it. In the case of a conductor of this type, thoughts of elegance of style, perfection of ensemble, delicacy of instrumental balance are all secondary; instead he is "singing" his way through the composition with a kind of concentration that does not allow for distractions of mere technical details. Such a reading, to be successful, must impose itself—must break down the resistance that may come from the thought that you or I might read the work differently. There can be no question of "aesthetic contemplation" here, either for the conductor or his listener. What he strives for is our involvement in a wholeness of experience—the sense that he and his listeners have lived through something important. This is the kind of performer who sometimes takes a meretricious piece and makes it sound better than it really is. The power of conviction behind such a performance tends to blot out critical reservations. We lend ourselves, and smile about it later. It was a good show, we got our money's worth, and no one was really fooled. But when the work merits it, and the reading is truly convincing, we are left with the impression that whether or not what we have heard is the only possible interpretation, we have at least heard one of the essential ways in which that music is to be understood.

I should like to invoke now another category of performer whose mind seems concentrated on a quite different artistic end; the performer whose approach to interpretation is more impersonal, more classic perhaps. Here the objective is an absolute clarity of texture, a euphonious ensemble, an infallible sense of timing, and above all, prime concern with continuity and flow—the sense of directional movement forward which is intrinsic to the nature and character of all music. Here it is not the musical measure being heard that is important but the musical measure to come. It is this concern with forward motion that carries a piece in one long trajectory from its beginning to its end and gives an interpretation inevitability.

The interpreter whose attention is focused on the road ahead is better able than others to give us the long line and sculptural shape of a composition. It is useless to explain this need for directional movement forward to performers who have no instinct for it. They may, and often do have clarity, but clarity taken by itself can easily decline in interest to that of a schoolroom demonstration — a laboratory taking-apart of the mechanics of a piece of music. We see how it ticks in its minutest part. For some reason, however, unless an inner fervor is generated, the performer becomes a schoolmaster who makes the composition clear for us but neglects somehow to turn it into music.

There is another attribute of the classic approach to the re-creation of music that should be mentioned: the species of deep satisfaction to be derived from a performance that has ease and relaxation. Effortless singing or playing is one of the major joys of music listening: it indicates a measure of mental confidence and a degree of physical assurance in the handling of the instrument, whatever it may be, that is not often found in combination in one human being. There are few qualities more grateful in execution than this sense of ease, the sense of powers completely adequate to the expressive purpose, but few things are more difficult to achieve for the performer. This is not at all a matter of the intellect, for certain performers in the field of popular music also have this kind of ease — in fact, they are more likely to possess it than are concert artists. I doubt whether it can be tricked. It must reflect a true inner relaxation, difficult to come by in view of the condition of public performance, which in itself makes for tension. But the master interpreters have it.

I have left until last the question of national characteristics in musical interpretation. Is there such a thing? Is there an American way of performing Schubert as distinguished from an Austrian way? It seems to me that there most definitely is. The quickest way of gauging this is to compare present-day American and European orchestral performance. Our orchestras, by comparison with those abroad, are energized and glamorized: they play with a golden sheen that reflects their material well-being. The European organization approaches orchestral performance in a more straightforward and natural way. There is less sense of strain, less need to make each execution the "world's greatest." In Europe it gives one a feeling of refreshment to come upon the frankly unglamorous playing of a solidly trained orchestra. I once heard such an orchestra in America, about fifteen years ago. It came out of the Middle West and played under a conductor of European origin in such a way that one felt the whole organization had just stepped out of the nineteenth century. Nowadays, when that approach is attempted, it generally results in a businesslike, shipshape rendition, without much artistic conviction behind it. More typical is the glorified tonal approach, although our orchestras still have not reached the steely brass perfection of a jazz combination's attack. But something of the same compulsion to "wow" an audience through the sheer power of tonal magnificence is present. Our symphonic organizations, as they become known in Europe, are admired for their live sound and their vitality in performance. It is only right that they should be. My object is not to belittle the outstanding qualities of our orchestras but merely to stress one factor in their playing which seems to me indicative of national flavor.

National characteristics are most clearly present in interpretation, I suppose, when it can be said that the execution is "in the true tradition." This comes about when the performer is either a contemporary of the composer and has received the correct style of rendition through association with the composer himself, or when, by birth and background, the performer is identified in our minds with the country and culture—sometimes even the city—of the composer in question. I realize that the phrase "in the true tradition" is at best a shaky one. For there is no positive proof that my conclusion of the "true tradition" is the really true one. Still, we are all mostly ready to concede that the conductor from Vienna has a special insight into the way in which Schubert should be played. Serge Koussevitzky once made an observation to me that I shall always remember. He said that our audiences would never entirely understand American orchestral compositions until they heard them conducted by American-born conductors. It seems clear, then, that if we can speak of national traits of character, inevitably those traits will form the interpreter's character as a human being and shine through the interpretation.

In sketching thus briefly various basic types of interpreter I have naturally been forced to oversimplification. The finest artists cannot be so neatly pigeonholed, as I am afraid I may have suggested. The reason we remain so alive to their qualities is just because in each case we are forced to balance and adjust subtle gradations of interpretative power. Every new artist, and for that matter every new composer, is a problem child—a composite of virtues and defects that challenges the keenness of mind of the listener.

I have mentioned what the composer expects from his interpreter. I should now logically state what the interpreter expects from the composer. Too often, however, the truth is that interpreters are not thinking about the composer at all—I mean the live composer. In the past it was different. There are numerous instances of a work being written simply because some outstanding instrumentalist inspired it. Paganini commissioning Berlioz, Joachim helping Brahms—instances such as these become more legendary as the years pass. Of course isolated examples still occur, but for the most part a regrettable gulf separates the interpreter and composer in present-day musical life. They are not interacting enough! A healthy musical state of affairs would include increased opportunities for interpreters and composers to meet and exchange ideas. This should begin at the school level, as often happened abroad. If I were an interpreter I think I should like to have the sense that I had been a part of the full musical experience of my time, which inevitably means an active part in the development of the composers of my time. Is this too utopian? I hope not, because the indissoluble link between interpreter and composer makes their interaction one of the conditions of a healthy functioning musical community.

Roy
Harris

[1898 - 1979]

The musical style of Roy Harris, like that of the more familiar Copland, has been shaped by a conscious involvement in the musical folk heritage of the United States. Harris is acutely sensitive to the indigenously "American" qualities in popular and folk culture, and has utilized these effectively in his own works. His music is strongly tonal, yet highly personal in its use of Medieval modes to shape melody and harmony. Rhythmically driving at times, particularly in evoking a boisterous "American" quality, Harris' music is more characteristically spacious in movement, more broadly expansive, and, in this respect, faithful to the symphonic tradition of the nineteenth century. These tendencies are tempered by a sense of rèstraint in orchestration, and a fondness for clean textures and uncluttered lines — all of which demonstrate the importance of his early training with Nadia Boulanger in Paris.

Harris' impact upon the American musical scene was initially overwhelming. This impact may have been occasioned not only by the undeniable quality of the music itself, but by the striking figure of Harris. He is the product of America's West rather than her cosmopolitan centers, a largely self-taught composer, a figure who has much to share with the "common man." Although he is no longer a major influence upon the younger composers, Harris' music remains an important body of work, and a landmark of its times. It vividly demonstrates the great creative energy of the United States in the 1930's, at the peak of the nationalistic resurgence of the arts in this country.

"Folksong — American Big Business," from *Modern Music* XVIII (November-December, 1940), pp. 8-11.

Folksong—
American Big Business

We had been dancing all night—putting the finishing touches to three of the most exciting days in my life. The Cowboys' Reunion came to an abrupt end as the pale blue-green dawn crept over the little Western town nestling into the foothills.

With whistling, shouting, singing and hollering they left by twos and threes and groups together, some by the West Road, some by the East, wagons and riders gradually disappearing and with them their clouds of prairie dust.

Nostalgia as lonesome as the prairies, and as old, too, led me back to the Fair Grounds. There was old Idaho Bill, well over sixty, directing his outfit. He had shipped in six carloads of wild horses from his mountain range for the wild horse race. During the race some had been saddle broken and had to be separated from the others. Idaho Bill figured he wouldn't come to any more Cowboy Reunions. The last time he went to Pendleton, Oregon he had felt the same way. The thing was getting a little too professional. "No question about it being real all right—the boys are the real bonafide article. You take that runt Shorty Kelsey—he broke the world's record for bulldogging this year. Now he figures he'll go professional. In a few years he won't be worth two toots in hell. It's getting to be cut and dried. When the boys ride hell-for-leather because their pardners, the old man or their girls and all the folks are a lookin' on—well that's one thing. That's real cowhide. When they calculate to make it pay for a livin'—that's a white horse of different color. You know there's somethin cussed-ornery about that, somehow. Taint decent to be ridin your heart out for pay."

Now that's what folksong is all about. Singing and dancing your heart out for yourself and the people you were born among—whose daily lives you share through the seasons, through thick and thin. From the hearts of our people they have come—our people living, loving, bearing, working, dying. These songs are as the people whom they express—salty, hilarious, sly, vulgar, gay, sad, weary, heroic, witty, prosaic, and often as eloquent as the silent poor burying their dead. They constitute a rich legacy of time-mellowed feelings and thoughts chosen through usage from the experiences of people who lived here and helped make America what she is today.

Many of our folksongs began as transplantations from European music.

Roy
Harris

Nearly everywhere one finds remnants of Protestant Church tunes and English, Irish and Scotch ballads. Spanish love songs have lingered. The French "Chant Populaire" turns up now and then. German chorales and folk tunes are part of our tradition. And then finally the ever growing influence of our black fellow-citizens — our one-tenth, leavening, hypnotizing us with voodoo rhythms and the indigo moods of the troubles they've seen.

All this and more too. The flavor added by the sun, moon and stars shining on our people as they built a nation in the wilderness. The smoldering excitable South, the vast lonesome West, bustling cities and man-killing industry. The old songs of our progenitors have been reborn. They are now more intense, sadder, wilder, more ribald, embodying much greater pitch variety and rhythmic freedom.

The pitch design in our best folksongs tends to lift beyond the banalities of obvious symmetrical sequences. Our best folksingers vary the sequence both rhythmically and tonally. They often end their phrases with characteristic "off pitch" ornamentations. Our popular bands also make a practice of this freedom in pitch design, especially the "spot" soloist when he "takes off."

But rhythmic freedom, asymmetry, is no doubt the greatest American contribution to folksong literature. (In that respect it most resembles Russian folksong.) This is probably due to the turbulence of our economic and social life. I cannot ascribe it to our language because we are doing the same thing to the English language that we have done to European folksong.

The basis of this rhythmic freedom is the sense of feeling rhythmic pulse in its smallest units, rather than in large arbitrary metrical denominations. Such a procedure can and does carry the rhythmic pulse into free moving groups of two and three with interspersed passing pulses of one, without in any way interrupting or complicating the clear intention of continuity. Our popular bands are so absolutely precise in their rhythmic ensemble for just that reason. Watch the players' feet for the smallest unit of rhythmic pulse.

In a sense our popular music is *urban* folk music. Both performers and audience have folksong characteristics. They have no esthetic attitudes, the music is produced only for enjoyment, they show a keen interest in the interpretive mannerisms of the performer, a lack of interest in all materials except those spontaneously improvised. There is emphasis on the lyrics, there are many word variations on nearly the same tune, a tremendous enthusiasm and desire to participate, a tendency to emphasize topics of current interest, a naive and aggressive self-sufficiency, and little respect for traditions other than their own.

Folksong —
American Big Business

But our popular music thrives on commercial exploitation. I doubt that folk music can do so but it now seems that it will be put to that test. The situation is as follows. For years the collecting of American folksong has quietly been going on. Credit must be given to such distinguished collectors as Cecil Sharp and to many others less acclaimed. But to the house of Lomax, father John and son Alan, goes the honor of bringing to records folksongs as they actually sound, and of placing before the public such folksingers as Leadbelly, Aunt Molly Jackson, Woodie Guthrie and Johnson of the Golden Gate Boys.

While this work of collection has been moving forward, radio has been increasingly hard put to supply fresh material for its omnivorous and voracious public. Now, since the big networks are planning to close their doors to all members of the American Society of Composers, Authors and Publishers, the problem becomes twice aggravated. So folksong is invited into the parlor. Also America has become a haven for expatriate musicians — one might almost say for the expatriated Muse herself. Some think she has now come to make her home with us. All these conditions have combined to high-light American folk music. It's rapidly becoming a new industry. Tossed into the commercial boiling pot, it is now being processed for radio and every conceivable outlet. The more obvious melodic idioms and the word ideas are put through the work-a-day wringer by crooners, bands, small orchestral groups, radio skits, folk-feature programs, records. Folk music is being used to "polish up the handle of the *Buy American* front door." This is America's way of getting acquainted — of applauding those she wants, for the time being. It may be, as it so often is, America's way of completely swallowing and digesting her oyster. In any case, our musical stream of consciousness will flow on with folksong intermingled.

Certain plastic residues will surely accrue to the sum total of usable materials. Unfortunately the tonal-sequential type of folksong — the *Jenny Jenkins* and *Lil Lizas* and *Sour Wood Mountains* are easiest to capture and exploit. There are some sentimentalists who try to make out a case for these banalities. They will deify folksong as descended from the Godhead of *the common people,* just as their prototypes have canonized the old masters, jazz or modern music according to their prejudices. But we need lose neither time nor space on these worthies. They are part of the Art Myth process too.

America will have many folksong vendors in the next few years. Some city boys may take a short motor trip through our land and return to write the Song of the Prairies — others will be folksong authorities after reading in a public library for a few weeks. "And though we have no talents here for hiring, we'll hire the robe out anyhow." We'll have Folk Song Hot and Cold and in the Pot with whiskers on it.

163

But all this mushroom exploitation of folksong will neither greatly aid nor hinder it. After the era has run itself out there will remain those composers who have been deeply influenced by the finest, clearest, strongest feeling of our best songs. Because these songs are identified with emotions deeply implicit in themselves, such composers will be enriched and stimulated. They may find a gold mine in the rhythmic resources of characteristic word combinations and of folk nonsense syllables, or in their polymodal-diatonic melody. They will absorb and use the idioms of folk music as naturally as the folk who unconsciously generated them. They will have learned that folksong is a native well-spring, an unlimited source of fresh material; that it can't be reduced to a few formulas to stir and mix to taste.

Those composers who are drawn to and richly satisfied with folksong will inherit the privilege of using it with the professional's resources and discipline and the amateur's enthusiasm and delight. For "here a great personal deed has room."

Samuel
Barber
[1910 -1981]

Perhaps the best known of those American composers working within the "mainstream," Barber has consistently produced works in a traditional idiom, highly lyric, definitely tonal, and only occasionally unsettling in their dissonances. His music, unlike that of Harris and early Copland, is not consciously evocative of America, but is allied, rather, to the traditions of European Romanticism. Similarly, his background and training are not identified with the Stravinsky-Boulanger school of neo-Classicism, but with Italian opera and vocal music in general.

Barber had at one time prepared for a career as a singer, and has composed a great deal of vocal music; his purely instrumental works also contain many passages of a strikingly lyric quality. He had not, however, composed a full-scale opera until recently. The present article recounts the events preceding the composition of that first opera, Vanessa.

"On Waiting for a Libretto," from *Opera News,* XXII/13 (January 27, 1958), pp. 4-6.

On Waiting
for a Libretto

For almost twenty-five years I have had a calm, often happy—in any case anonymous—existence composing symphonies, concerti, sonatas and songs, and I have never had to write a word about them. But now that I have composed an opera, things seem to be quite different! Honegger, the French composer, once said to me that there is a difficult transition in a composer's life between the ages of forty-five and fifty. Until then he is known as a "promising young composer." Suddenly, without any warning, he is called *un vieil imbécile* (an old fool). Why, just at this moment in my life, did I write my first opera?

Of course, I have always been interested in opera and attended the Metropolitan since childhood. Do you remember how vivid a child's first memories of the opera are? I was six and entranced. It was in New York. The opera: *Aida*. Caruso sang Radames and my aunt, Louise Homer, was the Amneris. Even the details are clear in my memory. We missed "Celeste Aida," due to parents' and uncle's irritating habit of lingering over coffee. Once arrived, there was the usual tussle as to who could keep the opera glasses longer (it seemed to me I always had to give them back at just the best moment). And then the kindly old Bishop in whose box we sat asked me, at the beginning of the Nile Scene, whether I could hear the mosquitoes. This was a signal for me to retrieve the glasses—the best ones. I looked and listened long and hard. I could hear no mosquitoes, only high violins. Ever since that day I have thought that people who listen for too much description in music are rather silly.

It pleases me now to think that I shall hear *Vanessa* in this old house of such memories. Actually it is not my first opera.

I began composing at seven and have never stopped. At nine I wrote my first opera, still in manuscript. I called it *The Rose Tree*. The libretto was by our cook, Annie Sullivan Brosius Noble. She had been imported from Ireland by my grandmother and was older than my mother, for whom she then worked. Whenever my mother dismissed her, she would say that she had no intention of leaving, as she had been in the family longer than Mother herself. Once when my mother asked her what we were having for dessert she answered, "Madam, a little something of my own. It is called a Bird's-Eye View of Death." (For the record, it was left-over cake with varying sauces.) Quick to pounce on literary talent—and miraculously close to home, at that—I asked her to write the text for me. She complied according to her moods, evasive or enthusiastic, like all librettists.

Thank heaven, this opera had an American setting. It took place no more than a mile from my own home, which was in Chester County, Pennsylvania. It concerned itself with, of all things, a band of wandering gypsies, apparently very prevalent along that Main Line at the time. The opening chorus, which seems to me now a good example of "opera-ese" (or a pre-Gutman translation), is as follows:

> A wandering gypsy we!
> The whole wide world is ours;
> We dance and sing with gladsome glee
> Through the sunny hours.
> We care not for the toilsome way
> The world so madly follows.
> Our hearts are light, our lives are gay
> And free from care as . . . swallows.

The hero was a tenor on vacation from the Metropolitan Opera Company who fell in love with a soprano by the good old Chester County name of Juanita Alverado.

This opera did not progress beyond Act I, not because the cook left, for they didn't leave in those days. Annie died.

I was about seventeen and deep in the study of composition, piano and even singing at the Curtis Institute of Music in Philadelphia. Yes, I had thought I should like to become a singer—a good way to earn a living while devoting myself to my first love, composing. But I soon found out that in order to be a great singer (and it is only amusing to be a great one) one must be either very intelligent or very stupid. It seemed to me I was neither. Although I smile now that I ever considered becoming a professional singer, how grateful I am, now that I am writing an opera, to my old teacher Emilio de Gogorza, who taught me so much about singing.

That year a young Italian from Milan, about my own age, arrived to study composition with my teacher, Scalero. He was very skinny, with a large nose—one of those noses that, as Isak Dinesen says, it takes 500 years to produce. He was not interested in opera; he had had enough of that, he said, at La Scala, and would devote himself to the purer forms, such as string quartets. He spent a solid year writing motets. I was in the same mood of abstraction, and, in fact, as we were very good friends, we signed a sort of blood pact never to write an opera. Thus life has its little revenges. As you may have guessed—but not from the nose, to which he

167

has now grown up—the young Italian was Menotti. And I hope that we will still be friends after the production of *Vanessa.*

As the years passed, he betrayed our pact and did write many operas. I continued in a non-operatic world; but now I was looking seriously for a libretto, and had been for some time. A couple of ballets were the closest I came to the stage. I had to turn down a Metropolitan commission because I did not like the libretto chosen for me by an earlier regime. A composer must make his own choice. Several long walks, mulling over the possibilities with Thornton Wilder, led to nothing, and the acceptance of Dylan Thomas, whose work I had early admired, to write for me was nullified by the outbreak of the war. I went into the service and an end was put to our possible collaboration.

I was more than delighted, therefore, when after all these years of searching for a libretto, Menotti suddenly offered to write one for me. We discussed many ideas and settled on what seemed to me a fascinating one. I think he wondered whether I really *would* do it, and I know I wondered whether I really *could.* I remembered what Poulenc said when he was starting his first opera: "Just throw yourself in!" It was decided that Menotti would write the first scene and we would see how that turned out. We left for the Maine seacoast, that summer of 1954, and I followed Poulenc's words with joy. At last I had a libretto! By late summer the scene was finished and my librettist seemed to approve. Now utterly engrossed, I asked him for more words in a hurry, to go full steam ahead.

Here was the beginning of a new trial of patience! He explained that I would have to wait until January, as he must leave for New York to produce *The Saint of Bleecker Street.* This was at the point in my opera when, after Vanessa's aria, Anatol first appears, silhouetted in semi-darkness in the doorway. She turns to him and screams. He remains standing.

And standing there in that drafty doorway in a northern country in deep winter, Anatol remained for four months until January. Once again my errant librettist asked for a reprieve, for now the *Saint* was to be done at La Scala. Not to mention the trials of Anatol (for no tenor must ever stand in a draft, even for a second), this composer was not fit to live with that winter. He fled to Greece and reorchestrated his *Medea.* And Anatol stood.

When the next spring, Menotti was at last *free,* I refused to write a *note* until the complete libretto was finished—a technique Menotti himself does not use. Doubly endowed, he has heretofore been in the privileged position of being both librettist and composer and could always jump to the defense of the underdog, as it were, whichever it was. My tactic succeeded brilliantly:. it made him so nervous that he sat on a rock by the Mediterranean every morning until, by summer's end, what I think is perhaps the finest and most chiseled of his libretti was finished. Now I could work without interruption until the end. My surroundings might change, from Mt. Kisco to Nantucket or Rome, but I was always with my characters. In the last scene, where they all say goodbye and leave forever, it was perhaps hardest of all for their composer to leave *them*.

Although Menotti and I often discussed twists and turns of plot and character, I had to change very few words. Menotti himself, perhaps with undue modesty, would say that a libretto is no more than a pretext for music. But this is an oversimplification. Interested as I have always been in any poetic texture I have set to music (Joyce, Hopkins, Yeats, Agee), I could immediately understand and appreciate the economy of Menotti's use of words, so necessary for the singing stage; their utter simplicity (how wonderful to set!) and his sense of theatrical timing, which seems to me indeed unique. I hope that I have done justice to his work and that his many admirers will not be disappointed by my intrusion. Actually, all I have really done in *Vanessa* besides the music was to choose the name. From Swift? people ask. Not at all. It came from a book I found in the Holliday Bookshop: *How to Name Your Child*!

Virgil Thomson

[1896 - 1989]

In the early nineteen-twenties, Thomson — like Copland, Roy Harris and others — went abroad to study with Nadia Boulanger in Paris, and learned, from her the austere techniques of Stravinskian neo-Classicism. Unlike Copland and Mme. Boulanger's other pupils, however, Thomson chose to remain in Paris, and, with the exception of one brief period, did not settle permanently in the United States until the outbreak of the Second World War. His music, therefore, reflects much of the wit and sophistication of his Parisian background, his contact with Cocteau, Picasso, Gertrude Stein, and Les Six. Nevertheless, it remains American in flavor, drawing upon Thomson's youth in Kansas City·as well. In its merging of simplicity and subtlety, folk air and cosmopolitan manner, it may well remind one of an urbane Ives — or a midwestern American Satie.

Virgil Thomson's musical activities have extended far beyond his composing. He has lectured extensively, helped to organize recitals of contemporary music, and actively supported the American movement of the 'thirties to improve the financial situation of composers. He is perhaps best known, apart from his composing, as a writer on musical subjects. As music critic, journalist, and essayist, Thomson has revealed his penetrating wit in words as well as in music.

Reprinted from Virgil Thomson, *The State of Music,* Second Edition, Revised (New York, Vintage Books, 1962), pp. 54-61, 63-65, 111-19. [Passages in brackets represent the author's 1962 additions to his original 1939 text.]

From
"The State
of Music"

Life among the Natives
or Musical Habits and Customs

Musical society consists of musicians who compose and musicians who do not. Those who do not are called "musical artists," "interpreters," executants, or merely "musicians." Those who do compose have all been executants at one time or another. One only learns to create performable works of music by first learning to perform. The longevity of musical works, however, is dependent on their being performable by executants other than the composer. This particular relation between design and execution is peculiar to music.

There is no such thing today as a serious painter who doesn't execute his own canvases. In the great days of Italian painting there was a tradition of workmanship that envisaged and even required the use of apprentice help. Veronese, for example, was a factory of which the large-scale execution and quantity production were only made possible, at that level of excellence, by the existence of such a tradition. The movie studios today produce as they do by means of a not dissimilar organization. Such formulas of collaboration are indispensable whenever a laborious art has to meet a heavy public demand. Even still the "mural" painters use assistants. But without an apprentice system of education, it is not possible to train assistants in a brush technique similar to the master's, or to depend on them for quick comprehension of his wishes. Hence the co-operation is not very efficient, and little important work can be delegated. Art-painting is really a one-man job today.

Poetry too is nowadays a one-man job. It neither derives from declamatory execution nor contemplates its necessity. Poets don't begin life as actors or elocutionists, and certainly actors and elocutionists do not commonly or normally take up poetic composition. Poetry, like prose writing, is not even recited at all for the most part. It is merely printed. Such reading of it as still goes on takes place privately, silently, in the breast; and although many efforts have been made to reinvigorate the art by bringing it out of the library and back to the stage and to the barrel-house (there is also a certain market for *viva voce* "readings" at women's clubs and on the radio and for recordings of the poet's voice), on the whole your enlightened poetry-fancier still prefers his poetry in a book. There are advantages and disadvantages in the situation, but discussion of them would be academic. The facts are the facts. And one of the cardinal facts about the poetic art today is that declamation is not essential to it.

Music is different from both poetry and painting in this respect. A musical manuscript is not music in the way that a written poem is poetry. It is merely a project for execution. It can correctly be said to consist of "notes" and to require "interpretation." It has about the same relation to real music that an architect's plan has to a real building. It is not a finished product. Auditive execution is the only possible test of its value.

Architects seem to get on perfectly well without having to pass their youth in the building trades. The successful composers of the past (and of the present) have all been musical artists, frequently virtuosos. The celebrated exceptions of Berlioz and Wagner are not exceptions at all, because Berlioz was master of the difficult Spanish guitar, and Wagner was a thoroughly trained conductor. (He could also play the piano well enough to compose quite difficult music at it, though not well enough to perform that music effectively after it was written.) Conducting, as we know it, was at least half his invention (Mendelssohn was partly responsible too), and he wrote the first treatise on the subject. He was one of the most competent executants of his century, unbeatable in an opera-pit.

A further special fact about music writing is that it is not only a matter of planning for execution but also of planning for execution by another, practically any other, musician. It may not be better so, but it is so. Interesting and authoritative as the composer's "interpretation" of his own work always is, necessary as it is frequently for the composer, in order to avoid misreading of his intentions, to perform or conduct his own piece the first time or two it is played in public, still a work has no real life of its own till it has been conducted or performed by persons other than the composer. Only in that collaborative form is it ripe, and ready to be assimilated by the whole body of music-consumers. A musical page must be translated into sound and, yes, interpreted, before it is much good to anybody.

At this point criticism enters. It used to amuse me in Spain that it should take three children to play bullfight. One plays bull and another plays torero, while the third stands on the side-lines and cries "ole!" Music is like that. It takes three people to make music properly, one man to write it, another to play it, and a third to criticize it. Anything else is just a rehearsal.

The third man, if he plays his rôle adequately, must analyze the audition into its two main components. He must separate in his own mind the personal charm or brilliance of the executant from the composer's material and construction. This separation is a critical act, and it is necessary to the comprehension of any collaborative art-work.

Criticism of the solitary arts is possible but never necessary. In the collaborative arts it is part of the assimilation-process. It it is not surprising, therefore, that the criticism of music and of the theater should be vigorously practiced in the daily press, and widely read, and that architectural criticism, which occupies whole magazines to itself, should be exercised by reputable scholars as well as by the most celebrated architects of our time, whereas the daily reporting of painting shows turns out to be almost nothing but merchants' blurbs and museum advertising. Poetry-reviewing, on account of poetry's small public, is pretty well limited to the advance-guard literary magazines. When verse is covered by the daily and weekly press, the reviewing of it is done by definitely minor poets, who fill up their columns with log-rolling.

The separateness of design and execution in the collaborative arts is not necessarily to the esthetic disadvantage of these, as the poets like to pretend. It is, on the whole, rather an advantage, I think; but we shall speak of that another time. Music's particular version of that duality, in any case, is what makes composers the kind of men they are. The necessity of being a good executant in order to compose effectively makes their education long and expensive. Of all the professional trainings, music is the most demanding. Even medicine, law, and scholarship, though they often delay a man's entry into married life, do not interefere with his childhood or adolescence.

Music does. No musician ever passes an average or normal infancy, with all that that means of abundant physical exercise and a certain mental passivity. He must work very hard indeed to learn his musical matters and to train his hand, all in addition to his schoolwork and his play-life. I do not think he is necessarily overworked. I think rather that he is just more elaborately educated than his neighbors. But he does have a different life from theirs, an extra life; and he grows up . . . to feel different from them on account of it. Sending music students to special public schools like New York's High School of Music and Art or the European municipal conservatories, where musical training is complemented by general studies, does not diminish the amount of real work to be got through. It merely trains the musician a little more harmoniously and keeps him from feeling inferior to his little friends because of his musical interests. In any case, musical training is long, elaborate, difficult, and intense. Nobody who has had it ever regrets it or forgets it. And it builds up in the heart of every musician a conviction that those who have had it are not only different from everybody else but definitely superior to most and that all musicians together somehow form an idealistic society in the midst of a tawdry world.

For all this idealism and feeling of superiority, there is nevertheless a rift in the society. The executant and the composer are mutually jealous.

The executant musician is a straight craftsman. His life consists of keeping his hand in, and caring for his tools. His relation to the composer is that of any skilled workman in industry to the engineer whose designs he executes. He often makes more money than the composer, and he refuses to be treated as a servant. He is a hard-working man who practices, performs, gives lessons, and travels. He not infrequently possesses literary cultivation. He is impressed by composers but handles them firmly and tries to understand their work. His secret ambition is to achieve enough leisure to indulge in musical composition himself. Failing that, to become an orchestral conductor. He doesn't mind teaching but on the whole prefers to play. He doesn't become a confirmed pedagogue except under economic pressure, when he can't earn a living by execution. He enjoys excellent health, can't afford to waste time being ill, in fact, and often lives to an advanced age. He pretends to a certain bohemianism, is really a petty bourgeois. His professional solidarity is complete. His trade-unions are terrifyingly powerful and not unenlightened. Economically, humanly, and politically the workman he most resembles is the printer.

The composer is a transmuted executant. He practices execution as little as possible, but he hasn't forgotten a thing. It is his business to know everything there is to know about executants, because he is dependent on them for the execution of his work. Executants, being embarrassed by the composer's broader knowledge, try to avoid the composer. Composers, on the other hand, fearing to be cut off from communication with the executant world, are always running after executants and paying them compliments and begging to be allowed to play chamber-music with them, in the hope of picking up some practical hints about instrumental technique. On the whole, composers and their interpreters get on politely but not too well. Composers find executants mean, vain, and petty. Executants find composers vain, petty, and mean. I suspect the executant's potential income level, which is much higher than the composer's, is at the bottom of all this jealousy and high-hatting.

Composers by themselves don't get on too badly either, but they don't like one another really. They are jovial, witty, back-biting. When young they keep up a courteous familiarity with one another's works. After thirty they preserve an equally courteous ignorance of one another's works. Their professional solidarity is nil. Even in the well-organized and very effective European societies for the collection of performing-rights fees, they are likely to let a few semi-racketeers do the work. They grumble no end about how they are robbed by managers, by performers, and by their own protective associations; but they don't do anything to change matters. Politely gregarious but really very little interested in one another, they are without any of that huddling tendency that poets have, without the simple camarderie of the painters, and with none of that solid fraternalism that is so impressive among the musical executants.

Composers . . . are always moving. A painter I know calls them "neat little men who live in hotel-rooms." They are frequently unmarried; but unmarried or not, they are super-old-maids about order. [Bachelor composers, to mention only the dead, include Handel, Beethoven, Schubert, Liszt, Chopin, Brahms, Moussorgsky, Rossini, and Ravel.] The papers on their desks are arranged in exact and equidistant piles. Their clothes are hung up in closets on hangers. Their shirts and ties are out of sight, and their towels are neatly folded. There is no food around. There isn't even much music around. It is all put away on shelves or in trunks. Ink and pencil are in evidence and some very efficient rulers. It looks as if everything were ready for work, but that work hadn't quite yet begun.

Living in hotels and temporary lodgings, and frequently being unmarried, your composer is a great diner-out. Of all the artist-workers, he is the most consistently social. Those painters who live in touch with the world of decorating and fashion are not infrequently snobs, for all their camaraderie and democratic ways. The composer is not a snob at all. He is simply a man of the world who dresses well, converses with some brilliance, and has charming manners. He is gracious in any house, however humble or grand; and he rarely makes love to the hostess. He eats and drinks everything but is a bit careful about alcohol, as sedentary workers have to be.

He has small illnesses often and gets over them. His diseases of a chronic nature are likely to be seated in the digestive organs. He rarely lives to a great age unless he keeps up his career as an executant. After all, the child who practices an instrument properly usually learns to live on what muscular exercise is involved in musical practice and in the ordinary errands of education. If he continues throughout his adult life some regular instrumental activity, he keeps well and lives to be old. If he gives up that minimum of muscular movement and alternates heavy eating with the introspective and sedentary practice of musical composition, he is likely to crack up in the fifties, no matter how strong his digestive system or his inherited organic constitution.

If he can survive the crack-up, he is good for another twenty years, frequently his finest and most productive. Your aged poet is rarely as vigorous a poet as your young poet. Your aged painter is tired, and his work is repetitive. The grandest monuments of musical art are not seldom the work of senescence. *Parsifal* was written at seventy, *Falstaff* after eighty. Brahms published his first symphony at forty. Rameau's whole operatic career took place after fifty. Beethoven's last quartets, Bach's *Art of the Fugue*, César Franck's entire remembered repertory, were all composed by men long past their physical prime.

The Appreciation-racket

Every composer is approached from time to time by representatives of the Appreciation-racket and offered money to lecture or to write books about the so-called Appreciation of Music. Unless he is already tied up with the pedagogical world, he usually refuses. If he makes his living as a teacher, refusal is difficult. I've seen many a private teacher forced out of business for refusing to "co-operate" with the publishers of Appreciation-books. Refusal of public-school credits for private music-study is the usual method of foreclosure. The composer who teaches in any educational institution except a straight conservatory is usually obliged to "co-operate." The racket muscles in on him. His name will be useful; his professional prestige will give a coloration of respectability to the shady business. He is offered a raise and some security in his job. He usually accepts.

Every branch of knowledge furnishes periodically to the layman digests of useful information about that branch of knowledge and elementary hand-books of its technique. Simplified explanations of the copyright laws, of general medicine for use in the home, of the mathematics of relativity, of how to build a canoe, a radio-set, or a glider, of home dressmaking, of garden-lore, of how to acquaint yourself with classical archaeology in ten volumes, and of how to see Paris in ten days—this literature is in every way legitimate. Some of the most advanced practitioners in every branch of knowledge have at one time or another paused to write down in non-technical language what was going on in those branches. The artistic professions have a large literature of this sort, the present book being an example. Biographies of celebrated musicians, histories of the symphony orchestra with descriptions of the commoner instruments, synopses of opera plots, memoirs of singers and their managers, even of musical hostesses, all go to swell the general knowledge about music and how it lives. Works of a scholarly or pedagogical nature, like treatises on harmony, on acoustics, on instrumentation, or bibliographies of historical documents, need no justification at all. They are instruments for the direct transmission of professional knowledge.

What needs some explaining is the Appreciation-literature, which

176

transmits no firm knowledge and describes no real practice. The thing nearest like it is the physical culture advertisement that proposes to augment the muscular and virile forces of any customer who will buy the book and do what it says for five minutes a day. Obviously, five minutes a day of gymnastics, any kind of gymnastics, with or without a book, will inside a week produce a temporary enlargement of the muscles exercised. Equally, the deliberate listening to music, any kind of music, five minutes a day for a week will sharpen momentarily the musical listening-ability. If the Appreciation-racket were no more than a pretext for habituating listeners to musical sounds, it would be a legitimate advertising device, destined, with luck, to swell the number of possible concert-customers.

What distinguishes it from the physical culture schemes is the large number of reputable musicians, philanthropic foundations, and institutions of learning connected with it and the large amounts of finance-capital behind it. So much money and so much respectability behind a business that hasn't very much instrinsically to recommend it is, to say the least, suspect.

When I say the books of Music-Appreciation transmit no firm knowledge and describe no real practice, you will either believe me or you won't. I have no intention of exposing in detail here the operating methods of that sinister conspiracy or of attacking by name the distinguished musicians who have signed its instruments of propaganda. If you are a musician, all I need say is, just take a look at the books. If you are not, avoid them as you would the appearance of evil.

It is as difficult for the laymen to avoid contact with Music-Appreciation as it is for the musician. Children in elementary schools get it handed out to them along with their sight-singing. So far as it is just a substitution of European folklore for American folklore and made-up exercises, not much real harm is done. At least, not as long as the center of attention remains instruction in sight-singing rather than the tastefulness of the pieces sung. It is in the secondary schools, with the introduction into education of mere listening, that is to say, of a passive musical experience, to replace performance, which is an active experience, that Appreciation begins to rear its ugly head. In secondary schools, especially in those where instruction is accomplished according to the pedagogic devices known as Progressive Education, passivity seems to be the chief result sought. A proper, that is to say, enthusiastic, receptivity to canned musical performance is highly prized by "progressive" educators.

In colleges the Appreciation of Music is a snap course, and as such it fills a need for many a busy (or lazy) student. As anything else it is hard to defend. For professional music-students it is confusing, because the explanations are esthetic rather than technical; and esthetics are a dangerous waste of time for young practical musicians. What they need is musical analysis and lots of execution according to the best living traditions of execution. For non-professional students also it is a waste of time that might be spent on musical practice. The layman's courses for adults in ordinary civil life are an abbreviated version of the collegiate Appreciation-courses. They offer nothing more (technically) than could be learned in one music lesson from any good private teacher. The rest is a lot of useless and highly inaccurate talk about fugues and sonata-form, sales-talk for canned music really.

The basic sales-trick in all these manifestations is the use of the religious technique. Music is neither taught nor defined. It is preached. A certain limited repertory of pieces, ninety per cent of them a hundred years old, is assumed to contain most that the world has to offer of musical beauty and authority. I shall explain in a moment how this repertory is chosen by persons unknown, some of them having no musical authority whatsoever. It is further assumed (on Platonic authority) that continued auditive subjection to this repertory harmonizes the mind and sweetens the character, and that the conscious paying of attention during the auditive process intensifies the favorable reaction. Every one of these assumptions is false, or at least highly disputable, including the Platonic one. The religious technique consists in a refusal to allow any questioning of any of them. Every psychological device is used to make the customer feel that musical non-consumption is sinful. As penance for his sins he must:

A. Buy a book.

B. Buy a gramophone.

C. Buy records for it.

D. Buy a radio.

E. Subscribe to the local orchestra, if there is one.

As you can see, not one of these actions is a musical action. They are at best therapeutic actions destined to correct the customer's musical defects without putting him through the labors of musical exercise. As you can see also, they entail spending a good deal more money than a moderate amount of musical exercise would entail. Persons whose viscera are not audito-sensitive need very little musical exercise anyway. To make them feel inferior for not needing it and then to supply them with musical massage as a substitute for what they don't need is, although a common enough commercial practice, professionally unethical.

If you will look at almost any of the Appreciation-books you will notice:

A. That the music discussed is nearly all symphonic. Chamber-music (except string-quartets) and the opera are equally neglected.

B. That the examples quoted are virtually the same in all the books.

178

C. That they are quoted from a small number of musical authors.
D. That 90% of them were written between 1775 and 1875 and are called Symphony Number Something-or-Other.

All this means that by tacit agreement Music is defined as the instrumental music of the Romantic era, predominantly symphonic and predominantly introspective. At least that that repertory contains a larger amount of the "best" music than any other. This last assumption would be hard to defend on any grounds other than the popularity of the symphony orchestras (plus their gramophone recordings and radio transmissions) performing this repertory.

A strange thing this symphonic repertory. From Tokyo to Lisbon, from Tel-Aviv to Seattle, ninety per cent of it is the same fifty pieces. The other ten is usually devoted to good-will performances of works by local celebrities. All the rest is standardized. So are the conductors, the players, the soloists. All the units of the system are interchangeable. The number of first class symphony orchestras in the world is well over a thousand. Europe, exclusive of the Soviet Union, counts more than two hundred. Japan alone is supposed to have forty. They all receive state, municipal, or private subsidy; and the top fifty have gramophone- and radio-contracts. All musical posts connected with them are highly honorific. Salaries, especially for conductors and management, are the largest paid anywhere today in music. The symphony orchestras are the king-pin of the international music-industry. Their limited repertory is a part of their standardization. The Appreciation-racket is a cog in their publicity machine.

It is not my intention here to go into the virtues and defects of the system beyond pointing out that the standardization of repertory, however advantageous commercially, is not a result of mere supply and demand. It has been reached by collusion between conductors and managers and is maintained mostly by the managers, as everybody knows who has ever had anything to do with the inside of orchestral concerts. To take that practical little schematization of Romanticism for the "best" in music is as naïve as taking chain-store groceries for what a gourmet's merchant should provide. For a composer to lend the prestige of his name and knowledge to any business so unethical as that is to accept the decisions of his professional inferiors on a matter gravely regarding his profession. I do not know whether it would be possible to publish a book or offer a course of instruction in music-appreciation that would question the main assumptions of the present highly organized racket and attempt to build up a listener's esthetic on other assumptions. I doubt if it would, and the experience of various well-intentioned persons in this regard tends to support my doubts. Their attempts to disseminate musical knowledge among musically illiterate adults seem to have led them eventually to substitute for instruction in listening some exercise in musical execution, such as choral singing or the practice of some simple instrument like the recorder. It would seem that such execution, which, however elementary, is a positive musical act, gives not only its own pleasure of personal achievement but also not inconsiderable insight into the substance of all music.

Do not confuse the Appreciation-racket with the practice of musical analysis or with the exposition of musical history. These are legitimate matters for both students and teachers to be occupied with. I am talking about a real racket that any American can recognize when I describe it. It is a fake-ecstatic, holier-than-thou thing. Every school and college, even the most aristocratically anti-musical, is flooded with it. Book-counters overflow with it. Mealy-mouthed men on the air serve it in little chunks between the numbers of every symphony-orchestra concert broadcast. It is dispensed in high academic places by embittered ex-composers who don't believe a word of it. It is uncritical, in its acceptance of imposed repertory as a criterion of musical excellence. It is formalist, in its insistence on preaching principles of sonata-form that every musician knows to be either non-existent or extremely inaccurate. It is obscurantist, because it pretends that a small section of music is either all of music or at least the heart of it, which is not true. It is dogmatic, because it pontificates about musical "taste." Whose taste? All I see is a repertory chosen for standardization purposes by conductors (who are musicians of the second category) and managers (who are not even musicians), and expounded by unsuccessful pianists, disappointed composers, and all the well-meaning but irresponsible little school-teachers who never had enough musical ability to learn to play any instrument correctly.

The musical ignorance of the army of teachers that is employed to disseminate Appreciation should be enough to warn any musician off it. Most composers are wary at first. Then it becomes tempting, because the money looks easy; and they think they at least will not be disseminating ignorance. Also in academic posts there is considerable straight pressure brought to bear. Nine times out of ten the young composer who is trying to make a modest living out of teaching harmony or piano-playing is ordered to get up a course in Appreciation (the tonier institutions are now calling it Listening) whether he wants to or not. He can make his own decision, of course; but I am telling him right now what will happen if he gets caught in those toils. He will cease to compose.

It always happens that way. No professional man can give himself to an activity so uncritical, so obscurantist, so dogmatic, so essentially venal, unless he does it to conceal his fundamental sterility, or unless he does it with his tongue in his cheek. In the latter case he gets out of it pretty quick. In the former case he gets out of composition instead. He gets out with some regret, because his professional status is lowered. But there is nothing to be done about that. Appreciation-teaching is not even a Special Skill of any kind. It is on the level of Minimum Musicality, as everybody in music knows.

So your composer who sticks at it becomes an ex-composer and an embittered man. Always beware of ex-composers. Their one aim in life is to discourage the writing of music.

Roger Sessions

[1896 - 1985]

Although not an experimentalist, Roger Sessions has long been regarded, until the last decade or so, as a relatively isolated figure in American music—highly respected, but often termed "complex" or "difficult" as a composer. This attitude, which is fortunately declining, may have resulted from Sessions' uncompromisingly personal approach to his art; he has produced comparatively few works, and each of these is of major proportions and represents a statement of deeply felt conviction. Secondly, his musical beliefs stem from a tradition alien to that of the neo-Classic, strongly nationalistic school of American composers who dominated the 1930's. He was closely associated with Ernest Bloch and, later in his career, more attracted to the work of the German Expressionists than to the French, Stravinsky-oriented circle of Nadia Boulanger. Sessions' music is, therefore, perhaps more intense and less "objective" than that of other Americans of his generation. It is also less straightforwardly tonal, and less consciously nationalistic—although, nonetheless, "American" in its rhythmic activity and directness of instrumentation.

With the decline of American neo-Classicism as a major force, and the emergence of the post-Webernian esthetic as an influence of international scope—particularly upon younger composers—the works of Sessions are beginning to enjoy widespread attention. Sessions' deep convictions about music as an expressive force are not only evident in his compositions, but in his teaching at Princeton University and in his forceful book, The Musical Experience of Composer, Performer, Listener. This volume consists of lectures delivered at the Julliard School of Music, New York City (summer 1949) and one of those lectures, "The Musical Impulse," is reprinted here.

The Music Experience of Composer, Performer, Listener (Princeton, Princeton University Press, New Jersey, 1950), pp. 3-20.

The
Musical
Impulse

How shall we explain the power that men and women of all times have recognized in music, or account for the enormous importance they have ascribed to it? Why did primitive peoples endow it with supernatural force and create legends, persisting into times and places far from primitive, in which musicians of surpassing ability were able to tame wild beasts, to move stones, and to soften the hard hearts of gods, demons, and even human tyrants? Why have serious and gifted men—in imaginative force and intellectual mastery the equals of any that ever lived—why have such men at all periods devoted their lives to music and found in it a supremely satisfying medium of expression?

Music, of all the arts, seems to be the most remote from the ordinary concerns and preoccupations of people; of all things created by man, its utility, as that word is generally understood, is least easy to demonstrate. Yet it is considered among the really important manifestations of our western culture, and possibly the one manifestation in which our western contribution has been unique. Those who have created its lasting values are honored as among the truly great. We defend our convictions concerning it with the utmost intensity; and at least in some parts of the world we bitterly excoriate those whose convictions differ, or seem to differ, from our own. We regard music as important, as vitally connected with ourselves and our fate as human beings. But what is the nature of our vital connection with it? What has impelled men to create music? What, in other words, are the sources of the musical impulse? I would like to explore here some approaches to an answer to this question.

Our way will be easier, I think, if we ask ourselves first: is music a matter of tones sung or played, or should we consider it rather from the standpoint of the listener? A close examination of this question leads to some rather surprising conclusions. We find that listening to music, as we understand it, is a relatively sophisticated, and even a rather artificial means of access to it, and that even until fairly recent times composers presumably did not think of their music primarily as being listened to, but rather as being played and sung, or at most as being heard incidentally as a part of an occasion, of which the center of attention for those who heard it lay elsewhere than in the qualities of the music as such.

183

In fact, composer, performer, and listener can, without undue exaggeration, be regarded not only as three types or degrees of relationship to music, but also as three successive stages of specialization. In the beginning, no doubt, the three were one. Music was vocal or instrumental improvisation; and while there were those who did not perform, and who therefore heard music, they were not listeners in our modern sense of the word. They heard the sounds as part of a ritual, a drama, or an epic narrative, and accepted it in its purely incidental or symbolic function, subordinate to the occasion of which it was a part. Music, in and for itself can hardly be said to have existed, and whatever individual character it may have had was essentially irrelevant.

Later, however, as certain patterns became fixed or traditional, the functions of composer and performer began to be differentiated. The composer existed precisely because he had introduced into the raw material of sound and rhythm patterns that became recognizable and therefore capable of repetition—which is only another way of saying that composers began to exist when music began to take shape. The composer began to emerge as a differentiated type exactly at the moment that a bit of musical material took on a form that its producer felt impelled to repeat.

The same event produced the performer in his separate function; the first performer was, in the strictest sense, the first musician who played or sang some-thing that had been played or sung before. His type became more pronounced in the individual who first played or sang music composed by someone other than himself. At both of these points the performer's problems began to emerge, and whether or not he was aware of the fact, his problems and his characteristic solutions and points of view began to appear at the same time. These will be discussed in detail later on. Here it is important only to envisage clearly that the differentiation of composer and performer represents already a second stage in the development of musical sophistication. The high degree of differentiation reached in the course of the development of music should not obscure the fact that in the last analysis composer and performer are not only collaborators in a common enterprise but participants in an essentially single experience.

I am not, of course, talking in terms of musical history. The developments I have cited are not in any precise sense historical, and I have not presented them even as hypothetically so. It would certainly be in accordance with historical fact, however, to think of them as a long, somewhat involved, gradual development, of which I have given a condensed and symbolical account. And this very qualification underlines better the point I am making: namely, that the performer, as distinct from the composer, is the product of already advanced musical refinement. While the relationship of the composer to music is a simple, direct, and primary one, that of the performer is already complex and even problematical. To be sure, the composer as an individual may be the most complex of creatures and the performer the simplest—I have personally known examples of both such types! But while the act of composition, of production, is a primary act, that of performance—that is, re-production—is already removed by one step. The music passes through the medium of a second personality, and necessarily undergoes something of what we call interpretation. I am not raising here the much discussed question of what interpretation is, or what it may or should be; whether it should be "personal" or "objective," whether it can be or should be historically accurate, and so forth. I am simply pointing to it as an inevitable aspect of the performer's activity, of which the other aspect is, of course, projection. The performer, in other words, not only interprets or reconceives the work, but, so to speak, processes it in terms of a specific occasion: he projects it as part of a recitation or a concert, as the embodiment of a dramatic moment or situation, a part of a ritual, or finally and perhaps most simply as a piece performed solely for his own delectation. Whether or not he is aware of the fact, the nature of his performance is conditioned by the circumstances under which it takes place.

It hardly need be pointed out that the relation to music of the listener is even more complex than that of the performer. As I have pointed out, the listener, as we think of him today, came fairly recently on the musical scene. Listening to music, as distinct from reproducing it, is the product of a very late stage in musical sophistication, and it might with reason be maintained that the listener has existed as such only for about three hundred and fifty years. The composers of the Middle Ages and the Renaissance composed their music for church services and for secular occasions, where it was accepted as part of the general background, in much the same manner as were the frescoes decorating the church walls or the sculptures adorning the public buildings. Or else they composed it for amateurs, who had received musical training as a part of general education, and whose relationship with it was that of the performer responding to it through active participation in its production. Even well into the nineteenth century the musical public consisted largely of people whose primary contact with music was through playing or singing in the privacy of their own homes. For them concerts were in a certain sense occasional rituals which they attended as adepts, and they were the better equipped as listeners because of their experience in participating, however humbly and however inadequately, in the actual process of musical production. By the "listener," I do not mean the person who simply hears music—who is present when it is performed and who, in a general way, may either enjoy or dislike it, but who is in no sense a real participant in it. To listen implies rather a real participation, a real response, a real sharing in the work of the composer and of the performer, and a greater or less degree of awareness of the individual and specific sense of the music performed. For the listener, in this sense, music is no longer an incident or an adjunct but an independent and self-sufficient medium of expression. His ideal aim is to apprehend to the fullest and most complete possible extent the musical utterance of the composer as the performer delivers it to him.

And how, through what means, does he do this? Let us think for a moment of a similar instance of artistic experience, which is however not quite so complex in structure. The reader of a poem does not generally receive the poem through the medium of an interpreter, nor does he, generally, actually "perform," i.e. read aloud, the poem himself. Yet the rhymes and the meters, as well as the sense of the words, are as vivid to him as they would be if the poem were actually read to or by him. What he does in fact is to "perform" it in imagination, imaginatively to re-create and re-experience it. The "listener" to music does fundamentally the same thing. In "following" a performance, he recreates it and makes it his own. He really listens precisely to the degree that he does this, and really hears to precisely the extent that he does it successfully.

I have discussed this question in some detail here not in order either to belittle the listener or to minimize the validity or the intensity of his relationship to music. What I do wish to point out is that if we are to get at the sources of the musical impulse, we must start with the impulse to make music; it is not a question of why music appeals to us, but why men and women in every generation have been impelled to create it. I have tried to show as clearly as possible that composer, performer, and listener each fulfill one of three separate functions in a total creative process, which was originally undifferentiated and which still is essentially indivisible. It is true that there are listeners — as, alas, there are composers and performers! — of every degree of talent and achievement. But the essential is that music is an activity: it is something done, an experience lived through, with varying intensity, by composer, performer, and listener alike.

An understanding of these matters will help us to seek and perhaps to understand the basic facts regarding the musical impulse. We will know better, for instance, than to seek them in the science of acoustics or even primarily with reference to sounds heard.

Let me make this a little clearer. A great deal of musical theory has been formulated by attempting to codify laws governing musical sound and musical rhythm, and from these to deduce musical principles. Sometimes these principles are even deduced from what we know of the physical nature of sound, and as a result are given what seems to me an essentially specious validity. I say "essentially specious" because while the physical facts are clear enough, there are always gaps, incomplete or unconvincing transitions, left between the realm of physics and the realm of musical experience, even if we leave "art" out of account. Many ingenious and even brilliant attempts, it is true, have been made to bridge these gaps. One of the difficulties of trying to do so, however, is apparent, in the way in which the physical fact of the overtone series has been used by various harmonic theorists to support very different and even diametrically contradictory ideas. Because the first six partial tones obviously correspond exactly with the tones composing the major triad, theorists are fond of calling the latter the "chord of nature." On that premise, Heinrich Schenker, for example, a brilliant and at times profound writer, has reconstructed the theory of tonality as basically an elaboration of that chord or its "artificial" counterpart, the minor triad. He bases what he considers the immutable laws of music on these deductions, even though in doing so he virtually excludes the music written before Bach, after Brahms, and outside of a rather narrowly Germanic orbit. Furthermore, what is perhaps even more problematical, he is forced to disregard the evolutionary factors within even those limits, and to regard the musical language of Bach and Mozart and Beethoven and Brahms in exactly the same light; and he remonstrates with even those composers whenever he catches them punching holes in the system he has thus established. Or again, Paul Hindemith, also a brilliant and certainly a more creative writer, has carefully examined the overtone series and made very interesting deductions regarding it, but he gives it an even more outspoken status than has Schenker, as a kind of musical court of last appeal, with the triad as final arbiter, on the basis not of musical experience, but of physical science. Other writers, however, noting that the overtone series extends well beyond the first six partials, have found in this fact justification for harmonic daring of a much more far-reaching type, and have in some cases sought to discover new harmonic principles based on the systematic use of these upper partials.

Such speculations have been in many cases the product of brilliant minds, of indisputable musical authority, and I do not wish in any way to minimize this fact. Yet it would be easy to point out that each author, in a manner quite consistent with his musical stature, found in the overtone series a tool he could adapt to his individual and peculiar purpose. Above all it seems to me clear that physics and music are different spheres, and that, though they certainly touch at moments, the connection between them is an occasional and circumstantial, not an essential, one. For the musician at any level of sophistication, it is his experience, his relationship with sound, not the physical properties of sound as such, which constitute his materials. Experience, and only experience, has always been his point of departure, and while it has often led him to results which find apparent confirmation in the non-human world, this is by no means always the case. Even when it is the case, it can be regarded as no more than an interesting coincidence until a clear connection with musical experience can be demonstrated.

What I wish to stress is the fact that since music is created by human beings, we must regard the sources, or raw materials, first of all as human facts. For it is not rhythm and sound as such but their nature as human facts which concern us. And if we look at them closely we perceive that they are actually human facts of the most intimate kind. We see that these basic facts—the raw materials, the primitive sources, of music—are facts of musical experience and not the physical facts of sound and rhythm.

Let us look at rhythm first, since it is perhaps the primary fact. It is quite customary to refer our feeling for rhythm to the many rhythmical impressions constantly received from experience—the non-human as well as the naïve and simple. Reference is made not only to the act of breathing and walking, but to the alternation of day and night, the precession of the equinoxes, and the movement of the tides; to the beating of the heart, to the dance, and to many another instance of rhythmic recurrence in nature and man, even the mechanical rhythms which everywhere impose themselves on our consciousness. Such illustrations certainly have their place and their relevance; anything so fundamental as our rhythmic sense certainly is nourished and no doubt refined by impressions of every kind, and I believe we may truly say that it remains impervious actually to none. It seems to me also, however, that such generalizations miss a fundamental point. For our rhythmic sense is based ultimately on something far more potent than mere observation.

It seems to me clear indeed that the basic rhythmic fact is not the fact simply of alternation, but of a specific type of alternation with which we are familiar from the first movement of our existence as separate beings. We celebrate that event by drawing a breath, which is required of us if existence is to be realized. The drawing of the breath is an act of cumulation, of tension which is then released by the alternative act of exhalation.

Is it, then, in any way far-fetched to say that our first effective experience of rhythm, and the one that remains most deeply and constantly with us, is characterized not only by alternation as such, but by the alternation of cumulative tension with its release in a complementary movement? This is, actually, the primary fact of musical rhythm too. We recognize it in the technical terms "up-beat" and "down-beat," arsis and thesis; and we apply it, consciously as well as instinctively, to our conception of larger musical structure, as well as to the more familiar matters of detail to which these terms are generally applied.

What, for instance, is a so-called "musical phrase" if not the portion of music that must be performed, so to speak, without letting go, or, figuratively, in a single breath? The phrase is a constant movement toward a goal—the cadence; and the rhythmic nature of the latter is admirably characterized in the term itself, derived from the Italian verb *cadere,* to fall: that is, the "falling" or down-beat, the movement of release.

I am tempted to call this the most important musical fact, and am sure I have done so on occasion. More than any other fact, it seems to me, it bears on the nature of what I shall call "musical movement"; on it depends the appropriateness to their context of harmonies, of melodic intervals, and details of rhythmic elaboration. From it are derived the principles on which satisfactory musical articulation is based; and many an otherwise excellent performance is ruined through inadequate attention to what it implies. How often, unfortunately, in the performance of music, do we hear so much emphasis put on the first part of the phrase that its conclusion is left dangling in the air! The phrase does not, if I may put it that way, sit: the effect is one of breathlessness because the tension is not quite released, or to put it a little differently, the goal of the phrase is not clearly felt. It is not a question of what is generally called accent, but rather of solidity and firmness.

For instance, I have sometimes been distressed to hear the following passages from Beethoven's Quartets played thus:

instead of thus:

Or, still more distressingly, I have heard the opening of the Scherzo of Beethoven's Fifth Symphony played thus:

(a)

instead of, correctly, thus:

(b)

In the first case (a) the "poco rit." for which Beethoven asks in the last two measures makes no sense whatever, and the effect is one of complete indecisiveness—the sense of the *ritenuto* cannot be communicated because it comes *after* the accent, and it therefore, as it were, trails off into space. In case (b) the *ritenuto* falls into place: it prolongs the tension before the final accent, and since it falls perfectly into place, its execution presents no problems whatever.

I am not implying that our rhythmic sense is derived from the act of breathing alone, or even from the alternation between tension and release which contributes such a tremendous part of our physiological and therefore of our psychological existence. Actually our sense of rhythm is a fundamental organic fact, the product of many forces within us working together toward a common end. Nor have I forgotten that the term "rhythm" is often used in an inclusive sense, embracing not only the facts I have described, but what we define more strictly as tempo and meter as well.

Once more I should like to emphasize that it is through our perception of these elements, our awareness of them, that they have meaning for us, and that we gain this perception through the experiences of our psychophysical organism. Here it is not a question of the alternation of tension and relaxation but of our experience of time itself. We gain our experience, our sensation of time, through movement, and it is movement, primarily, which gives it content for us. It is unnecessary to seek scientific proof of this. We need only a clear analysis of ordinary experience, and it is the latter, in any case, which is relevant to the nature of music. We judge tempo first of all by the relation of basic metrical pulsations to the speed with which we accomplish the ordinary actions of our existence, such as walking and speaking; but, in a more extended sense, we judge it by the amount of effort required to reproduce or respond to it. Heavy accents call forth more energy because we subconsciously assume more energy in producing them; they suggest, and therefore actually call forth in our imagination, greater effort, of which the physiology can be demonstrated many times and in many contexts. Similarly, music rich in detail or elaboration, whether melodic, rhythmic, harmonic, or polyphonic, requires greater effort on the part of the hearer than when the changes are less constant or the detail less elaborate. Consequently music of the former type performed at a fast tempo will seem energetic and strained, while music of simple texture may move along, however rapidly, with the utmost ease and grace.

Nietzsche, always a profound writer on music though not himself a musician, laments in his *Jenseits von Gut und Böse* ("Beyond Good and Evil") the passing of what he calls the "good old time" of Mozart and Haydn, when, to paraphrase his words, a true Presto movement was possible in music. He cites Mendelssohn as the last composer who could write a real Presto. To be sure, he did not know Verdi's "Falstaff"; and needless to say, he was speaking of the music of genuine composers and not of imitators of past styles. Everything, he said, had become ponderous, heavy in spirit, and weighted down with preoccupation; a vital ease had disappeared from the life and hence the culture of Europe. Leaving aside his psychological judgment, which does not concern us at this point, and translating his statements into analytic terms, is he not drawing true conclusions from the indisputable fact that the music of the nineteenth century was, actually, far richer in texture and in coloring than that which had preceded it, and that this fact in itself precluded the type of movement which Haydn embodied so often in his Finales, or Mozart in such a work as the Overture to "The Marriage of Figaro," in which detail is reduced to a minimum of elaboration, and contrasts are of the subtlest kind?

These few observations lay no claim to exhaustiveness. The subject of rhythm is a vast one, and indeed an adequate definition of rhythm comes close to defining music itself. It is a subject, too, that lends itself all too easily to oversimplification, a clear case of this being the abstraction of the rhythmic element in music from that of musical sound.

Now, if we consider musical sound from the standpoint of the impulse to produce it, we find that in a very real sense and to a very real degree this impulse, too, is rooted in our earliest, most constantly present and most intimate experiences. From almost the first moments of our existence the impulse to produce vocal sound is a familiar one, almost as familiar as the impulse to breathe, though not so indispensable. The sound, to be sure, is at first presumably a by-product. But is it not clear that much of our melodic feeling derives from this source; that is, from a vocal impulse which first of all is connected with the vital act of breathing and is subject to its nuances? In the second place melodic feeling undergoes vast refinement during the growth of even the most unmusical individuals. From the vocal impulse we acquire, for instance, our sensitive response to differences in pitch. I mean here powers not of discrimination, but of response, the kind of response that is instinctive and that precedes discrimination and possibly even precedes consciousness. In simple terms, when we raise our voices we increase the intensity of our vocal effort, a rise in pitch implies an increase in tension, and therefore in intensity of energy, or, in other terms, of expressiveness in one direction. When we lower our voices we make a different kind of effort, and gain an intensity of a different and more complex kind. Similarly, an increase in volume denotes, not only in terms of the physical effort of production, but in the sympathetic effort of response, also an increase in tension and hence of intensity. I have spoken of intensity of expression, which of course is synonymous or commensurable with the degree of contrast involved. If we like, we may speculate on the combinations possible between two directions of movement of pitch, and two directions of movement in volume. We may try to formulate, for instance, the effect of high or rising notes sung or played very softly, or of a descending passage sung or played crescendo. What I believe will be indisputable is the fact that with only slight qualifications we carry over these primitive responses from music produced vocally to our more complex response to that heard instrumentally, independently of the particular character of the instrument involved. Though subject to definition, qualification, and refinement, it is a very basic musical response of which I am speaking, and possibly more than any single factor it governs our response to melody in its largest features. I shall discuss actual discrimination, the refined sense of pitch, later; here I am referring to the purely instinctive bases of musical expression, as nearly as I can define them, quite apart from the coordinative function of the musical ear. It is true that the line of demarcation is an arbitrary one. But the discrimination of delicate shades of difference in pitch, such as all civilized musical systems demand, only refines these basic responses. It makes possible, through the fact of notes of fixed and definite pitch, greater precision in rhythmic and melodic contour.

Nevertheless, a melodic motif or phrase is in essence and origin a vocal gesture; it is a vocal movement with a clearly defined and therefore clearly expressed profile. And, one final point, it too is sensitive to infinitely delicate nuances of tension and relaxation, as these are embodied in the breathing which animates the vocal gesture and shapes its contours. Thus, agitated breathing will be reflected in agitated melodic and rhythmic movement; or conversely, sharp, irregular accents, or successive violent contrasts in pitch will call forth subconscious associations suggesting the kind of agitation which produces violent or irregular breathing, just as quieter melodic movement will evoke a more serene response.

I am oversimplifying, of course. These are not the only elements in musical expression, but I am deliberately restricting the discussion here to primitive, direct, and simple responses to music. Even at this level, may we not say that the basic ingredient of music is not so much sound as movement, conceived in the terms I have indicated? I would even go a step farther, and say that music is significant for us as human beings principally because it embodies movement of a specifically human type that goes to the roots of our being and takes shape in the inner gestures which embody our deepest and most intimate responses. This is of itself not yet art; it is not yet even language. But it is the material of which musical art is made, .and to which musical art gives significance.

If we appreciate these facts, we can understand the more readily why music is the art of sound. For of all the five senses, the sense of hearing is the only one inexorably associated with our sense of time. The gestures which music embodies are, after all, invisible gestures; one may almost define them as consisting of movement in the abstract, movement which exists in time but not in space, movement, in fact, which gives time its meaning and its significance for us. If this is true, then sound is its predestined vehicle. For what we apprehend through the eye is for us static, monumental. Even movement seen is bounded by our range of vision; we never can closely follow it off into space unless we ourselves move. Sound, at least in our experience, is never static, but invariably impermanent; it either ceases or changes. By its very nature it embodies for us movement in time, and as such imposes no inherent limits.

To sum up: the experience of music is essentially indivisible, whether it is embodied in the impulse to produce, or in the response, through reproduction, actual as by the performer or imaginary as by the listener, of the musical experience embodied in music already produced. Secondly, what we may call the raw, formal materials of music are also the expressive elements, and these, again, have their basis in certain of the most elementary, intimate, and vital experiences through which we live as human beings. Let us consider now the means through which these raw materials are coordinated, become coherent, and are rendered significant; through which, in other words, they begin to be music.

Edgard Varèse

[1885 - 1965]

For years known only to a handful of musical cognoscenti, the work of Varèse has recently become more widely appreciated, and its influence upon composers of the twentieth century is just beginning to be evaluated. Classically trained in his native France, Varèse came to America in 1915 and began to work in the cause of new music, organizing and presenting concerts in collaboration with such figures as Leopold Stokowski and his fellow composer Carlos Salzedo. After a period of almost twenty years of not composing, Varèse turned again to the creation of music, pioneering the use of electronic media. Recognition came rapidly during the last years of his life, and young composers the world over regard him as one of the major figures in new music.

Varèse was responsible for many innovations; among these were his use of electronic instruments and tape, as well as his concern with scientific developments and their reflection in musical forces.

Perhaps even more significant, however, was his approach to music not in terms of the doctrine of the affections but as sonoric and rhythmic balance—the brightness of sonority for its own sake. Varèse articulates this approach in great detail in the essays published here.

Excerpts from lectures by Edgard Varèse, compiled and edited with footnotes by Chou Wen-Chung.

The
Liberation
of Sound

I dream of instruments obedient to my thought and which with
their contribution of a whole new world of unsuspected sounds,
will lend themselves to the exigencies of my inner rhythm.[1]

New Instruments
and New Music
(From a lecture given at Mary Austin House, Santa Fe, 1936)

At a time when the very newness of the mechanism of life is forcing our
activities and our forms of human association to break with the traditions
and the methods of the past in the effort to adapt themselves to circumstances, the urgent choices which we have to make are concerned not with
the past but with the future. We cannot, even if we would, live much
longer by tradition. The world is changing, and we change with it. The
more we allow our minds the romantic luxury of treasuring the past in
memory, the less able we become to face the future and to determine the
new values which can be created in it.

Art's function is not to prove a formula or an esthetic dogma. Our
academic rules were taken out of the living works of former masters. As
Debussy has said, *works of art make rules but rules do not make works of*
art. Art exists only as a medium of expression.

The emotional impulse that moves a composer to write his scores
contains the same element of poetry that incites the scientist to his discoveries. There is solidarity between scientific development and the progress
of music. Throwing new light on nature, science permits music to progress—or rather to grow and change with changing times—by revealing to
our senses harmonies and sensations before unfelt. On the threshold of
beauty science and art collaborate. John Redfield voices the opinion of

[1] From "*391*"(periodical), No. 5 (June 1917); transl. from the French by Louise Varèse.

many when he says: "There should be at least one laboratory in the world where the fundamental facts of music could be investigated under conditions reasonably conducive to success. The interest in music is so widespread and intense, its appeal so intimate and poignant, and its significance for mankind so potent and profound, that it becomes unwise not to devote some portion of the enormous outlay for music to research in its fundamental questions."[2]

When new instruments will allow me to write music as I conceive it, the movement of sound-masses, of shifting planes, will be clearly perceived in my work, taking the place of the linear counterpoint. When these sound-masses collide, the phenomena of penetration or repulsion will seem to occur. Certain transmutations taking place on certain planes will seem to be projected onto other planes, moving at different speeds and at different angles. There will no longer be the old conception of melody or interplay of melodies. The entire work will be a melodic totality. The entire work will flow as a river flows.

We have actually three dimensions in music: horizontal, vertical, and dynamic swelling or decreasing. I shall add a fourth, sound projection — that feeling that sound is leaving us with no hope of being reflected back, a feeling akin to that aroused by beams of light sent forth by a powerful searchlight — for the ear as for the eye, that sense of projection, of a journey into space.

Today with the technical means that exist and are easily adaptable, the differentiation of the various masses and different planes as well as these beams of sound, could be made discernible to the listener by means of certain acoustical arrangements. Moreover, such an acoustical arrangement would permit the delimitation of what I call "zones of intensities." These zones would be differentiated by various timbres or colors and different loudnesses. Through such a physical process these zones would appear of different colors and of different magnitude, in different perspectives for our perception. The role of color or timbre would be completely changed from being incidental, anecdotal, sensual or picturesque; it would become an agent of delineation, like the different colors on a map separating different areas, and an integral part of form. These zones would be felt as isolated, and the hitherto unobtainable non-blending (or at least the sensation of non-blending) would become possible.

In the moving masses you would be conscious of their transmutations when they pass over different layers, when they penetrate certain opacities, or are dilated in certain rarefactions. Moreover, the new musical apparatus

[2] John Redfield, *Music, a Science and an Art* (New York, 1928).

197

I envisage, able to emit sounds of any number of frequencies, will extend the limits of the lowest and highest registers, hence new organizations of the vertical resultants: chords, their arrangements, their spacings—that is, their oxygenation. Not only will the harmonic possibilities of the overtones be revealed in all their splendor, but the use of certain interferences created by the partials will represent an appreciable contribution. The never-before-thought-of use of the inferior resultants and of the differential and additional sounds may also be expected. An entirely new magic of sound!

I am sure that the time will come when the composer, after he has graphically realized his score, will see this score automatically put on a machine that will faithfully transmit the musical content to the listener. As frequencies and new rhythms will have to be indicated on the score, our actual notation will be inadequate. The new notation will probably be seismographic. And here it is curious to note that at the beginning of two eras, the Mediaeval primitive and our own primitive era (for we are at a new primitive stage in music today), we are faced with an identical problem: the problem of finding graphic symbols for the transposition of the composer's thought into sound. At a distance of more than a thousand years we have this analogy: our still primitive electrical instruments find it necessary to abandon staff notation and to use a kind of seismographic writing much like the early ideographic writing originally used for the voice before the development of staff notation. Formerly the curves of the musical line indicated the melodic fluctuations of the voice; today the machine-instrument requires precise design indications.

Music as an Art-Science
(From a lecture given at the University of Southern California, 1939)

The philosophers of the Middle Ages separated the liberal arts into two branches: the *trivium,* or the Arts of Reason as applied to language—grammar, rhetoric and dialectic—and the *quadrivium,* or the Arts of Pure Reason, which today we would call the Sciences, and among which music has its place in the company of mathematics, geometry and astronomy.

Today, music is more apt to be rated with the arts of the *trivium.* At least, it seems to me that too much emphasis is placed on what might be called the grammar of music.

At different times and in different places music has been considered either as an Art or as a Science. In reality music partakes of both. Hoëne

The Liberation
of Sound

Wronsky and Camille Durutte,[3] in their treatise on harmony in the middle of the last century, were obliged to coin new words when they assigned music its place as an "Art-Science," and defined it as "the corporealization of the intelligence that is in sounds." Most people rather think of music solely as an art. But when you listen to music do you ever stop to realize that you are being subjected to a physical phenomenon? Not until the air between the listener's ear and the instrument has been disturbed does music occur. Do you realize that every time a printed score is brought to life it has to be re-created through the different sound machines, called musical instruments, that make up our orchestras, are subject to the same laws of physics as any other machine? In order to anticipate the result, a composer must understand the mechanics of the instruments and must know just as much as possible about acoustics. Music must live in sound. On the other hand, the possession of a perfectly pitched ear is only of a relative importance to a composer. What a composer must have, must have been born with, is what I call the "inner ear," the ear of imagination. The inner ear is the composer's Pole Star! Let us look at music as it is more popularly considered — as an Art — and inquire: what is composition?

Brahms has said that composition is the *organizing of disparate elements*. But what is the situation of the would-be creator today, shaken by the powerful impulses and rhythms of this age? How is he to accomplish this "organizing" in order to express himself and his epoch? Where is he to find those "disparate elements"? Are they to be found in the books he studies in his various courses in harmony, composition, and orchestration? Are they in the great works of the great masters that he pores over with love and admiration and, with all his might, means to emulate? Unfortunately too many composers have been led to believe that these elements can be found as easily as that.[4]

Eric Temple Bell, in a book called *The Search for Truth,* says: "Reverence for the past no doubt is a virtue that has had its uses, but if we are to go forward the reverent approach to old difficulties is the wrong one!" I should say that in music the "reverent approach" has done a great deal of harm: it has kept would-be appreciators from really appreciating! And it has created the music critic! The very basis of creative work is irreverence! The very basis of creative work is experimentation — bold experimentation.

[3] Hoëne Wronsky (1778-1853), also known as Joseph Marie Wronsky, was a Polish philosopher and mathematician, known for his system of *Messianism.* Camille Durutte (1803-1881), in his *Technie Harmonique* (1876), a treatise on "musical mathematics," quoted extensively from the writings of Wronsky.

[4] This, Varèse said in the same lecture, "undoubtedly accounts for one of the most deplorable trends of music today — the impotent return to the formulas of the past that has been called neo-Classicism."

199

**Edgard
Varèse**

You have only to turn to the revered past for the corroboration of my contention. The links in the chain of tradition are formed by men who have all been revolutionists! To the student of music I should say that the great examples of the past should serve as springboards from which he may leap free, into his own future.

In every domain of art, a work that corresponds to the need of its day carries a message of social and cultural value. Preceding ages show us that changes in art occur because societies and artists have new needs. New aspirations emanate from every epoch. The artist, being always of his own time, is influenced by it and, in turn, is an influence. It is the artist who crystallizes his age — who fixes his age in history. Contrary to general notion, the artist is never ahead of his own time, but is simply the only one who is not way behind.

Now let me come back to the subject of music as an Art-Science. The raw material of music is sound. That is what the "reverent approach" has made most people forget — even composers. Today, when science is equipped to help the composer realize what was never before possible — all that Beethoven dreamed, all that Berlioz gropingly imagined possible — the composer continues to be obsessed by the traditions that are nothing but the limitations of his predecessors. Composers, like everyone else today, are delighted to use the many gadgets continually put on the market for our daily comfort. But when they hear sounds that no violins, no woodwind or percussion instruments of the orchestra can produce, it does not occur to them to demand those sounds of science. Yet science is even now equipped to give them everything they may require.

Personally, for my conceptions, I need an entirely new medium of expression: a sound-*producing* machine (not a sound-*reproducing* one). Today it is possible to build such a machine with only a certain amount of added research.

If you are curious to know what such a machine could do that the orchestra with its man-powered instruments cannot do, I shall try briefly to tell you: whatever I write, whatever my message, it will reach the listener unadulterated by "interpretation." It will work something like this: after a composer has set down his score on paper by means of a new graphic notation, he will then, with the collaboration of a sound engineer, transfer the score directly to this electric machine. After that, anyone will be able to press a button to release the music exactly as the composer wrote it — exactly like opening a book.

And here are the advantages I anticipate from such a machine: liberation from the arbitrary, paralyzing tempered system; the possibility of obtaining any number of cycles or, if still desired, subdivisions of the

200

octave, and consequently the formation of any desired scale; unsuspected range in low and high registers; new harmonic splendors obtainable from the use of sub-harmonic combinations now impossible; the possibility of obtaining any differentiation of timbre, of sound-combinations; new dynamics far beyond the present human-powered orchestra; a sense of sound-projection in space by means of the emission of sound in any part or in many parts of the hall, as may be required by the score; cross-rhythms unrelated to each other, treated simultaneously, or, to use the old word, "contrapuntally," since the machine would be able to beat any number of desired notes, any subdivision of them, omission or fraction of them—all these in a given unit of measure or time that is humanly impossible to attain.

In conclusion, let me read to you something that Romain Rolland said in his *Jean Christophe* and which remains pertinent today. Jean Christophe, the hero of his novel, was a prototype of the modern composer and was modeled on different composers whom Romain Rolland knew—among others, myself.

> The difficulty began when he tried to cast his ideas in the ordinary musical forms: he made the discovery that none of the ancient molds were suited to them; if he wished to fix his visions with fidelity he had to begin by forgetting all the music he had heard, all that he had written, to make a clean slate of all the formalism he had learned, of traditional technique, to throw away those crutches of impotency, that bed, all prepared for the laziness of those who, fleeing the fatigue of thinking for themselves, lie down in other men's thoughts.[5]

Rhythm, Form and Content
(from a lecture given at Princeton University, 1959)

My fight for the liberation of sound and for my right to make music with any sound and all sounds has sometimes been construed as a desire to disparage and even to discard the great music of the past. But that is where my roots are. No matter how original, how different a composer may seem, he has only grafted a little bit of himself on the old plant. But this he should be allowed to do without being accused of wanting to kill the plant. He only wants to produce a new flower. It does not matter if at first it seems to some people more like a cactus than a rose. Many of the old masters are my intimate friends—all are respected colleagues. None of them are dead saints—in fact, none of them are dead—and the rules they made for them-

[5] Romain Rolland (1866–1944), *Jean Christophe* (1904–12); published in English as *John Christopher* (G. Cannan, tr.; 1910–13).

selves are not sacrosanct and are not everlasting laws. Listening to music by Perotin, Machaut, Monteverdi, Bach, or Beethoven, we are conscious of living substances; they are "alive in the present." But music written in the manner of another century is the result of culture and, desireable and comfortable as culture may be, an artist should not lie down in it. The best bit of criticism André Gide ever wrote was this confession, which must have been wrung from him by self-torture: "When I read Rimbaud or the Sixth Song of Maldoror, I am ashamed of my own works and everything that is only the result of culture."

Because for so many years I crusaded for new instruments[6] with what may have seemed fanatical zeal, I have been accused of desiring nothing less than the destruction of all musical instruments and even of all performers. This is, to say the least, an exaggeration. Our new liberating medium—the electronic—is not meant to replace the old musical instruments, which composers, including myself, will continue to use. Electronics is an additive, not a destructive, factor in the art and science of music. It is because new instruments have been constantly added to the old ones that Western music has such a rich and varied patrimony.

Grateful as we must be for the new medium, we should not expect miracles from machines. The machine can give out only what we put into it. The musical principles remain the same whether a composer writes for orchestra or tape. Rhythm and form are still his most important problems and the two elements in music most generally misunderstood.

Rhythm is too often confused with metrics. Cadence or the regular succession of beats and accents has little to do with the rhythm of a composition. Rhythm is the element in music that gives life to the work and holds it together. It is the element of stability, the generator of form. In my own works, for instance, rhythm derives from the simultaneous interplay of unrelated elements that intervene at calculated, but not regular, time-lapses. This corresponds more nearly to the definition of rhythm in physics and philosophy as "a succession of alternate and opposite or correlative states."

As for form, Busoni once wrote: "Is it not singular to demand of a composer originality in all things and to forbid it as regards form? No

---

[6] As early as 1916, Varèse was quoted in the New York *Morning Telegraph* as saying: Our musical alphabet must be enriched. We also need new instruments very badly. . . . In my own works I have always felt the need of new mediums of expression . . . which can lend themselves to every expression of thought and can keep up with thought." And in the *Christian Science Monitor,* in 1922: "The composer and the electrician will have to labor together to get it."

wonder that once he becomes original, he is accused of formlessness.'"[7]
    The misunderstanding has come from thinking of form as a point of departure, a pattern to be followed, a mold to be filled. Form is a result —the result of a process. Each of my works discovers its own form. I could never have fitted them into any of the historical containers. If you want to fill a rigid box of a definite shape, you must have something to put into it that is the same shape and size or that is elastic or soft enough to be made to fit in. But if you try to force into it something of a different shape and harder substance, even if its volume and size are the same, it will break the box. My music cannot be made to fit into any of the traditional music boxes.
    Conceiving musical form as a *resultant*—the result of a process—I was struck by what seemed to me an analogy between the formation of my compositions and the phenomenon of crystallization. Let me quote the crystallographic description given me by Nathaniel Arbiter, professor of minerology at Columbia University:

> The crystal is characterized by both a definite external form and a definite internal structure. The internal structure is based on the unit of crystal which is the smallest grouping of the atoms that has the order and composition of the substance. The extension of the unit into space forms the whole crystal. But in spite of the relatively limited variety of internal structures, the external forms of crystals are limitless.

Then Mr. Arbiter added in his own words:

> Crystal form itself is a *resultant* [the very word I have always used in reference to musical form] rather than a primary attribute. Crystal form is the consequence of the interaction of attractive and repulsive forces and the ordered packing of the atom.

This, I believe, suggests, better than any explanation I could give, the way my works are formed. There is an idea, the basis of an internal structure, expanded and split into different shapes or groups of sound constantly changing in shape, direction, and speed, attracted and repulsed by various forces. The form of the work is the consequence of this interaction. Possible musical forms are as limitless as the exterior forms of crystals.
    Connected with this contentious subject of form in music is the really futile question of the difference between form and content. There is no difference. Form and content are one. Take away form, and there is no content,

---

[7] Ferruccio Busoni, *Sketch of a New Esthetic of Music,* transl. by Dr. Theodore Baker (New York, 1911); reprinted in *Three Classics in the Aesthetic of Music* (New York, Dover Publications 1962), p. 79. Also reprinted in this book, see p. 3.

and if there is no content, there is only a rearrangement of musical patterns, but no form. Some people go so far as to suppose that the content of what is called program music is the subject described. This subject is only the ostensible motive I have spoken of, which in program music the composer chooses to reveal. The content is still only music. The same senseless bickering goes on over style and content in poetry. We could very well transfer to the question of music what Samuel Beckett has said of Proust: "For Proust the quality of language is more important than any system of ethics or esthetics. Indeed he makes no attempt to dissociate form from content. The one is the concretion of the other — the revelation of a world."[8] To reveal a new world is the function of creation in all the arts, but the act of creation defies analysis. A composer knows about as little as anyone else about where the substance of his work comes from.

As an epigraph to his book,[9] Busoni uses this verse from a poem by the Danish poet, Oelenschläger:

> What seek you? Say! And what do you expect?
> I know not what; the Unknown I would have!
> What's known to me is endless; I would go
> Beyond the known: The last word still is wanting.

(*Der mächtige Zauberer*)

And so it is for any artist.

Spatial Music
(From a lecture given at Sarah Lawrence College, 1959)

When I was about twenty, my own attitude toward music — at least toward what I wanted my music to be — became suddenly crystallized by Hoëne Wronsky's definition of music.[10] It was probably what first started me thinking of music as spatial — as bodies of intelligent sounds moving freely in space, a concept I gradually developed and made my own. Very early, musical ideas came to me that I realized would be difficult or impossible to express with the means available, and my thinking even then began turning around the idea of liberating music from the tempered system, from the limitations of musical instruments, and from years of bad

[8] Samuel Beckett, *Proust* (1957).
[9] Busoni, *op. cit.*, p. 75.
[10] See note 3 above.

habits, erroneously called tradition. I studied Helmholtz, and was fascinated by his experiments with sirens described in his *Physiology of Sound*.[11] I went to the *Marché aux Puces,* where you can find just about anything, in search of a siren, and picked up two small ones. With these, and using also children's whistles, I made my first experiments in what later I called *spatial music.*

In those formative years I had the good fortune to become a friend of Busoni. As everybody knows, or should know, Ferruccio Busoni was not only a great pianist, a great musician, but also a great and clairvoyant intelligence. I met Busoni when I was living in Berlin before the First World War. I was already familiar with his remarkable book, *Sketch of a New Esthetic of Music,* which was another milestone in my musical development. Imagine my excitement on reading these words of his: "Music was born free; and to win freedom is its destiny." Until then I had supposed no one but myself held such a theory. When I took Busoni my scores, he was at once interested and in spite of the great difference of age a friendship developed during the remaining years I was in Berlin. We talked at length on all the questions that were my chief preoccupation at the time—and still are. Although our views differed radically on many subjects connected with the art of music, I am convinced that it was those long talks with Busoni, during which new horizons were constantly opening for me, that helped crystallize my ideas and confirmed my belief that new means must be found to liberate sound, to free it from the limitations of the tempered system, make it possible to realize my conception of rhythm as an element of stability, and to achieve unrelated metrical simultaneity.

My first physical attempt to give music greater freedom was by the use of sirens in several of my scores (*Amériques,*[12] *Ionisation*[13]), and I think it was these parabolic and hyperbolic trajectories of sound that made certain writers as far back as 1925 grasp my conception of music as moving in space. For example, Zanotti Bianco, writing in *The Arts,* at that time spoke of "sound masses molded as though in space" and of "great masses in astral space."[14] Of course, it was still only a *trompe l'oreille,* an aural illusion, so to speak, and not yet literally true.

As early as 1927, I learned something of the possibilities of electronics

---

[11] Hermann L. F. Helmholtz (1821-1894), *Lehre von den Tonempfindungen als physiologische Grundlage für die Theorie der Musik* (1862); published in English as *On the Sensation of Tone as A Physiological Basis for the Theory of Music* (J. Ellis, tr.; 1873).

[12] Composed 1918-21; premiered April 9, 1926.

[13] Composed 1930-31; premiered March 6, 1933.

[14] Massimo Zanotti Bianco, "Edgard Varèse and the Geometry of Sound," in *The Arts,* 1924; "La Geometria sonora di Edgard Varèse," in *Il Pianoforte,* May 1925.

as a musical medium from Rene Bertrand,[15] inventor of the *Dynaphone* (this instrument was one of the precursors of the Martenot,[16] now widely used in Europe); and in 1934 Theremin,[17] a pioneer in this field, built two instruments to my specifications for my composition, *Ecuatorial,*[18] with a range up to 12544.2 cycles.[19] But it was not until 1954 that I had the opportunity of working in a studio with electronic equipment for composing on tape. In the fall of that year the Radiodiffusion Française[20] invited me to finish my tapes of *organized sound* for *Déserts*[21] in their studio in Paris. I had begun them on my one tape recorder in New York. This work is for both mediums, instrumental and tape. It contrasts the sounds of man-powered instruments with electronically treated sounds, alternating but never combining. In passing, I might say that the intervals in the instrumental sections, though they determine the constantly changing and contrasted volumes and planes, are not based on any fixed set of intervals such as a scale or a series. They are determined by the particular requirements of the work.

Now I come to the work you are going to hear tonight: *Poème Électronique.*[22] It is the musical part of a spectacle of sound and light, presented during the Brussels Exposition in the pavilion designed for the Philips Corporation of Holland by Le Corbusier, who was also the author of the visual

[15] Actually, Varèse first met Bertrand in the late spring of 1913. Varèse was naturally aware of Thaddeus Cahill's experiment mentioned in Busoni's book, but was disappointed when he saw it demonstrated in New York after his arrival in this country. In 1927, Varèse began seriously discussing with Harvey Fletcher, then Acoustical Research Director of the Bell Telephone Laboratories, the possibilities of developing an electronic instrument for composing. Subsequently, Varèse also tried to work at the sound studios in Hollywood. Tragically, these repeated attempts were all frustrated by the lack of understanding and financial support. Nevertheless, in the mid-thirties, he did make some very modest experiments with phonograph turntables by using motors of different speeds that could be operated simultaneously, as well as by running the records backward. In spite of the general apathy during those years, Varèse took another step forward and worked on and off on what may be called a "montage in space," entitled *Espace*, to be simultaneously broadcast from various points of the world.
[16] *Ondes Musicales* (generally referred to as *Ondes Martenot*), invented by Maurice Martenot (b. 1898).
[17] Leon Theremin (b. 1896) introduced his first electronic instrument in 1920. The instruments used in *Ecuatorial* are of a later type, belonging to the so-called "finger-board" models.
[18] Composed 1933-34; premiered April 15, 1934. In the published revised version, two Ondes Martenots are specified instead of the Theremins.
[19] An octave and a fifth above the highest C of the piano.
[20] The invitation was extended by Pierre Schaeffer, director of the Studio d'Essai of the French Radio.
[21] Composed 1949-54; premiered Dec. 2, 1954.
[22] Composed 1957-58, completed at Philips Laboratories, Eindhoven, Holland; premiered Brussels Exposition, May-October, 1958.

part.[23] It consisted of moving colored lights, images projected on the walls of the pavilion, and music. The music was distributed by 425 loudspeakers; there were twenty amplifier combinations. It was recorded on a three-track magnetic tape that could be varied in intensity and quality. The loud-speakers were mounted in groups and in what is called "sound routes" to achieve various effects such as that of the music running around the pavilion, as well as coming from different directions, reverberations, etc.

For the first time I heard my music literally projected into space.

The Electronic Medium
(From a lecture given at Yale University, 1962)

First of all, I should like you to consider what I believe is the best definition of music, because it is all-inclusive: "the corporealization of the intelligence that is in sound," as proposed by Hoëne Wronsky.[24] If you think about it you will realize that, unlike most dictionary definitions, which make use of such subjective terms as beauty, feelings, etc., it covers all music, Eastern or Western, past or present, including the music of our new electronic medium. Although this new music is being gradually accepted, there are still people who, while admitting that it is "interest-ing", say: "but is it music?" It is a question I am only too familiar with. Until quite recently I used to hear it so often in regard to my own works that, as far back as the twenties, I decided to call my music "organized sound" and myself, not a musician, but "a worker in rhythms, frequencies, and intensities." Indeed, to stubbornly conditioned ears, anything new in music has always been called noise. But after all, what is music but organ-ized noises? And a composer, like all artists, is an organizer of disparate elements. Subjectively, *noise* is any sound one doesn't like.

Our new medium has brought to composers almost endless possibilities of expression, and opened up for them the whole mysterious world of sound. For instance, I have always felt the need of a kind of continuous flowing curve that instruments could not give me. That is why I used sirens in several of my works. Today such effects are easily obtainable by elec-tronic means. In this connection, it is curious to note that it is this lack of flow that seems to disturb Eastern musicians in our Western music. To their

---

[23] The whole spectacle of light and sound, conceived by Le Corbusier, is called "Poème Électronique." Le Corbusier (Charles-Edouard Jeanneret-Gris) died on August 27, 1965, the day before the editing of this article was completed.

[24] See note 3.

ears, it does not glide, sounds jerky, composed of edges of intervals and holes and, as an Indian pupil of mine expressed it, "jumping like a bird from branch to branch." To them, apparently, our Western music seems to sound much as it sounds to us when a record is played backward. But playing a Hindu record of a melodic vocalization backward, I found that it had the same smooth flow as when played normally, scarcely altered at all.

The electronic medium is also adding an unbelievable variety of new timbres to our musical store, but most important of all, it has freed music from the tempered system, which has prevented music from keeping pace with the other arts and with science. Composers are now able, as never before, to satisfy the dictates of that inner ear of the imagination. They are also lucky so far in not being hampered by esthetic codification — at least not yet! But I am afraid it will not be long before some musical mortician begins embalming electronic music in rules.

We should also remember that no machine is a wizard, as we are beginning to think, and we must not expect our electronic devices to compose for us. Good music and bad music will be composed by electronic means, just as good and bad music have been composed for instruments. The computing machine is a marvelous invention and seems almost superhuman. But in reality it is as limited as the mind of the individual who feeds it material. Like the computer, the machines we use for making music can only give back what we put into them. But, considering the fact that our electronic devices were never meant for making music, but for the sole purpose of measuring and analyzing sound, it is remarkable that what has already been achieved is musically valid. These devices are still somewhat unwieldy and time-consuming, and not entirely satisfactory as an art-medium. But this new art is still in its infancy, and I hope and firmly believe, now that composers and physicists are at last working together and music is again linked with science as it was in the Middle Ages, that new and more musically efficient devices will be invented.

Harry
Partch
[1901 - 1974]

One of the most challenging yet generally overlooked figures in American music, Partch has devoted his career to the exploration of his unorthodox musical views. This has involved extensive experimentation in acoustics, construction of his own instruments, composition, and teaching. His conception of the acoustic basis of the scale, dividing the octave into 43 tones, was explained in great detail in his book Genesis of a Music, *from which the following chapter has been taken.*

As an experimentalist working in isolation, Partch has had to wait for time to catch up with his ideas. We cannot yet judge which of these ideas the course of new music will accept and which will be discarded. It is enough to note, now, that Partch remains a challenging figure on the American musical scene. In the best tradition of the experimenter he is dedicated, creative, and controversial.

Genesis of a Music (Madison, Wisconsin, University of Wisconsin Press, 1949), Chapter 13.

Experiments
in Notation

On the Horns
of Dilemma

In grappling with notation the composer-pioneer is continually on the horns of dilemma, a situation that becomes so thoroughly normal to him that when an integrated and rational solution seems to present itself he is more than likely to remain incredulously perched. And he has good reason. In a sense, a notation is the least of a music's ingredients, one that might be supplied on a moment's notice—literally. To provide a notation is a matter of paper and pencil and a good night's sleep—but to evolve a theory, to develop instruments upon it, and to write and present the music conceived therefrom is easily a matter of a lifetime.

An integrated notation involves much more than the mere invention of it; that would be easy, but to make it immediately comprehensible and translatable into physical acts is another thing. The status of Monophonic[1] notation after almost two decades of composing its music is unresolved, for it has no integrated notation. However anomalous this sounds, it is not unnatural. The first inclination is to sweep the boards clean and to start anew, and this procedure is practical so long as the composer depends solely upon himself for rendition of his music. That momentous time of departure from self-sufficiency into the complexities of ensemble work brings a totally different situation; from that time on he is quite effectively skewered by the education and conditioning of those whose assistance he seeks.

It is seldom possible to find a group of persons *en rapport* and to re-educate them, which in any case requires a great deal of time. A start must be made, somewhere along the line, in offering music that will stimulate the evolution of intonation. Without such music, problems in

[1] (Partch, in an earlier chapter, defines Monophony as "an organization of musical materials based upon the faculty of the human ear to perceive all intervals and to deduce all principles of musical relationship as an expansion from unity, as 1 is to 1, or—as it is expressed in this work—1/1. In this sense of growth from unity Monophony is a development of the theories deduced by Pythagoras of Samos . . . In another sense Monophony may be regarded as an organization deducible from the sounding of one tone; in this sense it is an evolved expression of the phenomenon of the overtone series . . . " [Editors].

theory could be solved on paper, and even in instruments, into time eternal without producing any noticeable evolution; the proof lies in the unique and "original" instruments in the museums of Europe. Stimulation will result only from a corpus of significant music, an emotionally dynamic music, which will win response from persons who don't give a tinker's damn that 3/2 is 1/50 of an equal semitone wider than the vibrational ratio they hear.

The composer who is moved to contribute to this stimulation bends every effort to get his music heard; and to get it heard (if he employs more than his own average talents in rendition) he must write his music in such a way that it will not require years, or even months, to connect fingers or lips or larynx to its execution. Here, however, the horns begin to hurt, because the hodgepodge of lines, numbers, and notes which results from this necessity is no sesame to an understanding of the fabric of theory which the composer has laboriously built up.

Nevertheless, music is composed on the basis of instruments, and instruments are individual. What is rational and well-integrated for one may be quite the opposite for another. Notes should represent, for the player, physical acts upon the strings, levers, wood blocks, or whatever vibratory bodies he has before him, but they do not represent such acts very well unless the peculiarities of his string patterns, or lever or block patterns, are taken into account as the basis for the figurations of those notes. Results would certainly be more immediate and might well be more rational as a whole if there were a separate notation for each type of instrument, based entirely upon its individuality, and, in addition, a common-denominator notation based upon ratios or clearly implying ratios. And students of the instruments would know both notations — the one for playing the music of a particular instrument, the other for studying and analyzing the total result.

This idea operates at least partially at present. Some of the parts are written in ratios, and those that are not so written are immediately translatable into ratios. The notations for each of the eight instruments constructed thus far have some or many similarities and some or many differences, but in each case the shortest and quickest means of bringing about the mastery of each instrument has been sought. This seems to be the only feasible course at present — to start the new notation in what may seem to be a nondescript fashion, and to hope that when enough persons are stimulated by the music to inquire into it, something closer to the ideal in notation will finally emerge. As evidence that this is not an indifferent shelving of the problem a brief account of various efforts to deal with Monophonic notation is here given.

Harry
Partch

First Experiments

The first notation consisted solely of numbers, from 1 to 29, for certain of the Monophonic ratios, deviations from these being lettered 1a, 1b, 1c, etc. This was soon abandoned because it tended to obliterate the meaning of ratios. The ratios themselves were next used, and looked something like this, in a line from a Li Po poem:[2]

Voice	I leave you and go —	when	shall	I	re -	turn?
10/9 ——————————— 10/7-10/9		9/8	8/7	7/6	6/5-11/9	
Viola (double stopping)	5/3 12/7 ———— 7/4 ———————	9/5	11/6 28/15 48/25 88/45 11/6			
	10/9 ————————————————————					

This notation is again being used for the Adapted Viola, and — with some differences — for the Adapted Guitars.[3] Thus far I have played these instruments myself, and within even a few years the ratios became as definitive as notes on a staff.

For ease of reading, however, the graphic quality seems very essential in notation, and from one to three or even five lines are sometimes added to show passage from one 2/1 to the next, lower or higher. The third experimental notation satisfied the graphic quality completely, having an eighteen-line staff — five pairs of lines visible, the other assumed, and having a line or space for each of thirty-nine ratios. A sample, with another fragment from Li Po,[4] is the upper of the two excerpts in the next example. Here the area the eye was obliged to cover defeated the object — easy reading through a completely graphic notation.

The next evolutionary step was the ordinary five-line staff, involving the same paper distance as in ordinary notation, and with altered note-heads, as in the lower of the two excerpts in the next example, also from Li Po.[5]

Now with the strokes of my inspired pen.

[2] Shigeyoshi Obata, *The Works of Li Po, the Chinese Poet* (copyright, 1922), 117; this and the two following quotations in the illustrative notation are used by permission of E. P. Dutton and Company.
[3] These, and the other instruments mentioned, were developed and built by Partch [Editors].
[4] Shigeyoshi Obata, *The Works of Li Po, the Chinese Poet* (copyright, 1922), 25.
[5] *Ibid.*, 104.

212

It is obvious that it would take months, if not years, to acquire facility in reading these notations. For the two small instruments, the Adapted Guitar and the Adapted Viola, a return was made to straight ratios, and an occasional horizontal line was used to indicate the 2/1. In the viola score, numbers enclosed in squares indicate the 2/1 register, and appear on each new line of music as a reminder.

Chromelodeon I Notation

The notation for Chromelodeon I is the present everyday variety, requiring nothing more than a psychological adjustment, since the keyboard is the usual 7-White—5-Black (color bands on the keys excepted).

When the notation is the composer knows that this repre-

sents the ratio 11/7, but the player—whether he knows this or not—merely plays what is written, namely, "F#," which is now simply the name of a key or lever and has no significance as a pitch. The keyboard distance for intervals is now approximately quadrupled, since an octave (the keyboard distance) is now only in the neighborhood of a 6/5 (true "minor third"). To translate into current values the note distance is quartered,

213

since which looks like an "octave," is actually a 6/5.

This realization has the effect of taking the seat out from under the player, but after a little groping, and with the aid of music especially written for the new intonation, he soon quiets down. The player has a familiar keyboard under his fingers and familiar notes before him; only the sounds are strange, and his eyes and fingers are too well correlated to let that strangeness disturb him once the reconditioning process has begun. In this we find proof that the automatic acceptance of a certain note distance as an exact intonational quantity is not very deep-seated in the trained musician, a stimulating discovery to anyone interested in advancing the cause of new instruments.

The familiar notation is a track over which to run a newly conceived train. The designers of new trains—engines and coaches—might wish they had rails closer together or farther apart, or a track of an entirely different nature, but the wish is futile because the new trains, if they are to run in the service of public transportation, must use the system of tracks available. Chromelodeon I is a new train offering different values on the same old track—which it cannot escape using, at least for the present, to get anywhere.

Chromelodeon II Notation

The Clavicymbalum Universale was constructed and tuned so that "sharps" and "flats" were different tones, and—although the Chromelodeon is not concerned with the tuning of the Clavicymbalum—this characteristic together with its nineteen keys in the distance of an octave fits neatly into Monophony's effort to find a familiar keyboard with fewer impossible stretches than those on Chromelodeon I, and one amenable to a familiar notation. It does not offer quite the same degree of familiarity to the player, but he still has the old dependable groups of blacks—twos and threes—and from the standpoint of notation it is almost if not quite as feasible as the Chromelodeon I keyboard.

The keys of Chromelodeon II are in four planes (disregarding the sub-bass keys): the usual plane of white keys, the usual plane of black keys, a higher plane of red keys set slightly to the right and back from the blacks, a red key appearing between each pair of whites, and, finally, a sub-plane of five short yellow keys in each 2/1. Notes "flatted" signify red keys, notes "sharped" black keys, notes without accidental marks white keys, and "naturals" yellow sub-keys.

An alternative to this plan—and one that should appeal to the meridional temperament—is a notation in conformity with the color characteristics of the keyboard: incarnadined notes to represent incarnadined keys, black notes for black keys, open, or hollow, notes—white, that is, if on white paper—for white keys, saffron notes for saffron keys, and blue notes for blue keys (thus far, since there are only thirteen of these sub-bass keys, they have been expressed in ratios). In the conventional notation hollow notes carry a rhythmic meaning, but since the same meaning is at least partially carried by the stems or connecting lines it can be ignored; also, if the present rhythmic indications are retained, those symbols representing half or whole notes could be considerably larger than those representing quarter and eighth notes. Here is an example of the individuality of an instrument, mentioned above, and the desirability of suggesting its out-standing characteristics in the notation for it.

The cost of publishing such a score would of course be close to prohib-itive, but at present the objection is academic, since the instrument and its notation are merely the means of an isolated composer and his expres-sion; in any case, if such instruments ever became common, the making of color plates would perhaps have been considerably simplified. As for the color-blind, they can always revert to "sharps," "flats," and "naturals."

Voice Notations

Monophonic voice parts are written in two ways. They are always present in the Chromelodeon score in Chromelodeon notation so that in rehearsals the voice or voices may be aided by the chromelodeonist in getting precise tones, whereas the voice scores are in the usual nota-tion with the usual pitch values, as close as these can be figured to the actual Monophonic ratios. These scores are then used simply as guides to movement, or direction, very much as neumes were used in the days of plain-song.

The voice, having an unfixed gamut, is trained, when it sees the interval

to sing the 2/1 "D-D" and, unlike the chromelodeon-

ist, in whom the mental image unconsciously evokes the corresponding physical reaction, must consciously work for the intonation intended. Hence, in the separate score, if the sequence 5/4 – 7/6 – 6/5 is required of the

voice, it is written which notes do not represent the

ratios above but do indicate in a general way the movement of the voice part, and the approximate pitch of the above ratios.

In my music I have frequently limited the voice parts to "steps" and

215

"half-steps" which correspond to Monophonic intervals in the Ptolemaic Sequence. Since the voice is very easily inclined to sing true intervals anyway, rectification from the notes of the separate score to the actual ratios is comparatively easy. When the voice is required on other than Ptolemaic Sequence degrees, the process of rectification demands a longer period of rehearsal, but is by no means impossible. With six singers —much above average to be sure, but highly diverse personalities—I have obtained satisfactory if not phenomenal results even when the vocal requirements were most exacting.

In conventional practice the voice part of a song is generally supported in 2/1 or unison, or in various of the implied 5-limit ratios, by the chords of the accompanying piano. Likewise, in my music the voice is supported in easy-to-hear intervals by the accompanying instruments; there is no demand for unaided vocal rendition of forty-three tones to the 2/1.

Our Lack of Candor—Why Blame Singers?

Much of the oft-heard railing against the intonation of singers is scandalously lacking in candor. As composers and educators we give them an accompanying instrument—the piano—which is continually at odds with their instincts. After they have mastered this incongruity we pose them in an *a cappella* choir or before an orchestra, where they are at the mercy of each intonational whim of concertmasters and conductors (who are by no means agreed on intonational rectitude), and proceed to criticize them for their "bad" intonation. As musicians we have no intonational norm, and we vent our annoyance over this situation upon innocent singers, who have no norm simply because we have none.

Many musicians regard as inconsequential the seventh of a semitone falsity of the "thirds" and "sixths" (ratios of 5) on the piano—to which singers are trained; but we will see how so "inconsequential" a falsity as 1/50 of a semitone—2 cents—creates out-of-tuneness. The great need for a better instrument than the piano in the training of singers and for the accompaniment of songs is too self-evident to be labored.

Notations for the Kithara,
Harmonic Canon, and Diamond Marimba

The notation for the Kithara might be called a number-correlation system at least partially divorced from ratios. If the instrument were cut through horizontally the strings would give the appearance of seventy-two dots in twelve series of six each, thus:

216

1	2	3	4	5	6	7	8	9	10	11	12

PLAYING SIDE

If we then set this pattern of dots on an ordinary five-line staff without clef or "key signature," it would appear as below — another example of a distinctive notation demanded by the individuality of an instrument.

The corresponding number of each hexad shown above in notation is found on the ledge at the top of the hollow base on the playing side of the Kithara. Consequently, when a full quick chord is desired it is written, for example, [image: chord notation marked 9] If it is to be played with plectrum, "plec." is written above it; if it is to be played in running style away from the player, it is written [image: notation marked (plec.) 9] ; if desired in running style toward the player, [image: notation marked 9] and if a single tone is wanted, say the third string from the playing side in the third hexad, it is written [image: single note marked 3]

The forty-four uniform strings of the Harmonic Canon lend themselves less easily than the Kithara hexads to notation patterns. Thus far only ratios have been used. Notation for the Diamond Marimba represents no problem, its tuning being based on the same twelve hexads as the Kithara.

217

Harry
Partch

Rhythmic Notation

We have previously observed that the human race has advanced through the number 5 in its harmonic music, and is now hovering somewhere between that eminence and the number 7. With respect to the element of rhythm, however, we modern Westerners are primitives; as compared with the subtle speech rhythms of the Middle Ages, ancient Greece, and classic China and Japan, and also with the dance rhythms of the American Indians, our rhythms are aboriginal.

In the thirteenth and fourteenth centuries, shortly after the introduction of mensural music, the number 3 became endowed with the same magic as in the Pythagorean intonational system. Hawkins quotes an unnamed author of the thirteenth century to the effect that, in rhythm, 3 (the Trinity) is "perfect," and therefore 243 is "five times perfect" because 3 is involved five times in arriving at 243 by the factor of 3.[6] Fortunately our forebears abandoned 3-ism in rhythm more readily than 3-ism in intonation.

From the standpoint of the intriguing metric forms which are attained within the rhythms of 2,3, and 4 — the basis of virtually all Western music — much can be said in extenuation of our present "aboriginal" condition, especially as regards the dance rhythms of the Latin Americans or Negroid Latin Americans.

Although Westerners have used basic rhythms of 5 and 7 to good effect, the field for exploration in the more complex forms of 5 and 7, the simple impulses of 11 and 13, and the rhythms of speech, is fabulously extensive. An example of a simple 13 rhythm — a strong impulse followed by twelve weaker pulsations, or an alternate six-seven or seven-six rhythm — is found in an old Edison cylinder record of the "Stick Game Song" from the Hoopa (or Hupa) Indians of northern California. This, and other such records which I examined at the Southwest Museum in Los Angeles in 1933, showed a wealth of rhythms more complex than anything Westerners have thus far attempted.

I have used the present orthodox rhythm notation almost without modification except as follows: 0, enclosed in a diamond, indicates the natural, easy rhythm of speech, and the notes following it are generally written without stems, at least in the voice parts; a hollow note without stem is used to represent a tone that covers two or more syllables — a solid one when a single syllable is sung to it. Duple rhythms are indicated by a 2 or 4 enclosed in a diamond, an eighth or a quarter note being the unit; the usual signs 4/4, 2/4, and 3/4 are not used because they might lead to confusion in a score in which ratios are common. The other rhythms — triple, quintuple, septuple, undecimal — are indicated on the same unit basis, the number being enclosed in a diamond.

[6] *History of the Science and Practice of Music*, 1:248.

Music's Determinants — the Ear, the Hand

Our system of notation must be held partially responsible for the inelasticity of our present musical theory, and for the misdirection of many intonational ideas that have been proposed — it is so "easy" for the notation of "quartertones," for example. But historically, in the establishment of current musical habits, there was little if any causal relation. Significant developments in notation, naturally enough, followed the development of musical artifices. The Middle Ages made two notable advances over the awkward alphabetical notation of the Greeks — both in line with harmonic innovations. Graphic notation was probably the direct result of organum; it was a translation onto paper of the pitch separation of two voice parts. Again, the rhythmic division of music was probably the direct result of part-singing; it filled the need for an indication of a steady accent, so that the several voices could keep together.

Viewed from an acoustic standpoint these developments have little or no relation to the long, sometimes agonizing, evolution of musical theory and the science of intonation. They were — and notation is — a clumsy prescript and a clumsy record; just how clumsy we can appreciate if we analyze our own translation of notes into actions, and perceive how many of those actions are not indicated in any absolute way, often not at all. Hence the latitude of "interpretation."

A musical system does not evolve as it does because it lends itself to being translated into notation. It evolves, basically, from the capacity of the ear, and is formulated and articulated by scientific insight and creative speculation. In the modern procedure the criterion of the ear — its basic capacity, uninfluenced by conditioning factors or education — is partially disregarded in the interest of recently acquired desires, such as facility of modulation. And, finally, it is disregarded in application to instruments; the nature of the human anatomy, particularly the hand, has been allowed to pass as an argument for adulteration, especially in keyboards.[7] Hence, three factors mold our theory: the primal criterion of the ear; the condi-

---

[7] It could perhaps be said that the criterion of the ear is also disregarded in the formulation of a musical theory, in order that it may be simple enough to be comprehensible to the least intelligent of its potential devotees. This is frequently the attitude of the moderns: "But how can we expect students to learn ratios when we have so much difficulty teaching them the A-B-C's of music?" What is overlooked is that simple superficialities are both more difficult to teach and to learn than complex fundamentals. It is not surprising that they do not differentiate — today's teachers were yesterday's students, and yesterday's musical curriculum was simply a segment of the vicious circle. But I am sure that the more influential theorists of the formative period of the sixteenth and seventeenth centuries did not advise the course of temperament because of its superficial simplicity. The persistent searches of Zarlino, Mersenne, Rameau, and many others indicate that they had a zeal for the truth whatever the cost to a fallaciously simple concept.

tioned desires of the ear; the tyranny of the hand.

Does man maintain that in practice he cannot reconcile the last two of these factors with the first, the criterion of the ear? The history of the men who have undertaken to do this, extending back through hundreds of years B.C., offers a good deal of encouragement.

Henry
Brant

[1913 -   ]

Bearing out the indications of his first works, published in the New
Music Quarterly when he was in his teens, Brant has remained a witty
and immensely inventive composer and theorist. Long before the European post-Webernian composers "discovered" them, Brant developed the
ideas of antiphonal music. These include the use of a full performance
area for single players or sometimes the wide separation of groups of
musicians. Unlike many composers today, Brant has no prejudice
against writing for anyone who is interested, whether he be the rankest
amateur or the most skilled professional virtuoso. His music achieves an
extensive gamut of musical expression while remaining easy to play.
Often, this constitutes a refreshing change from the increasing notational
complexity of the last two decades. In the following essay, Brant reviews
his years of work with antiphonal concepts of music.

This article was written especially for the present volume.

Space
as an Essential Aspect of
Musical Composition

Fifteen years ago, in 1950, a discussion of the space factor in Western music would have resembled a discussion of chords and harmonic progressions from the viewpoint of Chinese classical music, where harmony in the Western sense does not appear at all. In both cases the arguments would have to have been based largely on speculation, and perhaps on a few isolated examples — special cases, rather outside the normal spheres of both musical cultures.

As of 1951, my own experience of spatial effects in music was limited to the following:

I had conducted Gabrieli canzonas, with performing groups placed at the front and back of the hall.

I had conducted Ives' *Unanswered Question*, with strings backstage led by a separate sub-conductor, flutes in a "box" halfway down the hall, and the trumpet solo at the very back of a high balcony.

I had heard the Berlioz *Requiem* in Paris, with the four brass groups placed in the four corners of a continuous balcony.

I had also heard a not very spatial performance of Mozart's *Serenade for Four Orchestras*. One was on stage, two were backstage, and the fourth was in a "box."

I did not come to hear Tallis' *Spem in Alium Nunquam Habui* until 1958; in that year I persuaded Ralph Hunter to present a circular performance of this forty-voice contrapuntal piece, with the audience enclosed.

Even today (1965) the resource of space is still, by most composers, considered an optional or peripheral aspect of music, in some cases applicable, but requiring no essential fixed scheme or extensive fund of detailed knowledge based on practical experiment. This view, as it now seems to me, places serious restrictions on musical expressiveness — it could almost be compared to a method of composing which made no specific provision for the control of time values or of pitches.

The observations that follow are made on the basis of rehearsals and performances of my own recent music, composed since 1951, and in reference to experiments I have carried out in connection with these works. In all of them, the spatial distribution of the performers throughout the hall is a planned, required, and essential element of the music. I have also supplied brief descriptions of characteristic examples of spatial technique in the existing literature.

A previous report

In 1954, after performances of five large-scale spatial compositions, I offered the following conclusions in an article on spatial composing technique in the *American Composers Alliance Bulletin*. All these points have been verified in numerous rehearsals and performances of my subsequent works.

1. The difficulty of combining several active but contrasted textures, each with its own distinctive sonority scheme, *over the same octave range*, arises out of the unison tones, made by the different textures sounding together, that are bound to occur in the course of such a combination. If the various sonorities used are highly contrasted, then these casually-occuring, by-product unisons are apt to be of poor and confusing tone quality and hence disturbing to the overall harmonic effect. This impression will be strongly felt if the sound comes from the same source and direction, as when all the performers are placed close together on one stage. If these same textures are now disentangled by distributing their respective performing groups into widely separated positions in the hall, the unisons occuring between the contrasted textures are no longer perceived, because the groups at this distance can no longer make harmonic contact between the tones that they simultaneously sound, and their respective tone qualities are now so diffused that no connection between them can impress itself on the listener.

2. A unison passage between instruments of two or more *separated* groups will face obvious ensemble difficulties because of the distances involved; if the overall ensemble is not exact, then the unison as an amalgam (which it must be by definition) cannot be brought about at all.

3. The total impression of spatially distributed music, in its clarity of effect and in the special kind of relationships produced, is to some extent equivalent to setting up the performers close together on a stage, as usual, but writing the music in such a way that each texture remains in its own octave range, with no collision or crossing of textures permitted. The spatial procedure, however, permits a greatly expanded overall complexity, since separated and contrasting textures may be superimposed freely over the same octave range, irrespective of passing unisons thus formed, with no loss of clarity.

4. Spatial music must be conceived in accordance with the premise that there is no one optimum position in the hall for each listener, and no one optimum distribution of the players in only one ideal hall. However, if a precise and controlled musical result is desired, *spatial arrangements may not be considered optional,* but must be carried out in accordance with an exactly specified plan that still allows for some practical adjustment in detail. Spatial music must be written in such a way that the composer is able to accept what he hears as a listener, regardless of his position in the hall.

224

*Comparing the effect of one sound source with that of
many: a recent example (1964) in which the same
music was rehearsed in two different spatial arrangements in the same hall.*

The diagram below shows the distribution plan for my *Voyage Four,* as
originally conceived, and as exactly carried out at the first performance.

back of top balcony

3 flutes   voice

violins   cellos   bass
viola   saxophone
oboes   English horn
                  back of 1st balcony   small clarinet

ground floor level

VIOLIN
CONDUCTOR   double basses   double basses

contrabassoon

bassoons
                                          chimes*

side balcony   side balcony

tuba*
                                                            violas
24 violins   Diagram of approximate distribution
                  of performers in Woolsey Hall   cellos
                  for Henry Brant's Voyage Four

under vents in floor   timpani

                                          VIOLA-'CELLO
                                          CONDUCTOR

mandolin   glockenspiel
harpsichord   xylophone
         harp   piano

trombones
                          STAGE
                                          horns
trumpets
              CHIEF
              CONDUCTOR

organ pipes (high up)

227

Henry
Brant

At the first rehearsal, the entire forces were jammed together on the stage in a conventional symphonic seating arrangement. The effects of this procedure were as follows:

Resonance was limited, sonorities were "cramped"—there seemed to be comparatively little volume even in the large tuttis, and that seemed "thin" in quality. Balances were poor, not all the parts being audible; the complex textures were unclear—the numerous impinging contrasted tone qualities sounding over the same octave, from closely adjacent positions, produced an irritating effect of meaningless non-relationship.

When the instrumentalists later took their places in the hall as indicated in the diagram:

There was an immediate and startling increase in volume and resonance from all the sections;

heights and depths of pitch became immediately vivid;

balances in volume between the superimposed but now separated textures immediately righted themselves;

contrapuntal amalgams, even in the most complex places, became easily clear, and individual parts easily identifiable by direction.

Distance

Is the effect of distance absolute (measurable in feet), or is its effect proportionate to the size of the hall? I think the latter, on the whole, and I think that the size of the hall affects horizontal distances more than vertical ones.

1. *St. Catherine's Wheel* is a tape-recorded piece. There are four independent tapes, each proceeding from a separate speaker, with one speaker in each corner. When the speakers are set up this way in a living room, the direction and clear identity of each position are strongly felt. If one or two speakers are placed at the ceiling level (11 feet) the resulting vertical contrast is very marked. If the four speakers are closely bunched together, there is an immediate loss of clarity and overall resonance.

2. *The same music* is performed, but now projected into a hall 40 feet by 70 feet by 25 feet. First, use the same limited distances of the living room in placing the speakers. When heard *inside* the square outlined by the four speakers, the sound now seems much less clear and even in resonance than in the small room, although the distances between the speakers are the same as before.

Next, place the speakers in the four corners of the large room. The effect, anywhere in the hall, is now as clear as what was heard in the small room, but much more sonorous and able to sustain more volume. The vertical distance of 11 feet still means something when transferred to the larger room, but the effect

228

is somewhat ambiguous-at 16 feet a definite vertical identity of position becomes perceptible.

In general, *vertical height creates a persuasive impression of higher pitch,*
even when the pitches are *not* actually higher than those being simultaneously
produced at a lower positional level.

The following are general propositions, which have had frequent
application in my own work.

1. *Two small groups* (three to five performers) are placed one at each
extreme side of the stage, in a medium-sized concert hall. When one stands on
the stage between the two groups, the direction of the sounds is quite apparent,
and some connection between them is felt, but these distinctions are *not*
emphatic from any point in the audience, and are principally made evident if
the musical material and timbre of the two groups are highly contrasted. If the
effect is to be noted at all, then no sound should simultaneously originate from
the middle in-between space. The space impression works better in this case
with single instruments or voices. On a very large stage the following set-up
will give a clear spatial result:

2. *Two groups, either one, or both, being small or large,* each with its own
independent musical material and (preferably) its own special instrumentation.
One group on stage, the other at the extreme rear of the hall. They must, of
course, be balanced for volume; the spatial separation will not accomplish this.
No account need be taken of the position of each listener in the house—the
volumes of the two groups need merely be equated exactly as though they were
side by side, all on the stage. When these conditions have been met, the result
is *maximum separation,* which I think of as the *locus classicus* of spatial music.
It is unmistakeable in its startlingly clear effect:

(a) of equally projected distant identities;

(b) of additional resonance and sonority resulting from simultaneous
converging projections from two widely separated points of origin.

The impression of separation becomes still more marked if the two
vertical levels are contrasted, one being higher by at least one-third the
height of the hall, if it is of large size (approximately 2000–2500 seats); by
one half the height, if the hall is of medium size (approximately 1200–1500
seats). In very large halls, or in those where the proportion of wall dimensions is more square than rectangular,

Henry Brant

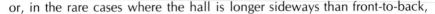

or, in the rare cases where the hall is longer sideways than front-to-back,

a positioning of the two groups on opposite *sides* of the hall will give a striking impression of separation, similar to front-back under normal circumstances. The side-to-side method is enhanced if *both* groups are placed at a balcony level.

Reaction of performers to distance

Singers and instrumentalists participating for the first time in music that requires unusual and extreme separations of performing groups, distributed throughout the hall, often experience an initial uneasiness, since they strain to hear all the parts in some kind of harmonic relationship, as they are accustomed to do in music that is conventionally set up with all the performers together on a stage.

In spatial music where the distances and separations are substantial, it is not always possible for each performer to hear all the parts. Musicians accustom themselves to this fact with little difficulty, and do not find performance disagreeable under such a condition, once they understand that it is the result of a planned element and not a mere oversight in the overall balance of volumes; and that precision in their efforts is as essential to the total effect as it is in conventionally placed music.

Projection

As a safe general working axiom: live performers placed close to a wall, *unimpeded by overhang*, project *about equally* from any point in the hall, assuming that the stage area is not of superior resonance. If the player stands out in the open, there is usually a noticeable loss of resonance and volume. If the player stands in an open doorway, or in a room or lobby outside open doors, projection and resonance are definitely impaired, and the sound is distant.

If the players can be distributed vertically from floor to ceiling, playing simultaneously in an even spread over a substantial part of the area of an entire wall, the result, especially if the instruments are arranged vertically in order or pitch (lowest notes at lowest level, etc.), will be quite as hoped for—the entire wall space will seem to be sounding at once, an extremely vivid and concentrated directional effect.

violins		3rd balcony level
violas		2nd balcony level
cellos		1st balcony level
basses		ground floor level

It thus begins to appear that one achieves, spatially, pretty much what one expects in a commonsense anticipation of the probable effect, if the problem is a straightforward and natural one in the sense of those thus far described.

One exception to this is the placement of performers under the audience floor, with the sound coming up through grilled openings in the floor. Far from sounding subterranean or submerged, the instruments, astoundingly, appear to be emitting their sounds from points in midair above the audience's heads.

High and low pitches as related to high and low vertical levels

There is no mistaking the compelling naturalness of effect when high pitches originate in a high location (e.g. a piccolo in a top balcony), or low pitches from a low position—the latter effect being *enhanced*, not detracted from, if the sounds originate from under a projecting level (e.g. tympani placed in back of the ground floor audience section, which in many halls is under a balcony). However, the actual *pitch* need not be high or low, as the case may be; if the *register* in which the instrument plays is *proportionately* acute or deep, this will substitute very well for absolute height or depth in pitch, and the instrument (or voice) may be situated in, respectively, high or low positions accordingly.

Spill

1. Harmonic possibilities: the sole example of this, to my knowledge, is the "Tuba Mirum" from the Berlioz *Requiem*. The four brass ensembles, placed in the corners of a continuous balcony (as at the Invalides in Paris), present a common tone-quality participating in a common harmonic texture. They seem to reach out to each other when all are sounding, to extend the brass-harmonic texture continuously over the *entire* balcony area, not merely confining it to the corners of the balcony where the sounds originate.

2. "Non-spill counterpoint: if groups with highly contrasted tone-qualities, each with rhythms contrasted to the others (and especially if no rhythmic co-ordination is required between the groups) are assigned to widely separated positions, *no spill at all will result* (i.e. no influence, or real or imagined extension, of one texture on the others).

Recent harmonic experiments involving sustained chords

Each test involved only one tone-quality throughout, and in each test each performer sounded a different note of the chord.

(A)   The chord was arranged vertically, one performer placed above the other:

(1)   the above arrangement against a wall, and (2) this arrangement out in the open, both tried with a quartet of violins, with a quartet of clarinets, and with a group of twelve women's voices.

(3)   the vertical chord, assuming a more oblique position, but still compact, moved up the stairs on to a new level, sustaining its tones during the climb. (This experiment was tried only with voices.)

In the experiments thus far, the top notes seemed physically high, the bottom notes physically low. In (1) the listener could walk around the chord; in both (1) and (2) he could experience its "height" or "depth" by standing in different vertical locations.

(B)   The performers in the chord were arranged horizontally.

(1)   The performers were in a close horizontal row. Two possibilities: facing as in single file, and all facing forward. These were tried with voices and with instruments.

(2)   The performers gathered in a tight circular huddle, football style, all facing inwards; these were also tried with voices and with instruments.

(3)   The performers were evenly spaced out against the four walls (this experiment tried only with voices). The listener experienced a definite, clear sensation of being "surrounded" by the chord.

(4)   The position of experiment (2) moving into that of experiment (3), all the tones being sounded continuously throughout the maneuver, this being tried only with voices. The motion of the sound was easily perceptible to the listener.

The tests with quartets of instruments were done with triads and 7th chords; I also tried dissonant chords consisting of three superimposed major 7ths. In the tests with singers, two different chords were used, one of

them consonant the other consisting of the twelve adjacent

semitones.

Harmony — rhythm — ensemble — co-ordination

Whether the spatial separation is small or great, it will cause a *deterioration* in the rhythmic co-ordination (keeping together) of the separated groups, and hence in their harmonic connection. At the same time, if the music is so written that the separated groups are in a contrasted polyphonic-rhythmic relation to each other, the separation will *enhance* contrapuntal clarity and distinctness to a marked degree.

In moderate-to-large-sized halls there may also be a time lag, so that if one conductor is to be followed by all the performers, the groups situated at a distance from him will produce their sounds fractionally — and sometimes noticeably — later than those groups close to him. However, the ensemble in each of the groups will remain *accurate in itself,* so long as the players in each group are close together. If this possible slight "rubato" between individually co-ordinated groups is anticipated by the composer, effective results may be obtained, even if a common overall meter and tempo are retained.

In such situations, the only serious difficulty that might occur would be that involving co-ordinated *marcato* attacks required simultaneously from the entire aggregate of performers. Even aside from this particular problem, the time lag may at first glance appear to be a discouraging obstacle to the practical and controlled use of spatial materials in music. However, it can be turned into a unique advantage if the composer will go one step further, and plan his music in such a way that *no exact rhythmic correspondence is intended* between the separated groups. This permits simultaneous contrasted meters and tempi, easily controlled either by assistant conductors, soloists, or section leaders. Extreme overall rhythmic intricacy and a sense of great rhythmic freedom are attainable by this kind of procedure; at the same time, maximum control within well-defined limits, as well as ease and naturalness in playing, is retained. This idea of non-co-ordinated, but in-its-essential-parts-controlled, rhythm was a novelty when I first described it in my 1954 article. At that time, the only examples of it known to me were Ives' *The Unanswered Question* and the antiphonal pieces of my own that I had thus far presented in public, plus Teo Macero's *Areas.* The conception is opposed to what later came to be termed "aleatoric" or "indeterminate" music, in which accident and chance are looked upon as primary musical ingredients. When non-co-ordinated rhythm is combined with spatial distribution, accident is no more a factor than it is in the performance of rubato in a complex Chopin ratio.

Examples of spatial technique
in the existing literature

1. A sometimes unsatisfactory solution occurs when Gabrieli's 8-part and 12-part canzonas are played in large halls, with wide separations between the groups. In the final sections of these works, where the harmonic changes are fairly rapid and the counterpoint is intricate but harmonically related, a total and exact rhythmic co-ordination is required. This is destroyed by a time lag, which cannot be accurately rectified by having the more distant groups attempt to "anticipate" the conductor's beats.

2. An easy solution, reached principally by avoiding the combination problem, is found in Mozart's "Echo" Serenade for four orchestral groups, which are mostly heard separately, one at a time.

3. A solution with limited spatial resource: Mozart's passages for three simultaneous orchestras in *Don Giovanni*. One group is in the orchestra pit, another is on stage, and a third backstage. From an eighteenth-century viewpoint, the musical materials assigned to the respective groups are highly contrasted — three actual different meters are combined. Exact rhythmic co-ordination is harmonically essential. There is no spatial obstacle to the overall ensemble co-ordination, since no great distances are involved in the separations. In a very large theater with a deep orchestra pit, some spatial effect is perceptible from pit level to stage level, and from the direct onstage projection to the muffled backstage projection. But the whole procedure lacks emphatic spatial impact, since the entire amalgam of sound originates from points in front of the audience.

4. A twentieth-century solution: Ives' *The Unanswered Question*. This unique, unprecedented little work, written in 1908, presents, with extraordinary economy and concentration, the entire twentieth-century spatial spectrum in music, and offers guidelines for solving all the practical problems involved. There are two groups, intended to be separated, and one isolated soloist. There is complete contrast between the three elements: in tone quality, tempo (which includes speedups, retards and rubato), meter, range, harmonic, melodic, and contrapuntal material. No rhythmic coordination exists between the three constituents, except an approximate one at points of entrance. No matter how great the distances in position, two conductors can maintain the simultaneous independence of all the participating musical elements with utmost precision and control.

The spatial-contrapuntal-polytemporal principles so brilliantly exem-

plified in this piece are the basis for the more complicated spatial superim-
positions present in all my own recent large-scale works.

5.   In 1953, shortly after my Juilliard School performances of *The
Unanswered Question,* I discussed with Teo Macero the program of a
proposed Juilliard concert, to be devoted entirely to new works exploiting
jazz materials. I suggested that he compose for this concert a large jazz
piece using spatial devices, and the result was his *Areas,* which requires
five separated groups, four of winds and one of percussion. The greater
portion of the texture is highly contrapuntal, with carefully notated jazz
figurations in all the parts, but there are also moments of total improvisation. The co-ordination problems were worked out in such a way that the
composer was able to lead the entire amalgam of forces himself at the
performance.

Spatial uses of recorded music

Loudspeakers can be placed in parts of the hall where live performers
cannot work, and can thus add considerably to the versatility of spatial
arrangements.

The essential differences between live and speaker projection are very
marked. They are noticeable not so much in the recording's lack of fidelity
to the original, but in the extremely concentrated and directional projection which proceeds from loudspeakers, which is totally at variance, in its
effect, with the immediate and extensive diffusion of the sounds emitted by
a live player or singer. The difference in impression, if the listener stands in
front or in back of the speaker, is violent: the front producing a compact
blast, the back nothing. On the other hand, the listener may walk around
the live player or stand above or below him, and from each position hear
a substantial diffusion of the sounds. For these reasons, if a recording-
through-speakers simulates or imitates a live performer who is *simultaneously* heard, a want of correspondence in projection is felt, and the mixture
of live and recorded sound either seems not to take place at all or to be
unsatisfactory. If, however, the recorded sound is purposely planned for
maximum musical *contrast* with the simultaneous live sound, then a *wide*
spatial distance between speakers, and between speakers and live sound
sources, will enhance the contrast and make the total impression more
intelligible and resonant.

If a convincing naturalness of effect is desired, plus a maximum diffusion of the sound, an extremely satisfactory position for a loudspeaker is in
the ceiling. Oddly enough, however, this position does not always promote
a clear directionality of the sound.

The duplication of the identical musical texture in different speakers, or the identical material recorded simultaneously from different microphone positions (overlapping or "spill" being permitted between the various areas covered by the microphones), although by now an accepted convention in commercial recording and playback reproduction ("stereophony"), does *not* promote maximum clarity in precise individual details, since whatever *directional* guide was originally present has now been cancelled out.

If what emerges from any given speaker is not sufficiently differentiated from the musical content assigned to other speakers, in relation to texture, range and tone quality, mere bewilderment and a sense of "wasted" space result, and one of the principal advantages of spatial distribution is lost. *The listener's senses strongly urge him to assign a particular musical texture to a particular location in the hall.*

Outdoor music

Live outdoor performance requires favorably placed rebounding surfaces and is sometimes diffused to the point of inaudibility by wind interference. The location of the rebounding surfaces is particularly difficult to control if the performers move. All these conditions make the calculation of effect for outdoor live music an almost hopeless task, since the probable variability in each situation is so great. The matter is not solved by the amplification of live sound; this merely creates distortions in tone quality and balance, since, if the sound-sources are placed outdoors, the area of sound to be amplified cannot be precisely limited or controlled. (The problem would be a different one if the sounds, recorded live in a controlled studio, were simultaneously projected from speakers placed outdoors; but in this case the sounds might just as well be pre-recorded, and projected later, with much greater facility and variety of resource.)

Pre-recorded sound is much more practicable than live sound for outdoor use. It can resist wind interference to a considerable degree, and can make itself heard without favorably placed rebounding surfaces, by reason of its more concentrated projection, and because of the possibility of stepping up the volume, without distortion, to levels unattainable with naturally produced sound. Pre-recorded sound is obviously superior to amplified live sound, both for high volumes and for the quality of timbre as reproduced.

Even so, the conditions of outdoor sound production cause variations of projection during the progress of the sound itself, and usually cause much diffusion of a complex kind, sometimes making the sound appear to proceed from the wrong direction, or from two places at once when there is only one actual source, and often with a continuing minimum of shifting volume. For these reasons conventional "stereophony" (the identical

237

musical material proceeding from separated speaker sources) is even more confusing in its effects outdoors than in.

How much complexity of texture should emerge from a single highly amplified speaker, placed outdoors at the usual, and effective, substantial height (20-40 feet)? The *amount* of volume and amplified fullness suggests the power of a substantial group of performers, but the sense of being too tightly jammed together, as in a closet or sardine can, is identical to that felt when a recorded symphony comes out of an 8-inch radio speaker placed in a living room. The most natural and compelling impression outdoors thus seems, as indoors, as though it should be limited to a *single performer from each speaker*. The resulting effect, as of a giant or celestial voice or instrument, seems commensurate with the greatly expanded space-range involved. Extensive distances between speakers, unattainable in enclosed spaces, can be impressively encompassed outdoors, when individual musical material is assigned to each speaker. The premises outlined above should be the basis for many outdoor, non-stereophonic, spatial experiments, using powerfully amplified speakers, separated over substantial distances—a city block or more apart.

Travel and "filling-up" (density)

When instruments placed in fixed positions as shown below, begin playing one at a time and *accumulating* (staying in) as indicated by the arrows in the diagram, there is a compelling impression of the hall tangibly *filling* up with sound, principally along the walls, but also with some feeling of the center being progressively saturated, especially as the accumulation proceeds towards its maximum point.

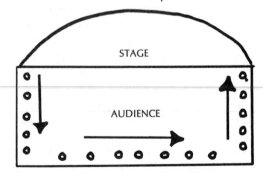

The impression of the sound *travelling* gradually down the first wall is very strong; this impression of moving direction becomes less well defined as the further entrances and accumulations occur.

If this total procedure is carried out entirely at a balcony level, it will seem that the "travel" and "filling-up" are limited to the upper vertical region of the hall. What would result if sound were somehow made to originate in the middle empty area of the hall, above the ground-floor seats and between side balcony areas?

One experiment which almost fulfilled this condition indicated straightforward and realistic results: my *Grand Universal Circus,* at Mc-Millan Theater in New York. The audience seated beneath the "sphere" of total sound noted a tangible "submersion"; those listeners situated vertically midway had a feeling of being "immersed"; those seated above experienced a "resting-on-clouds" sensation. These sensations of "submersion" and "immersion" seemed particularly pronounced when voices participated.

Travel with moving performers

This is encountered occasionally in the theater as an exit-fadeout device (a soloist or group leaving the hall by exits, or backstage and out, while still playing, speaking, or singing). When a performer walks playing or singing through a large hall, it is difficult to note any definite aural-spatial motion whatever. The explanation has to do with the speed of the performer's walk — a sound-source moving at the speed of human walking is not rapid enough to register spatially with any emphatic impact on the senses, except in a comparatively restricted space.

In December 1964 a number of experiments were conducted with moving performers. In all of these tests, the listeners kept their eyes closed, so as to eliminate the influence of the visual image as much as possible.

1. In a room 20 feet by 20 feet and 12 feet high, a flutist walks around the walls, playing continuously. He takes various vertical positions while playing, by means of climbing ladders, standing on tables, and sitting on the floor. Listeners adopt stationary positions of their own choice, but are free to move from one to the other as they wish. *An unmistakeable impression of travelling sound and of vertical positions.*

239

Henry
Brant

2. In this same room, four flutists, playing E soprano, C, alto and bass flutes, take positions in the four corners of the room, and perform a Bach fugue. Listeners are free to take any positions they choose, to move from one place to another, and to walk about as they listen. *The directional impression is definite, and a connection is felt between the four flutes; but the harmonic relationship, although definitely present, takes on an elusive character difficult to describe. The polyphony seems almost unnecessarily clear.*

3. In the same room, four flutists, all playing C flutes in the first octave, improvise lyric lines that are similar but independent. They begin with each player in the middle of a wall, and play continuously, walking in a circle and keeping the same distance from each other. The audience is stationary in the middle of the room. Flutists now halt, stand still, but continue playing. Flutists start walking again, in the opposite direction. *A compelling impression of musical circular motion; differences in the melodic material played by each flute provide points of directional identification. A change is immediately apparent when the flutes play in a stationary position; the reversed direction is equally identifiable.*

4. This and the following tests were made in the entrance hall of a large old-fashioned mansion — 30 feet by 30 feet and 15 feet high. Two long narrow corridors extend into the entrance hall from opposite sides, each corridor opening into rooms of different sizes. The doors into these rooms are open for this test. Two flutists, playing independent material, begin six feet apart in the entrance hall, then walk away into the corridors in opposite directions, going in and out of each room they pass on the way. Each flutist, having reached the end of his corridor, reverses the process and returns to the entrance hall, where they meet and pass each other, each continuing in his own direction into the corridor just ahead. Both flutists play continuously throughout the experiment. Listeners remain in the entrance hall. *Impressions of diverging and converging separations, of increasing and decreasing distance, of decreasing and increasing volume, and of suddenly intensified resonance as a player goes from an open room into a corridor — all very vivid and marked. The moment when the players meet is strongly felt by the listeners as a climax of unusual intensity, but of a character difficult to describe.*

5. An unplanned variant of the above test. Four flutists go aimlessly all over the entrance hall, corridor and adjoining room areas. Listeners follow them with no prearranged route. *No particular aural sensation results; the procedure quickly becomes tedious both to players and hearers.*

6. The entrance hall is at the bottom of a wide, open, winding staircase going up two floors. The vertical distance to the second floor is 20 feet, and from the second to the third floor another 20 feet. Three flutists participate. When the first player reaches the first landing, the second player begins; when the first player reaches the second floor, the third player begins. Each player starts in the low register of his instrument, gradually ascending in range, so that at the third floor he is in his highest register. As each player reaches the top, he waits and keeps playing until all three have assembled there. (The musical material of the three players is independent, the playing continuous.) Now the

240

procedure is reversed, one player starting downstairs at a time, and this time they all begin in their lowest register and proceed towards the highest, *as they descend* the stairs. (The exact reverse would have started each flute in its highest register, with a downward progression in range.) Listeners remained in the entrance hall throughout both parts of the experiment.

The first test produced an extremely realistic *physical feeling of ascent, vertical distance combined with musical pitch ascent* creating an unusually vivid impression. This was made more intense by the fact that the instruments did not lose volume as they ascended, since a progression into the highest register of the flute will naturally produce a crescendo.

The second part of the test produced a conflict of impressions, but of a positive kind. It seemed disturbing that the strong sense of *physical descent* should be associated with an *ascent in pitch,* but this contradiction, combined with the *increase in volume and intensity* as the instruments approached the listeners at the bottom of the steps, created a satisfying conflict.

All the tests in the above series were carried out in spaces of comparatively modest dimensions. They were effective partly because a proper ratio could be maintained between the speed of the moving sound and the distance to be travelled. The problem of transferring effects such as these to large concert areas has no easy practical solution, since the larger distances involved would require speeds considerably beyond that which a walking (or even running) musician or singer could accomplish, except by superhuman means. If faster speeds for moving sources of sound are not achieved when working in larger halls, then little or no impact of musico-spatial motion will be experienced by the listener.

The corridor, or tunnel, has special properties for musico-spatial motion that cannot be duplicated in a normally rectangular space. It also appears, on the basis of preliminary experiments, that the extended rectangle (such as 80 feet by 30 feet) is less favorable for the comprehension of spatial motion than the more normal rectangle (80 feet by 60 feet).

Visual aspects of musical space

Schemes for spatial distribution that are conceived in terms of their *visual expressiveness on paper* cannot be expected to produce any effect on the *aural* mechanism, and hence any *musically* expressive result, unless they happen to coincide with procedures such as those set forth in detail above, which in all cases are based solely on *what strikes the ear* during the process of actual performance.

The spatial elements in concert music, if exploited fully and expressively, could make their points much more strongly if the sounds could be heard in complete darkness, without the disturbing and confusing intervention of merely functional visual impressions — such as the appearance and motions of performers and audience, and the decor and lighting of the hall — that are irrelevant to the actual communication of the music in terms of its sound. Totally invisible spatial music, *in the theater,* would leave the visual senses free to concentrate on visual material planned for its dramatic expressiveness, which theatrical technique can accomplish with complete and varied control.

Conclusions

Questions of melody, harmony and counterpoint are not initially decided, for the practicing musician, by the acoustician, the anatomist or the psychologist. Textbooks written by musicians are not scientific studies; at best they describe a working knowhow based on everyday practice, which has to take into account many inconsistencies and vagaries, both human and mechanical. Wherever musical phenomena can be demonstrated with sufficient consistency and stability, the musicians' findings will of course be supportable and explainable in acoustical, anatomical, and psychological terms.

In most cases, a working procedure useful to the musician is first discovered and retried in practical, do-it-yourself experiments — it may then, in some instances, be verified scientifically. This is also true of the space factor, of which investigation, expressive use, and control are still in the beginning stages.

Except for the brief discussion of outdoor possibilities, nothing in the foregoing has progressed beyond an essentially rectangular view of musical space. More importantly, this view is limited to a one-room conception of musical space — even the most elaborate and complex events in Western musical culture still take place in single, four-walled, all-enclosed halls. Why need we stop here? What might be the next steps? In the not too distant future I hope to describe some promising lines of procedure, and their practical working out, in terms of new music in new spaces.

Milton Babbitt

[1916 -   ]

In addition to being Professor of Music at Princeton University and a director of the Columbia-Princeton Electronic Music Center, Milton Babbitt is a professional mathematician. He has, in fact, taught mathematics as well as music at Princeton. It is understandable, therefore, that Babbitt brings to music a scholarly, analytic, relentlessly probing attitude such as one would normally associate with pure research in a scientific area.

In his own music, which exerts great influence upon younger composers, he has set out to explore the possibilities inherent in the serialization of dynamics, timbres, and the temporal elements of rhythm, pulse, and duration—that is, the extension of Webern's technique of pitch organization to dimensions other than pitch. This mathematically precise control over all the variables in the musical fabric is a goal more attainable, perhaps, through electronic composition than the intermediary of fallible human performers; Babbitt has, in fact, become increasingly active in the area of electronic music.

His esthetic approach and conception of the composer's role further demonstrate his scientific orientation. In the essay reprinted here, Babbitt rejects the popular notion that the composer must necessarily communicate with the layman. On the contrary, the composer's first obligation is to his art, to the evolution of music and the advancement of new musical concepts. Advanced musical concepts, furthermore, are no more intended for the average man than advanced theories of astrophysics. In advancing this thesis, Babbitt and the younger composers stimulated by his work propose an objectivity allied with that of Stravinsky, and far removed from the Romantic expressionism of Schoenberg or the Gebrauchmusik of Hindemith.

"Who Cares if You Listen?," from *High Fidelity*, VIII/2 (February, 1958), 38-40, 126-27.

Who Cares
if You Listen?

This article might have been entitled "The Composer as Specialist" or, alternatively, and perhaps less contentiously, "The Composer as Anachronism." For I am concerned with stating an attitude towards the indisputable facts of the status and condition of the composer of what we will, for the moment, designate as "serious," "advanced," contemporary music. This composer expends an enormous amount of time and energy—and, usually, considerable money—on the creation of a commodity which has little, no, or negative commodity value. He is, in essence, a "vanity" composer. The general public is largely unaware of and uninterested in his music. The majority of performers shun it and resent it. Consequently, the music is little performed, and then primarily at poorly attended concerts before an audience consisting in the main of fellow professionals. At best, the music would appear to be for, of, and by specialists.

Towards this condition of musical and societal "isolation," a variety of attitudes has been expressed, usually with the purpose of assigning blame, often to the music itself, occasionally to critics or performers, and very occasionally to the public. But to assign blame is to imply that this isolation is unnecessary and undesirable. It is my contention that, on the contrary, this condition is not only inevitable, but potentially advantageous for the composer and his music. From my point of view, the composer would do well to consider means of realizing, consolidating, and extending the advantages.

The unprecedented divergence between contemporary serious music and its listeners, on the one hand, and traditional music and its following, on the other, is not accidental and—most probably—not transitory. Rather, it is a result of a half-century of revolution in musical thought, a revolution whose nature and consequences can be compared only with, and in many respects are closely analogous to, those of the mid-nineteenth-century revolution in theoretical physics. The immediate and profound effect has been the necessity for the informed musician to reexamine and probe the very foundations of his art. He has been obliged to recognize the possibility, and actuality, of alternatives to what were once regarded as musical absolutes. He lives no longer in a unitary musical universe of "common practice," but in a variety of universes of diverse practice.

This fall from musical innocence is, understandably, as disquieting to some as it is challenging to others, but in any event the process is irreversible; and the music that reflects the full impact of this revolution is, in many significant respects, a truly "new" music. Apart from the often highly sophisticated and complex constructive methods of any one composition, or group of compositions, the very minimal properties characterizing this body of music are the sources of its "difficulty," "unintelligibility," and — isolation. In indicating the most general of these properties, I shall make reference to no specific works, since I wish to avoid the independent issue of evaluation. The reader is at liberty to supply his own instances; if he cannot (and, granted the condition under discussion, this is a very real possibility), let him be assured that such music does exist.

First. This music employs a tonal vocabulary which is more "efficient" than that of the music of the past, or its derivatives. This is not necessarily a virtue in itself, but it does make possible a greatly increased number of pitch simultaneities, successions, and relationships. This increase in efficiency necessarily reduces the "redundancy" of the language, and as a result the intelligible communication of the work demands increased accuracy from the transmitter (the performer) and activity from the receiver (the listener). Incidentally, it is this circumstance, among many others, that has created the need for purely electronic media of "performance." More importantly for us, it makes ever heavier demands upon the training of the listener's perceptual capacities.

Second. Along with this increase of meaningful pitch materials, the number of functions associated with each component of the musical event also has been multiplied. In the simplest possible terms, each such "atomic" event is located in a five-dimensional musical space determined by pitch-class, register, dynamic, duration, and timbre. These five components not only together define the single event, but, in the course of a work, the successive values of each component create an individually coherent structure, frequently in parallel with the corresponding structures created by each of the other components. Inability to perceive and remember precisely the values of any of these components results in a dislocation of the event in the work's musical space, an alternation of its relation to all other events in the work, and — thus — a falsification of the composition's total structure. For example, an incorrectly performed or perceived dynamic value results in destruction of the work's dynamic pattern, but also in false identification of other components of the event (of which this dynamic value is a part) with corresponding components of other events, so creating incorrect pitch, registral, timbral, and durational associations. It is this high degree of "determinancy" that most strikingly differentiates such music from, for example, a popular song. A popular song is only very partially determined, since it would appear to retain its germane characteristics under considerable alteration of register, rhythmic texture, dynamics, harmonic structure, timbre, and other qualities.

The preliminary differentiation of musical categories by means of this reasonable and usable criterion of "degree of determinacy" offends those who take it to be a definition of qualitative categories, which—of course—it need not always be. Curiously, their demurrers usually take the familiar form of some such "democratic" counterdefinition as: "There is no such thing as 'serious' and 'popular' music." There is only 'good' and 'bad' music." As a public service, let me offer those who still patiently await the revelation of the criteria of Absolute Good an alternative criterion which possesses, at least, the virtue of immediate and irrefutable applicability: "There is no such thing as 'serious' and 'popular' music. There is only music whose title begins with the letter 'X,' and music whose title does not."

Third. Musical compositions of the kind under discussion possess a high degree of contextuality and autonomy. That is, the structural characteristics of a given work are less representative of a general class of characteristics than they are unique to the individual work itself. Particularly, principles of relatedness, upon which depends immediate coherence of continuity, are more likely to evolve in the course of the work than to be derived from generalized assumptions. Here again greater and new demands are made upon the perceptual and conceptual abilities of the listener.

Fourth, and finally. Although in many fundamental respects this music is "new," it often also represents a vast extension of the methods of other musics, derived from a considered and extensive knowledge of their dynamic principles. For, concomitant with the "revolution in music," perhaps even an integral aspect thereof, has been the development of analytical theory, concerned with the systematic formulation of such principles to the end of greater efficiency, economy, and understanding. Compositions so rooted necessarily ask comparable knowledge and experience from the listener. Like all communication, this music presupposes a suitably equipped receptor. I am aware that "tradition" has it that the lay listener, by virtue of some undefined, transcendental faculty, always is able to arrive at a musical judgment absolute in its wisdom if not always permanent in its validity. I regret my inability to accord this declaration of faith the respect due its advanced age.

Deviation from this tradition is bound to dismiss the contemporary music of which I have been talking into "isolation." Nor do I see how or why the situation should be otherwise. Why should the layman be other than bored and puzzled by what he is unable to understand, music or anything else? It is only the translation of this boredom and puzzlement into resentment and denunciation that seems to me indefensible. After all, the public does have its own music, its ubiquitous music: music to eat by, to read by, to dance by, and to be impressed by. Why refuse to recognize the possibility that contemporary music has reached a stage long since attained by other forms of activity? The time has passed when the normally well-educated man without special preparation could understand the most advanced work in, for example, mathematics, philosophy, and physics. Advanced music, to the extent that it reflects the knowledge and originality of the informed composer, scarcely can be expected to appear more intelligible than these arts and sciences to the person whose musical education usually has been even less extensive than his background in other fields. But to this, a double standard is invoked, with the words "music is music," implying also that "music is *just* music." Why not, then, equate the activities of the radio repairman with those of the theoretical physicist, on the basis of the dictum that "physics is physics"? It is not difficult to find statements like the following, from the *New York Times* of September 8, 1957: "The scientific level of the conference is so high . . . that there are in the world only 120 mathematicians special-izing in the field who could contribute." Specialized music on the other hand, far from signifying "height" of musical level, has been charged with "decadence," even as evidence of an insidious "conspiracy."

It often has been remarked that only in politics and the "arts" does the layman regard himself as an expert, with the right to have his opinion heard. In the realm of politics he knows that this right, in the form of a vote, is guaranteed by fiat. Comparably, in the realm of public music, the concertgoer is secure in the knowledge that the amenities of concert going protect his firmly stated "I didn't like it" from further scrutiny. Imagine, if you can, a layman chancing upon a lecture on "Pointwise Periodic Homeomorphisms." At the conclusion, he announces: "I didn't like it." Social conventions being what they are in such circles, someone might dare inquire: "Why not?" Under duress, our layman discloses precise reasons for his failure to enjoy himself; he found the hall chilly, the lec-turer's voice unpleasant, and he was suffering the digestive aftermath of a poor dinner. His interlocutor understandably disqualifies these reasons as irrelevant to the content and value of the lecture, and the development of mathematics is left undisturbed. If the concertgoer is at all versed in the ways of musical lifesmanship, he also will offer reasons for his "I didn't like it" — in the form of assertions that the work in question is "inexpres-sive," "undramatic," "lacking in poetry," etc., etc., tapping that store of vacuous equivalents hallowed by time for: "I don't like it, and I cannot or will not state why." The concertgoer's critical authority is established beyond the possibility of further inquiry. Certainly he is not responsible for the circumstance that musical discourse is a never-never land of semantic confusion, the last resting place of all those verbal and formal fallacies, those hoary dualisms that have been banished from rational discourse. Perhaps he has read, in a widely consulted and respected book on the history of music, the following: "to call him (Tchaikovsky) the 'modern Russian Beethoven' is footless, Beethoven being patently neither modern nor Russian. . . ." Or, the following, by an eminent "nonanalytic" philosopher: "The music of Lourié is an ontological music. . . . It is born in the singular roots of being, the nearest possible juncture of the soul and the spirit. . . . " How unexceptionable the verbal peccadilloes of the average concertgoer appear beside these masterful models. Or, perhaps, in search of "real" authority, he has acquired his critical vocabulary from the pronouncements of officially "eminent" composers, whose eminence, in turn, is founded largely upon just such assertions as the concertgoer has learned to regurgitate. This cycle is of slight moment in a world where circularity is one of the norms of criticism. Composers (and performers), wittingly or unwittingly assuming the character of "talented children" and "inspired idiots" generally ascribed to them, are singularly adept at the conversion of personal tastes into general principles. Music they do not like is "not music," composers whose music they do not like are "not composers."

In search of what to think and how to say it, the layman may turn to newspapers and magazines. Here he finds conclusive evidence for the proposition that "music is music." The science editor of such publications contents himself with straightforward reporting, usually news of the "factual" sciences; books and articles not intended for popular consumption are not reviewed. Whatever the reason, such matters are left to professional journals. The music critic admits no comparable differentiation. He may feel, with some justice, that music which presents itself in the market place of the concert hall automatically offers itself to public approval or disapproval. He may feel, again with some justice, that to omit the expected criticism of the "advanced" work would be to do the composer an injustice in his assumed quest for, if nothing else, public notice and "professional recognition." The critic, at least to this extent, is himself a victim of the leveling of categories.

Here, then, are some of the factors determining the climate of the public world of music. Perhaps we should not have overlooked those pockets of "power" where prizes, awards, and commissions are dispensed, where music is adjudged guilty, not only without the right to be confronted by its accuser, but without the right to be confronted by the accusations. Or those well-meaning souls who exhort the public "just to *listen* to more contemporary music," apparently on the theory that familiarity breeds

248

passive acceptance. Or those, often the same well-meaning souls, who remind the composer of his "obligation to the public," while the public's obligation to the composer is fulfilled, manifestly, by mere physical presence in the concert hall or before a loudspeaker or—more authoritatively—by committing to memory the numbers of phonograph records and amplifier models. Or the intricate social world within this musical world, where the salon becomes bazaar, and music itself becomes an ingredient of verbal canapés for cocktail conversation.

I say all this not to present a picture of a virtuous music in a sinful world, but to point up the problems of a special music in an alien and inapposite world. And so, I dare suggest that the composer would do himself and his music an immediate and eventual service by total, resolute, and voluntary withdrawal from this public world to one of private performance and electronic media, with its very real possibility of complete elimination of the public and social aspects of musical composition. By so doing, the separation between the domains would be defined beyond any possibility of confusion of categories, and the composer would be free to pursue a private life of professional achievement, as opposed to a public life of unprofessional compromise and exhibitionism.

But how, it may be asked, will this serve to secure the means of survival for the composer and his music? One answer is that after all such a private life is what the university provides the scholar and the scientist. It is only proper that the university, which—significantly—has provided so many contemporary composers with their professional training and general education, should provide a home for the "complex," "difficult," and "problematical" in music. Indeed, the process has begun; and if it appears to proceed too slowly, I take consolation in the knowledge that in this respect, too, music seems to be in historically retarded parallel with now sacrosanct fields of endeavor. In E. T. Bell's *Men of Mathematics,* we read: "In the eighteenth century the universities were not the principal centers of research in Europe. They might have become such sooner than they did but for the classical tradition and its understandable hostility to science. Mathematics was close enough to antiquity to be respectable, but physics, being more recent, was suspect. Further, a mathematician in a university of the time would have been expected to put much of his effort on elementary teaching; his research, if any, would have been an unprofitable luxury. . . ." A simple substitution of "musical composition" for "research," of "academic" for "classical," of "music" for "physics," and of "composer" for "mathematician," provides a strikingly accurate picture of the current situation. And as long as the confusion I have described continues to exist, how can the university and its community assume other than that the composer welcomes and courts public competition with the historically certified products of the past, and the commercially certified products of the present?

Perhaps for the same reason, the various institutes of advanced research and the large majority of foundations have disregarded this music's need for means of survival. I do not wish to appear to obscure the obvious differences between musical composition and scholarly research, although it can be contended that these differences are no more fundamental than the differences among the various fields of study. I do question whether these differences, by their nature, justify the denial to music's development of assistance granted these other fields. Immediate "practical" applicability (which may be said to have its musical analogue in "immediate extensibility of a compositional technique") is certainly not a necessary condition for the support of scientific research. And if it be contended that such research is so supported because in the past it has yielded eventual applications, one can counter with, for example, the music of Anton Webern, which during the composer's lifetime was regarded (to the very limited extent that it was regarded at all) as the ultimate in hermetic, specialized, and idiosyncratic composition; today, some dozen years after the composer's death, his complete works have been recorded by a major record company, primarily—I suspect—as a result of the enormous influence this music has had on the postwar, nonpopular, musical world. I doubt that scientific research is any more secure against predictions of ultimate significance than is musical composition. Finally, if it be contended that research, even in its least "practical" phases, contributes to the sum of knowledge in the particular realm, what possibly can contribute more to our knowledge of music than a genuinely original composition?

Granting to music the position accorded other arts and sciences promises the sole substantial means of survival for the music I have been describing. Admittedly, if this music is not supported, the whistling repertory of the man in the street will be little affected, the concert-going activity of the conspicuous consumer of musical culture will be little disturbed. But music will cease to evolve, and, in that important sense, will cease to live.

Otto
Luening
[1900 - 1996]

In the course of his own career as a composer, and in the development of his musical style, Otto Luening represents most vividly the continuity underlying the musical changes of the past fifty years. A student of Busoni, Luening absorbed from his teacher both the rigorous craft of neo-Classic technique and the experimental bent that sought to liberate sounds from the restrictions of conventional scales and instruments. Luening thus represents both the conservative and the revolutionary tendencies of contemporary music, and has fused the two in his own work.

After many years of composing music for conventional instrumental forces (songs, chamber music, symphonic and operatic scores) in a strongly linear, dissonant yet tonal idiom, Luening became increasingly interested in composition by electronic means, primarily the manipulation of pre-recorded sounds by splicing, speed alteration, and other means. He produced a number of works using this technique in the early 1950's, and has continued to explore the field of electronic music through his own compositions, research, and writings. Presently one of the directors of the Columbia-Princeton Electronic Music Center, Luening has lectured widely on this subject and contributed a number of articles to music journals; one of these is reprinted here.

"Some Random Remarks on Electronic Music," from *The Journal of Music Theory*, VIII/1 (Spring, 1964), pp. 89–98.

Some
Random Remarks
About Electronic Music

Electronic music has gone along a zig-zag path. This article may follow suit. But first a definition of electronic music will serve as a starting point. Electronic Music is music which uses electronically generated sound or sound modified by electronic means, with or without voices or musical instruments, live or over speakers. My effort here is to highlight events from the past that have a bearing on the present or point to the future. Essential to a fuller understanding of the broad developments within the field are the readings given. . . .[1,2,3]

Recently I have had numerous conversations about much new music with many composers, some of them young. In order to communicate with them I found that in addition to the standard contemporary music vocabulary as approved and used by our best music journals I had to be able to follow and even use a new one. The New has become an end in itself. But can we really be sure that our latest novelty has not been beaten by a month, a week, or a minute as we practice our Olympic Gamesmanship? Have I any assurance that I am ahead of the man in Iceland? Nowadays possibilities are limitless. Is the starting point limitless, too, or are we looking for totally planned spontaneity? I understand that this is the age for squaring the circle and circling the squares.

Electronic music is part of the avant-garde mystique. Yet, as we enter the race for the newest we remember that it takes a long time to produce works in this medium. One wonders whether newness organized and an end in itself is conservatism under a new label. Perhaps a glance into the past will help to clarify things. At worst, in the end we can take a stand by accepting all or by avoiding whatever it is that connects us to it. Do we want an all-purpose music, with or without sound and/or silence, or are such conscious positions unimportant after all?

Preoccupation with acoustics is not new. I Ching and Chinese acoustical studies both stem from approximately 2800 B.C., and King Fang tried a fifty-three-tone scale within an octave over fifteen centuries before the West

[1] H. Partch, *Genesis of a Music* (University of Wisconsin Press, 1949).
[2] F. K. Prieberg, *Musik des technischen Zeitalters* (Atlantis Musikbücherei, 1956).
[3] F. K. Prieberg, *Musica ex Machina* (Ullstein Verlag, 1960).

got around to it. The work of the Sanskrit grammarian Panini of the third or fourth century B.C. has survived. In addition to making purely linguistic studies he found the relationship between language sounds and physical positions of the mouth. Ptolemy and Pythagoras are so well advertised that they need only brief mention. As we move forward in time a number of interesting experiments come to mind.

Don Nicola Vicentino's (c. 1550 A.D.) "Archicembalo" was a harpsichordlike instrument with thirty-one steps within an octave. With it he hoped to revive the ancient Greek modes. Although there was at least one organist who played the instrument with great skill and Vicentino's ideas were received with favor in some quarters, he could not prevail against the taste of his time. His influence, however, was felt.

Athanasius Kircher, another inventor, moved in still other directions. In 1660 he constructed a composing machine with the fine name "Arca Musarithmica." Scale, rhythm, and tempo relations were represented by numbers and number relations, indeed arithmetic, from which the machine got its name.

A hundred years after Kircher had built his composing machine the drive toward machine music had produced not only instruments like the mechanical organs, trumpets, musical clocks, and glass harmonicas that interested Mozart, Kirnberger, Haydn, and Handel but also those practical and playing instruments, the perfected organ and pianoforte. The "Electric Harpsichord," invented by J. B. Delaborde in Paris (1761), Hipp's "Electromechanical Piano" in Neuchatel (1867), Elisha Gray's "Electroharmonic Piano" demonstrated in Chicago in 1876, the same year that Koenig's "Tonametric" apparatus (which divided four octaves into six hundred seventy equal parts) was demonstrated in Philadelphia, and Julian Carrillo's theories of microtones and preoccupation with a ninety-six-tone scale (Mexico, 1895) bring us to the threshold of the twentieth century.

Edison's patent for the phonograph (1878), the Emile Berliner telephone transmitter and disc record (1877), the development of various acoustical principles by Alexander Melville Bell (1867), Helmholtz's *Sensations of Tone* (1885), and the work of W. C. Sabin, P. M. Morse, Lord Rayleigh, Dayton Miller, Harvey Fletcher, and other scientists gave focus to experiments of the past and influence us to this day.

On March 10, 1906, an editorial in the professional electrotechnical journal, *Electrical World*, published in New York, described a demonstration that took place in Mount Holyoke, Massachusetts, on that date. A machine, the "Dynamophone," produced music made by a group of dynamos run by alternating current. The editorial was signed L. Stokowski.

Other reporters wrote that the machine, also called "Telharmonium," was the largest musical instrument in the world. It weighed two hundred tons. The electrically generated music was transmitted over telephone wire systems, but these proved to be too fragile to carry such an array of signals. Upon the complaint of the regular telephone subscribers this "extraordinary electrical invention for the production of scientifically perfect music" stopped functioning.

The experiments of Thaddeus Cahill, who invented this instrument, were presented first in 1900. They came to the attention of Ferruccio Busoni when he read the July, 1906, article in *McClure's Magazine*, "New Music for an Old World," by R. S. Baker. At that time Busoni was writing his *Sketch of a New Esthetic of Music* which was published in 1907. In this remarkable collection of "notes," as he called the booklet, he questioned much of the prevailing music practice and pointed out some new possibilities. He wrote that art forms last longer if they stay close to the essence of each individual species. He suggested that music is almost incorporeal (he called it "sonorous air"), almost like Nature herself. He opposed formalism, systems, and routine, but asserted that each musical motive contains within itself its "life germ," the embryo of its fully developed form, each one different from all the others. He proclaimed that the creative artist did not follow laws already made; he made laws. Busoni decried a too rigid adherence to existing notation and said that the terms consonance and dissonance were too confining. He suggested an expansion of the major-minor-chromatic scale and assembled one hundred thirteen other scale formations within the octave C-C. (Ernest Bacon expanded this number by using algebraic permutations. Using intervals no larger than a major third he found one thousand four hundred ninety possibilities. See "Our Musical Idiom", *The Monist,* 1917, about this and other interesting matters.) Busoni predicted a revolution in the field of harmony. He was convinced that instrumental music had come to a dead end and that new instruments were needed, and he suggested a scale of thirty-six divisions within the octave as an interesting possibility for new music.

In Cahill's instrument Busoni saw a way out of the impasse which instrumental music had reached. However, he warned that a lengthy and careful series of experiments and further ear-training was necessary to make the unfamiliar material plastic and useful for coming generations. Two years after Busoni made these statements the Italian Marinetti published in *Le Figaro* in Paris his "Futurist Manifesto" which called for a world-wide artists' revolt against the ossified values of the past. The movement spread rapidly to Germany, Russia, and Switzerland.

"The Art of Noises," compiled in 1913 by Luigi Russolo, a painter, is still of interest. He suggested fixing the pitch of noise sounds and classi-fied them as follows:

Group 1	Group 2	Group 3
Booms	Whistles	Whispers
Thunder claps	Hisses	Murmers
Explosions	Snorts	Mutterings
Crashes		Bustling noises
Splashes		Gurgles
Roars		

Group 4	Group 5	Group 6
Screams	Noises obtained by	Voices of
Screeches	percussion or	animals, men
Rustlings	metals, wood,	Shouts
Buzzes	stone, and	Shrieks
Cracklings	terracotta	Groans
Sounds by		Howls
friction		Laughs
		Wheezes
		Sobs

In his diary about "Concrete Music"[4] Pierre Schaeffer names the precursor of the noise montage as it developed at the Centre d'Étude of the Radiodiffusion-Télévision Française by mid-century. Russolo imple-mented his catalogue of noises by building a whole collection of noise-making instruments. Futurism became Dadaism when Tristan Tzara coined the term in 1916 in Zurich. His recipe for making a poem still has a bear-ing on some of today's artistic manifestions: ". . . cut out the single words of a newspaper article, shake well in a bag, take them out one by one and copy them down in the order in which you picked them."

Between Busoni's booklet and the advent of Dadaism Schoenberg wrote his *Harmonielehre* (1911). In this important book triadic harmony evolved systematically and logically to a system of chords built on perfect fourths. The work ends with a prophetic statement about timbre melodies. And in 1913 the Paris premiere of Stravinsky's *Rite of Spring* took place. Orchestral rhythm and timbre were given a new dimension and the work had a profound effect on composers, indeed, on the art world in general.

When I met Busoni in Zürich in 1917, his views about composition had changed since 1907. On tour he had seen the German-American theorist Bernhard Ziehn in Chicago. Ziehn had published in 1887 a remarkable

[4] *Répértoire International des Musiques Experimentales* (Service de la Radio-Télévision Francaise, 1962).

harmony text which developed a system of symmetrical inversion based on the old Contrarium Reversum. When Busoni met him in 1910, he was engaged in developing a system of canonical techniques.

In his Zürich years Busoni assumed that composers who showed him scores would have mastered technical problems more or less by themselves. He expected experimentation and analysis; novelty for its own sake interested him no longer. He talked of form, not formula, and spoke, as he had written in the past, of taste, style, economy, temperament (human, not musical!), intelligence, and equipoise.

Edgard Varèse, friend and protégé of Busoni, and precursor of much that has happened, suggested in the early 1920's that greater cooperation between engineers and composers would be both desirable and necessary if the art were to reach new heights. Curiously enough, Carlos Chavez in his *Toward a New Music* (W. W. Norton, 1937) also expressed the hope that a collaboration between engineers and musicians would take place. Some of the results of this kind of cooperation have been and still are far reaching.

Joerg Mager built an electronic "Spharophon" in Germany which was presented at the Donaueschingen Festival in 1926. Supported by the city of Darmstadt he later developed a "Partiturophon" and a "Kaleidophon." All these useful electronic instruments had been tried in theatrical productions, and although all were destroyed in World War II, Mager's example animated others to explore the field. It was Friedrich Trautwein who introduced his "Trautonium" a few years later. It became a practical instrument that was used by a number of composers including Hindemith, Richard Strauss, and Werner Egk. Hindemith, in his *Craft of Musical Composition,* acknowledges his debt to Trautwein and his instrument for providing the foundation for many of the theses that he expresses in his book. The Hindemith-Trautwein research team was discontinued because of the war and was never active again, but improvements of the "Trautonium" by Oscar Sala resuled in the "Mixtur-Trautonium," a very brilliant instrument which Sala plays and for which he composes with skill. The German composers Henze, Orff, Erbse, and others have also composed for this instrument.

Leon Theremin introduced to Russia in 1923 the instrument bearing his name. A number of composers have used it in their compositions, among them Paschtschenko, Schillinger, Slonimski, Varèse, Grainger, Martinu, and Fuleihan. The Theremin-Cowell Rhythmicon, for which Cowell composed several pieces in 1932, could perform the most complicated kinds of polyrhythmic formations with clarity. Henry Cowell's tone-clusters, introduced to the wider public in the early 1920's, became the starting point for further extensions of piano resonance, for other preparations of the piano useful as sound sources for experimental music.

Just before and during the 1920's various kinds of research were brought into focus. For example, in the field of theory Ernst Kurth published his *Grundlagen des Linearen Kontrapunkts* (1917) and other works that dealt with musical form in Busoni's sense of the term, and in 1920 Josef Mathias Hauer presented his *Vom Wesen des Musikalischen: ein Lehrbuch der Zwölftonmusik*, followed by his *Zwölfton technik: die Lehre Von der Tropen* (1926). Schoenberg's ideas about a method for composing with twelve tones had crystallized by 1921. In France, Maurice Martenot demonstrated his Ondes Martenot in the Paris Opera on April 20, 1928. Nineteen years later he was Professor at the Paris Conservatoire, instructing classes in Ondes playing. A long list of composers have used the Ondes Martenot. They include Honegger, Milhaud, Messiaen, Jolivet, Koechlin, and Varèse. The inventor built a special model of the instrument in 1938 following specifications of Rabindranath Tagore and Alain Daniélou for the purpose of reproducing the microtonal refinements of Hindu music. Another invention of far reaching importance must be mentioned here. Lee DeForest, with inspired vision, thought first of the Audion (1906), now called the Triode. This and his three hundred other patents had a deciding influence on modern communications.

At the 1926 Chamber Music Festival in Donaueschingen in Germany it was suggested that recordings might be used as creative tools for musical composition. Two years later a research program was established at the Hochschule für Musik in Berlin to examine this and related problems. By 1930 Paul Hindemith and Ernst Toch had produced short montages based on phonographic speed-up and slow-down, sound transposition and mixing, as well as polyrhythmic experiments. Toch produced his *Fuge aus der Geographie*, a work based on four-part vocal choral writing. Hindemith used instruments and solo voice as his sound sources. Robert Beyer, in the article "Das Problem der Kommenden Musik", (*Die Musik,* Volume 19, 1928) had expressed new idea on space or room music but without having gained significant reactions from professionals and the public.

From the 1930's until after World War II much attention was given to producing electric instruments that could imitate existing instruments. At the same time the tape recorder was perfected and seemed destined to be used for creative purposes. Research and development took place, in part, at great institutions like the Bell Telephone Laboratories, the Brookhaven National Laboratories, the University of California, and the Institutes of Physics in Berlin and Moscow.

Pierre Schaeffer, an engineer in Paris, had presented a "Concert of

Noises" over the French Radio in 1948. He had arranged sounds from natural and instrumental sources into a series of montages, somewhat like the experiments by Hindemith and Toch in Berlin but with much greater freedom in sound and noise selection. The sounds were treated, manipulated, and presented from phonograph records. By 1952 Schaeffer was director of the research center of Radio-Diffusion Francaise and had associated himself with the engineer Poulin and, among others, the composers Jolivet, Messiaen, Pierre Henry, and Boulez. This group presented two concerts of Musique Concrete in the hall of the Conservatoire in May, 1952. A year later Schaeffer's *Orpheus* was first performed at the Donaueschingen Festival. The resulting scandal focused international attention on the new music. Since then the Paris radio has organized study groups, produced much music over the air and in concert, and built a concert hall to perform the music. Schaeffer has taken out many patents, notably those for the Phonogene and Morphophone, both used in the Paris center.

Valdimir Ussachevsky, born in China of Russian parents and educated in the United States, first experimented with tape in 1951, independent of the Paris group. His experiments were presented at Columbia University in May, 1952. At the Bennington Composers Conference in the fall of 1952 some short compositions by Ussachevsky and the present writer were performed. On October 28, 1952, in a concert at the Museum of Modern Art in New York, Leopold Stokowski introduced a work by Ussachevsky and three by this writer. Both composers used tape techniques, with flute and piano as sound sources. Thus, the pieces were called tape music. (For a description of the techniques see Vladimir Ussachevsky, "The Processes of Experimental Music," *Journal of the Audio Engineering Society*, July, 1958.)

The first public performance of a work for tape recorder and symphony orchestra was *Rhapsodic Variations* by the present writer and Vladimir Ussachevsky, a work commissioned by the Louisville Orchestra and programmed there March 20, 1954. It was during these years that the Columbia Studio was first established and the earlier works by Ussachevsky and Luening were produced with Peter Mauzey as consulting engineer. In 1959 with the help of a Rockefeller grant the Columbia-Princeton Electronic Music Center was established under the direction of Milton Babbitt and Roger Sessions from Princeton and Vladimir Ussachevsky and the present writer from Columbia. The Center has been active in advising other institutions about establishing studios. There are now seven in the United States and more are planned.

In 1955 the Radio Corporation of America demonstrated the Olson-Belar "Electronic Music Synthesizer" for the American Institute of Electrical

Engineers in New York. The concept of almost limitless possibilities of tonal synthesis was impressive. In 1958 Babbitt, Ussachevsky, and this author did research with the Synthesizer at RCA. A second model, Mark II, was lent to the Columbia-Princeton Center in 1959. My work *Dynamophonic Suite,* based on material from the Synthesizer manipulated on tape, was presented at the American Academy in Rome in 1958. Babbitt, who has been concerned with electronic music since the late 1930's, presented the first extended work for this medium, entitled *Composition for Synthesizer,* on May 9, 1961, at Columbia University. The output of the Synthesizer provided the sole material for the piece and it was not subjected to any further modifications.

On the same program my composition entitled *Gargoyles,* for violin and synthesized sound, was performed. The violin is played live; the sounds from the Synthesizer have been manipulated on tape. Appearing also on this program was Ussachesky's *Creation,* a work which combines a live chorus and solo voice with electronic sounds. The voices sing a tri-lingual text.

In Germany in 1948 H. W. Dudley from the Bell Telephone Laboratories demonstrated the "Vocoder," a composite device consisting of an analyzer and an artificial talker. This instrument and *The Mathematical Theory of Communication* (1949) by Claude Shannon and Warren Weaver made a strong impression on Dr. Werner Meyer-Eppler at the Phonetic Institute of Bonn University. Meyer-Eppler presented the "Vocoder" at the Northwest German Music Academy in Detmold where he gave a lecture," Developmental Possibilities of Sound," in 1949.

In 1950 Beyer, who had been present at Meyer-Eppler's lecture in Detmold, gave two lectures and Meyer-Eppler gave one lecture on "The World of Sound of Electronic Music." Varèse and Herbert Eimert attended. The next year Meyer-Eppler produced models of synthetic sounds at Bonn University and presented them at Darmstadt. On October 18 these experiments were broadcast over the Cologne Radio station and the staff recommended" . . . to follow the process suggested by Dr. Meyer-Eppler to compose directly onto magnetic tape." These events led to the creation of the "Electronic Studio" at the Northwest German Radio in Cologne. In 1952 Bruno Maderna composed his *Musica su due Dimensioni* for live instruments and electronic sounds. The preparation of the tape was made with the help of Meyer-Eppler. Pierre Boulez and Karlheinz Stockhausen heard the work in Darmstadt.

May 26, 1953, saw the first performance of works from the Cologne studio, works by Eimert and Beyer. Then in 1954 the studio gave a concert of purely electronic works by Goeyvaerts Pousseur, Gredinger, Eimert, and

Stockhausen. The compositions used a strict serial technique. The Cologne studio has had a study group for some time and last year appointed Stockhausen Artistic Director.

Luciano Berio first heard electronic music in 1956 at the Museum of Modern Art concert in New York. Two years later the "Studio de Phonologie Musicale de Milan" (RAI) was founded. Berio's *Mutazioni* and Maderna's *Sequenzi a Strutture* were performed that year, and since that time the studio has been opened to a number of composers from various countries.

The present state of electronic studio facilities has fairly complete documentation from 1948 through 1962 in the publication *Répértoire International des Musiques Experimentales*[5] which lists twenty-one studios in 1962. Since then another dozen have come to my attention including those at Brandeis, Yale, Wayne State, Pennsylvania, Michigan, San Francisco Conservatory of Music, and Bennington College.

[5] See footnote 4.

Elliott
Carter

[1908 -   ]

After majoring in English as a Harvard undergraduate, Carter began his musical studies at the graduate level, with Walter Piston, then went on to Paris for work with Nadia Boulanger. His position at St. John's College, in the early forties, where he developed the music part of the curriculum, was followed by other teaching work; at the same time, Carter was an active contributor to such journals as Modern Music. Not a facile composer, he did not begin to gain a major reputation for some years; today, however, he is one of the most important figures in contemporary music.

Carter's composition has developed slowly and consistently from a strong and cleanly orchestrated "American" style into a highly personal, tightly developed rhetoric that achieves originality on all levels of musical craftsmanship. One of the most influential of Carter's innovations has been "metric modulation," a means of obtaining overall structural rhythmic coherence in a composition by relating tempo in succeeding sections of a piece: a group of five notes against the two in a 2/2 bar, for example, becomes the norm for an immediately succeeding 5/4 section, and this in turn, perhaps re-signatured in 3/4, is once again used for another such change, each change shifting the fundamental pulse of the music. This facilitates in turn an immense range of subtlety of rhythmic interaction and voicing.

As a theoretician, Carter is eminently rational, eminently humanistic, eminently concerned with theory only as a vehicle for what will sound. He is a fluent and coherent writer and speaker, as the following material, from a Princeton seminar on new music, amply demonstrates.

"Shop Talk by an American Composer," from The Musical Quarterly, XLVI/2 (April 1960), 189-201.

Shop Talk
by an American
Composer

When I agreed to discuss the rhythmic procedures I use in my music, I had forgotten, for the moment, the serious doubts I have about just such kinds of discussion when carried on by the composer himself. That a composer can write music that is thought to be of some interest is, of course, no guarantee that he can talk illuminatingly about it. It is especially hard for him to be articulate because inevitably his compositions are the result of innumerable choices—many unconscious, many conscious, some quickly made, others after long deliberation, all mostly forgotten when they have served their purpose. At some time or other, this sorting and combining of notes finally becomes a composition. By that time many of its conceptions and techniques have become almost a matter of habit for the composer and he is only dimly aware of the choices that first caused him to adopt them. Finally, in an effort to judge the work as an entity, as another might listen to it, he tries to forget his intentions and listen with fresh ears. What he is aiming at, after all, is a whole in which all the technical workings are interdependent and combine to produce the kind of artistic experience that gives a work its validity and in so doing makes all its procedures relevant. There is no short-cut to achieving this final artistic relevance. No technique is of much intrinsic value; its importance for the composer and his listeners lies only in the particular use made of it to further the artistic qualities and character of an actual work. If in discussing his works, therefore, he points out a procedure, he is bound to feel that he is drawing attention to something of secondary importance and by dwelling on it misleading others into thinking of it as primary. Schoenberg expressed such doubts in essays on his use of the twelve-tone method. And he was right, for certainly the twelve-tone aspect of his works accounts for only a part of their interest, perhaps not the most important part. For from Opus 25 to his last works the number of different kinds of compositions he wrote illustrates the very broad range of expression and conception and the wide variety of musical techniques that can incorporate the system and yet be distinguished from it.

In any discussion of specifically contemporary procedures, there are a few serious risks involved that must be constantly borne in mind. The first is the danger of rapid and wide dissemination of oversimplified formulas that shortens their life. It is obvious that one technical fad after another has

swept over 20th-century music as the music of each of its leading composers has come to be intimately known. Each fad lasted a few years, only
to be discarded by the succeeding generation of composers, then by the
music profession, and finally by certain parts of the interested public. So
that through over-use many of the striking features of the best works lost
freshness; it was hard for those close to music to listen to these works for a
time, and many of the better works disappeared from the repertory without a
trace. Such a formula as the Impressionists' parallel ninth chords, for instance, wore itself out in the tedious arrangements of popular music current
until recently. Each of the trends of our recent past—primitivism, machinism,
neo-Classicism, *Gebrauchsmusik,* the styles of Bartók and Berg and now
those of Schoenberg and Webern—has left and will leave in its trail numbers of really gifted composers whose music, skillful and effective as it is, is
suffocated, at least for a time, by its similarity to other music of the same
type. Of course, ultimately this faddishness is trivial, but its mercurial
changes today have made the life of many a composer a great trial, more
even than in the time of Rossini, who is now generally thought to have
been one of the first outstanding composers to have given up composing
because he could not change with the times.

The tendency to fad has been greatly encouraged by the promulgation
of systems, particularly harmonic systems. Many recent composers following Schoenberg, Hindemith, and Messiaen have gained renown by circu-
lating descriptions of their systems even in places where their music was
not known. This kind of intellectual publicity can lead to a dead end even
more quickly than the older fads derived from the actual sound of music in
styles the composer did not even bother to explain.

The popularity of modern harmonic systems is, unfortunately, easy to
understand. Textbooks led music students to think of harmony as a well-
ordered routine, and when they found it to be less and less so in the years
from Wagner to the present, they were much troubled—and still are—by
the gap between what they learn and what they hear in modern music. For
mature composers, lack of system is usually not much of a problem since
they write, as they probably always have, what sounds right to them. This
"rightness" has come, I suppose, from a developed sensitivity and experience that take time to acquire. When modern systems of harmony that
were orderly and easy to explain appeared they filled an important pedagogical need for the inexperienced.

The very ease with which any of these systems can be used has its
obvious dangers, as I have said. With the help of these and other shortcuts
a vast amount of music is being written today, far more than can ever be
played, than can ever be judged or widely known. At the same time there
seems to be little corresponding development of discrimination, or even of

ability or desire to listen to new music, little expansion of opportunities for performance, at least in this country. The struggle to be performed and to be recognized makes it very hard for one not to become, even against one's will, some kind of system-monger, particularly if one uses certain procedures that are considered effective. For among students there is today a hunger for new formulas, and they constitute an interested public.

Obviously the only way to withstand the disturbing prospect of being swept away by a change in fad is to plunge into the even more disturbing situation of trying to be an individual and finding one's own way, as most of us have tried to do, not bothering too much about what is or will be sanctioned at any given moment by the profession and the public. We may then have to lead our lives producing works "too soon" for their time as Webern did, if they are not really "too late" since, if professional, they presuppose an attentive public which seems to be getting rarer. We are caught in a development dictated by convictions impossible to change with the fads.

All this is to say that I do not consider my rhythmic procedures a trick or a formula. I do not even feel that they are an integral part of my musical personality, especially in the way I used them in my First String Quartet (1951), which delves elaborately into polyrhythms. As I have suggested, all aspects of a composition are closely bound together, and for this reason I cannot give an orderly exposition of any without bringing in a large perspective of ideas. So I do not know where to begin, and I need your help in directing this discussion to regions that will be interesting and useful to you. Almost anything I might say, I suppose, preferably on musical subjects, might be considered relevant to the subject you have so kindly invited me to discuss here.

• *Question: In the program notes of your Variations for Orchestra which you wrote for the Louisville performance, you described your method of variation as being a method of transformation, which you compared to the transformation from one life-stage to another of some marine animals. What did you mean by this?*

• *Answer:*   As musicians you are all familiar with the problems of program notes. Technical discussions baffle the greater part of the audience and the few who do understand are apt to feel that the composer is a calculating monster, particularly since musical terms are ponderous, not always very definite in meaning, and too often give the impression of complexity when describing something very obvious to the ear. If I had described the augmentations, diminutions, retrograde inversions as they occur, this would have been positively bewildering to the public and would not have helped it to listen—certainly not the first time. So I tried to find a comparison that would help the listener to grasp my general approach. Serious music must appeal in different ways. Its main appeal, however, emerges from the quality of the musical material or ideas and perhaps even more from their use in significant continuities, but does not always depend on grasping the logic of the latter on first hearing. There has to be something left for the second time, if there ever is a second time.

As in all my works, I conceived this one as a large, unified musical action or gesture. In it, definition and contrast of character decrease during the first variations, arriving at a point of neutrality in the central variation, then increase again to the finale, which comprises many different speeds and characters. This work was thought of as a series of character studies in various states of interaction with each other both within each variation and between one and the next. Activity, development, type of emphasis, clearness or vagueness of definition, I hoped would also contribute to characterization. Form, rhythmic and development processes as well as texture and thematic material differ in each one for this reason.

The characteristic effort of the serious composer, as I see it, is not so much in the invention of musical ideas in themselves, as in the invention of interesting ideas that will also fill certain compositional requirements and allow for imaginative continuations. Serious music appeals to a longer span of attention and to a more highly developed auditory memory than do the more popular kinds of music. In making this appeal, it uses many contrasts, coherences, and contexts that give it a wide scope of expression, great emotional power and variety, direction, uniqueness, and a fascination of design with many shadings and qualities far beyond the range of popular or folk music. Every moment must count somehow, as must every detail. For a composer it is not always easy to find a passage that fits the particular situation and moment at which it appears in the composition, that carries to a further point some idea previously stated, that has the appropriate expressive quality motivated by what has been heard and yet is a passage that sounds fresh and alive.

As far as I am concerned, I am always interested in a composer's phrases and their shape and content, the way he joins them, the type of articulation he uses, as well as the general drift or continuity of a large section, and the construction of a whole work. The small details of harmony, rhythm, and texture fall naturally into place when one has interesting conceptions of these larger shapes.

- Q: *What do you mean by metric modulation?*
- A: If you listen to or look at any part of the first or last movement of my First String Quartet, you will find that there is a constant change of pulse. This is caused by an overlapping of speeds. Say, one part in triplets will enter against another part in quintuplets and the quintuplets will fade

265

into the background and the triplets will establish a new speed that will become the springboard for another such operation. The structure of such speeds is correlated throughout the work and gives the impression of varying rates of flux and change of material and character, qualities I seek in my recent works. The wish to accomplish this in the domain of heavily emphasized contrapuntal contrasts led me to work out the plan of metric modulation described by Richard Goldman.[1]

- Q: *Why are the contrapuntal lines in your quartet so much alike, using equal note-values?*
- A: You cannot have listened to the work very carefully or looked at the score. Of the nine notes in the first four measures, there are seven different lengths, the longest 18 times the shortest. There are, it is true, a few places near the beginning in which several contrapuntal parts each of equal note-values are combined, but in complete polyrhythmic contrast emphasized by intervallic, bowing, and expressive contrasts. In these I was particularly anxious to present to the listener the idea of polyrhythmic textures in its most definite form, for even this quality of texture develops during the work, leading, in the second movement, to a four-part fragmented canon in continuous sixteenths and, in later movements, to lines of much notational irregularity. But even if the values were more frequently equal than they are, as for instance in the polyrhythmic, posthumous Etudes of Chopin, I cannot see that this would be a real objection, as you imply. Many a fine work has dealt in continuous streams of equal note-values.

- Q: *Does your music have any harmonic plan?*
- A: A chord, a vertical group of pitches either simultaneously sounded or arpeggiated, like a motif, is a combination to be more or less clearly remembered and related to previous and future chords heard in the same work. Whether the composer is conscious of it or not, a field of operation with its principles of motion and of interaction is stated or suggested at the beginning of any work. The field may be tonal, employ traditional harmony, or it may be unrelated to traditional harmony, as my music seems to be nowadays, in which case I feel it imperative to establish clearly, near the beginning, the principles upon which the composition moves. Once this field of operation is established, its possibilities are explored, interesting new aspects of it are revealed, patterns of action of contrasting types emerge as the work goes along. A work whose world is not clearly defined loses a great deal of possible power and interest, one whose world is too narrow and restricted runs the risk of being thin, although if the world is unusual enough this narrowness can produce a kind of hallucinatory

[1] Richard Goldman, *The Music of Elliott Carter*, in *The Musical Quarterly*, XLIII (1957), 151.

quality—one that I do not concern myself with in my own works. This extension of the traditional methods of coherence can rarely be attained nowadays solely by intuition, I think, because of the vast number of musical means, new and old, that we know. Some composers, it is true, insulate themselves from new musical experiences in an effort not to be distracted. Others, whose curiosity and interest prompt them to follow what is going on, feeling, perhaps, as Charles Ives did, that "eclecticism is part of his duty—sorting potatoes means 'a better crop next year,'"[2] have to make a number of conscious choices and establish the frame in which to work before they can compose at all.

In my First String Quartet, I did use a "key" four-note chord, one of the two four-note groups, that joins all the two-note intervals into pairs, thus allowing for the total range of interval qualities that still can be referred back to a basic chord-sound. This chord is not used at every moment in the work but occurs frequently enough, especially in important places, to function, I hope, as a formative factor. It is presented in various kinds of part-writing and interval combination, the number of notes is increased and diminished in it, in ways familiar to all of you. The chord, here in its closest position, showing its content of intervals of a diminished fifth and less, is also used both in many intervallic inversions and in total inversion:

Here is an example of its use in counterpoint that occurs in measure 477 of the last movement, where the quality of the chord is strongly dwelt on —each vertical combination except the last being made up of it:

• Q: *Did you try to shape the free writing found in your quartet into formal patterns?*
• A: Since I consider form an integral part of serious music, I certainly did. Strange as it may seem, the intention of composing a work that depended so much on change of movement and polyrhythmic texture in-

---

[2] Charles Ives, *Essays Before a Sonata*, New York, 1920, p. 94.

volved me not only in special questions of clarity and audibility that one does not usually have to face, but in special problems of form also. One of the solutions I tried, to keep this rather free-sounding technique from seeming haphazard and thus lose its connection with the progress of the work and the attentive listener's ear, was to establish thematic patterns made up of components of different ideas that could be separated. This feature emerges in the last movement, many of whose motifs are disintegrated to produce polyrhythms. This is only one of the many ways I tried, hoping to give the impression of that combination of freedom and control that I greatly admire in many works of art.

- Q: *Do you use the twelve-tone system?*
- A: Some critics have said that I do, but since I have never analyzed my works from this point of view, I cannot say. I assume that if I am not conscious of it, I do not. Naturally out of interest and out of professional responsibility I have studied the important works of the type and admire many of them a great deal. I have found that it is apparently inapplicable to what I am trying to do, and is more of a hindrance than a help. Its nature is often misunderstood, it is a building material and not the building, and it allows, I think, for certain greater freedoms than were possible using traditional harmony with its very strict rules of part-writing, just as reinforced concrete allows for certain construction patterns impossible with stone. I must also say that having known many of these works all of my adult life, I hope the recent fad will not cause them to seem commonplace too soon. The results of total serialization are more recalcitrant to musical handling, I think.
- Q: *Do you mean to say that your rhythmic method is not a product of serialization?*
- A: It is not. But it is true that like all music, mine goes from one thing to another — the pattern on which serialization is based, but my choices of where to start and where to go are controlled by a general plan of action that directs both the continuity and the expression. Single details, chords, rhythmic patterns, motifs, textures, registers follow each other in a way that combines them into clearly perceivable larger patterns and then patterns of these patterns, and to me this cannot be easily accomplished with total serialization, at least the kind I study my way through in European articles these days. Perhaps another more useful and not so arbitrary kind of serialization could be devised. The present one resembles the turning of a

kaleidoscope and usually produces not much more—or less—interesting results. Indeed it can be fascinating to listen to the total repertory of pitches, note-values, timbres, registers, and dynamics being touched upon in rapid succession and from a point of view we are unaccustomed to. But the cumulative effect of this is self-defeating since neither the attention nor the memory is appealed to. For who can decipher, by ear, the complexities of total serialization in most works of the sort? On the other hand, those in which this process can be followed are too obvious to be of any interest.

• *Q: What is your attitude about performance difficulty?*

• *A:* I realize with brutal clarity that orchestral music requiring a lot of rehearsal can, by the nature of American musical life, find very few, if any, performances. This is not true of difficult music for soloists or small standardized instrumental groups, for obvious reasons. Our orchestral musicians are trained to play in the demanding scores of Strauss, Mahler, Debussy, Ravel, and early Stravinsky. One might imagine that one of the obligations of a present-day composer would be to use the skills of these excellently trained musicians to their full, lest their abilities deteriorate for want of use; that the challenge of good, effective yet technically advanced scores would be helpful in maintaining high performance standards in an orchestra, if not in raising them, as it did in the past. But this does not seem to be a consideration here, and, as you and I know, new works that make an immediate effect with a minimum of effort and time are favored. The real effort goes into the standard repertory, where it is more widely appreciated. Therefore, a composer who wishes to write orchestral music and get it played here has to tailor his work to these practical conditions, whether his ideas are suitable to such exploitation or not. Those who find that they can do nothing of interest under these conditions either give up writing orchestral music or, if they cannot, hope for European performances of their works. For these reasons, the scores of our composers often show a lack of practical experience that reveals itself in conventionality and timidity. How can a man be adventurous, under the circumstances that obtain here? Any casual look at the European scores written since the war will show how far in advance of us even beginners are there in this respect. As in many other things, we may be willing to accept the final, accomplished results of European training and experimental efforts but we cannot afford and are impatient with the step-by-step experience needed to produce them.

Naturally, music that is both difficult and yet practical to play is not easy to write, and it may even be difficult to listen to. It does not make for a comfortable life to have this as one's mode of expression. There is an undoubted beauty in reducing things to their essentials or to their simplest form if something is gained thereby. When a composer cannot find an interesting and satisfying way of writing easy music, he is at least free,

here, to use the level of difficulty he needs to set forth his ideas completely
—even if this results in no performances. But I see no reason for being
just difficult. Whenever difficult passages seem imperative in my works, I
try to make them especially rewarding once they are played correctly.

For I regard my scores as scenarios, auditory scenarios, for performers
to act out with their instruments, dramatizing the players as individuals and
participants in the ensemble. To me the special teamwork of ensemble
playing is very wonderful and moving, and this feeling is always an important expressive consideration in my chamber music.

• Q: *Have you ever thought of composing electronic music?*

• A: Naturally, I have often been intrigued with the idea of electronic
music and have visited the Milan electronic studio several times to find out
what is being done. I must say that almost all I have heard seems to me to
be in a primary stage, and has not resolved some fundamental problems of
matching and comparison of sounds that would raise it above the physical
scariness that makes this music useful for television science fiction and
horror programs. As far as composing it myself is concerned, you can
imagine that since I am very enmeshed in the human aspect of musical
performance, I would find it hard to think in terms of the impersonal sound
patterns of electronic music. Certainly, impatience at not being able to
hear my works in performance and impatience at the inaccuracies of some
performances have occasionally made me wish that I could have a machine that would perform my music correctly and without all the trouble
and possible disappointments associated with live performances.

• Q: *What do you think of Charles Ives now?*

• A: My opinions about Charles Ives as a composer have changed
many times since I first came to know him during my high-school years in
1924-25, but my admiration for him as a man never has. No one who
knew him can ever forget his remarkable enthusiasm, his wit, his serious
concern and love for music, and his many truly noble qualities which one
came to notice gradually because they appeared casually, without a trace
of pompousness, pretention, or "showing off." Attracted to him by a
youthful enthusiasm for contemporary music, I first admired, and still do,
the few advanced scores privately available in those days, the *Concord
Sonata,* the *Three Places in New England,* and some of the *114 Songs.*
However, after I had completed strict musical studies here and abroad, I
saw these works in a different light. Misgivings arose which I expressed
with considerable regret in several articles in *Modern Music* after the first
performance of the *Concord Sonata* in New York in 1939. My doubts were
of two kinds. First, there seemed to be very large amounts of undifferentiated confusion, especially in the orchestral works, during which many
conflicting things happen at once without apparent concern either for the

total effect or for the distinguishability of various levels. Yet in each score such as the *Robert Browning Overture,* the *Fourth of July,* and the second and fourth movements of the Fourth Symphony where this confusion is most frequent, it is the more puzzling because side by side with it is a number of passages of great beauty and originality. Even more disturbing to me then was his frequent reliance on musical quotations for their literary effect. In spite of these doubts, I continued for many years to help bring Ives's music before the public since he would do nothing for himself, rescuing, among other things, *The Unanswered Question* and *Central Park in the Dark* from the photostat volumes of his work he had left with the American Music Center. I arranged for first performances of these at a Ditson Fund Concert at Columbia University in, I think, 1949.

What interests me now is his vigorous presentation in music and essays of the conflict between the composer with vision and original ideas, the musical profession, and the American public. It is the living out of this conflict, made poignant by his strong convictions, the anger it produced, the various actions and attitudes it led him to, the retreat into a subjective world, and, unfortunately, the terrible toll of energy and health it took, that makes of Ives an artist really characteristic of America, not unlike Melville. Without the dimension of this struggle and the quality it gave his scores, his *Emersons* and *Hallowe'ens* would be of superficial and transitory interest.

His rage, which explodes between the waves of his transcendental visions in prose as it does in the scribbled comments in the margin of his musical manuscripts, reveals troubled concern over the problems of the American composer and his relations with the public. The music profession is castigated in one place as being more hide-bound, more materialistic, petty, bigotted, and unprincipled than the business world. The latter, his refuge from the bleak, meager life of the conventional American musician of his time, he respected and identified himself with enough to adopt an American business man's view of the artistic profession, one that was especially characteristic of that time of wealthy art-collectors. Making of the artist an anti-business man, Ives saw him as a prophet living in the pure, transcendent world of the spirit, above the mundane matters of money, practicality, and artistic experience. The 19th-century American dream of art and high culture, which Henry James liked to project against the sordid European background from which it came, was the source, as Aaron Copland and Wilfrid Mellers have pointed out, of Ives' greatest misfortune. In gradually retiring into this dream, he cut himself off from music's reality. Too many of his scores, consequently, were never brought to the precision of presentation and scoring necessary to be completely communicative to the listener — or so it seems now. One could say that

271

Ives was unable completely to digest his experience as an American and make it into a unified and meaningful musical expression. The effort of remodelling the musical vocabulary to meet his own personal vision, almost without encouragement or help, was too great, and too often he had to let hymn tunes and patriotic songs stand for his experience without comment.

As I have said, Ives's life vividly presents the special conflicts inherent in the American composer's situation. Today, even more than in his time, the division between the musician's professional code of ethics, his traditional standards of skill and imagination established at another time in another place, and the present standards of behavior respected, sanctioned, and rewarded by the society that surrounds us, is very pronounced. The familiar training of a composer giving him knowledge and skill in the accumulation of musical techniques, past and present, and the development of skill in notating them, presupposes trained copyists and performers who can grasp what he means and respect his notations. It also presupposes critics and, if not a large public, at least an influential élite that will be able to perceive the sense of the composer's efforts and skill, value them and enable him to develop them further, by giving them careful consideration. When one or more of the links in this chain is not sufficiently developed or non-existent, as is often the case here today, the composer has a bitter fight just to keep his skill, let alone develop it.

This misfortune can be laid to the general lack of unanimity about and concern for the profession of composing on the part of the mass musical public that plays such an influential financial role in America. By training, the composer learns to write for a musically educated public that is also an influential élite, which does not exist and may never exist here. He cannot help but feel that he will be heard by a large majority of listeners and even performers that disagree with him, if they have any opinions at all, on the most fundamental issues of his art. Questions of style, system, consonance, dissonance, themes, non-themes, being original or an imitator, which imply some agreement on fundamentals, are not the stumbling blocks. A professional composer has today, as Ives certainly had, the training to be "communicative," "melodious," "expressive," qualities considered to have a wide appeal, just as he is now trained to use advanced techniques that will be appreciated by only a few professionals. How shall he decide? He is free, here, to do what he likes, of course, but it does not take him long to realize that whatever he chooses to do, radical or conservative, his music will further divide into small sub-groups the handful of people who will listen to contemporary music at all. Not one of these small sub-groups has the power or the interest to convince the large public by publicity or other means of the validity of its opinions, as happens in the other arts here. While diversity of opinion is much to be welcomed, where so little support exists such decimation of interest, one hesitates regretfully to conclude, can lead to cancelling of efforts and ultimately to their negation.

Even America's panacea, publicity, seems strangely useless in this field. Good reviews do not, often, lead to further performances, but they do help to sell more recordings. One might have thought that Ives, now so much discussed and publicly admired, would be often heard. That a number of his recordings have been discontinued, that only a few of his easiest pieces are heard while some of his more remarkable works are still unplayed or scarcely known, is surely an indication of how confused and desperate is the relation between the composer, the profession, publicity, and the musical public.

Stefan Wolpe

[1902 - 1972]

Born in Berlin, a student of Ferruccio Busoni, Anton Webern, and Hermann Scherchen, Stefan Wolpe emigrated from Nazi Germany in 1934 and taught composition at the Jerusalem Conservatory. In 1938 he came to the United States, where for years he was known to only a few fellow composers. Wolpe's music began to receive more frequent performances in the years following World War II, and today he is regarded as one of the major influences on the younger composer.

Thinking Twice, one of a group of lectures on Wolpe's musical poetics, presents the composer's highly individual approach and personal solutions to problems raised by the serial hypothesis, including questions of pitch-set selection, intervallic grouping, formal processes, and historical contingency. Wolpe's exposition charges the quantitative with the qualitative by always engaging the musical medium as a whole. It is revealing that in his speech, as in his music, structure is everywhere expressive and expression is always structured.

Originally presented as a lecture at the University of California, Los Angeles, in 1959, *Thinking Twice* was edited by Austin Clarkson, under the author's supervision, for the present volume.

Thinking
Twice

No one can blur the evidence of the light's ravishing speed. No one can dissuade an apple from falling as no one has the strength to withhold his breath.

Laws of nature can't be bent into modifying the nature of laws, but one can sit out history and its yesterdays' implications. Many have tried so. But, having taken their judgments for granted, they find themselves confronted by the turntables of history and, being like waves that try to stick to the ground, they fight or give up or wither away. The better among them are dissatisfied by the images of their art which have become flat and dull.

One has to practice one's art with a knowing sense of its radical nature. Because substance is radical (as the nerves are, and the mind that attests to the making of substance) one is touched, initiated, formed by experiencing the traces, pressures, compressions of musical substance. This substance behaves with all its fierce contractions:

interhinging the sequences of tones into cogent levels of shapes, interlapping them into internalized, center-bound, concentric rows of pitches, pitch-aggregates, of sounds, of sound-aggregates. It also behaves as an outwardly spreading, extensively trajecting force,

impulse-driven, eccentric, in full release of width, of an outside spatial dimension, of furtherness and farness. The substance affirms the double-content of nature: to be core and inwardly held, to be form and mould which are extended into and outwardly grasped.

These are basic manifestations of musical substance, and one's attitude must remain ever alerted by examining, rigorously and without fear, how much history one carries along with oneself, and whether this load, in effect, interferes with a radical attack on all genuinely fresh musical problems. The less history is repeated, the more unique is the moment's time and all that rests wholly on the moment's total dedication. A moment will crystallize as history after it has existed within all its momentary actuality. Then truly will the moment be rallied into the vast depths of time which history is: the ever-restored and ever-advancing moment.

Since the twelve-tone chromatic set has become the master set and the principal source of generating musical material, one acquiesces to the state of balance for which its closed circuit provides. Each tone, each collection of tones within this circuit is complementary to the remaining tones. Thus the remaining tones that close the circuit are, in turn, complementary to the succeeding tones, which force the circuit open again. This mechanical chromatic rotation of the static quantity of twelve tones is offset by the shift of grouping that takes place among the tones and that accounts for the change of course of the tones and their aggregates.

Thinking
Twice

The saturated balance of twelve tones is partly very mechanistic and neutral in quality, though the order of the twelve undoubtedly renders the circuit as particular. Yet the relationship between the static character of the material and the dynamics of its structural formations remains problematical in view of its fixed and unalterable content of pitches. No amount of transposition, permutation, and the various modes of projection and exposure of a twelve-tone set, no amount of dislocation or multiplication of sets in motion can relieve the ear from hypertrophic abundance of a pitch-totality that, in this exclusive form, must stagnate.

The tempo of structural transformation should influence the tempo of chromatic circulation, and every possible modification of speed of chromatic circulation shall be built into the structural chart of pitch-operations. Generally, one understands the all-chromatic circuit as an equilibrium of tones whose centralizing effects result from consecutive realizations of complementary pitch relations. Through progressive summations of single pitch-strands, the center is extended throughout the compositional space. The concept of the permanence of a fully packed twelve-tone circuit, and of its total reproduction (with all its unrelieved finality), the concept that the coherence of the whole-of-the-unity-of-pitches has to be continually restored — such a concept of an equilibrium of unified pitches, of a pitch-totality, is classical thinking. As such, it is, at least at this moment, an undissolved remainder of the contextual properties of tonality and of that obsessive preoccupation (in an early phase of atonality) with decomposing historically-encrusted formations of sound.

If the center is extended throughout the compositional space, then all the sectors in it, fed by their share of the center, become centers themselves. From this one can infer that the all-chromatic chain

can be unhinged, its sections interrupted, isolated, and arrested.

**Stefan
Wolpe**

A constellatory space (to avoid the term "thematic space") will then be established in which the elements – the tones – are fashioned according to the degree of precompositional selectivity.

One may decide to give to a certain number of tones a greater preponderance in time, to enhance acutely the plasticity of their pitch arrangements. This requires revising one's attitude toward the multiplication of tones on different registers (levels). Every new pitch combination involving the same tone alters its former identity. A tone's identity shifts according to its context. The dynamics of its response changes when changes take place in its intervallic engagements.

Thus a given tone may appear with different frequencies at different levels; it may appear freely at any level, fixed at a particular level, or alternating between levels. This is valid as a means of disconnecting, disturbing – thereby differentiating – the exclusive continuum of the all-chromatic

278

circuit. Either pitch-sectors are isolated and their performance sustained, their articulation focused, or the orbit of twelve is widened to a larger one of fifteen or more tones.

A given tone may then be presented either several times under conditions of different intervallic constellations, or in isolated position,

[All pitches repeated in various registers]

or it may be given a particular order in regard to frequency or repetition,

Stefan
Wolpe

sust. ped.

spatial position,

In wide spaces

rather quick ♩ = ca. 66

**Thinking
Twice**

place within a sound, function within an ensemble, etc. Any axis interval of a seventh or ninth can paralyze the zero qualities of octaves or octave multiples.

Likewise, any complex interval (meaning a combination of an axis interval of a seventh or ninth with one of the remaining, differentiating intervals) can do the same.

Or any other more diversified intervallic conglomerations can equally well interfere with, counter-focus, all those variants of a prime which are congruous with each other.

282

Octaves and their multiples are no longer heard with a tonal ear as being the aggrandizing extension of a fundamental tone. The growing complex of intervallic conglomeration effects the progressive differentiation of the minimum tone, the minimum axis interval, or the minimum complex interval.

Its maximum extension of chromatic growth indicates either its qualitatively most supreme and non-exceedable stage,

or its most neutral and average one. If whatever happens does happen
within an arc whose opposite poles are equivalent, and thus interchangeable, then the total chroma (colorfulness) of a tone must equal its minimum
chroma, and must also equal all the multiple exposures of this tone in all
its manifold octave levels.

The maximum pitch differentiation within a conglomeration of sound (the maximum chroma)

may be adjacent to the single tone and its many congruities (the minimum chroma).

Since both are equivalent they are also ambiguous and interchangeable. Either one is capable of being the extreme at either end of the arc; either may be the average and neutral,

Stefan
Wolpe

or the exceptional and the most "differentiated".

The most densified mass of a most diversified, all-intervallic sound corresponds to the shrivel of a shredded tone. The concept of equivalence of opposites has led to the practice of a discontinuum, which also could be understood as instantaneous transformation. Provided one allows for a change of speed in the tempo of transformation, the classical concept of gradualness will be on one end of the arc which stretches through the gamut of speedier transformations to the other end where the instant conversions magically take place. In a continuum of adjacent opposites, the asymmetry in the sequences of sensations of mass and chroma of sound is not the only asymmetry. Every element, in an ensemble of those elements that constitute the musical language, is affected by it: time, space, inflection, proportion, course and character of events and of their coordinations, the level of articulation of ideas, their organic quality, their generic quality—all these defining factors are affected by it.

Every pitch constellation smaller than the all-chromatic circuit is either a delay in completing the whole,

or is an autonomous fragment which can exist outside of the total circuit.

It may be first unhinged as a part of the total circuit, later hinged back at various degrees of speed, either absorbing stepwise the remaining parts of the circuit, or taking them over in chunks or as a whole. In any way, the modified speed of the all-chromatic circuit points to a concept of modulatory circulation, to an increase or decrease of pitch quantities. This happens either within a given total-set,

or within autonomous fragments of such a set. It may then generate complementary, transpositional units to approach, at various degrees of speed, the total or near-total chromatic circuit.

Stefan
Wolpe

Slow accumulation of the total chromatic circuit

[O] [I] [O] [O]
1 new pitch 2 new pitches 3 new pitches

Quick accumulation of the total chromatic circuit

[O] [RI] [R]
4 new pitches 2 new pitches

These are diversionary tactics, certainly, yet the slower the speed of complementary circulation, the more focal the various pitch regions become. A distinct spectralization of pitches is the result. The concept of an autonomous fragment could also help shape multiple twelve-tone extensions of homogeneous or heterogeneous intervallic groups, as I have shown in my *Passacaglia for Piano* from the year 1936.[1]

[from my Passacaglia]

thirds fourths

major sixths minor sevenths

major sevenths

Here are sets of thirds, of fourths, of major sixths, of minor sevenths, and of major sevenths. An interval or an intervallic group that otherwise belongs to a larger set just breaks off and generates the series of intervals of which it is part. It is a kind of revived neighbor-note action — that is, it

[1] Published in *New Music Edition*, 1946. *Passacaglia* is discussed by Edward Levy in "Stefan Wolpe," *Perspectives of New Music* (Fall-Winter 1963), p. 56.

includes and activates subdivisionary orbits within the more central and obligatory ones. Here, for example, is a fragment from a larger pitch-set.

The extension into a twelve-tone set of the minor sixth, the minor seventh, and the major seventh, or of possibly any other interval, neutralizes for a moment the entire set.

**Stefan
Wolpe**

They exist, if one recognizes them, as a vocabulary of a stationary character. There are others, like thirdless four-tone aggregates of two tritones, that will result either in similar homogeneous intervallic twelve-tone structures,

or in the all-interval set obtained through stepwise contractions of intervals from a major seventh downward.

Thinking Twice

It is not for reasons of any distributive (and combinatorial) fancy that I speak about the autonomous fragment and its distinct spectrumlike distribution of pitches. Neither have I in mind to mention merely as technicalities the divergent and parenthetical projection of homogeneous intervallic twelve-tone structures. In this respect, it is important to have an area of neutralization that uses pitch-orders of a more common or lower grade. Important, too, is the structuring of pitches in accordance with specific organizational modes, categorical arrangements in respect to everything that pertains to any kind of pitch structure either inside or outside the all-chromatic circuit. The same applies to constellations whose number of pitches is reduced to, say, five or seven tones. They exist then under conditions of a sort of rotary omnipresence. To have a more systematic differentiation of formalized quantitative and qualitative—that is, morphological—relationships is significant: frequency of performance of certain intervallic groups (their numerical fate), the type of their spatial performance, their structural behavior.

I in 3 different ways II at wide, open distances III canonic plus verticalized sound, diagonal

Since the chromatic totality of pitches is an assumption of complementary conditions, fragmentary units either strive to restore the all-chromatic equilibrium, or may strive for a more gradual restoration, possibly delayed and possibly interrupted. All of it matters, and all of it becomes regulatory. The autonomous fragment, released from the larger total set, feeds on itself and exists in terms of its own equilibrium, although every pitch-body, even the smallest and even the least chromatic, rests ultimately within the total chromatic orbit.

This chromatic orbit is a twelve-tone-functioning, self-enclosed circuit in which each of the twelve tones is a complementary condition of the other tones. But every pitch-body, even the smallest and even the least chromatic, though resting within the total chromatic orbit, can also dispense with that orbit, provided a pitch-field reduced to any smaller size is set up containing the necessary fixed pitches, which then maintain the equilibrium with their inter-rotating moves. Equilibrium is not a matter of quantities but of a specific condition under which these pitch quantities act. Where one deals with an autonomous fragment, the attitude toward the all-chromatic set is one of decentralization—the set is loaded with possibly shifting focal areas. Decentralization, or the interference with a total-pitch continuum, is a form of its differentiation.

The quantitative modification of the set, whether by regulating the tempo of chromatic circulation or by isolating autonomous fragments, disturbs the total chromatic equilibrium. This modification also disturbs the tautological forms of the set's chromatic accumulation. Such selectivity and specialization in the nature of pitch-sequences are of great value in sharpening the distinctness of varied pitch-group sensations. It is also of great value in lessening fatigue from constantly excessive pitch combinations. By excess is meant the constant feeding of a tone with the total chromatic range of its complementary tones. The all-chromatic circuit, or the all-chromatic engagement of a tone, derives its basis from historical conditions of a material that formerly required the radical liquidation of even faintly tonal traces and patterns. Only a hermetically closed chromatic circuit with all its chromatic provisions, its all-chromatic space, seems then to be the guarantee of complete alienation from a historical climate of elements and patterns.

Historical properties don't remain the same. A third today is not the third of a triad, and the triad is not the triad of the triad. Those sounds are produced by engagements with at least one axis interval of a seventh or ninth.

Whether these are actually, or only associatively, engaged with them, makes no difference. They are alienated from their former sources and though classical phenomena can—and cannot—be interpreted in contemporary terms, contemporary phenomena can—and often cannot—be interpreted in classical terms. Take that old babe, the scale fragment C to G:

It now is either part of the whole chromatic gamut:

or, as an autonomous fragment, it is a pitch-fixed settlement, a definite pitch constellation, with all the attributes of its structural content.

293

**Stefan
Wolpe**

Historical unsettlings, derangements of concepts, the anti-dogmas, always take place as history leaps into successive phases. Changed then are anticipatory expectations that are connected with the notion of conceptual attitudes. The all-chromatic continuum becomes questionable or insufficient as the exclusive source for content-making material.

As one accepts the adherence of the discontinuum to the practice of the all-chromatic continuum, one will have freed oneself from a fatal obsession. Take any twelve-tone series. I have already spoken about the possible extension into fifteen or more tones, or the working with multiple exposures of a series — multiple series. There is no reason why more radical manifestations shouldn't exist on a more elemental level: the series is an order of succession of tones that gives to each of them a precise position and formal reference. A serial tone is not a thing merely evincing sensations of general audibilities, but as a tone it is a specific pitch link within the context of others. From this context is derived the tone's acute reality as a pitch. The further enhancement of the pitch's reality is then accomplished in shaping pitch combinations and pitch distributions into shapes, forms, states, and processes.

Since the musical space is multi-dimensional, the series (though seen as a horizontal progression)

unfolds in simultaneous, multidimensional moves.

One is used to thinking of a series in terms of a maximum amount of combinatorial flexibility. The crystallizing and interconnecting of ever-freshly-conceived, generated, released aspects is precisely what keeps it from being stagnant and dropping dead. Or, to put it differently, being a series means a relentless mobility of cutting, folding, stratifying serial aspects, layers, levels. Each tone within the set is equally aroused to do it, equally capable, an equal spatial component. Each serial tone's faculty is of the *same* order, of the *same* serial fate: to be focused or unfocused. Because of each tone's serial omnipresence, there are perhaps no focuses. Yet the organizational mode, the organizational assignment of serial tones or serial segments could be radically different.

Instead of hexachordal, tetrachordal, or other divisions that only satisfy claims for symmetrical correspondences or for reductions in the number of intervallic cells within the series, the reproductive, combinatorial activity is applied to zones—that is, half of the serial area is, for example, dynamic and progressive, the other half is stagnant, repetitive, and fixed. One zone is in motion, the other is motionless, one mobile, the other dead, one warm, the other cold. While one is freed from the order of stepwise pitch successions, the other clings to the protocol of the serial, the alphabetical order. One invites restrictive obligations. For what? To sharpen one's attentions. Why? To enter different levels of consciousness, different stages of sensibilities, to become aware that difference is a difference in degrees of an actual internal depth, of an actual internal stretch that separates a musical object from the ultimate reduction to its core. This is what is meant if one speaks of optimal conditions to which a musical event has been raised. The idea of a musical process has to be understood in these terms: that it takes time, musically composed time, to break the resistance that those very different stages of a not-yet-fully-revealed musical idea offer. In setting up areas of committed serial material, boundary situations offer that resistance which the musical mind is trying to break. In trying to reach inside of it, the mind grows. If the mind grows, the mind will move towards those concentrated and most summary stages on which any musical object's self-identity rests.

Serial limitations are areas of defined sensibilities.

No series is an absolute continuum. Such it is if one needs it to be. If one doesn't, it isn't.

Parts, segments, zones of the series (the autonomous fragments) take over a shrunken continuum. The one is reasonable, its serial order is stable and reliable. The other, if in use, is a dis-continuum. The serial order is anarchic, ambiguous, at random. It is convertible and alternate.

A pitch can turn into a noise, a noise into a diphthong, a diphthong into a fragmented word, a fragmented word into quoting anything, because everything is open and everything becomes adjacent. The bird sits on the typewriter that settles on a river's bed and the ripples of water reflect the smile of children carrying an antenna to listen to sermons given long, long, long ago.

Thus wonders can happen, and the containment of pitches is fighting for an exit away from pitch into noise, away from noise into sensations whose complicity with the community of senses can be traced back to abandoned and daily neglected rituals.

The discontinuum may show strange features. In opposition to the inviolable order of pitch sequence in what was called the continuum, tones may be dropped, later resumed. They may exist in bundles of alternatives, of noise or other sensations. They may multiply themselves, run out of gear in any other way. They may exist only under special level conditions (and their alternatives). Their pitch elements may exhibit the strangest possible musical climate with formations decomposed into slang or quotational material; or authentic formations may simultaneously run together with their decomposed formations — and so on.

It would require the vast lucidities of aural anticipation to codify in advance all that could happen if a serial continuum were connected to a serial, half-serial, non-serial discontinuum.

I am reminded of the lines by William Blake:

To cast off Rational Demonstration by Faith in the saviour,
To cast off the rotten rags of Memory by Inspiration.

I am tempted to paraphrase Blake's lines:

To cast off rational demonstration by purging oneself of expectations,

— yes! To retain the witnessing memory which evades the sling of the past, to enter the never-cohering moment,

With none of the terms and none of the seasons of time
A disorientation of dreams
An experience of suspension.

If the discontinuum takes that turn, it is not to depose the pride of man's rationale, it is to invite him to observe and take notes in the dark, to watch the game of disengaged sensations, the infinite intercourse of conditions, of scattered calls, moves, haunted responses, of shape, of stuff, of pulse — of failures, of death, secretive cues, incredible transformations — a leaf caught in the mouth — a tone caught in silence.

Art indeed moves on excessive grounds of exaggerated restraint and of violent exaggerations. Every problem defines itself within a total arc of interrelated opposite poles — that is, that opposites become adjacent to each other. Since the non-exceedable extreme lies on both ends of the arc (and both ends have become adjacent to each other), and the extremes of both sides are each other's equivalents, a concept of fusion, or elimination of irreconcilable opposites, reveals itself as the norm.

A sound's protrusion and recession
violence and stillness

A sound's mass and its fraction all become contiguous.
The leap is next to the step,
The infinite farness recoils into infinite closeness.

Manifest become the breakages in the continuum of form: the ruptures of dynamics, the accumulation of perspectives and a sort of expansion in reverse, where, in the shortness of projection, a shrinking time is revealed within the sum of intensely heightened moments.

The consequences are penetrating, because the double content of a single phase of action points to the multidimensional space. Its multiple dimensions are simultaneously in motion, meeting and intersecting at points of highly diverse and diverging directions. The total spatial traffic is engaged. The zig-zags and curves and multispatial moves, the manifold opposites, with all their multiple modifications — isn't this the oneness of space in action?

Expanding, contracting, interrotating, interlayering
all-complementary opposites
oneness of space.
Void also, and nothing may happen
or a state of stasis
or impulses of a shortest while,
   a sound
   a noise
   a soundless duration.

That lost gradualness, the slow evolution, the anticipatory cause of action, the syntactical organization (bringing about the slowly cohering thoughts and their progressive persistence in the dimension of time), they all may come back as strange wonders separated from an elaborate system of an earlier architecture of quickly grasped but slowly evolving relations. They all may come back (and they do) as an extreme condition, as a terrorizing *ennui*, as a trap, as an organism with a low structure and a mediocre purpose, a broken needle, a torn stamp, a potato peel.

Thinking
Twice

The very core of even the smallest intent of action is antinomic, by which is meant the concept of adjacency of otherwise irreconcilable opposites. Where there is unified, centrally guided coordination of elements within a functional ensemble, there is its breakdown:

> dissociation of activities
> non-gradualness
> decentralization
> shift of centers — of multiple centers —

of a release of forces independent of each other to the extent of bringing about new types of contrasting modes of action, of contrasting organic modes. They will determine a proper kind of fluctuating continuity. The re-orientation demands asymmetry in the sequence of events. Since the sequence of events must ultimately have something to do with content — a making of some kind, of any kind, or of a very rarefied kind — an asymmetrical sequence of events brings together all possible — possibly all most disparate, incompatible, incongruous — aspects of one, or more than one, event.

Since every situation exists anticipatorily within reach of its latent extreme, and extremes are adjacent equivalents, then there is no longer necessarily any definite order in the sequence of events. As to the space, whatever may be the summary interplay of its dimensions, you are in it or out of it. If you are in it, then you grasp its total condition, and wherever you start, it's neither a beginning nor an end, it is its partial condition. You are always in a situation which cannot exist without the complementary conditions of its participating dimensions. Space does not know of any difinite or more tangible order of dimensions.

The concept of an asymmetrical sequence of events means, in simplér words, a particular disinterest in affirming what is, unless it includes the affirmation of not being it, though it is. The statement moves in inverse directions. It is the minumum step within the space of thoughts, comparable to the participating complementary dimensions of space itself.

One makes a statement and destroys it.

**Stefan
Wolpe**

One makes a statement and can't recall it.

One delays a statement and then makes it.

One can't recall the statement one wants to make, and then one makes it just the same.

There is a space-like omnipresence of a great many aspects of an event. The empirical notion of any one-dimensional (that is, causal and argumentative) connection between aspects of an event renders the event conditional and one-sided. The process of gradual approach serves only to narrow the view.

To move in all directions, because all aspects are exposed to each other in that space of omnipresent notions, will yield the view from all sides. Everything becomes connectable, and, because there is no hierarchic order of succession, everything is equally prophetic, and all-inclusively discovered and revealed. Development, or the course of action, would then be the incessant exposure of aspects and their spatial integration (which is another incessancy).

An audacious sense for a highly elastic shiftiness of quantitative action will replace the older predictable numerical deals:

> much with nothing
> little with none
> more with nothing.
> nothing with much.

An audacious sense for an extreme shiftiness of qualitative action will replace the older complacency that sits near one's grave. It will replace the causal order of its forces, of its naturalistic sequences, where it seems that the climactic state does not precede the state of averages, where growth cannot result from diffuse or interrupted forces, where randomness cannot agree with and cannot be correlated to procedures of intentional organization. Of course it can—by the very plain fact that every action and every problem defines itself within an arc of interrelated opposite poles in which they become adjacent and equivalent.

The form must be ripped endlessly open and self-renewed by interacting extremes of opposites. There is nothing to develop because everything is already there in reach of one's ears. If one has enough milk in the house, one doesn't go to the grocery store. One doesn't need to sit on the moon if one can write a poem about it with the twitch of one's senses. One is there where one directs oneself to be. On the back of a bird, inside of an apple, dancing on the sun's ray, speaking to Machaut, and holding the skeleton's hand of the incredible Cézanne—there is what there was and what there isn't is also. Don't get backed too much into a reality that has fashioned your senses with too many realistic claims. When art promises you this sort of reliability, this sort of prognostic security, drop it. It is good to know how not to know how much one is knowing. One should know about all the structures of fantasy and all the fantasies of structures, and mix surprise and enigma, magic and shock, intelligence and abandon, form and antiform.

The non-cohering moment is to read simultaneously in different directions of meanings, to let everything in but to make decisions beforehand and appoint areas toward which to direct the meanings:

What is flat and what is dense, and what flat-with-dense can do.

What is thick and what is brittle, and what the thick can take from the brittle.

What is inert and what is a flickering, and how the flickering can tap the inert.

What one, what two, what four, what seven pitch trajectories can do. Where the first flies rapidly, the second flies in hesitation, the third halfway collapses, and the seventh is an interferer.

Through all this sound moves—free, liberated, unhinged sounds of a hundred changing volumes, or of the inertness of a doubly-dead rat. Sounds of an utter inevitability, or an utter soberness, of strictly selected, codifiable distinction, sounds moving in multi-dimensional space formations, in multiple exposures, sounds composed of special proportions of width, narrowness, curvature, accumulation, dissolution, fragmentation, interference: all simultaneous, or all separate.

The projection of these and similar adjacent opposites is not the only cause for concern, although a concept of non-gradualness, of non-causal, non-transitional, non-process-like thinking leads to a regeneration of expressive musical phenomena. It offers the cold, the shabby, the hard, the sudden, the inanimate, the rigid, the confused, the joke, the excess, the dense, the dropping; the most general, unlayered, flat; the extraordinary, highly layered, highly charged; the loose, the tattered, the inordinate, nothing much, the perpetual, the always interrupted; shock and the ever-extending opposites; the simultaneous, the quotational; the noise.

The connection of these phenomena of expressive conditions is, of course, based on a reasoning that promotes causes, yet with consequences in reverse. Virtually everything, then, is admitted, provided it is included in an asymmetrical sequence of events that no hierarchic order either precedes or controls, for, in a total-dimensional space of events, all dimensions (that is, all their aspects) equal each other. The inter-relation of adjacent opposites — supremely distinct as they both are — must lead to a state of undifferentiation, centralization, and loss of scope — that is, loss of compelling choice. In that total-dimensional space of infinite aspects of events and their shifting positions, there are also infinite choices for which there is either an infinite number of necessities or none — that is to say, an infinite number of ambiguities.

One observes, perhaps with amazement (or with discomfort), the replaceable necessities. Though it is true that only those things are happening which one wishes to happen, one discovers with amazement (or with discomfort) that that which is happening can exist (without changing one's wishes) under infinitely replaceable conditions. Entangled in a dilemma of infinite replaceabilities of happenings, and confined to the unalterable changingness of ambiguous decisions, one either gives up and uses decisions (however ambiguous) for the evidence and celebration of nonsense, or each of the happenings will hence be assigned to, and incarnated in, the structural and expressive phenomena of particular pitch sets.

Thus organic modes or *generic sets* are created, and for each of them certain definite organic manifestations are appointed, a particular constitutional range of behavior is drawn up which is predeterminedly inter-linked with the transpositions and transformations of a master set. Thus, to a pitch set is given an additional fundamental function to provide for the organic conditions (I call them organic modes) of musical-matter-making shapes, events, and a course of action. Sets are no longer merely generators of distributive, combinational, and formally related pitch material. Each of the transpositions, transformations, constellations, and autonomous fragments is appointed for specific organic tasks or organic habits. For example:

1) A certain organic mode may act within a major seventh. All manifestations then take place within an extremely constricted and narrowed area. As an organic, structural phenomenon it signifies jammed densities in action. As a pictorial sensation it is the doodle, the beehive. As an expressive sensation it is the symbolic retreat into sub-miniature forms of human beings the size of ants.
2) A certain organic mode may act under exclusive conditions on the whole gamut of canonical interplays, canonical reflexes, contractions, intersections. As an organic, structural phenomenon it signifies proliferation, multiplicity, and linkage. As a pictorial

sensation it is the multiple layering of rose leaves, all held together.
As an expressive sensation it is freedom and commitment.

3) An organic mode may only conglomerate into its total sound.
It may be repeated in definite, prescribed ways, redefining its
proportions—that is, its weight, mass and radiance. As an organic,
structural phenomenon it signifies aggregation, mass, accumulation; it is also throw, accent, reflex, temperature. As a pictorial
sensation it is wall, color-focus, containment-form. As an expressive
sensation it is body, eye, center.

4) A certain organic mode may exist only in ever-expanding trajectory
curves, or in double, triple, or multiple curves that are clearly
regulated. For example, two may move up a small distance, while
one moves down a large distance and another moves forward and
backward. As an organic, structural phenomenon it signifies an
interplay of curves, a simultaneous release of impulses. As a
pictorial sensation it is birds' flight, movement of waves. As an
expressive sensation it is extension on all sides, giving and being
given.

5) A certain organic mode may repel any cohesion of tones into
subsequent patterns. It may exist only under conditions of their
extreme separateness for the purpose of dispersion of positions.
The locus of a tone, its spatial area, the constellation of points,
manifest themselves as being non-linear. Movement is stopped, and
a non-sounding time, as well as vast stretches of distances and their
inter-traffic, are structured by sets of proportions. As an organic,
structural phenomenon it signifies a constellation of disparate
points, a distancing of space. As a pictorial sensation it is emptiness
and interference. As an expressive sensation it is sleep and certainty.

6) A certain organic mode may exist under the highest symmetrical
conditions of its linear and sound grouping, yet two tones may
interfere with and disturb the balance at never-predictable points.
Every time the set is in operation, the two previous tones alternate
with two new ones. As an organic, structural phenomenon it
signifies an act of unpredictably disturbing symmetrical organization; it is a faulty organism. As a pictorial sensation it is a sequence
of realistic objects with two offsetting points. As an expressive
sensation it is a threat.

Certain modes join other sets to create jumbles; certain modes dis-
integrate and fragment; certain modes are polymorphic; certain others
alternate with noises and jump off their pitch rails; and certain other modes
are double-minded in their language behaviour—while one part of the
mode (the continuum earlier described) is speaking the language of its
contemporary tongue, the other part resets the material for quotational
language; one mode is strict, ceremoniously strict, the other set has no

order, is willful, anarchic and ill. And so it goes, on and on and on, and in that universe of organic possibilities there are no codes of selection, not even preferences. Observe the patterns of intentional order. Is one better than the other? Observe the patterns of non-intentional order, which are the patterns of disorder. Is one better than the other? Also observe the combined patterns of intentional and non-intentional order. Can one say one is better than the other?

Who is going to rule over the sequences of a hundred released simultaneities? I have already pointed out the reading in different directions! How serious must be the intersecting passages when each of the goals is an honest and exposed one! There is a formal pathos in an ashtray, on an old wall, on a cluttered table, in the junk store, on a beach with stones, and shells, and the foot writing in the sand, and the theater of shifting positions of bathers, and the motions of waves, and the deadened meaning of inter-chasing voices, and pieces of cheese and the newspaper flying off, and an observer shaking off the pains of change, and the hetero-coincidences of the guideless, total-proportional world.

But what offering of profusions, recessions, interceptions, interstices, intermixtures, interpositions, inter — in — inter — outer — out — ex — off! What sequences of fleeting fields, of intervals of haps — happenings! which all render the total scope within the total field. And each of the single happenings has each digested the total field, and comprehends its own singular totality of aspects.

The supreme eye, the supreme ear grasps the whole! The singular situation, supporting the never-vanishing axes of the whole, is alien to itself, yet, inside the whole, its identity is deeply proven and vivified. It is the unfolding of adjacent opposites. A world where all aspects are available to themselves in any given stretch of a continuum of time or in its instant conversion into the all-inclusive moment.

As I have already said, each event pre-exists within the entire reach of its dormant extremes. It is the unfolding and evolving of contrarieties that are now complementary. It is the universe of the altered values of opposites, it is ineffectual extremes that render the state of averages rare and strangely fresh. With the inclusion of a state of averages into the generic set (which decides the organic mode for the pitch set), with the inclusion of the classical tempo of transformation, the conditional contrast, the reciprocating relationship, the concept of progressive differentiation, the concept of preservation in moments of development and of development in moments of preservation, all these classical concepts and their adaptation by generic sets, when coordinated with other more antithetical and contemporary positions, will be stood on their heads.

**Thinking
Twice**

The use of history is an act of dehistorizing history. The concept of dissociation of aspects becomes easily the dissociation of an omnipresent, total time. The profound actuality of historical epochs feeds on an interpretation in contemporary terms because the settling in historical soil of some contemporary manifestations evolves from interpreting them in terms of earlier preoccupations. If the use of what belongs to the content-making of earlier times offers organic sensations of an extreme kind, then the intercourse of conceptually different events will convey to us history's only worthwhile actuality:

the ever-restored and the ever-advancing moment.

Chou
Wen-Chung

[1923 -   ]

When Chou came to this country from Shanghai, his original purpose
was the study of architecture at Yale University. Deciding upon a musical
career, he studied at the New England Conservatory and at Columbia,
working primarily with Slonimsky, Varèse and Luening. His early works
were based upon a framework of traditional Chinese folk and art music;
he has since incorporated these earlier tendencies into a larger, more
comprehensive style that utilizes advanced Western techniques as well.
The basis, both philosophical and musical, of this stylistic evolution is
discussed at length in the present essay.

The fusion of Eastern and Western musical languages has been a subject of great interest in this century. Both Europeans and Americans,
ranging from Debussy and Messiaen to Cowell, Partch, and Lou Harrison
have been concerned with its problems and implications. Chou's approach, with its roots in Chinese music, presents a unique and fresh
viewpoint, presented with great clarity in the following essay.

An interview taped for broadcast on radio WBAI, New York, 1965,
revised by the author especially for the present volume.

Towards a
Re-Merger
in Music

Like the Chinese calligrapher and painter, I have always regarded the technique of a composer as a spontaneous manifestation of his gradually crystallizing esthetic concepts. This is perhaps in agreement with the Confucian concept: *Music* is "born of emotion"; *tones* are the "substance of music"; *melody and rhythm* are the "appearance of tones." *Greatness of music* lies not in "perfection of artistry" but in attainment of "spiritual power inherent in nature."

The last quotation is a free rendition of the word *Te* in the original text.[1] According to the modern Chinese philosopher Fung Yu-lan, *Te* is " translated as 'virtue' but better rendered as the 'power' that inheres in any individual thing."[2] Fung translates the double term, *Tao* and *Te*, as the Way and its spiritual power, and he quotes Chuang Tzu (c. 369–c. 286 B.C.) in saying that "he who links himself with *Tao* and *Te* is 'using things as things, but not being used by things as things.'"[3] Discussing *Tao* and *Te* as opposed to methods of self-preservation, Fung continues, "if a man cannot see things from a higher point of view, none of these methods can absolutely guarantee him from danger and harm." It seems to me that, if we read "these methods" as "these systems or isms," we could perhaps understand why so many artists tend to be *used by* things as things rather than *using* things as things, thus causing danger and harm not only to themselves as artists but also to their art.

To see things from a higher point of view, i.e. to know the power inherent in any individual thing and to use things as things, is then the technique of a higher level that a composer should aspire to. But once the ultimate purpose of communication is achieved through the score, then, to paraphrase a fundamental Buddhist concept, "the material is immaterial, the immaterial material." Technique is merely the catalyst—indeed, the momentary and illusory vehicle, as the Buddhists say—that precipitates the necessary sensory stimulation. As the material evaporates—that is to say, as the auditory sensation fades away in the listener's ear—a crystallization of

---

[1] *Li Chi (Record of Rites)*. Transl. J. Legge; F. S. Couvreur; R. Wilhelm.
[2] Fung Yu-lan, *A Short History of Chinese Philosophy*. Cf. Fung, *A History of Chinese Philosophy*, vol. I.
[3] *Chuang Tzu*. Trans. Fung; J. Legge; Lin; L. Wieger.

perception emerges[4]: a transitory condensation of a transitory experience. Therefore, in discussing the catalyst, the material that is immaterial, it will serve us well not to lose sight of the immaterial that is material, the condensation itself.[5]

Since, in my opinion, Chinese poetry and painting, among all art forms, seem to have come closest to the idea of knowing the power inherent in any individual thing and of using things as things, I first tried in my early works to convey through sound the qualities of Chinese poetry and painting, and to achieve this end with the same economy of means. In these works, I was influenced by the same philosophy that guides every Chinese artist, be he poet, painter or musician: affinity to nature in conception, allusiveness in expression, and terseness in realization.

This is particularly manifest in my first orchestral score, Landscapes[6] (1949), in which each of the three movements is based upon a traditional Chinese melodic pattern (ch'ü tiao), which, in turn, is associated with a poem. The poems are linked to the Landscapes in much the same manner as poems are affixed to Chinese paintings. For example, the last poem reads as follows:

Green, green the grass west of the pavilion,
The clouds low, the cries of the wild geese faint,
Two lines of sparse willows,
One streak of dying light,
Hundreds of homing ravens dotting the sky.
(Dialogue d'Eluthère)

Needless to say, the poem is rich in its terse allusions to nature's sight, sound, and poetry. Small in dimension but deep in expression, economical in means but spacious in feeling, it immediately evokes — in ink and in music — dots, lines, delicate shadings, open space, and motion.

In the two subsequent orchestral scores, All In The Spring Wind (1953) and And The Fallen Petals (1954), there is a marked change in the use of tonal material and instrumental resources. Line, mass, and their interaction, together with such elements as articulation, duration, intensity, and timbre,

---

[4] It should be of interest to note that Varèse says, "A composition develops like a crystal". Of course Varèse's reference to "crystallization" is from a physical rather than perceptual point of view. However, Varèse also speaks of what he calls the "inner life" as opposed to the "appearance" (sic) of sound.

[5] In recent times, such views have been not totally unknown in the West. As Varèse has pointed out in one of his lectures, Julien Benda (1867-1936), the French philosopher and critic, once said: "The idea peculiar to music and which music gives is that of immaterial existence presenting, in short, the condition of being a being [italics mine] without being an object" (Dialogue d'Eluthère). Related observations on a limited scale are also found here and there in the writings of Whitehead, Maritain, F. H. Bradley, and Heidegger, among others.

[6] All compositions cited are published by C. F. Peters.

are organized into an integrated body of sound that ebbs and flows—in the manner of a tonal brushwork in space—with ever-changing motion, tension, texture, and sonority. It seems to me that these works reflect not only the fundamental concept of the Chinese painter in general but also that of the Chinese musician in particular. The ancient Chinese musician believed that each single tone or aggregate of tones is a musical entity in itself and a living spark of expression as long as it lasts.[7] Therefore, it was also believed that the meaning in music lies intrinsically in the tones themselves, that maximum expressiveness can be derived from a succession of tones without resorting to extraneous procedures.

Consequently, in the late fifties, I became more and more interested in the principles that are best demonstrated by the art of Chinese calligraphy, in which the controlled flow of ink—through the interaction of movement and energy, the modulation of line and texture—creates a continuum of motion and tension in a spatial equilibrium. These principles are first employed in the piano piece *The Willows Are New* (1957), the thematic material of which is based upon a traditional composition for *ch'in,* the Chinese zither, a unique instrument capable of the most subtle inflections in its tone quality, to which we shall return shortly.

This interest in the controlled flow of sound through organized complexity and ordered interplay of all of its properties led me to *Metaphors* (1960), for wind symphony orchestra. The conception of this work is influenced by the philosophy of *I Ching* or the *Book of Changes,*[8] the foundation of which is a system of eight symbolic images (*kua*). Each of these images is a trilinear arrangement of the two polar opposites, the *yin* and the *yang,*[9] represented by a broken (– –) and an unbroken line (–), respectively. These images (e.g. ☰) represent the continually transforming forces that germinate all in the universe. The images interact with each other in a state of perpetual transformation and superimposition. The interplay of the images at any specific moment signifies a unique but predictable situation in the constancy of nature—the changing microcosm in the unchanging macrocosm. The meaning of these composite images (e.g.☶) is interpreted through metaphors, hence the title of my composition.

Eight *pien,* or *mutable* modes, each constantly mutating within itself, are constructed according to the concept of the eight images. These

---

[7] Again, it is remarkable to note that Varèse also speaks of music as "a living, evolving substance," or "bodies of intelligent sounds," and maintains that the slightest change in the manner of producing a tone changes the quality, and consequently the meaning, of the tone.
[8] Transl. C. de Harlez; J. Legge; R. Wilhelm. Cf. J. Needham, *Science and Civilization in China,* Vol. II.
[9] The terms *yin* and *yang* have many connotations such as negative and positive, dark and light, etc., according to the context. As definition, I prefer the connotation given by the eleventh-century philosopher Chou Tun-yi: *quiescence* and *movement.*

311

modes, as more fully developed in subsequent works, are based upon three disjunct segments of the octave that are either unbroken (a minor third) or broken (a major and a minor second, i.e. the minor third interpolated with a *pien*-tone).[10] These segments are reciprocally mutable according to whether the movement is ascending or descending: the order of the two seconds also depends on the direction of movement.[11] In other words, each segment in the ascending order is reflected in mutation in the descending order—the intervals being mutually complementary, the pitches being mutually exclusive. These modes, with similar coordination in duration and register, are woven into a fabric of the transitory and changing within a continuum of the timeless and unchanging—like the shifting patterns in a steadily flowing current, for example. This means that the contour of the work is the summation of modal interaction in space and time—a process of constant transmutation and superimposition. In principle, this process follows that of binary arithmetic, upon which the concept of change in *I Ching* is founded.[12]

A moment ago, I mentioned the *ch'in*. This long fretted zither[13] has been the favorite instrument of Chinese scholars and artists, as well as musicians, ever since the time of Confucius. The music of this instrument has thus enjoyed a unique position and an uninterrupted tradition. It is also the most characteristic of Chinese music. Over one hundred symbols (*chien tzu*) are used in its finger notation for achieving the essential yet elusive qualities of this music: subtle inflections in the production and control of its tones as a means of expression. They indicate the articulation and timbre of either a single tone or a series of tones; they specify the occurrence of variable microtones between fixed scale tones; and they control the rhythmic and dynamic organization within each tonal aggregate. In fact, they even evoke a certain state of mind to the performer for the execution of each detail. Such a system naturally makes possible in its music a wealth of resources that has been beyond the realm of pre-electronic Western music.

To make this clear, let us examine a short characteristic phrase in *Yu Ko*

[10] *Pien* means "to change," "to transform." In music, it refers specifically to the interpolation of a minor third with a semitone below the upper tone. This interpolated tone is called a *pien*-tone. Cf. Joseph Yasser, *A Theory of Evolving Tonality*; Gustave Reese, *Music in the Middle Ages.*

[11] Although this procedure is derived from *I Ching*, a practical precedent may be found in the Indian ragas, where the mutation in ascending and descending scalar orders generally follow the same principles.

[12] It is now recognized that *I Ching* uses a binary system in its images for "computing" its immense store of knowledge.

[13] Actually no frets are used. Instead, thirteen studs are inlaid in the sound-board, indicating the first seven harmonics.

by Mao Min-chung (c. 1280). In the score, this phrase is indicated by a single *chien tzu*, which, in this case, denotes only one excitation of the string. Consequently, the changes in pitch and timbre are achieved *during the decay*. The finger technique involved may be described briefly as follows: as the right middle finger pulls the string inward, the left ring finger glides up quickly from the whole tone below the given note. At first, it glides very lightly, barely touching the string; then, when the finger is just less than a semitone below, it glides more firmly, pressing down on the string. This is referred to as "hiding the head (of the tone)" and is described as "a flying seagull touching down."[14] Once the finger reaches the given note, it pauses to ring out the tone, which should be "as pure as a pond in autumn, as bright as the clear moon, as resonant as waterfalls, as remote as echoes in a valley." Then the finger again quickly glides up to the whole tone above and back "like a gust of wind." It then glides down to the whole tone below and executes there a broad and accentuated vibrato, which is described as "the cry of a monkey climbing a tree" and is expected to sound as crisply as "pearls rolling in a bowl." Afterwards, the finger glides back to the given note once again, when the decay as well as this transitory musical expression of a "single tone" is completed. The excitation itself, which, as we have noticed, is carefully "hidden" in this case, is described as "a solitary wild duck looking back at the flock," meaning that the right middle finger should be curved and supple like the neck of the duck. The subtle dynamic modulation that goes hand in hand with the finger movement is obvious and will materialize naturally if the finger technique is executed properly. Equally obvious is the rhythmic structure within the phrase. A proper durational organizational within the limited time span of the decay is clearly indicated by the sequence of events.

Early in 1965, I adapted this composition for the following instruments: piano, violin, alto flute, English horn, bass clarinet, trombone, bass trombone, and a battery of twenty percussion instruments. In this adaption, I have magnified, as closely to the original as possible, these inflections in pitch, articulation, timbre, dynamics, and rhythm to a more perceptible level, by expanding the articulations and timbres possible on each instrument used and by controlling the microtonal modifications in pitch according to the nature of each instrument.[15]

These ideas and those in *Metaphors* are combined in *Cursive* (1963), for flute and piano. "Cursive" refers to the type of script in which the

[14] All quotations in this paragraph are from the following treatises on *ch'in: Ch'in Sheng Shih Lui Fa; Ch'in Shu Tai Ch'uan; T'ai Ku I Yin; Yang Ch'un T'ang Ch'in P'u.* Cf. R. H. van Gulik, *The Lore of the Chinese Lute.*

[15] A concept perhaps not unlike that of the Greek *chroai*, to cite a case somewhat related to the tradition of Western music.

joined strokes and rounded angles result in expressive and contrasting curves and loops. The cursive script represents the ultimate in the art of Chinese calligraphy, as its power of expression depends solely upon the spontaneous manifestation of the power inherent in the controlled flow of ink. In this score, the *cursive concept* has influenced the use of specified but indefinite pitches and durations, and the use of regulated but variable tempo and intensity. Throughout the score, the piano is treated as a combination keyboard, string and, percussion instrument, while the flute is required to use controlled microtonal modifications in pitch. An attempt is made to treat the individual sound as a "living matter" through inflections in its production and control. A sense of freedom and independence for each instrument is also obtained through the use of individual but coordinated tempi for the two instruments, the use of non-proportional note-values, and the use of intensity according to the natural character of each instrument.

When coordinated individual tempi are used, the two parts, having arrived at the same beat, move on at different tempi with *accelerando* and *rallentando* as indicated, meeting eventually on the first beat of the next passage. Thus, between the two synchronizing points, a living but controlled rhythmic interplay is set free.[16] When qualitative rather than proportional note-values are used, when intensities according to the natural character of the instruments are used, not only the durational elasticity and the dynamic interaction are set to work, but also the state of mind of each of the performers is encouraged to exert its power. In other words, an attempt is made to recognize the "natural power" of every individual matter that is part of the music to bring forth a condensation of experience.

Now, in conclusion, let me add the following: if I seem to have dwelt on certain Chinese philosophical ideas, it is because of my conviction that we have reached the stage where a true *re*-merger of Oriental and Occidental musical concepts and practices—which at one time shared a common foundation[17]—can and should take place. It seems to me that the music of China, India, Varèse,[18] the Balinese *gamelan* music, the Japanese *gagaku*, the Korean *ah ahk*, and even our new electronic music all have much in common, sharing the same family traits. If I seem to have dwelt on certain

[16] We again find a precedence in the Indian practice of *tálas*, especially in the lengthy ones, when the soloist and the drummer carry on an improvised rhythmic interplay, synchronizing only at the *samas*, or initial beats.

[17] For a recent study on this matter, see Walter Wiora, *The Four Ages of Music*; also Curt Sachs, "The Lore of Non-Western Music" (in Mendel, Sachs, and Pratt, *Some Aspects of Musicology*; also partly incorporated in Sachs, *The Wellsprings of Music*); Mantle Hood, "Music, the Unknown" (in Harrison, Hood and Palisca, *Musicology*).

[18] I would naturally have included Webern, had he not been so ubiquitously cited and deserving to be respectfully left alone, at least in the course of this writing.

314

aspects of music, it is because the West in its preoccupation with polyphonic concepts has more or less ignored those particular aspects in which
the East has remained master. As a matter of fact, these are aspects that not
a few composers today are beginning to explore. Unfortunately, these are
often used merely as a matter of extraneous procedure and constructivist
calculation. Indeed, Chuang Tzu's teaching, "using things as things, but
not being used by things as things," can never be overstated. In this respect, I believe there is still much that we can learn from the music of the
various Eastern cultures.

Of course, no matter what one's philosophy and technique in composition, the result must stand on its merit as an abstract art-work in sound. In
other words, we are concerned with the crystallization rather than the
catalyst. Let me cite a little poem from the T'ang Dynasty:

> Wild geese
>   flying across the blue sky above
> Their image
>   reflected on the water below
> The geese
>   do not mean to cast their image on the water
> Nor the water
>   mirror the image of the geese.

Yet in that instant, the beauty of the flight is truly mirrored by the water.
Such is a moment of pure reflection in Nature, when time and space merge
and a spark is struck from Nature's rock. Such is a moment of true perception
in art, when a transitory condensation of a transitory experience is born.

Jack
Beeson

[1921 -   ]

Not all of the musical developments of the past twenty years are concerned with the avant-garde. Contributions of importance are being
made as well within the "mainstream" traditions; these often deal with
questions of large-scale form and structure rather than problems of the
musical language per se. Many composers working within the relatively
conventional forms and media of symphony, program music, and opera
are continually reshaping these into vehicles more suited to twentieth-
century modes of expression, less reminiscent of an earlier generation's
rhetoric.

Jack Beeson, one of the very few American students of Bartók, is a
highly successful composer of operas, including many that have been
widely performed and recorded. He has written a number of articles on
the subject of opera, particularly opera in the United States, and in many
instances, as in the essay printed here, has addressed himself to the
problems of the American opera composer seeking to adapt the form not
only to his times but to his language.

"Grand and Not So Grand," from Opera News, 27/9 (January 5, 1963),
pp. 8-13.

Grand
and not
So Grand

One or two generations ago, when opera in the U.S. was performed regularly in only a few large cities and but sporadically elsewhere, it was sufficient for the times that everything that went on in the few legitimate opera houses be known as "grand opera" and that the few and classiest (and most expensive, best-dressed and dullest) events in the Grand Old Op'ry Houses on Main Streets also be called "grand opera."

If distinctions were not made in those days, it was in part because they were not called for. The same kinds of sets, costumes, stage direction and singing were used in widely differing styles of operas, emphasis being always laid on the large, the impressive and the loud — in other words, the grand. So long as the tenor bawled passionately enough, it mattered little whether he was singing "Vesti la giubba" in a bloody, realistic Italian opera or "M'appari" in a flimsy little romantic comedy kept alive by frequent transfusions of "The Last Rose of Summer." But an objection is heard: the era that found the term "grand opera" good enough for everything from Suppe to *Casse-Noisette* was, after all, the Golden Age of Song. One might concede that had it been the Golden Age of Opera it would have been more precise about naming its treasures. But the Golden Age of Song always remains about thirty years behind the times — the number of years separating an authority on things vocal from the singers of his youth. We of the sixties are beginning to hallow the singers of the thirties.

Changes in nomenclature are only the conversational symptoms of more basic changes that have taken place on the American operatic scene in the last generation or two. The same old opera houses are with us, but the Grand Old Op'ry Houses, with few exceptions, have been razed, turned into movie theaters, supermarkets or warehouses. And the old-fashioned, puffed-up idea of all opera as something so grand as to be unrelated to music, language, drama or common sense has become as dated as the buildings.

The deflation of "grand opera" in the last few years has not implied any lack of faith in musical theater as a source of pleasure and instruction. Quite the reverse: American interest in the writing, producing and enjoyment of opera is more widespread and seriously regarded now than at any other time in our history. And part of the serious interest in opera as a viable medium is a curiosity concerning its historical guises and the forms it may take in the future.

A casual glance at the standard repertory shows that its components are not "just operas"—not all of one kind, and certainly not all of the grand variety. For with the exception of isolated works of singular character, the repertory can be divided into large, easily recognized and accurately named categories. With a little investigation, the singular pieces turn out to be the hardiest representatives of yet other categories that did not retain musical or dramatic vitality beyond the era that gave them birth.

An operatic genre that seemed vigorous in its heyday but turned out more than usually mortal is true grand opera—the serious, dialogue-less French opera of the second third of the nineteenth century. It survives chiefly in the symbolism of the large Parisian theater, its monument and mausoleum, where it is no longer performed. Opera is one of the most transitory of the arts. Like gastronomy, it is subject to the gross desires of the multitudes as well as the special tastes of the elect. Sensation-seeking Parisians of the time of Louis Philippe reveled in the succession of *coups de théâtre* invented by such librettist-playwrights as Scribe, capitalized upon by such composers as Meyerbeer and Halévy. French theater had always been notable for its reliance on scenic display, choral effects and ballet, but the nineteenth century found ingenious (and sometimes ingenuous) means of enlarging the number of floods, conflagrations and battle scenes in stories of even higher and lower passion and romantic derring-do. Singers were required to carry out vocal feats quite as heroic as the deeds of the paladins and Amazons they represented. If vocalists could be found today to encompass their roles, the audiences who were once thrilled by the operatic equivalents of *Les Misérables* and *The Count of Monte Cristo* would not be found to go elsewhere for such entertainment. For three centuries opera was not only the chief musical (vocal) entertainment but also the chief theatrical display; today the equivalent of the costumed histrionics of *Les Huguenots* can be seen weekly at the movies.

There was nevertheless room on the Parisian musical scene for the creation of such an impressive work as Berlioz' *Troyens*, while those who looked to the musical theater for comedy, high spirits and topical allusion could find them in Offenbach. Then too, set apart from grand opera by the convention of spoken dialogue, there was the *opéra-comique*—which, despite its name, was not necessarily comic but maintained a middle ground. Both *Carmen* and *Faust* began life as *opéra-comique;* but provided at birth with a prevailing lyricism and outfitted soon after with recitatives to clothe the spoken dialogue, they took on the characteristics of yet another genre of the time, *opéra lyrique*.

318

Grand
and not So Grand

The trouble with categorization is, of course, that once one has passed the necessary first step of finding similarities in apparent diversity and diversities in apparent similarity, categories proliferate as distinctions become clearer and more numerous. Somewhere between the dreary fact that dozens of eighteenth-century *buffo* operas seem to have been fabricated by the same copyist and the exciting truth that Mozart's *Figaro* and *Così* transcend their categorization as *buffo* operas lies the usefulness of finding likenesses and unlikenesses among works of art, only the greatest of which ever seem to be autonomous.

Operas, characterized by the languages and customs of national groups, are more parochial than varieties of instrumental music. One can point to traits that characterize national schools throughout three centuries. Italian opera, for example, has never strayed far from the sound of the vocal cords vibrating sympathetically with the heartstrings. Careful musical construction, with emphasis on orchestral elaboration, has characterized most German opera since its beginnings. The French infatuation with stage splendor has been mentioned; in addition, the French have always insisted on literary excellence in librettos and a clear, correct text setting. Surely no genetic determinants account for these hardy personality traits. If they did, how then could one explain the fact that almost all the composers who shaped the French style, from Lully to Offenbach, were Italians or Germans? It is rather the stabilizing effect of shared language and habits of mind and feeling that bends the desires of creators, the tastes of critics and audiences, along parallel, sometimes converging, lines.

That languages in themselves can profoundly influence musico-dramatic forms is clear from even one example, the varying treatment of recitative from country to country. The difference between singing and speaking is smaller in Italian than in other languages. A street-corner discussion in Naples, though certainly no organized ensemble, is often almost a *recitativo secco*. It is therefore perfectly natural for an Italian composer to use recitative for passages concerned with plot or other mundane matters that do not require or permit musical expansiveness. The Germans and English, on the other hand, have long troubled themselves over what to do with such passages, frequently resorting to a clear demarcation between the emotionally expansive parts of the text that become musical numbers (arias and ensembles) and simple speech for the necessities. More recently, German-speaking composers have found another solution, whereby words are purveyed by the voice, singing more or less, while musical interest is relegated to the orchestra.

Aesthetic standards and ideals, being related to the social status of creators and audiences, have also played a part in the creation of operatic styles. In the early eighteenth century, when those who underwrote opera

Jack
Beeson

came from the highest, most rigidly formalized elements of society, the stylization necessary to English and German recitative was accepted. The even higher degree of stylization implied by *opera seria* (sung in Italian) proved acceptable to German and English, even Russian and Polish aristocratic circles. The French, however, with their great pride of language, would have little to do with opera in a foreign tongue. Their attention to the jealous demands of good prosody led them to find a middle ground between the pleasures of song and the clarity of speech. Meanwhile, nonaristocratic circles outside Italy took their pleasure in works making little use of recitative but alternating song with speech (the ballad opera in England, *Singspiel* in Germany and *opéra-comique* in France). In their reliance on sprightly comedy and realistically drawn characters, they offered the vernacular equivalents of *opera buffa*, which got along unselfconsciously with the patter of dry recitative.

Operatic styles have come into being, then, not only as a result of differing languages and musico-dramatic customs but also as a reflection of the differing habits and wishes of differing classes of society within language groups. For 250 years the aristocratic and plebeian musical theaters remained distinct, corresponding roughly to the worlds of serious and comic opera; then, not surprisingly, the breakdown of the old order erased the line between serious and comic operas. But the definitive social history of opera has yet to be written; this is not the place to adumbrate its contents, nor is it necessary to enumerate further the myriad forms the lyric theater has taken in the past. It is sufficient if one realizes that opera — like other theater, though more slowly — reflects the changing and disappearing scene even as it comments on and helps to create that scene. Only occasionally does a work capture more than the surface of its times. When it does, it may remain alive to enrapture later generations.

During the first half of our century, composers and writers of the first rank were not often attracted to the operatic form, but since World War II there has been a revival of interest. This creative renewal coincides in our own country with mushrooming performance and attendance, activity that is chronicled each autumn in *Opera News*. Opera in English is not new, but it has had no continuity since its brief and intense beginnings toward the end of the seventeenth century. Except for the works of Blow and Purcell, dating from those early days, *The Beggar's Opera* from a generation later and the comic operas of Gilbert and Sullivan, now barely out of copyright, the repertory conceived in English is only now being created. What kinds of lyric theater are being shaped by the forces of our language, our theatrical and musical customs and social organization, the imagination of our composers and librettists?

The strongest influence on vocal style is, as always, language. The only

singers and audiences who believe that ours is a language unfit for singing
are the uninformed, the lazy or the snobbish. For a musical style based
primarily on the continuation of sensuous vocal tone through long phrases,
Italian or Church Latin are undeniably the best Western languages. But
opera does not consist entirely of lyrical effusion. Often enough one has
the feeling that Italian librettists and composers have worked hard and
unsuccessfully to find a verbal line with sufficient strong consonants and
short vowels to provide the required dramatic thrust. If Italian singers are
known for their lack of rhythmic precision, it is not because they are less
adept than other singers but because Italian vocal music, like the language
itself, invites rhythmic imprecision. One has only to examine an Italian
opera score to see that the rhythmic organization of successions of vowels
is frequently left to the taste of the singer and his knowledge of performance
conventions. It is a rare composer who would notate the vowel arrangements of such a phrase as "miei gioielli"; no matter what a singer does
to such words they remain euphonious, even if euphony is not the effect desired.

English, on the other hand, is a language that has rhythmic strength and
vitality built into it. For this reason one might even say that it is better
suited to musical drama than Italian! It is surely as good as German, and
much better than French, for singing. It offers strongly articulated consonants that do not, however, occur in such large combinations as in Russian, and vowels of varying length that ensure rhythmic crispness and a
certain quickness of pace. To a greater extent than in most other languages,
the meaning of an English phrase is dependent upon its accentuation.
There is only one way of saying, "How do you do?" without meaning
anything. "How do you *do?*" expresses real interest, even curiosity. "How
do you do?" is either affected or funny. "How do *you* do?" forces attention
on one person. In such lines as the following, there is an immanent rhythmical phrase without implying that the composer's setting was predestined:

> Thus on the fatal banks of Nile
> Weeps the deceitful crocodile! (*Dido and Aeneas.*)

> I dreamt that I dwelt in marble halls,
> With vassals and serfs at my side (*The Bohemian Girl*)

> I got plenty o' nuttin'
> And Nuttin's plenty for me (*Porgy and Bess*)

> Love, too frequently betrayed
> For some plausible desire (*The Rake's Progress*)

The frequent combination of an accented first syllable on a short vowel
followed by an unaccented long vowel forces syncopation. That cake-

walks, ragtime and jazz grew up among English-speaking people is not surprising when one remembers such a line as "If a body meet a body comin' thro' the rye" — syncopated, even *sans* music.

Language affects style in more general ways than melodic construction and rhythmic turns of phrase. I believe that it is likely to be a more important determining factor in lyric theater here than in other countries, France perhaps excepted; for our new repertory is being created at a time when all the musico-dramatic media insist on word clarity. In the casting of musical comedies, almost anybody who is good box office will do for the lead. If he can't carry a tune, it can be put in the orchestra; but he should be able to speak in rhythm. On radio and records the engineers are instructed to play down the accompaniment and boost the voices. Already the new generation of record collectors finds unacceptable the traditional balance of voice and orchestra in concert halls and opera houses. Television audio equipment is adequate only for the spoken voice. In televised opera the practice of playing down the orchestra and keeping the singers' mouths half-closed, even when high notes are being sung, tends to focus attention on the words, though it also serves to prevent the close-up singer from sounding and looking ridiculous. Those of us who are deaf to the "beauties" of operatic singing when they are unrelated to the expressive values of the understood word applaud the attempt to make the text clear — even while we deplore the tendency to make it an end in itself.

Large orchestras and improperly used small orchestras obscure words; neither will be welcome in the America opera of the future. Even if the large orchestra should again become an economic possibility, it is not likely to be required often, for the subject matter that attracts American composers and librettists invites intimacy between stage and audience, ruling out large orchestras in huge theaters. Acousticians tells us there cannot be good, unamplified diction in halls beyond a certain size; common sense tells us that an amplified voice from a faceless singer is ridiculous. And furthermore, it goes without saying that composers and singers will have to pay more attention to good prosody and diction than has been their habit. If listeners expect to understand the libretto, they will not want to be embarrassed by its foolishness.

Already composers are showing a sharpened critical sense in their choice of librettos. Successful plays are sought, as are experienced writers with the special talents necessary to a librettist. There are no surer signs of an emergent, dramatically viable American lyric theater than that playwrights are beginning to release adaptation rights to their plays and that professional writers are at last beginning to equip themselves for the specialized task of writing for composers. They know very well that there is little or no chance of monetary reward, though the financial success of a few pieces and projects such as the present Ford Foundation aid to American opera suggests that where there is smoke there may be fire.

The American scene changes so radically and rapidly that one can suggest only tentatively some of the directions our opera may take in the near future. In the past, opera has sometimes been the most advanced theatrical medium and at other times lagged behind the spoken theater; which of these positions it will hold here depends on rapidly changing audience tastes and theater economics. If one believes that American opera will grow directly out of the excitements and simplicities of musical comedy (I do not), one could point out that at the moment the most solvent aspect of the absurd Broadway setup is its musical theater. But it is precisely the hit-or-flop aspect of the musical comedy scene that prevents the emergence of "serious" lyric theater from such a source. Because the personality of an opera is usually neither recognized nor understood at first hearing, most operas have not been assured long life on their first night or in the papers the next morning.

If our lyric theater is not to be found on Broadway's doorstep, neither will it be found in the foyers of the long-established opera houses. These are too stodgy, too snobbish and—for a variety of complicated social and economic reasons—too preoccupied with the polishing of dead composers' tombstones to take part in the present, not to speak of the future. The operatic Establishment has enough difficulty tending its legitimate functions as a museum, offering some of the best and some of the mediocre pieces from the past for rehearing and revaluation, without taking under its wing new, problematic works that cannot exist on or off Broadway or in the more transient opera companies. Our numerous university and civic workshops and their audiences cannot yet cope with large-scale operas making use of the more advanced musical idioms. In Germany, audiences and heavily subsidized opera companies are interested in little else, and within the last year European houses have shown interest in several American works unperformed here. If our situation continues for long, the effect will be to send "advanced" composers back to their symphonies and quartets and to solidify the present conservative personality of American opera, directing it even more strongly toward popular theater.

The wish to provide a very broad basis for culture is as much a passion among us as it is a duty in the Soviet Union. What are and should be primarily local institutions—the Metropolitan Opera and Lincoln Center, for example—are sold to, and in part paid for by, the nation at large. There seems to be a collective guilty conscience when the arts must be paid for, unless they are to be enjoyed by, the whole population. It is permissible (and possible, it should be added) for a film to be budgeted at ten million dollars provided that a hundred million people go to see it. It is improper

Jack
Beeson

(and impossible, it should be added) to mount a new opera if only ten thousand go to see it; and a corollary is that the millions must not be taxed to pay for the pleasures of the thousand. The effect of such a state of mind and pocketbook on the formation of a native style of lyric theater will be disastrous, for it has yet to be proved that opera is for everybody, even though it may be for very many and need not be restricted to a special few.

Musical theater is one of the masks of time and space. It often hides the individual features of the society behind it, but the broad outlines of its personality are apparent, even as the facture of the mask shows the quality of its artists. No one kind of musical theater, and certainly no one kind of opera, can represent the changing faces of our society. The discontinuous past of opera in English and the personality of the language itself suggest some of the features, as do some of our special musical and theatrical habits. But what beauties and strengths of workmanship our composers and librettists will be able to contribute remains, as always, unpredictable. To the person who is curious as to what the next chapters in the history of American opera will contain, one can only counsel: wait and see—or, better, wait and listen.

Lukas
Foss

[1922 -   ]

Coming to America from his native Germany in 1937, Foss began almost immediately a career as enfant prodigue both as composer and pianist, later as teacher and conductor as well. His earlier work unites the best of European neo-Classicism and a Copland-like Americanism. Recently he has become concerned with the power of controlled improvisation in music, and as composer-pianist he works with a highly trained chamber group to develop new music through these techniques.

Unlike the "chance" composers who formulated their ideas in New York in the early 1950's, Foss puts forth in his work no revolutionary esthetic. It retains the lyricism and rhythmic interest of his earlier music and is not concerned with sound solely as such, freed from other organizational processes. In all Foss' work there may be seen a constant probing and provocative intelligence, which is reflected in the essay here presented.

"The Changing Composer-Performer Relationship: A Monologue and a Dialogue," from Perspectives of New Music, I/2 (Spring, 1963), pp. 45-53.

The Changing
Composer-Performer Relationship:
a Monologue and a Dialogue

I

On the heels of the invaluable discovery of what is commonly referred to as electronic music there followed a diametrically opposed movement endeavoring to draw the performer closer into the composer's laboratory, to build performance at times "into" the composition. This movement consists of a series of efforts in different directions, efforts so full of vague, half-understood implications, that an attempt at objective critical assessment would seem to be premature. Also, I hardly qualify as an objective observer, having been steadily involved with new performance ideas for some time. Thus my remarks here may best be understood as observations made from "within."

Progress in the arts: a series of gifted mistakes perhaps. We owe our greatest musical achievements to an unmusical idea: the division of what is an indivisible whole, "music," into two separate processes: composition (the making of the music) and performance (the making of music), a division as nonsensical as the division of form and content. The history of music is a series of violations, untenable positions, each opening doors, as it were: the well-tempered scale, Wagner's music drama, Stravinsky's neoclassicism, Schoenberg's twelve-tone method, to name but a few. ("My method does not quite work . . . that makes it interesting," Arnold Schoenberg to Gustave Arlt, U.C.L.A.) The methodical division of labor (I write it, you play it) served us well, until composer and performer became like two halves of a worm separated by a knife, each proceeding obliviously on its course.

Around 1915, composition withdrew underground, leaving the field to the performer and to the music of the past. That this created a sterile state of affairs "above" ground was perfectly clear to the more educated virtuoso, who has been trying ever since to resolve the conflict, often leading a Jekyll and Hyde existence on account of it. Thus, Arthur Schnabel gave his audience Beethoven and Schubert; his lifelong involvement with Schoenberg was kept scrupulously to himself. His 1960 counterpart, Glenn Gould, rebels, openly attacks our "narcissistic listening," despises our applause, threatens to retire from the concert circuit at the age of thirty. Leonard Bernstein, deeply aware of the missing element of urgency in our symphonic culture, consoles himself with the musical theater—and so on.

The conflict still rages, and yet the feud between composition and performance is over. The factor which led to the conflict, the division of labor (performance/composition), will remain with us. The procedural advantages are too great to be sacrificed. But a creative investigation is in full swing, and correction of the sterilizing aspects is under way. Composers have had to abandon Beethoven's proud position: "Does he think I have his silly fiddle in mind when the spirit talks to me?" Composers are again involved in performance, with performance. More—they work with handpicked performers toward a common goal. Among the new composer-performer teams: Cage and Tudor, Boulez and the Südwestfunk, Berio and Cathy Berberian, Babbitt and Bethany Beardslee, Pousseur and a group of seven, my own Improvisation Chamber Ensemble. Each of the teams mentioned is involved in a search, what we might call a joint enterprise in new music. Characteristic here is the composer's fascination with the possibility of new tasks for his new-found partner and confidant. The new tasks demand new ideas of coordination. In fact, the creation of a new vocabulary requires that the composer give constant attention to all performance problems in connection with his score. As a result, a thorough overhauling of conducting technique is in the making, new instrumental discoveries have antiquated every existing orchestration treatise,—traditional limitations of voice and instrument have proved to be mythical: the piano was the first instrument to expand, the flute underwent a change of personality (due largely to Gazzeloni). The human voice followed; percussion came into its own.[1]

The emancipation of percussion and, for that matter, the new use of flute, voice, strings (Penderecki), and *Sprechchor* (Kagel) must actually be attributed to yet another factor: I began by observing that the performance movement directly followed the discovery of electronic music. Paradoxically, it is the advent of electronic music which sparked the performance renaissance.

Electronic music showed up the limitations of live performance, the limitations of traditional tone production, the restrictiveness of a rhythm forever bound to meter and bar line, notation tied to a system of counting. Electronic music introduced untried possibilities, and in so doing presented

[1] The extent to which percussion has begun to preoccupy the composer can be illustrated by the recent mania for acquiring one's own percussion instruments, then lending them out to percussionists. Stockhausen bought a Degan vibraphone, Berio brought a marimba from San Francisco to Milan, Boulez owns a whole collection of percussion instruments. Can we imagine composers twenty years ago going to such pains to ensure faithful performance?

a challenge, shocked live music out of its inertia, kindled in musicians the desire to prove that live music "can do it too." When I say: "I like my electronic music live," the somewhat flippant remark contains a tribute. Via electronic music came a new approach not only to the above-mentioned instruments and voices, but to their placement on stage, to phonetics, to notation. Percussion found a new climate in a "handmade" white noise. Today, it appears to some that electronic music has served its purpose in thus pointing the way. "Tape fails," says Morton Feldman. And I remember reading in Thomas Mann: "Everything, even nature, turns into mere scenery, background, the instant the human being steps forward."

II

"I beg your pardon if I may be so bold as to interrupt: this new team, this joint 'composer-performer enterprise in new music,' is it to replace the composer's former, solitary work?"

"Give up solitude, and you have given up composition. But performance is always *with* or *for* or both. As to the team (I dislike the word as much as you do), it complements the composer's work, it is a bridge . . ."

"Then all is as it always was, it would seem."

"Yes and no. When I advise a young composer—one so young and foolish as to seek advice—I say: Study old and new music, work by yourself. When you grow up, find your performer(s)—and then work by yourself again."

"I am a performer. I am intrigued by the 'laboratory' approach of recent music, but I must admit that I find my powers as an instrumentalist, the capabilities of my instrument, more often abused than used. Playing behind the bridge, inside the piano, slapping the wood, this is not a new task, it is withdrawal to mere marginal possibilities."

"Marginal possibilities are good for marginal purposes . . ."

"And as to the new freedoms and choices suddenly handed to the performer, they seem intriguing and dangerous at first, but soon reveal an inane foolproofness. They are safe, either because the given entities control the desired result, neutralizing my own additions, or because the result does not concern the composer (only the "situation" does). In either instance, I am given choice because 'it matters not what I do.'"

"And that you resent, understandably. But performer-choices where it matters can be accomplished only after years of study. My colleagues of the Improvisation Ensemble and I undertook such a study five years ago. In spite of this experience, or perhaps because of it, I am among the most reluctant of composers when it comes to introducing performer-freedom into my composition. Moments of incomplete notation do exist, but only—to quote you—where it is safe."

"Then why have them at all?"

"For the same reason that figured bass was 'filled in' by the performer. As you know, solo parts plus *basso continuo,* reasonably insured the harmonic result. Figured bass was never conceived as a performer-freedom but as a form of shorthand for composer and performer; one avoids cluttering up the score with unessentials. Today our scores are more cluttered. Schoenberg invented H⁻ and N⁻ to clarify the *Notenbild* (a makeshift device, to be sure). This brings me to the notational dilemma of the 1940's and 1950's: the precise notation which results in imprecise performance. Can we speak at all of precise notation if the practical realization can but approximate the complexities on the page? The dilemma lies in the need to notate every minute detail . . . Take a rubato. Here is a comparatively vague notation:

The accelerando, ritardando, written out would produce:

This seemingly precise notation puts the performer in a strait jacket. It is a translation of the supple into the realm of the rigid. A rigid rubato: contradiction in terms. Imagine asking the performer to feel a moment 'out of time,' as it were, when it is notated slavishly 'in time.' Similarly, an effect of, say, chaos, must not be notated in terms of a subtle order. To learn to play the disorderly in orderly fashion is to multiply rehearsal time by one hundred."

"Allow me to be the devil's advocate here. Is not the orderly fashion the only way to play the disorderly? Is not all notation a translation? Is it not a sign of sophistication that this is so? I know of some recent experiments in which the notation simply consists of showing changes in the position of the hands on a keyboard . . ."

"You mean Ligeti's organ pieces."

"Is this not an infinitely more primitive notational concept? It is our

traditional notation's ability to translate subtleties like a rubato into measured exactitude which makes it a highly developed tool. Inspired notation is
inspired translation, transposition of the inexpressible to the domain of the
exact. Take Beethoven's introduction to the last movement in Opus 106,
those chords in both hands, that no one can feel as anticipating the beat,
because the beat becomes a mere abstraction, as in Webern a hundred
years later. I marvel at the surrealism of this notation, implying—without
footnotes—the tentative no-beat feeling of a music in search of . . . the
fugue theme. Not to mention the ingenious

in the *Grosse Fuge.* As to the complexities of the 1940's and 1950's, agreed,
I am yet to hear a precise and spirited performance of Boulez's *Marteau,*
instead of all the counting, watching, and approximating. But at least it's
all there on paper. The function of notation is not only to serve the immediate performance efficiently, but to keep, to conserve. What will happen
to all the aleatory scores in a hundred years?"

"It is perhaps typical and commendable that you, the performer, should
be concerned with the composition's immortality. For the composer the
issue is how to make it, not how to keep it. New tasks: new performance,
new notation. Let me forget the 'masterwork.' We have new problems
—some of them perhaps primitive, hence primitively notated. But here I
must clear up a misunderstanding. I should like to see traditional notation expanded, not replaced. For instance: I am well aware of the inherent subtlety
of the relationship of bar line and beat to the music, which 'overcomes'
them. But we also need moments of no bar line and no beat—notes held not
by mutual agreement as to the number of counts, but via a spontaneous reaction of one performer to the other. Here is a germ of a performance task
capable of much development; and, as yet, far from resolved in the notation-
coordination domain: a music where the instruments or voices either individually or in groups, act and react to and against one another, like characters in a play, at times turning the concert stage into a battlefield. This idea
proved to be fertile ground for ensemble improvisation. It is easier to
improvise in that manner than to compose. On the other hand, one can go
much further with it in actual composition. One can develop it into a
veritable polyphony of musics, with each music independent of the tempo
and pulse of the other. I repeat, this presents a coordination-notation
problem. Ives wrestled with this problem, not without reward, but, lacking
practical performance experience, he could only derive certain limited
effects. Carter found a useful device in 'metrical modulation,' but one that

330

demands concentration by each performer on his own part to the point of shutting out the conflicting pulse of the others; hence, a genuine reacting, in my sense of the word, cannot take place (isn't supposed to, perhaps). Stockhausen's *Gruppen* is the most daring attempt, with its three orchestras, but here the composer relies on the makeshift method of metronome watching, a method which completely isolates one group from the other. I am convinced that genuine coordination must ultimately be obtained via 'reaction,' in other words, via *musical* points of reference, via listening and playing accordingly. Such interplay would constitute a task capable of engaging the performer's entire musical being."

"Is it not perhaps too schizoid a task, forcing upon the performer a role of simultaneous support and opposition? While you ask two players to play *at* each other, you still expect them to play *with* each other."

"Why not? Performance always required the ability to combine, say, passive and active, leading and following. Every downbeat is also an upbeat; our senses take in, enjoy what is just moving into the past, as our mind is shaping the next sounds. Performance also requires the ability to 'interpret' while at the same time allowing the music to 'speak for itself.'[2] And the degree of tension in a performance is dependent on the presence of such a dual effort on the performer's part. A crescendo to a climax is dramatic only if the performer is both the racehorse and the horseman holding the reins. Playing *at* as well as *with* is simply an extension of the duality principle inherent in the drama of musical performance."

"Are there any examples in your recent music which bear out this principle?"

"There is the clarinet, barking in the foreground at a distant tune in the background of *Echoi III,* a piece in which the foreground is much of the time in conflict with the background. But do not stress the 'conflict' aspect of these notions. We are dealing here with a variation of the old idea of different things going on at the same time, and the somewhat newer idea of what may be called a montage. The unforeseen relationships forming between the mounted elements interest us today, open up new possibilities. There is a moment in Bach's *Matthew* Passion which always struck me as unique and prophetic. A concert-duet, a setting of a poem of meditative nature, is suddenly blotted out (without preparation) by the chorus shouting: 'Bind him not!' Meanwhile, the concert-duet continues under the shouting, unperturbed; a form of superimposition, this; a montage of two musics, that stand in opposition to one another, yet miraculously relate, the

---

[2] At the root of this paradox is a phenomenon experienced by all performers: the emergence of the interpreter's originality through identification with the author and submersion in his work.

way everything relates if one but finds the key, the nonsense can make sense and 'open doors' in the hands of genius."

"You mentioned the notation-coordination difficulties arising with the realization of these ideas. Can you show this on paper?"

"It would take the space of a book to do it."

"You mentioned the need for notation to expand, as indeed it does today. Is this in the direction of the performer's choice, in the direction of 'less notation'?"

"A hundred different composers will devise a hundred different ways. But the new approach to notation can certainly not be equated with 'avoidance of notation.' Moreover, granting the performer limited areas of freedom and choice is primarily a formal and textural, not a notational idea."

"When one looks at the beautiful calligraphy, the graphic originality of recent scores, is it not as if the notation, the 'writing' of the score had become an end unto itself?"

"An end perhaps not, but here too, we have a performance of sorts. . ."

"What did you mean earlier by 'moments of incomplete notation'?"

"Unessentials to be filled in by the performer."

"I meant to ask then what could possibly be unessential in a composition, outside of the filling in of a self-evident harmony (as in figured bass)."

"Take a very fast run, for example, low to high and back to low: lowest and highest notes may be essential. Intermediate notes may, under certain circumstances (tempo, style) be unessential:

Leave it as above, and there is immediate clarity regarding the important low and high notes. The performer will realize that the in-between notes need hardly be discernible; the seemingly sketchy notation actually clarifies. I mentioned the barking of the clarinet in *Echoi*. This is to be done by way of a tone distortion, rendering pitches unrecognizable. Hence, I do not write them in, I indicate the approximate height, but erase the staff lines:

In his *Tempi Concertati,* Berio uses the word 'tutta' to indicate that the percussionist is to hit everything, as fast as possible; try to notate this exactly, and you force the percussionist to wrestle with an unessential: the 'order' in which these instruments are to be hit; the resulting performance will seem studied, whereas the effect in the composer's mind was one of abandonment, of eruption. Of course, choices allotted to the performer need not be confined to such detail."

"Where draw the line? At what point does the performer begin to be smothered by unsolicited freedoms, handed to him with a gesture of: 'You do it.'"

"Never draw the line and say: 'beyond this line there is no art.' But I sympathize with you. Many a new task is an old, or worse, a poor task in disguise. It sounds good in theory, fails in practice. Desk-experiment one may call it; choices allotted to the performer by a composer who has no live experience with performance problems, and who works out a new task like a chess problem. Freedom—choice—dangerous words. Yet the aleatory idea is no idle invention, and quite naturally follows the serial idea. In fact the two complement one another, share the basic premise of an ingenious 'pre-ordering,' which guarantees a particular result. Both involve a *canvassing* of possibilities, or games of numerology. Both run the risk of self-deceit, serial music in the direction of a would-be order, aleatory music in the direction of a would-be freedom. In our most recent music the two techniques join forces, producing perhaps the most interesting 'laboratory situation' of all times."

"And the music sounds like a 'laboratory situation' some of the time."

"I would not 'object to all this, on principle.' Object if you will, but not on principle. Object if you must to the extra work without extra credit demanded of the performer by the most extreme aleatoric music. Here a situation of 'musical indeterminacy' may well oblige you to decide for yourself what, where, and when to play, perhaps even write out your own part. In the program book there will be no mention of this 'overlapping' of performance and composition. One might call it 'Action-music,' or even, if you wish, 'Gebrauchsmusik.'[3]

"How closely related are your improvisations to the situation of musical indeterminacy?"

"The latter lays the emphasis on the 'situation' giving birth to the performance. Chamber improvisation lays the emphasis on the 'performance' resulting from the situation, and puts the responsibility for the

[3] In a number of Cage's compositions one may play as much or as little of the music as is convenient, use all instruments or only a few, depending on available performance time and personnel.

choices squarely on the shoulders of the performer. It by-passes the composer. It is composition become performance, *performer's music.*"

"Age of performance, laboratory obsessed!"

"Yes! 'All the world's a performance.' A monkey performs, lovers perform, Picasso's drawings are a marvel of performance, and the President of the United States performs his office. The word is growing old under my pen. Give me young words . . .'

"Like: situation, event, statement, variant, resultant, parameter?"

"These are 'borrowed' words. One uses them and blushes a little."

"I wonder why you neglected to mention 'chance' in this essay?"

"Quite by chance, I assure you . . .''

John Cage

[1912 - 1992]

Perhaps the most controversial composer of our time, John Cage is often dismissed as an incompetent and a fraud. The first charge can be answered simply by referring to Cage's musical background. He has had a sound academic training in music, and was for a time a pupil of Schoenberg and Cowell. With regard to the second accusation, it should be noted that Cage's interest in the unusual is by no means a recent development in his career or a hastily considered whim. On the contrary, his entire life's work — the early use of percussion ensembles, music for radios, the "prepared piano," and his present concern with improvisation, random choices, and visual effects akin to a new theatre — has been consistently experimental and in accord with his stated beliefs. This is hardly the mark of a fraud.

Cage has also been described as a "philosopher" rather than a composer, but the distinction is one which he would probably consider irrelevant. Music is, for him, not the restricted art form that our civilization has always assumed, but a vastly enlarged area of speculation that emerges as both a branch of theatre and a branch of philosophy. His experiments in this area are often moving, amusing, at times frightening, occasionally enlightening, always entertaining, and undeniably related to the uses of sounds. Whether the works are "music" or not is an unimportant question; they function much as music does, they teach us much about music — as music does, in the abstract — and, in their own right, they demand our attention and consideration.

"Interview with Roger Reynolds," originally published in *Generation* magazine (Ann Arbor, Michigan), 1962. Reprinted in the C. F. Peters Co.'s *John Cage* catalog (New York, 1962), pp. 45-52.

Interview
with Roger Reynolds,
1962

[*The questions are primarily based on material from Cage's new book* Silence. *The numbers in brackets which occur periodically in the text refer to relevant page numbers in the book.*]

- *Roger Reynolds:* Would you say something about your early musical training and tastes? I was amused to read that, at one time, you had hoped to devote your life to playing the works of Grieg. [115]
- *John Cage:* My first experience with music was through neighborhood piano teachers, and particularly my Aunt Phoebe. She said of the work of Bach and Beethoven that it couldn't possibly interest me, she herself being devoted to the music of the nineteenth century. She introduced me to Moszkowski and what you might call the piano music the whole world loves to play. In that volume, it seemed to me that the works of Grieg were more interesting than the others.
- *RR:* You remark in *45′ For A Speaker* [163] that "when [you] first tossed coins [you] sometimes thought: I hope such and such will turn up," and elsewhere in the same lecture [170] that "an error is simply a failure to adjust immediately from a preconception to an actuality." Are you still troubled occasionally by practical difficulties in implementing your philosophical positions?
- *JC:* I find that question a little difficult to deal with.
  When I first made the transition from a continuity that I was directing, as it were, to one which I wasn't directing, I still had a certain knowledge of the possibilities. And so, seeing that there were some that would be pleasing, I did, at first, wish that they would come up, rather than the ones I didn't know were pleasing. What actually happened was that when things happened that were not in line with my views as to what would be pleasing, I discovered that they altered my awareness. That is to say, I saw that things which I didn't think would be pleasing were in fact pleasing, and so my views gradually changed from particular ideas as to what would be pleasing, toward no ideas as to what would be pleasing. Therefore, when you ask at the end, do I "have difficulty in implementing" my philosophical positions: I don't try to have any of those things.

336

In other words, I try, rather, to keep my curiosity and my awareness with regard to what's happening open, and I try to arrange my composing means so that I won't have any knowledge of what might happen. And that, by the way, is what you might call the technical difference between indeterminacy and chance operations. In the case of chance operations, one knows more or less the elements of the universe with which one is dealing, wheras in indeterminacy, I like to think (and perhaps I fool myself and pull the wool over my eyes) that I'm outside the circle of a known universe, and dealing with things that I literally don't know anything about.
• RR: What do you think about the terms "meaning" and "symbolism" in connection with Art?
• JC: Well . . . About symbolism: I have never particularly liked it.
I'm beginning to have a different view of it. I don't like it when it is a one to one relationship. That is to say, that a particular thing is a symbol of a particular other thing. But if each thing in the world can be seen as a symbol of every other thing in the world, then I do like it.

As for meaning, I'm afraid that word means how one's experience affects a given individual with respect to his faculty of observing relationships. I think that is a rather private matter, and I often refer, in this case, to the title of Pirandello's play, *Right You Are, If You Think You Are.*
• RR: Would you comment on your statement in *Silence:* "when we separate music from life, what we get is art."
• JC: I cite [*in Silence*] the hexagram on grace in the Chinese book, the *I Ching.* That is generally held to be the hexagram on Art, and Art is viewed there as a light shining on top of a mountain, illuminating, to a certain extent, the surrounding darkness. That would place Art in a position where it penetrated, to a certain extent, life. Now if you separate the two, let us say, if you deal with this light—this thing that is better than the darkness or lighter than the darkness—and call that Art . . . then all you have is that lightness. Whereas what we need is to fumble around in the darkness [45-46], because that's where our lives (not necessarily all of the time, but at least some of the time, and particularly when life gets problematical for us) take place: in the darkness, or as they said in Christianity, "the dark night of the soul." It is in those situations that Art must act, and then it won't be just Art, but will be useful to our lives.
• RR: In *Lecture on Something* [139] you write that "when we remove the world from our shoulders, we notice it doesn't drop. Where is the responsibility? Responsibility is to oneself which is to say the calm acceptance of whatever responsibility to others and things comes along." Has not man traditionally operated on the assumption that his responsibility was to force Nature or life to conform to his needs?

• *JC:* Not man in general, but man as European. Man as Asiatic had a different view, which I refer to several times in the book. And in particular to that lecture by Fuller in which he points out that, just as if setting out from Asia to America you go with the wind, so the philosophies that grow up in Europe are in opposition to Nature, and toward the control of Nature. Whereas, the philosophies that grow up in Asia and increasingly so toward the Far East, are concerned with the acceptance of Nature, not its control. These two things meet in America, and so it is possible for us, I think, as Americans, more than it is possible for Europeans, to see the possibility of what you might call irresponsibility.

• *RR:* I notice that, at one time [30], you found the sounds of Beethoven, Italian *bel canto,* jazz, and the vibraphone distasteful, but that you had come to terms with all excepting the vibraphone. What is the present state of your relation to the vibraphone?

• *JC:* I can see perfectly well that, if I liked the vibraphone, the world would be more open to me. In the same way that if I liked Muzak, which I also don't like, the world would be more open to me. I intend to work on it. The simplest thing for me to do in order to come to terms with both those things would be to use them in my work, and this was, I believe, how so-called primitive people dealt with animals which frightened them.

• *RR:* In spite of some of the charges which have been hurled at you, it seems that your activities could be interpreted as a battle against the superficial: a reaction against a society which seems bent on increasing its insulation from direct experience and involvement in life.

• *JC:* I don't hear that as a question.

• *RR:* Well, its perhaps a proposal for comment . . .

• *JC:* Yes, maybe this will act as an answer. Nowadays more and more people are beginning to protest against society. Is that what you're talking about?

• *RR:* No, not exactly . . .

• *JC:* Or an objection to what you call the superficiality of so much of our society . . .

Well, I have decided that it is frequently difficult to know how to steer one's course in social situations; and I've decided to use this as a kind of compass: To make affirmative actions and not to make what I call negative, or, you might say, critical or polemical actions, even when the thing being criticized or fought against is patently evil. In other words, I shall not attack the evil but rather promote what seems to me to be what I call affirmative.

• *RR:* What I had in mind with this question was to get at what seems to me to be true of your work. That is, although there are many uninformed

338

and unthinking criticisms and comments about what people think your work does — not what you intend it to do — it could be viewed as a positive attempt to get at the rejection of experience.

• *JC:* Now I understand a little better. Let me put it this way, and it's in direct relation to the book [*Silence*]. I've had more response from the book than I've ever had from the publication of a record, the publication of music, the giving of a concert, the giving of a lecture or anything. Many, many people write or telephone to say that they have responded to a particular part of the book. It puzzled me at first — why they should respond more to a book than to any other action — and then it occurred to me that they are, in a sense, performers when they read. That is to say, they engage in an activity of their own, and so have a direct experience.

Most people mistakenly think that when they hear a piece of music, that they're not *doing* anything, but that something is being done *to* them. Now this is not true, and we must arrange our music, we must arrange our Art, we must arrange everything, I believe, so that people realize that they themselves are doing it, and not that something is being done to them.

• *RR:* I notice, in that connection, that you refer somewhere to your compositions as "occasions for experience" involving the eyes as well as the ears.

While noting the influence that Zen has had on you, in the foreword to *Silence,* you absolve it of responsibility for your activities. This was interesting, and brought to mind the disparities between the concept of Art in societies influenced by Zen, and your views. Would you comment on which aspects of Zen you find stimulating and acceptable, and which are not useful?

I notice, for example, that several times in the book you mention that the *I Ching* expresses a certain view with which you cannot agree.

• *JC:* That is rather difficult for me to answer because it's a process that I'm involved in continually. What I do, and what I have done since about 1947 when I got involved with Oriental philosophy is this: I try to see how something I read or something I experience works outside of its context (in, say, the context of music) and then, again, in the context of daily life. If I can see that it works, then a kind of thing you might call *acceptance* goes on. But if it doesn't work somewhere . . . it seems to me that there must have crept in some bug. Then I will lay it aside, become skeptical about it, and try to examine it further.

One can't do this all the time but it's a useful process. For instance, if, in our dealings with our composition of music, we find that it distorts our daily life, then there must be something wrong with the way we're composing, it seems to me. Whereas, if the way we compose is applicable to our daily life, and changes it, then it seems to me that there is something useful in the way we're composing music.

• *RR:* Which is the most important element of music?

• *JC:* The element of time.

• *RR:* I was hoping that you would talk a little about your provocative ideas on this subject.

• *JC:* My reasons [for believing that time is the most important], I have often given;namely, that if you take what the Europeans call the various parameters of sound, you find that only one of them exists in what we call silence, and that is time. Nevertheless, our views of time are suffering alteration, so that it is almost becoming less tangible than it was.

• *RR:* Would you elaborate?

• *JC:* Well, as I say somewhere in the book [38-40] we not only can go forward in time but we are able to go backwards in time. We must find some way to be able to go in all directions. Or in the work, for instance, of Christian Wolff, a thing which is difficult to rationally conceive takes place, namely, zero time.

You see, if music is conceived as an *object,* then it has a beginning, middle, and end, and one can feel rather confident when he makes measurements of the time. But when it [music] is *process,* those measurements become less meaningful, and the process itself, involving if it happened to, the idea of Zero Time (that is to say no time at all), becomes mysterious and therefore eminently useful.

• *RR:* You have said that [62] "normally the choice of sounds is determined by what is pleasing and attractive to the ear: delight in the giving or receiving of pain being an indication of sickness." You also mention that "when the war came along, [you] decided to use only quiet sounds," because, "there seemed to [you] to be no truth, no good, in anything big in society." Do you still hold these views, and, if so, what about the subjective and purposeful nature of such choice?

• *JC:* Both of those views were preliminary to my present point of view, which brings it about that I use, frequently, very loud sounds now. Even the view expressed about the giving of pain and pleasure . . . I don't agree with that any longer. We do give and receive pain and we might as well recognize the fact.

• *RR:* A question that has often been asked of you, and one to which you give interesting answers is: What is the purpose of writing music?

• *JC:* —

• *RR:* Perhaps it should be phrased, what is your purpose in writing music now?

• *JC:* I frequently say that I don't have any purposes, and that I'm dealing with sounds, but that's obviously not the case. On the other hand it is. That is to say, that I believe that by eliminating purpose, what I call *awareness* increases. Therefore my purpose is to remove purpose.

It's very simple to show, and we've already talked about it. If I have a particular purpose, and then a series of actions comes about, and all I get is an approximation of my purpose, then nothing but a sort of compromise or disappointment can take place. And perhaps that still takes place when my purpose is to remove purpose, namely, I see that I haven't really done it. But at least I'm going along in that general direction.

• RR: What is an experimental act, and how does it relate to so-called experimental music?

• JC: Experimental music can have many definitions [17 & 31], but I use the word *experimental* to mean making an action the outcome of which is not foreseen.

• RR: In your lecture *Experimental Music* [15] you answer a question concerning the impracticability of performing your music by saying: "Composing's one thing, performing's another, and listening's a third. What can they have to do with one another?" It would seem that they are very intimately connected.

• JC: We normally think that the composer makes something, the performer is faithful to it, and that the business of the listener is to understand it. Yet the act of listening is clearly not the same as the act of performing, nor is either one of them the same as the act of composing. I have found that by saying that they have nothing to do with one another, that each one of those activities can become more centered in itself, and so more open to its natural experience. Referring to what we said earlier, about people generally thinking that something is being done *to* them, well, when they listen, they think that the composer, through the performer, has done something to them, forgetting that they are doing it themselves.

• RR: Since it would seem that human beings have uniquely developed capacities for expressiveness (no matter how crude they may sometimes seem to us to be), how can you advocate abandoning expressivity in music?

• JC: Coming back to what we said about symbolism, everything is expressive. But *what* it expresses grows up in each person who has the experience. If the person performs in such a way that the events he brings into existence are free, completely around them, to be viewed in any way, then the optimum of a desirable situation seems to me to have arisen. Whereas, if in his expressivity, he forces the viewer to respond in a particular way, then he has cramped and narrowed the situation of possibilities.

• RR: Then the sounds the performer makes should be free of intention in order to allow them . . .

- *JC:* . . . to be fully expressive!
- *RR:* A key term which appears in many of your writings is "Theater." What does "theater" imply to you?
- *JC:* It simply means the use of all one's senses. But the senses we use primarily are seeing and hearing. Theater is distinct from music in that it calls seeing strongly into play with hearing.
- *RR:* In other words, physical actions in space take on a significance equal to that of sounds in the air.
- *JC:* Yes.
- *RR:* Do you think that lack of theater may be partially responsible for some of the negative response to electronic music?
- *JC:* Definitely. I think that the most important thing to do with electronic music now is to somehow make it theatrical, and not through such means as turning the lights out, but rather through introducing live performance elements. That is to say, people actually doing things.
- *RR:* Do you think that perhaps a degree of encroachment on the traditionally ritualistic atmosphere of public concerts would help? That is, should listeners not be artificially separated from sound sources by stereotyped seating arrangements, stages, formal clothing, and so on?
- *JC:* That too. But I also mean the actual, visible manipulation of the machines, to begin with; the distinct giving to the audience of the impression that something is happening then which is unique to that particular experience. If the audience, if any of us, feel that what is being played at that time can be played at any other time, and result in the same experience, then a kind of *deadliness* falls over everyone.
- *RR:* This strikes me as being the case in traditional concert programs such as those given by the Choral Union Series here in Ann Arbor. When you can hear Beethoven's Fifth Symphony on any one of forty different recordings, how strong is the need to listen carefully at a concert? Urgency is missing because the sound of a familiar piece of music is such a relatively common experience, especially since various "interpretations" are so remarkably similar.
- *JC:* In this connection, David Tudor and I were discussing on our way from New York, the possibility of his resolving not to make any records in the future, unless they result in actions which could not possibly be made otherwise. I don't think that this would be a full answer to the problem, but at least it would be an answer to the problem as it confronts him, in his musical life; namely, he is frequently asked to make records, and now he could refuse to make them.
- *RR:* Yes, though such a resolve could be hard on those of us who do not live in New York.
- *JC:* But you see through the kind of activity that you are making here

in Ann Arbor, the deficit of music that records have seemed to offset is being offset here, through the concerts that you give;* and if this will spring up over the whole country—or even just what you're doing here—then there will be inevitably an exchange of live music, in the places where it is produced. The more people see the liveliness of this, the more it will crop up in other places. This is, again, what I refer to as affirmative action.

• *RR:* In a lecture in 1937 [5], you said, "the principle of form will be our only constant connection with the past." You went on to identify this connection as "the principle of organization, or man's common ability to think." Later [35] you would associate form with the "morphology of a continuity" and "expressive content." Would you trace your developing view of form?

• *JC:* I'm now more involved in *dis*organization and a state of mind which in Zen is called *no-mindedness.*

Those statements, given in 1937, are given as a sort of landmark to let the reader know from where I set out. There are certain things in that lecture that I would agree with and some that I would not. I imagine that when I used the word *form* then, that I meant what I later called *structure* (the divisibility of a whole into parts). Later I used *form* in the same sense that people generally use the word *content* (that aspect of composition which is best able to be free, spontaneous, heartfelt, and so on).

That attitude towards form is sort of in the middle, between my present thought and my early thought. Now I don't bother to use the word form, since I am involved in making processes, the nature of which I don't foresee. How can I speak of form?

• *RR:* A chronological sampling of your work would seem to indicate that each successive composition implements a new idea. That is, instead of a fresh manipulation or reordering of accepted terms within a style, you manipulate styles or ideas within a developing philosophical view.

• *JC:* I don't understand the question.

• *RR:* Most composers operate within a certain style or idiom, and they have set materials which they manipulate. Their compositions, each one after the other, become no more, nor less, than a careful new ordering of the same factors. It has seemed to me in looking at your activities chronologically that your works continually evince a new manipulation of *ideas* on a level abstracted from *things*. Each new piece puts into effect a new manifestation of style or idea in some way, and that the continuity in your work is a developing view of desirable actions.

• *JC:* Oh, yes, I'm devoted to the principle of originality. Not originality in the egoistic sense, but originality in the sense of doing something which

*[Ed. Note: Mr. Cage refers here to the activities of the ONCE organization.]

it is necessary to do. Now, obviously, the things that it is necessary to do are not the things that have been done, but the ones that have not yet been done. This applies not only to other people's work, but seriously to my own work; that is to say, if I have done something, then I consider it my business not to do that, but to find what must be done next.

• *RR:* Why are you in the habit of presenting your lectures in some unusual manner? As an example, in the extremely repetitious *Lecture On Nothing*, you periodically say, "if anybody is sleepy let him go to sleep."

• *JC:* If a lecture is informative, then people can easily think that something is being done to them, and that they don't need to do anything about it except receive. Wereas, if I give a lecture in such a way that it is not clear what is being given, then people have to do something about it.

• *RR:* In the lecture *Composition As Process*, you state that, around 1950, you viewed composition as "an activity integrating the opposites, the rational and the irrational, bringing about, ideally, a freely moving continuity within a strict division of parts, the sounds, their combinations and succession being logically related or arbitrarily chosen." Later you refer to composition [71] as involving processes not objects. Would you comment on how your view has altered during the last few years?

• *JC:* Yes. It is still involved with process and not with object. The difference is specifically the difference, say, between an ash tray and the whole room. Ash tray can be seen as having beginning and end, and you can concentrate on it. But when you begin to experience the whole room—not object, but many things—then: where is the beginning? where is the middle? where is the end? It is clearly a question not of an object but rather of a process, and finally, that process has to be seen as subjective to each individual.

• *RR:* It is the process of one's observation, not the physical fact . . .

• *JC:* Yes, and that is why I want to get it so that people realize that they themselves are doing their experience, and that it's not being done to them.

Then coming back to that question on form. I thought of something else to say. When I say that, "I am not interested in form," or "how can I use the word form," I have to ask another question, namely, where do we see any formlessness? Particularly nowadays with telescopes, with microscopes, etc., as one of my painter friends, Jasper Johns, says, "the world is very busy." Form everywhere.

• *RR:* What relation has "cause and effect" to your work?

• *JC:* That, again, is like the attitude toward symbol; rather than see that one thing has a given effect, we want to see that one thing has *all* effects.

• *RR:* The notion of causality has been much too simple in the past, there is such a multitude of causes and effects, and their interrelationships are so complex . . .

• *JC:* That is the real situation: that everything causes everything else. In other words, it is much more complicated than our scientists like to admit.

• *RR:* For example, the development of relativity has put Newton's laws in an unexpected perspective. One discovers that the neat mottos which we have for dealing with life are often inaccurate.

• *JC:* And if I feel the weight, for instance, of my responsibility, then I'm simply ignorant of the effects of my actions, because they have effects which don't happen to cause me to think about them.

• *RR:* Some composers recently have admitted a degree of chance to their compositions but have retained generally traditional methods by and large. You have noted that this practice reveals a "carelessness with regard to the outcome." [138] Would you elaborate on that comment?

• *JC:* If one is making an object and then proceeds in an indeterminate fashion, to let happen what will, outside of one's control, then one is simply being careless about the making of that object.

• *RR:* You don't think, then, that it is valid for a composer to wish that a certain aspect or section of his work will have a changing face while the general language and substance remains controlled?

• *JC:* I think I know what you're referring to and it's a very popular field of activity among composers at the present time. That is to say, to have certain aspects of a composition controlled, if I understand you, and others uncontrolled. Well, what is maintained here is the concept of *pairs of opposites:* having black and white, as it were, and then composing with the play of these opposites. One can then engage in all of the games that academic composition has led us to know how to play. One can balance this with that, produce climaxes, and so on. I'm afraid all I can say is that it doesn't interest me.

It doesn't seem to me to radically change the situation from the familiar convention. It simply takes these new ways of working and consolidates them with the old knowledges, so that one remains at home with one's familiar ideas of the drama — of the play of the opposites. So, one wouldn't have to change one's mind. Whereas, I think we are in a more urgent situation, where it is absolutely essential for us to change our minds fundamentally. And in this sense, I could be likened to a fundamentalist Protestant preacher.

Stockhausen has recently employed a system of composition which involves the selection of one technique at a time from a number of different ways of working, and an attempt to let any one of them move into play. This gives the impression of a rich reservoir of contemporary techniques, so that in a repertoire of say seven or eight compositional techniques, indeterminacy would play the part of one, and you could call on it, as it were, when you had some use for it. But, that doesn't require a change of mind from what one previously had, and so nothing fundamentally different is taking place. I think one could see it very clearly in terms of painting. You could have certain parts of a canvas controlled and others quite chaotic, and so you would be able to play, as it were, in the same way in which you had played before. What we need is a use of our Art which alters our lives—is useful in our lives. We are familiar with those plays of balance, so they couldn't possibly do anything more to us, no matter how novel they were, than they already have done. "New wine in old bottles."

• *Robert Ashley:** It seems to me that your influence on contemporary music, on "musicians," is such that the entire metaphor of music could change to such an extent that—time being uppermost as a definition of music—the ultimate result would be a music that wouldn't necessarily involve anything but the presence of people. That is, it seems to me that the most radical redefinition of music that I could think of would be one that defines "music" without reference to sound.

• *JC:* Oh yes, I made some use of that in my silent piece [Ed. Note: Mr. Cage has written a piece (4'33") which directs the performer (if he is a pianist) to come on stage, seat himself at a piano for a specified time without engaging in any other activity than the delineation, by some means, of the 3 movements of the composition. At the end of the designated time, the performer rises and leaves the room without having made any intentional sounds.]

• *RA:* It doesn't strike me as being that.

• *JC:* But that involves a number of people being together, and there are no special sounds.

• *RA:* If our awareness of time increased to such a degree that it didn't require that we be informed of time through the medium of sound—if our awareness of time became enlarged or changed to a really radical degree—then it's conceivable that we would do away with sound.

• *JC:* But we can't. You see there are always sounds. [8]

• *RR:* This has to do with the distinction that Mr. Cage has made between *sound* and *silence*: that the former consists of sounds that are *intended*, while the latter allows the sound which occurs unbidden in the environment to be heard.

• *JC:* Yes.

---

*Mr. Ashley, a composer living in Ann Arbor, is one of the organizers of the ONCE activities. He was enjoying the interview, which took place in his living room, and asked if he might comment on this point.

• *RR:*   So that what you are saying, in essence, is that we might do away with intended sounds.

• *RA:*   Well . . . Let me put it this way. We might have a piece from which one participant would come,and, upon being questioned, would say that the occasion was marked by certain sounds. Another person might say that he didn't remember any sounds. There was something else. But they both would agree that a performance of music had taken place.

• *RR:*   This seems to have more to do with what we've discussed as theater.

• *RA:*   It seems that the use of "theater" in this connection is a sort of transitional definition, to condition people to other possibilities.

• *JC:*   And that the experience itself becomes markedly more subjective.

• *RA:*   Markedly more subjective and particularly involved with a sort of indefinable sense of where your time information was coming from.

• *JC:*   Exactly.

• *RR:*   This would certainly take place if one could do away with the obvious hierarchy of importances which is usually intended when you come to a musical experience. If the experience is unpurposeful, and undirected, then response becomes totally a question of the listener's individual sensitivities and conditioning.

• *JC:*   La Monte Young is doing something quite different from what I am doing, and it strikes me as being very important. Through the few pieces of his I've heard, I've had, actually, utterly different experiences of listening than I've had with any other music. He is able either through the repetition of a single sound or through the continued performance of a single sound for a period like twenty minutes, to bring it about that after, say, five minutes, I discover that what I have all along been thinking was the same thing is not the same thing after all, but full of variety. I find his work remarkable almost in the same sense that the change in experience of seeing is when you look through a microscope. You see that there is something other than what you thought there was.

On the other hand, La Monte Young's music can be heard by Europeans as being European. For example, take the repetition of a tone cluster or a single sound at a seemingly constant amplitude over, say, a ten-minute period. The European listener is able to think, "Well, that is what we've always had, minus all the elements of variation." So they imagine, you see, that something is being done to them, namely a simplification of what they're familiar with. My response is not that he is doing something to me, but that I am able to hear differently than I ever heard.

• *RR:*   Do you think that America has yet begun to further its most striking and characteristic resource which you summarize as [74] "its capacity to break easily with tradition, to move easily into the air, its capacity for the unforeseen, its capacity for experimentation"? Are not some Europeans capitalizing on a limited exploration of what is a fundamentally American impulse?

• *JC:*   There are two questions. We are clearly going to have a great deal of lively activity in America, and already are having it. And I also agree that Europeans will be capitalizing on it. What I hope is that the Europeans will become more American.

Richard
Maxfield

[1924 -   ]

Richard Maxfield has been a major influence in the second generation of American composers following the ideas of Cage, Feldman, and their associates. With a sound formal musical education here and abroad, Maxfield has thoroughly worked through both post-Webernian and post-Cageian musical approaches, coming at last to his own solution through electronic and theater music — the latter, as it is written today, concerning the manner in which the actions of the performers or participants contribute varyingly to the total effect of the piece. Maxfield's challenging and original scores, unfortunately known only slightly even now, reflect the same pervasive concern for personal statement in music to be found in the following short essays.

"Composers, Performance and Publication" and "Music, Electronic and Performed," from *An Anthology of Chance Operations* edited by La Monte Young (New York, LaMonte Young and Jackson MacLow, 1963), unpaged.

Composers,
Performance
and Publication

When music is published for people to play
composers often obtain performances utterly lacking in style.

For one reason or another
performers frequently find themselves playing
music they don't like
but go through with it because after all it's their job.
This hostility projects itself to the audience
and the public and the music are done disservice.

Well-meaning artists
who have an extensive training in the standard repertory
but no understanding of new music
sometimes believe that it is their duty to introduce contemporary fare
(which it is not!)
and dutifully offer
with equal probability something of good or vulgar taste
and perhaps play it with style, but in greater probability not
to an audience with their minds elsewhere
dutifully sitting it out;
and this is a disservice.

Composers might do well to avoid these embarrassments.

Artists don't publish directions
for painting their paintings or sculpting their sculptures
except in the form of children's coloring books and toys.

And in the event of a showing of paintings
one may expect some unity of painter, group, movement, subject or
    culture,
but is not required to run the gamut of familiar and diverse period pieces
beginning with a baroque or rococo piece or two
a Gainsborough
a popular van Gogh
a dutiful representation of Bauhaus

350

and a rousing nude or lovely sunset to cap it off at the end.
Yet concert programs full of clashing works are the rule.

I can remember having considered myself lucky
to have one of my pieces mixed into the usual variety show.
It may not occur to the composer
to limit his works to appropriate circumstances;
when music is published for people to play
he could not if he would.

Yet nobody suggests that he shouldn't publish his music.
There is the general assumption that he should by all means
hope to sell lots of copies
and strive always to be performed anywhere and everywhere
to obtain in return a small token income and increased fame.

One is made to feel that to be part of our society
one must fit into the general picture:
It is everyone's business to make things as fast as possible
then sell them somehow:
employ psychologists, promoters, statisticians;
advertize; distribute. POUR the products out.
There's a market for anything.

And so we have too much art, too many concerts, records,
    radio broadcasts,
like we have too many potatoes, newspapers, city-dwellers.
Consequently things are of little value, and never built to last.

But it seems to me that the time allotted to each of us is so short
that it becomes a serious waste to spend it in the slightest superfluous act;
if art is worth producing (there is already such an accumulation!)
it must be of superior quality.
It will require great ingenuity to compete with all the rest.
Looked at in this way, what is worth doing
is worth our best concentration, discipline, integrity, style.
We might try to do less
and better
and take care that our effort counts for more
and be happier and healthier.

If composers see it as their duty to limit their performances
to programs where they fit and strengthen
and to performers who can be counted upon
they would find their music in greater demand.

to publishers and performers concerned with business and box office
and with pleasing the mass taste,
if instead of hustling to push themselves into public consciousness
they were to become more modest and more proud,
then people would start seeking them out.
Interested people do this.
And so their public would become an interested one.

Like an art showing, a concert is a unified experience
if only through the unity of its time and place and those assembled.
It may be a unifying experience as well
if the work of one composer only
or a group of composers with essentially similar spirit
are placed together on the same program.
But for heaven's sake what kind of unified experience can anyone obtain
from the usual programming of our well-meaning (we suppose) performers:
a motley concatenation of this and that for every (or average) taste.
It is an ordeal like having to take in the whole Metropolitan Museum in
    one day
as if one were born with but this one day to live.
Then one would do better not to spend it in a museum.

Another means toward control of his fate in performance
is offered the composer by so-called electronic music.
I mean the new techniques of sound production and montage
by which the composer is enabled to produce his own musical
    performance
without dependence on anybody else for interpretation and execution.
(And he gains in the bargain access to the whole continuum of sound for
    his palette
instead of being limited to acoustic inventions a few centuries old
and the agility with which they can be bowed, plucked, beaten and
    blown.)
Working directly with sound with his new sensitive electronic tools,
he has no further need of the universal but obsolete symbols on score
    paper
(do-it-yourself performance recipes suitable for voluminous publication).
By this means, his terminal art product is no longer just plan
but definitive realization in a recorded form
which can be trotted out like a piece of sculpture to show anybody.
It thus becomes far easier to present his work publicly or privately
not having to depend on the patronizing publisher and the dutiful
    performer.

352

Composers,
Performance and Publication

In so extricating himself from these dependencies
the artist is rewarded by liberation from the enervating conflict
between integrity and the compromising demand of merchandise
  salability.
Destructive inhibitions arise in that mind
which under all other considerations and activities is constantly
  remembering
that in the end its work must be acceptable to the publisher
who is not interested in risk but in monetary profit.

The few pennies so patronizingly offered the composer for his work
amount to payment so meager as to be totally absurd;
no sane person would give his time for such a pittance.
And this in return for all rights and control over the fate of the music!
The publisher does not serve the composer
by printing and disseminating his music:
it becomes the property of the publisher,
and its use governed by big business not artists.
Serious art is hardly likely to thrive in such an impossible system.

John Cage said that composers are like princes
who bestow priceless gifts to humanity without hope of return.
Since the matter is beyond price
no sense in giving any thought to collecting miserable little token fees.
Better find another means to get fed.
A properly effective means.

An audience is best served by presenting a challenging occasion
suitable to the most sophisticated connoisseur.
The more special and atypical the fare
the more it offers by virtue of being extraordinary.

Rather than popularizing such concerts,
warn the audience away.
Then only those who are receptive to the extraordinary will come
and the atmosphere will be alert and open.
The majority who mainly seek familiar entertainment
will help by staying away
until they become properly curious as to what the informed are talking
  about.
There is more satisfaction in that calmer atmosphere
of an audience come prepared to listen
than in the cool reception of a very much larger audience
who aren't really interested.

**Richard
Maxfield**

Never mind adverse press.
It is predominantly the voice of conventionality
and exerts, if anything, a negative effect on thinking people.

And especially never mind how much applause.
It is not so much correlated with the quality of the music
as it is a conditioned response
elicited by the bravura of a strong personality on stage
or the clangor of a loud and vigorous finale.

Music,
Electronic
and Performed

The use of sound recording as a compositional medium
with its attendant techniques
of electronic manipulation and tape montage
called electronic music for want of a better term
has been censured
as producing a degree of rigidity in its sounds
much as in a recording of a Beethoven symphony or Ives quartet.

There is, however, a fundamental difference.
Formal instrumental music is generally embodied in written score
the notation of which is not to be taken as complete or exact;
thus room is left its interpreter
to decide nuance of detail
anew for each performance.

But although a performance of an instrumental work
merely projects a *given performance,*
in this new art form
it is the composer himself
working directly with the recorded sounds
who selects every nuance;
there may indeed be no score
and later interpretations not desired:
the recording, instead, becomes the terminal object of creation.

Even so, music in this medium is not necessarily rigid.
There are means here too
for allowing a certain mobility in detail.
Thus, when it is completely fixed
it is at the choosing of the composer.

A rigid structure is a property rather than a fault.
Writing, painting, and sculpture preserve fixed shapes,
while theatre, dance, and sculptural mobiles
are intended to change in certain respects from time to time.
The creator normally selects his medium or usage

Richard
Maxfield

according to his intentions
as to fixity or flux.

And even when an art object is completely fixed
the aesthetic experience it induces
is never the same on two different occasions.
Moreover, music by nature moves in time
and can project its rigidity
only upon *second* hearing
(and even then only by comparison with the memory of the first).

In any case, one can avoid any such effect
by never listening twice to the same recording of the work.
(I frequently compose a new realization
for each presentation of a given work.)

Connected to the objection of rigidity in recordings
is the felt absence of live performers.
Tradition has conditioned us to expect their presence
and without them we feel less at home;
and so we must
until we are as used to something else.

The missing element
is the live contact between audience and performer
and the awareness that both affect each other.

This loss to the audience:
hearing electronic music,
but not being able to influence its creation
(because it was prerecorded on tape)
can be felt, too, by reading a poem
aloud, but to oneself, alone.

We become both audience and interpreter
face to face with the poet's own writing
without intermediary.

Rightfully, the final, crucial interpretation of any work
(whether performed in our presence or finished beforehand)
must take place in the mind of the beholder;
all the skill of the finest artist would be to no avail
if all his audience had closed and unresponsive minds.

If the poem we had read alone
were read to us instead by someone other than the poet

there would now be interposed a third personality
and the words would come to us second hand.

Traditionally, composers had no choice
since notation was by nature inexact and incomplete
but to delegate interpretation to the performer.
Nowadays very exact and complete notation can be made
with the aid of acoustic measuring devices
but since performers are not mere machines
we treat them with due respect and ask their collaboration,
turning to our machines on those occasions
when we would completely predetermine the result.

The recorded means allow a greater unity
since there is no compromising the creator's intentions by a latter hand.
No matter how expert and sensitive this latter hand
its impulses do not derive from the mind which conceived the work.

A higher degree of perfection is inherent, too,
in the possibility of correction and revision
which the electronic composer may effect in the calm of his studio;
but a prerogative not granted the live performer
whose every nuance is irrevocably made under the scrutiny of an audience
simultaneously with its reaching their ears.

This perilous condition
wherein the final act of creation
depends upon such exigencies of the moment
as states of digestion, nerves, mood,
how the audience and performer get on together and the like,
may produce its off days
its unforgettable lapses and mistakes
as well as inspiration.
In fact, a live performance of an exacting work
is seldom completely in order.
Not even a Toscanini could reliably produce such a risky miracle.

Certainly catastrophe may be extremely interesting
and to include its possibility or even probability
might well be a composer's intention.

Risk of catastrophe, degrees of indeterminacy or mobility of detail
may also be obtained in electronic music if desired.

In *Fontana Mix,* John Cage provides four tapes

Richard
Maxfield

to be played on four machines simultaneously.
He suggests that (optionally) during the playing
tape speed, volume and tone controls may be freely altered
and that the machines may be stopped and started
between each recorded sound event.
White paper leader is spliced into the silences on each tape
to mark the places where these changes might occur.

If live performers play the machines
imaginatively altering the structural detail
through interpretations of the composer's instructions,
we now have a hybrid form
yielding the increased palette available on tape
as well as improvisatory freedom through human performance.

There is also a literature in existence
combining tape and instrumental players.

In its simplest form,
as in the old "add-a-part" records of the standard repertory
with missing part to be supplied by amateur or student,
our instrumentalists may play along
in luxury of the captive, if unresponsive, mechanical collaboration.

By comparison with either medium alone
such usage may lose more than it gain.
The loss is particularly felt
the more the taped sounds imitate an instrumental style.
Electronic resources are utterly different by nature,
their limits and idiomatic use having nothing whatever to do
with those imposed by the instruments or the human voice.
Its abuse as a financially expedient novelty
to substitute for additional live performers
is serving us dinner with the decoy instead of duck.

And if the soloists have to coordinate with the tape
following its rhythm and nuance like the accompanist,
lost is tape's freedom to transcend the old ensemble limitations
and the live performer is effectively straitjacketed in the bargain.
I view the situation as demanding quite another approach
than pretending that prerecorded sounds on a tape machine
can be treated like a responsive ensemble player.
And I shall here risk attempting some description
of my own approaches to this fusion
believing the issues to be sufficiently new and problematic
that these examples will not be unwelcome.

**Music,
Electronic and Performed**

It seems to me that pure electronic music
is self-sufficient as an art form
without any visual added attractions or distractions.
I view as irrelevant
the repetitious sawing on strings and baton wielding spectacle
we focus our eyes upon during a conventional concert.

Much more sensible
either no visual counterpart
or one more imaginatively selected
such as lighting
cinema, choreography
fireworks
trees . . .

To interject the human personality
on stage before the audience's eyes
only to have him play a musical instrument
would normally be uninteresting and gratuitous
unless he might pursue activities visually effective
yet relevant or contributive to the total effect.

In short, if we watch the soloist while we hear the music he makes,
we experience a theater piece rather than pure music.
Traditionally we pretend otherwise
and little imagination is tolerated in his demeanor;
but a more interesting alternative
might be for acceptance of this reality.
It begins already with Haydn,
where the players depart one at a time
at the end of the Farewell Quartet.

In this opera for players instead of singers,
the performers, most ideally, would play themselves,
and the composition integrated with such an expression.
(That most jazz players achieve this effect to some extent
explains a good deal about their popularity and communicative power.)

Basic to the composition of the *Piano Concert for David Tudor*
and also in *Perspectives for La Monte Young*
is the consideration of the distinctive stage personality
of the soloist who will be seen, heard, felt during the music.

I therefore began the composition of each of these two works
by recording the performer's improvisation,
but otherwise endeavoring not to influence his choice.

Richard
Maxfield

Thus was obtained a library of material
much larger than might be needed
so that for each new presentation
I could select a fresh combination from the collection
to be treated anew
in montage and electronic manipulation.

In concert the performer, having the last turn,
is to combine similar but new live sounds
in freely improvised rapport with this montage.
He should not be forewarned
as to how I have structured his sounds
nor indeed which of them are to appear on the occasion.
Though he will be familiar with each
having made it
he cannot anticipate the alterations I shall have made.
The effect is to enter a world at once familiar and strange.

The result is a creative collaboration
between composer and performer
in which the two personalities alternately predominate
in the successive layers of activity
by which the final structure is produced.

I will only add that these performers characteristically employ
unconventional modes of performance
beautiful and fascinating to watch;
and that the recorded montage does not imitate an instrumental texture
(on the contrary, its components originate in it
from which they radically deviate and extend).

In another work, *Clarinet Music,*
for five clarinetists and five tapes,
the theatre situation
is more an abstract choreography than portrait of the artist.
Here I prescribe certain unconventional modes of playing
(chosen for both visual and sonic value)
to be freely used by each performer
except that they are not to coincide
with timbres, pitches, rhythms, or dynamics
heard from the other performers
or suggested by the tapes.

Finally, a third example
representing an almost opposite approach

Music,
Electronic and Performed

was used in *Dromenon* for James Waring,
"a concert for music, dance, and lights."

Here the visual focus is upon two independent media:
modern dance and a composition of lighting.
Again the aural counterpart presents two opposing sources of activity:
the instrumental ensemble and synthetic sounds on tape.

My treatment is of course related to an Ivesian device
whereby independent groups play simultaneously
each in different character and tempo
and without attending to synchronization
one group with the other.

My score for the five instrumental performers
indicates definite time areas (in numbers of seconds)
and within each, which instruments may play and in which register;
but nothing more

Which five is left undetermined,
and may be different for each presentation.
Each performer may play as much or as little as he wishes,
but is asked to produce a variety
in pitch, duration, dynamics and timbre
within his own part and in rapport with the others.

The tape parts contain the same durational areas
of density and tessitura,
except structured in a different permutation.
Its texture is kept transparent
so as not to mask the instrumental forces,
but its timbres mostly complex and strident,
so as to compete with them in richness and brilliance.
The sounds were tuned to notes from unconventional scales
and avoid standard pitches expected from the instrumental forces.

To facilitate the opposition,
the five instruments play from the pit
preferably situated to hear the electronic tapes but dimly
and each other well.

The separateness in nature of these two media
is thus accepted and heightened
to produce in combination an antiphonal collage
serving like a back-drop fabric
decorative but independent of the lights and dance.

Morton
Feldman

[1926 - 1987]

One of America's most important and original contributions to new music was developed in New York in the early 1950's by a group of composers including John Cage and Morton Feldman. Not so much concerned with chance as a compositional method as with the nature of sound itself, Feldman attempts to present sonorities objectively without the complexities and superfluities of process or "message." This concern has enabled him to perfect a music whose rationale is solely sonoric, demonstrating a singular clarity and texture.

Feldman's concern with the implications of the composer's task is reflected in the present interview, conducted by Robert Ashley. Ashley is one of a group of young composers who have organized the important ONCE festivals of new music in Ann Arbor, Michigan; another composer active in the ONCE group is Roger Reynolds, whose interview with John Cage is reprinted elsewhere in this volume.

This interview was conducted expressly for the present volume, and printed with the editors' permission in *Kulchur* 18 (Summer, 1965), 20-24.

An Interview
with Robert Ashley,
August 1964

• *Feldman:* During the past few years I am continually reminded of Peguy's remark, "Everything begins as a mystique and ends in politics." It seems that about ten or fifteen years after something new and original is done and has its first impact, that impact becomes a political one. That is to say, by the time the young composer gets in touch with a particular work, it is already in a power struggle with other works and other ideas. The intention, the *aesthetic* of the work may be a complete mystery to this young composer. But in the form of politics it is not a mystery. It is very concrete. So what the young composer does is to become a *revisionist*. We know from history that it is the revisionist who takes things from that mysterious region of originality and gives those things a man-made rationale. It was true of Christ; same thing with Luther; what was pure, for example, in the ancient Hebrew belief was too mysterious for many people. It came from a divine being. It wasn't human. Christ made it human. For Luther it had to be even more human. I mean that the human comes in and makes a synthesis which he can work with comfortably—a concrete synthesis. And so what happens is that the original—that which was pure, that which was like Nature, that which didn't seem to reflect a "human" point of view—is cast aside, or rather, to be more precise, is *incorporated* by the revisionist mind. Stockhausen is a perfect example of the revisionist mind. His whole attitude to the work, for example, that John Cage has done and the work that I have done is really not unlike Toynbee's evaluation of history seen through a Christian bias—that the Jews are a fossil race. I'm quite sure that Stockhausen feels that "chance" is now a fossil aesthetic. But then I must not even use the word "aesthetic." Remember that the revisionists do not see chance as an aesthetic. They see it as a process that they must "humanize" and present only in a very portentous technical fashion. This, of course, is done without any aesthetic goals in mind. What the revisionist wants to do is to make a political impact. The revisionist wants power. It is in the nature of a revisionist to want power. It is in the nature of a revisionist to start a "school." It is the nature of a revisionist to want to convert. For example, it is very interesting how much Stockhausen enjoys having around him a large coterie of young people, and how much he enjoys talking and lecturing—converting people. The

363

revisionists are fanatics. But what they are fanatic about is always amazing to me, because they have created nothing new.

• *Ashley:* How does this change from aesthetics to politics affect you? That is, when you began working—if I understand your analogy—your concern was primarily aesthetic. But now your aesthetic has become one of the ingredients in the political struggle. How does this affect your work?

• *Feldman:* I find that the only way I can work today is not to think of the present, but only to think of the past, the past of my own life, where I worked without being conscious of the ramifications of my own actions in the world. I certainly don't want to create the impression by those religious analogies that I think *I* was some sort of deity. But there was a deity in my life, and that was *sound.* Everything else was after the fact. All "realization" was after the fact. Process was after the fact. Of course, what happens in the world when your work starts to become well known is that you have to justify it. You have to make some sort of rationale. And even the most banal rationale is accepted—welcomed—by people who should know better. For example, in some of my music I leave the rhythmic situation quite free. That is, there are variable degrees of slowness, and the performer has freedom of duration. Several years ago I mentioned to a very renowned colleague that in a certain piece I had made a metronome marking of "between 40 and 70"—which is still relatively slow—and it was amazing to me how relieved this brilliant man was.

• *Ashley:* You mean that to rationalize your art puts it into the political struggle. Certainly most composers are aware of "chance" now, and a lot of recent music uses chance in some fashion—to some degree—combined with other ideas. This, I guess, would be "revisionist" music. Most of it does seem sick—I mean ailing, without conviction. The composers seem uncertain about just why they are using chance. In quoting Péguy do you mean that when a musical idea, like chance, gets to be part of the political struggle, its value really "ends?"

• *Feldman:* Well, that's what happens when a composer gets caught up in the political struggle. The whole temperament of this period is basically an academic one, academic because it is based on other people's work. That alone makes it academic. For me there is no difference between the extreme, mechanistic writing of Milton Babbitt and the extreme, compulsive writing of La Monte Young. The reason that music is ailing is that everybody is still following the same historical process—that Malraux idea—that Art comes from Art. Now, anybody who was around in the early '50s with the painters saw that these men had started to explore their own sensibilities, their own plastic language, each one very different. It's almost laughable when you read the criticism of the work of those days, when they were all lumped together as the "New York School." Actually, the thing that made it a school was a powerful, mysterious aesthetic. That is, they all searched within their own sensibilities for those energies, for everything connected with the painting. Now, again, a few years later what the young people all started to take from the work was its most superficial mannerisms — its brushstrokes — that which they thought was "calligraphy" — that which they thought were objects (which weren't objects). They started to build on the work of these people with what they could recognize as technical achievements. Now, never before was there an aesthetic movement as fresh and new as the abstract painting of the '50s: that complete independence from other art, that complete inner security to work with that which was unknown to them. That was a fantastic aesthetic accomplishment

I feel that John Cage, Earle Brown, Christian Wolff, and I were very much in that particular spirit. We didn't exchange intellectual ideas. Ideas didn't make the work. Unfortunately for most people who pursue art, ideas become their opium. The sickness that you feel about the situation today is a piling up of multitudinous suggestions and multitudinous misconceptions, each tumbling over the other. There is no security to be one's self. There is only a total insecurity because people don't know who they want to be. This is not only true of the young people. This is true of Boulez. This is true of Stockhausen. You can see this in the way they have approached American "chance" music. They began by finding rationalizations for how they could incorporate chance and still keep their precious integrity. How can you have integrity when your whole life is based on the accumulation of ideas? Boulez began to work out a complicated schematic situation of systematizing chance by way of Mallarmé and Kafka. He tried to give it a literary justification. Stockhausen talks about science, about all the "improbable" things that become "probable," and about all those things that are "justifiably improbable" in his work. But this work did not come through science. It didn't come through Kafka and Mallarmé. It came through a completely different world that did not *need* justification! That's what is important. When I wrote what I wrote, when I write what I write, I do not have to talk about Kafka. I don't have to make it human. I don't have to revise history.

• *Ashley:* Then, in order for the young composer to reach that situation where he doesn't have to justify himself, what direction do you think he should take? What prospects are there for him?

• *Feldman:* In *The Magic Mountain* the last paragraph begins " . . . if thou livest or diest, thy prospects are poor." I feel that the prospects of the young composer are very, very poor, because all he can salvage, even from the work that he finds important, the work that he actually loves, is the furthering of his technical facility. And the demands on that technical facility are becoming greater and greater. This is the age of Picasso, and we know what Picasso did as a young man! After 15 or 20 years he started to look at Cézanne and to develop cubism. What has that got to do with Cézanne? We all say, "Yes, look at what he learned from Cézanne." And that is exactly what is happening now in music. You go to the various festivals and you see fantastic technical equipment. And all the time you feel that the young composer has immorally been given the moral license to lead a parasitic life. You find the same thing in the universities. You find it in important centers like Tanglewood, where they're given this immoral basis for a really unproductive life. Quite recently Lukas Foss tried to get me an appointment. It was for a "chair" at a large university. When he mentioned my name, the consensus was, "Yes, he's a very colorful figure, but what can he teach?" What the schools and the important pedagogues are doing is just perpetuating a tragic syndrome, a tragic misunderstanding about what it is to be a composer. But then, perhaps they don't think of themselves as composers. I think that composing for them is just an incidental activity in the power struggle of ideas. You used the word "sick." The word "sick" is not sick enough. There's a perpetual cultural insanity feeding itself on everything it can use, without any feeling of obligation.

• *Ashley:* What you've said implies, I think, that even if a composer today saw music as a religious "calling" and chose to keep himself apart from the professional situation and from musical politics, he would still be "discovered" — and discussed and imitated — before very long. And worse, he would probably get more publicity for being a "religious figure." In other words, the composer today can't go very long without having to contend with his own "image."

• *Feldman:* Well, this is something that Rilke was always running away from. In fact, I think there is a legend that he feigned his death in order to be left in peace to work. It's certainly more in keeping with the temperament of a painter or a poet, but it's something new for the composer to face.

Charles
Wuorinen

[1938 -   ]

Wuorinen is reminiscent of the eighteenth-century musical virtuoso-of-all-trades. At an age when most composers are just finding themselves, he has made his mark as composer, performer, teacher, impresario, and musical commentator. He is not unique in this, but, rather, represents a new breed of talented player-composers who have been effective in bringing new music back to the concert stage, often as collaborators in chamber performances.

Like other composers of his generation—the youngest generation of composers represented here—Wuorinen has synthesized the musical resources of the last twenty years into a highly forceful personal rhetoric, moving steadily toward a style of strong individuality. His vigor as a musical thinker is shown in his ideas on music as well as in his actual compositions; in the following interview, many provocative statements on performances, audiences, and the future of music—representative of other young composers' opinions as well as Wuorinen's—are presented.

This interview was originally published under the title *What Concerns Me Is Music,* in *Genesis West* 1 (Fall, 1962), pp. 11-18, and revised especially for the present volume.

An Interview
with Barney Childs,
1962

- *Childs:* What happened to Gebrauchsmusik?
- *Wuorinen:* It certainly has changed, hasn't it? In the old days, there was not a very great stylistic difference between music for use and "art" music—in fact, even the distinction of types was not very strong. Gebrauchsmusik than was simply a little less demanding in performance, and a little less formidable conceptually, than "art" music. But today, of course, the term signifies a horrid, watered-down, conventional pap. It has come to mean *easy* music, not useful—and therefore it is easy, not so much in a technical as in a conceptual sense. That's why Gebrauchsmusik is generally so repulsive: its basic aesthetic is that it must not sound different from that music most familiar to the audience to whom it is addressed. It must be familiar before it's even been heard. And nowadays, of course, it is also almost impossible to write music for use in a relevant contemporary idiom, because playing technique is currently about fifty years behind composing.
- *Childs:* Isn't the instrumental musician today the composer's best friend?
- *Wuorinen:* No, there is, it is true, a handful of excellent performers of contemporary music—and not only in New York—and it is these people who are friends of the composer, friends because they understand what he is doing. But most instrumentalists are like most listeners: lazy, uneducated, pretentious—contemptible. Contemptible because they submit to the conditioning they received in their training; contemptible because it is their duty to understand the composers, because therefore they are infinitely less to be excused for succumbing to brainwashing than are others.
- *Childs:* Then you feel that the average instrumentalist is too "square" to like or to play contemporary music, that he's apt to return home after playing a concert to turn on the television and watch something like *The Beverly Hillbillies?*
- *Wuorinen:* Well, most people are lazy; but in the case of the performer we must mainly hold his attitudes to the account of the reactionary teaching to which he has been subjected in the conservatories and similar institutions. That there *has* been a sturdy expansion of instrumental technique since, say, 1940, is the result of the activities of only a very few

performers who have been playing contemporary music, and it is as unknown to most professional musicians as is the comparable twentieth-century revolution in composition to most listeners. Incidentally, we are now witnessing what I think is a very healthy and significant trend in this area: composers, having gotten sick of waiting for performers to do their job correctly, have, many of them, decided to do the performing themselves. Thus today you will find an increasing number of us who are complete musicians in the old sense. We write the music, set up the concerts where it is to be played, perform it ourselves, and even — for we are also sick of waiting for critics and musicologists to do *their* job intelligently — write about it ourselves.

- *Childs:* What about the listeners? Do you really care much what the audience thinks? Should any of us?
- *Wuorinen:* Which audience?
- *Childs:* The normal concert-going audience.
- *Wuorinen:* That's still pretty vague, but taking the "average" audience for major symphony concerts, and speaking personally, I can say that I care no more about them and their reactions than I do about the audience for juke boxes in bars. Indeed the latter are preferable because they really enjoy what they hear (I think), and in any case are not under the impression that their passive reception of "music" qualifies them for literate judgment. Besides this, one can drink in bars; symphony orchestras, whose programs are enough to drive any sensible man to drink, unfortunately do not provide alcoholic anesthesia during performances, as they should — but then considering the amount of sleeping at symphony programs that gets done by our "normal concert-going audience" I suppose the orchestras may be excused for not seeing the need. There is, however, an audience about whom I care very much indeed, and if I may be cautiously optimistic, I should say it is growing. This audience, made up mostly of composers, but increasingly of players and even non-musicians, is the one which has been exposed to enough twentieth-century music to accept it naturally, as it should be accepted — as the most important music there is, because it is *ours*. Mostly this audience is made up of cultivated individuals, and generally I respect their judgment. This of course is not to say that their reactions could ever influence what I compose or the way I do it — but the way they feel does somehow influence my overall attitude to music. They are colleagues.
- *Childs:* Why don't composers like each other?
- *Wuorinen:* Actually, some do. I can even claim to like a few myself. But it is certainly true that there is abroad much jealousy. Aside from obvious human-nature-type causes it seems to me that a good deal of this petty competitiveness has resulted from the fact that there really has been

369

absolutely nothing to gain from it. I think humans squabble most with each other when the winner gets no more than the loser. As far as composers are concerned, perhaps we can hope that should some of the tentative and timid moves now being contemplated for discussion during the next century to improve his lot actually come to pass, some of the jealousy might diminish.

• *Childs:* Is what's happening in New York today more or less vital and interesting than what's happening in Florence, Cologne, Darmstadt?

• *Wuorinen:* There seems to be a consensus now that New York is the center of the musical world. We can hold such a position because we are quite careful to inform ourselves of what is going on abroad. Many Europeans who come here will grudgingly admit to our primacy. But unfortunately, as is well known, Europeans are appallingly ignorant of musical composition and activity in this country, and for this reason you will be unlikely to find any Europeans who have not been here willing to admit merit in American music.

Apart from all this, it seems to me that American music today presents in the large an unparalleled richness, diversity, and multiformity; and since New York in some ways represents a concentrated picture of the musical life of the whole country, one can say the same of the city. As for "Florence, Cologne, Darmstadt," we seem to be hearing less of them these days than we once did. Some of the promotional machinery has apparently broken down, and these poor revolutions have run out of steam.

• *Childs:* But hasn't American music entered a new period of dependency on the European tradition, a dependency which may prove as stultifying as that which clouded the years before World War I? That is, half the bright young students at music schools are now new twelve-tone people, derivatively so?

• *Wuorinen:* No, I don't think so at all. First of all, most of the Europeans say that they have "gone beyond" and "exhausted" the twelve-tone system, so that the interest shown here in that mode of composition is strictly indigenous. I think myself that it is a very healthy interest, because in this country—mostly due to the work of Milton Babbitt—the twelve-tone system has been carefully studied and generalized into an edifice more impressive than any hitherto known, including the tonal system, needless to say. There is, it is true, a small group of ill-informed (mostly in the provinces these days) who imitate some European compositional conceits—the most obvious of these being "aleatoric" music. But don't forget that even this latter originated here in the "work" of John Cage and some of his friends.

Also, the presence of a great composer here like Elliott Carter (although his work is less subject to rationalization than is twelve-tone music) serves,

370

I think, to overshadow possible influences from Europe, which could hardly be very strong in any event nowadays in view of the paltriness of present continental composing talent.

• *Childs:* How come so many young American composers feel they must go to Europe?

• *Wuorinen:* I don't think many do. It is rare these days to see an American go to Europe to study. Whom would he study with? I am certain that the only reason anyone bothers any more is that what with Fulbright grants, Rome prizes, etc., a certain kind of cheap tourism can be indulged in by those who wish to put off growing up as professional composers for a few years.

Aside from this, the musical life of Europe is simply too poverty-stricken for us to abandon what we have here (in spite of our manifold problems) to go there.

• *Childs:* Is there, then, an American music as such? Why don't we forget about this cliche left over from the '30s?

• *Wuorinen:* There's an American music mostly in the geographical sense, I think. At any rate, the overt cliche that used to characterize a substantial amount of American music has vanished. We are now writing in some sort of "international style" — although I don't mean the same thing by this that the Europeans do. But apart from this, it seems to me that there are certain qualities of American music — mostly in the rhythmic area — that set most of it off from other music; but I couldn't be more precise in identifying them than that. Finally it should be said that most of us are not particularly conscious of our nationality — except when we are attacked for the mere fact of our living and working in this country.

• *Childs:* Isn't dodecaphony merely a crutch for the chap who can't write "pretty" music or who wants to be "avant-garde"?

• *Wuorinen:* No. In the first place, you can write "pretty" music using any technique you like, if that's the kind of music you want to write; in the second, dodecaphony is not considered "avant-garde" any more by those who make a profession of the same.

• *Childs:* Is there, then, really an "avant-garde"?

• *Wuorinen:* I don't think there is any more. To be sure, there are some composers here and abroad who have made it their business to discover some new revolution every week, but a lot of them seem to be running down and out. How can you make a revolution when the revolution before last has already said that anything goes? These musicians are indulging, I think, in what Pierre Boulez has aptly called "escape into the future." To me its opposite number, escape into the past, and the temperaments attracted by either asininity seem to me curiously similar.

• *Childs:* Why do you like working with the Synthesizer?

Charles
Wuorinen

• *Wuorinen:* Because of its design, it offers presently unique possibilities for the realization of musical structures accurately, as specified, to almost any degree of desired complexity. Now while I have come to believe that anything human beings can hear, they can play (given appropriate instruments), the fact still remains that the realization of some musical structures is impossible for human performers to accomplish without communicating at the same time a possibly unwanted atmosphere of strain. It is the elimination of this sense of strain that makes the whole electronic medium — and the Synthesizer in particular — valuable for me. For the music I compose in this medium is precisely that whose structure is to be perceived through hearing "objectively," and brooks no dramatic interference from the effects of performance.

• *Childs:* Is "indeterminacy" a passing fancy?

• *Wuorinen:* I suppose so. I'm not really competent to speak about it, as it bores me so much that I've not bothered with it particularly. I did try "indeterminacy" out once, but found it too limiting and predictable to engage my interest for long. It seems to me that it can't last, because the number of possible musical situations diminishes so drastically when you specify them in the terribly general ways that are your only choices in "indeterminate" composition. For example, if you specify, with respect to timbre, only that a piece may be played by any number of instruments, you remove that element from the composition. it is true of course that there are then, in this gross domain, an infinite number of ways to perform that *piece;* but at the same time, there are no longer an infinite number of ways to *compose* the piece with respect to timbre. There are *no* ways. Soon, I should imagine, the number of interesting choices will be therefore exhausted, and "indeterminate" composers will turn to something else, if they can.

• *Childs:* Does a bad review disturb you?

• *Wuorinen:* Certainly, in the sense that one would rather be complimented than criticized. But certainly not because one could ever take seriously something a critic said. They're just too stupid for that.

• *Childs:* Why are there so many critics who haven't a clue what they're hearing?

• *Wuorinen:* Unfortunately the ranks of critics are formed from failed musicians. Every one of them tried to be a composer or performer and failed. This establishes two things at once: first, that critics are to a man mediocre musicians and hence have bad ears and worse minds — after all, if a man can't make it as a professional in a field as devoid of standards of competence as the present world of music, he must be pretty bad — and second, because they've failed at *doing,* and now make their livings evaluating that very doing at which they've failed, they are bound to be bitterly jealous, spiteful, and destructive — as indeed most of them are. Most

372

of them are not better with words than they were with notes, but some, alas, *can* write a little bit. They are the most dangerous sort, for they cloak their bitter hatred of the art under semi-skilled sentence structure.

• *Childs:* John Osborne says in the dedication of one of his plays something to the effect that nobody has ever dedicated a string quartet to a donkey although books have been dedicated to critics.

• *Wuorinen:* You point out a serious injustice that we ought to correct. No reason to favor the asses over the donkeys.

• *Childs:* You mentioned to me once that you were esthetically left of center. Any further comment?

• *Wuorinen:* I simply mean that I'm a little more radical than conservative. Maybe I'm a member of what some have called the "intellectual avant-garde." But self-classification is pointless and I resist doing it.

• *Childs:* Is Webern really that good or bad?

• *Wuorinen:* Webern is of course a very interesting and important composer. But I don't think he's really all so significant as our European friends have suggested. Naturally, they are hardly to be blamed for so overestimating him, as they "discovered" him after World War II. We of course have known him since Varèse first introduced his works here in the 'twenties. But for Americans, anyway, the (as one person has put it) "perhaps richer and more suggestive polyphony" of Schoenberg is really the important thing. And I'm sure as time passes (and I say this without at all downgrading Webern's music, which I love very much) we will see more and more how crucial and overwhelming is Schoenberg's influence — either directly or as transmuted through the important work of such composers as Milton Babbitt.

• *Childs:* Is Webern's influence harmful?

• *Wuorinen:* In what way?

• *Childs:* I mean to suggest that a young composer might find it too simple to shirk his own development by accepting some predetermined style whole-hog, without consideration.

• *Wuorinen:* Well, first of all, I don't think you're really talking about this country. Here, you can't accept a style whole-hog — because there's no advancement to be gained from it, and because the multiformist pressures of our musical life here are simply too fragmenting to permit the elevation of any one "style" to that of possible whole-hog acceptance, let alone Webern's, for reasons I indicated already. Furthermore, I don't think anyone here would go to the enormous trouble of being a composer simply to find an excuse to "shirk his own development."

• *Childs:* What about jazz: is it or isn't it?

• *Wuorinen:* Awful? yes it is. I find it very boring to listen to. I think the reason is that in jazz of almost any type, two irreconcilables are in conflict:

the tonal-oriented vertical approach of recent western music, and the improvisatory instinct. The trouble here is that vertical thought—chord changes and their more modern derivatives—are inextricably part of a musical *ambiance* which is "goal-oriented," to use a bourgeois solecism: the whole point of functional harmony and modes of musical thought derived from it is that it gets somewhere (usually to a "home" key) in a certain specified period of time. Now this, it seems to me, is absolutely contrary to the marvelous improvisatory spirit of *real* "spontaneously" created music. The result of the tension in jazz between these two is immobility that pretends to motion, which I find very irritating. I'd much rather hear Karnatic music, for there the pretentions of jazz are actualized.

Furthermore, I resent the claim of some present-day jazz to being part of the serious progressive movement. It just isn't, nor could it be, as most of its practitioners are far too untutored to have any idea at all of what goes on in present music.

- *Childs:* Which pieces of yours do you like best? Why?
- *Wuorinen:* I like the latest pieces best. All one's compositions are chunks of oneself detached and frozen. Therefore the older such pieces are, the more one has grown away from them and hence the more alien they seem. Now it's perfectly possible to *like* such far-removed pieces; one does this in the same way one likes the work of someone else—for that of course is whose it really is. But the recent pieces are different. They are children, and one *loves* them.
- *Childs:* Do you agree with Ives that prizes are the badges of mediocrity?
- *Wuorinen:* Most of the time.
- *Childs:* Otherwise do you agree with Ives at all?
- *Wuorinen:* I like Ives' irascibility and his lack of respect for authority, his ingenuousness and his great genius. But also I fear he was really too amateur to do more than amaze us with how far his general ideas were in advance of his time. Aside from this, his music usually fails to satisfy me. And naturally I resist approving of the cult that has grown up around his name.
- *Childs:* Do you feel you could write as well elsewhere as in New York?
- *Wuorinen:* I suppose so. But I like New York—not only because I was born here, but also because there is more new music being made here than anywhere else in the world. There are great composers living here, and many others with whom it is worthwhile and continually stimulating to be in contact.
- *Childs:* Which do you find more difficult, beginnings or endings?
- *Wuorinen:* I can't generalize.
- *Childs:* Is academic training worthwhile for a composer?

• *Wuorinen:* It is essential; but by "academic" training I mean something quite different from what the term usually signifies: I refer to mental discipline, to training of the musical intellect, and to its admission as the principal determinant of musical significance. This does not mean harmony-and-counterpoint.

Composers have always been "intellectuals" and this stance is absolutely unavoidable today, for music has grown too rich and complex to be handled by the illiterate. (Santayana rightly observes that those who are ignorant of the past are condemned to repeat it.)

And I wish to see united all aspects of music, in a single person, who will be known simply as a *musician*. Some of us are already starting this; we perform, administer, write (words) and speculate on theoretic, historic, etc., subjects—all of these musical functions along with the central preoccupation of composition.

• *Childs:* Is it whom one knows rather than what one does?
• *Wuorinen:* Both.
• *Childs:* Should anything be done about it? Is it worth bothering about?
• *Wuorinen:* I'd rather compose.

III

POSTMODERNISM
AND
RECENT CONCERNS

Karlheinz Stockhausen

[1928 -   ]

Stockhausen is perhaps the most well-known European avant-garde composer to have come to prominence during the 1950s. His music has embraced both total serialism and indeterminacy while working with such resources as electronics, small chamber groupings, and massive multi-orchestra forces.

Though considered by some to have almost single-handedly developed much of the formal and notational language of the European avant-garde period, a substantial portion of his musical thinking may have been informed by two of his important influences—Olivier Messiaen, with whom he studied in 1952, and John Cage, whom he befriended in the 1950s.

Among Stockhausen's noted works of the fifties are Kreuzspiel *(1951), which involved the serial manipulation of pitch, rhythm, and register;* Gesang der Jünglinge *(1956), which mixed electronics and processed human voice; and* Klavierstück XI *(1956) and* Zyklus *(1959), which explored various avenues of chance and the use of the performer's discretion.*

From the mid-sixties onward, Stockhausen's music moved further away from traditional European concert models and toward what might be considered a grander philosophical/spiritual intent as in Hymnen *(1967), which combined electronically processed national anthems from around the world in a tape collage that was meant to inspire international brotherhood, and* LICHT *(1978 through the 1990s), a series of works that employ aspects of theater, dance, opera, and ritual performance and are based on myths from around the world.*

"Five Revolutions Since 1950" (program note) written October 10, 1986, for the premiere of *Evas Zauber;* updated February 3, 1995. From *Stockhausen, 60, Geburstag* (Kürten, 1988).

379

Five
Revolutions
Since 1950

I have used mobile synthesizers in compositions ever since *Sternklang* (1970).

In the version of *Michaels Reise* for ten soloists (premiered on May 8, 1986 at Bremen's *Pro Musica Nova*), two synthesizers took on all the functions served by the orchestra in the original 1978 score as well as expanding the timbral family and all the notated parameter modulations.

In *Evas Lied* (September 3, 1986 in the Berlin Philharmonie during the Berlin Festival) and *Evas Zauber* (November 20, 1986 in the Théâtre Municipal during the *Rencontres Internationales de Musique Contemporaine* at Metz) I composed over 150 "timbre" programmes for 3 x 2 synthesizers, developing completely new methods of sound regulation and modulation, space projection and notation.

Invasion (September 29, 1991—Alte Oper, Frankfurt) and *Synthi-Fou* (May 20, 1992—Grande Auditorio of the Gulbenkian Foundation, Lisbon) employ ten synthesizers and samplers (plus additional equipment). The production of *FREITAG aus LICHT* (Leipzig Opera, 1996) involves numerous electronic keyboard instruments and supplementary equipment.

Since the beginning of 1986 I feel myself confronted by innumerable unknown compositional situations in which one literally does not know where to make a start—as had previously been the case in 1952 at the ORTF's Musique Concrète Studio in Paris, and from May 1953 in the WDR Studio for Electronic Music at Cologne.

The fifth revolution within my work as a composer since 1950 is in fact now under way.

1) The first revolution occurred from 1952/53 as musique concrète, electronic tape music, and space music, entailing composition with transformers, generators, modulators, magnetophones, etc; the integration of all concrete and abstract (synthetic) possibilities within sound (also all noises) and the controlled projection of sound in space (*Konkrete Etude, Elektronische Studien I-II, Gesang der Jünglinge, Kontakte, Gruppen* for three orchestras, *Carré* for four choirs and orchestras, etc.).

2) From around 1963 I started expanding this into live electronic music utilising a group of experimental interpreters. That resulted

380

in many compositions involving new processes of modulation, transformation, and spatial projection of the orchestra (*Mixtur, Stop, Hymnen, Sternklang,* etc.); such individual instruments as the tamtam, piano, viola, electronium, electrochord, etc. (*Mikrophonie I, Solo, Prozession, Kurzwellen, Spiral, Pole, Expo, Mantra,* etc.); and choral singers (*Mikrophonie II, Stimmung,* etc.) with the sound-projectionist taking on a completely new function, enormously expanding the traditional role of the 'conductor'.

This development also includes the intermodulation technique employed in such works as *Hymnen* and *Telemusik,* which is carried further in *Sirius* and throughout the whole of *LICHT* (and again now in the sound-scenes from *MONTAG aus LICHT*).

3) The third revolution occurred during work on *Sirius* in the WDR Studio, utilizing the big EMS Synthi 100 and the perfected eight-channel rotation table. For three years I had to relearn everything about regulating sound-formation processes in real time and utilizing highly complex eight-track equipment.

4) A fourth new beginning came in 1984 through composing with the PDP 11 computer and 4X synthesizer at IRCAM in Paris for the six-channel version of *Kathinkas Gesang* for flute and electronic music. Once again I had to learn a new way of thinking, sign language, notation, performance practice, etc.—and that development has only just begun.

5) And now the explosion of the mobile electronic studio is getting under way—a far-reaching, unpredictable transformation of the craft of composition now that use of the modifiable synthesizer, sampler, etc., has become technically and financially possible. That may be a natural further development of everything I have implemented over the past forty-three years, but mastery of the various synthesizer systems demands the greatest skill, imagination, and patience.

"Timbre Composition" has now become a misleading term because composing a single "timbre" (today a "sound programme") is indivisibly linked with the composition of an entire work. One cannot in fact make a "timbre programme" determining all the modulations without devoting detailed attention to the duration, dynamics, spatial projection, etc., of this sound with regard to all the other simultaneous, preceding, and subsequent sound-events within an organic context.

That is why composition of a single sound at the synthesizer—in conjunction with interpreters experienced in this specific synthesizer—often demands many hours of work, and also usually several changes during rehearsals.

That development is leading in precisely the direction I time and again predicted from the very start: that every composer—both alone and with qualified interpreters—composes an *intrinsic* sound-world for every *new* work (as I have done for years), constantly trying out on the synthesizer what he is writing, and constantly listening on headphones, day and night, to his catalogued sound-programmes. Even then one makes indescribably many mistakes, which can only be put right in numerous rehearsals—extending over 300 or so hours for the entire ensemble of eight soloists and seven child singers in the case of *Evas Lied*. Never before in history has composition been in such an experimental state!

Another aspect is of importance in that context. I utilized twenty-two sound-scenes in *Evas Zauber*, composed and spatially projected (four channels) at the WDR Studio in 1985. In these acoustic scenes, "concrete sound-scenes" from all conceivable spheres of life, which normally could never contact one another, are composed in a completely unpredictable and trans-causal fashion. A technique I gradually learned in *Gesang der Jünglinge*, *Hymnen*, *Telemusik*, *Kurzwellen*, *Spiral*, and *Sirius* served me there. The twelve-channel composition and realization of sound-scenes in *FREITAG aus LICHT* go further than in all earlier works.

What the solo flute, the children, the percussionists, and the three synthesizer performers play or sing is based on the sound-scenes in *Evas Zauber*, identifying with, imitating, and transforming the structure.

Synthesizer player I uses two synthesizers: a PPG Wave 2.2 with an Oberheim XK 1 master keyboard, a Prophet VS, both with SPLIT, enabling four different simultaneous programmes, and a Roland digital effects processor DER-3.

Synthesizer player II uses two Yamaha DX7-II FD synthesizers, a Casio FZ 1 sampler, and an ART ProVERB effects device.

Synthesizer player III uses two synthesizers: an Oberheim XPANDER with an XK 1 master keyboard, a Yamaha DX7-II, a Casio FZ-1 sampler, and an ART ProVERB effects device.

All those synthesizers are equipped for Midi link-ups.

For each synthesizer I composed individual programmes which are stored on cassette, cartridge, and diskettes, and—like the "sheet music"—are part of the performance material.

For all my compositions during the past seventeen years I have regularly spent months (several hours daily) working with instrumentalists, trying out new micro-scales as well as voiced and unvoiced (rushing) consonantal timbres. Quarter, sixth, and eighth tones, and intervals no longer definable in simple numbers (with up to 26 steps within a major third—quasi "13th tones"), with all of the indescribable timbral variations, occur in these new compositions. To this are added movements integrated in the spatial sounds.

Spatial composition has moved on from such early quadrophonic works as *Gesang der Jünglinge* (1955-56), *Kontakte* (1958-60), and *Hymnen* (1966-7) by way of the five-track *Telemusik* (1966), the eight-track *Sirius* (1975-7), and a large number of other eight-track works to *Oktophonie* (1990-1) for a cube-like arrangement of eight loudspeaker groups with all possible vertical and diagonal movements of sound, and then to *Dodekaphonie* (1992-4) with twelve spatial sources of pyramidic projection.

In all my compositional work I constantly feel that I am a student on the threshold of a new development in instrumental practice. One does not normally talk in public about ongoing daily advancement of this metier, but such crucial experiences should also transform the awareness of those who ill-informedly hold forth on new compositions.

"He that hath ears to hear, let him hear."

Today one must add: Get hold of some new ears, or else you will soon no longer hear what is new but merely the records of your leaky, centuries-old memory.

Michael
Tippett

[1905 -   ]

Sir Michael Tippett is a worthy successor to Benjamin Britten as the elder statesman of British music. Like Britten, Tippett has shown marked sensitivity to English word-setting, and draws upon historical references in his work. But Tippett's music only rarely projects the fluid, graceful affect of Britten's. Rather, it is often angular, thorny, texturally dense, and profoundly thoughtful—perhaps closer to his American contemporary Elliott Carter, or to later generations of British composers such as Harrison Birtwistle.

Tippett's eclectic mix of sources can be heard in the relatively early oratorio A Child of our Time, *which incorporates black American spirituals, and in his later years he has demonstrated insatiable curiosity about Middle Eastern, Native American, African, and Pacific cultures. Popular and vernacular art enters his musical world, too, as in his opera* The Knot Garden, *or the 1972 Third Symphony which marries a telling fragment of the Beethoven Ninth's finale to the blues.*

He often creates both words and music for his major vocal, choral, and operatic ventures, as he did for A Child of our Time, *which premiered in 1944. For much of his career Tippett was also a dedicated musical citizen, active as a teacher, administrator, and conductor, often working with amateur and youth ensembles. Highly articulate, and endowed with an unusually strong social conscience, he regards the artistic experience as a challenging endeavor of moral, ethical proportions.*

"Dreaming on Things to Come . . ." reprinted from *Tippett on Music,* edited by Meirion Bowen (Oxford University Press, 1995).

"Dreaming
on Things
to Come . . . "

*Not mine own fears, nor the prophetic soul
Of the wide world dreaming on things to come . . .*
Shakespeare, Sonnet 107

At the end of a filmed interview in Paris in 1994, I was asked a final throwaway question: Do you think it possible for there to be another Tippett in the next millennium? My reply, perhaps rightly, was dismissive: one is enough! But then I began to think what indeed might be the future for a composer embarking on a career, as I had early in this century, with high aspirations and ideals and a determination to sustain them through thick and thin. Of course, I could not predict the course of world events in a century I might be just lucky enough to glimpse, though not to experience to any degree.

Young composers and performing musicians today are obviously starting out in circumstances quite dissimilar to my own. My generation had no radio, no discs, no television; communications and travel were infinitely slower; access to professional music-making limited. Composers now grow up with an ever more versatile array of technologies, adaptable to musical purposes and increasingly central to everyday living. Every parent is daunted by the speed and assurance with which their tiny children learn to use computers. In a more specialized context like that of music, a radical transformation is under way, such are the facilities for dreaming up, exploring, setting down, publishing, and reproducing new music. The interaction of cultures across the globe is prodigious and intricate. What guidelines, thus, could one possibly hope to offer succeeding generations? Is all that one has struggled to accomplish over many decades anachronistic? It might well seem to many that the historical archetypes of symphony and concerto, of the standard orchestra and other genres, are exhausted. With what are they to be replaced? The composition of notional archetypes extending and replacing the old is even more of a leap in the dark.

Others have also faced this challenge, and set down their thoughts about the kind of musical future they think might lie ahead. A notable example is Pierre Boulez, whose voluminous writings offer a quite comprehensive guide to the issues that have to be faced. Boulez's formidably ratioci-native approach to these issues commands respect, and has won him many admirers. Boulez has a vision of history. It has a direct, undeviating trajectory. Moreover, it is identified with his own intellectual and artistic evolution. He chooses carefully his own antecedents. He is aware of the obstacles to continuing along a directly evolutionary path: the nature of existing musical institutions, of concerts and of concert-halls as presently conceived, of programme building, of the restrictions imposed by musical instruments in satisfying the imaginative demands of composers—and so on. Boulez has greatly enlivened the musical scene with his conducting, his programme-planning, and so on. His consummate solution, as he sees it, to the problems he as a composer has faced has been the creation of a Bauhaus-style research centre—IRCAM. It is not for me to judge the products of that utopian institution; on the contrary, how wonderful that a society somewhere has assigned such value, allotted such immense financial resources, to the fulfillment of an artistic dream.

But there are, it seems to me, certain underlying drawbacks within the Boulez prescription. Chief amongst them, Boulez assumes a centripetal thrust within our musical culture, rather than a centrifugal one. All roads lead, if not to Boulez, at least to IRCAM. There I part company. Some roads lead away from IRCAM, and quite decisively so. And the question that then demands attention is: what is the basis for an alternative to IR-CAM—a medium for plurality and diversity?

My temperament draws me thus back to the theatre—to what Peter Brook encapsulates as "the empty space."[1] A composer dreaming on things to come is probably best occupied thinking how to fill that empty space, and can certainly derive stimulus, as I have, from Brook's example and ideas. To begin with, the danger to the music of the future lies not with prescriptive dogma or centralization by Boulez or anyone else, but rather with commerce. What Brook calls "The Deadly Theatre,"[2] subordinating artistic innovations to a network of legal and financial transactions, is more prevalent than ever before. The musical theatre tradition, so gloriously vital from Gershwin right up to Sondheim, has tended of late to become an excuse simply for investment in the technology of the spectacular. Dramatic and musical contents are reduced to an anodyne level, but the lighting, special effects, and so on are amazing. What remains, in artistic terms, is an empty shell. The marketing methods of rock music, as applied to art music, have also been immensely beneficial, but they too have their dangers. In my time I have seen an abundance of trends and fashions, schools

[1]Peter Brook, *The Empty Space* (London, 1968).
[2]Title of ibid., ch. 1.

and coteries, come and go. But those of today seem to acquire incredible commercial backing, even they also evaporate equally quickly. Composers may be more tempted than ever before to surrender to the falsity of commercial hyperbole. And who can blame them in a period of nasty, selfish monetarism? They want to survive. Composers certainly have higher material expectations than when I started out.

On the other hand, a wonderful realm of creativity beckons. The extension of the realm of notional archetypes is made possible just by starting with an awareness of established theatrical genres—what Brook calls "The Rough Theatre," "The Holy Theatre," and "The Immediate Theatre."[3] These are not tightly defined exclusion zones, let alone a final, exhaustive list. One of their excitements lies in their potential for intermixture and development through new genres of presentation. New concert music inevitably follows as an off-shoot of this, just as new genres of concert will follow, too. In this way, as much room is available for the quasi-scientific approach, such as that of Boulez, as might be allowed for the quasi-primal or the improvisatory.

I dream, therefore, not of the Tippett of the future, but of the successors to the holy theatre of Harrison Birtwistle's *The Mask of Orpheus,* the rough theatre of Mark-Anthony Turnage's *Greek,* the video-documentary theatre of Steve Reich. . . . The list can go on and on, and I have only hinted at where it might begin. My dream is indeed that there will be a new plurality of theatrical genres beyond my immediate apprehension.

In the present day, architecture has been perhaps the most obvious point of fusion between artistic and technological innovation, and, as such, constantly at the crossroads of intellectual revolution. If this leads us to expect of its most successful practitioners an ultimate visionary proteanism, it is rarely so. To take but two examples, the polarity between Norman Foster and Richard Rodgers, the one commercially well focused, the other dreaming less immediately realizable projects, is acute.

In musical theatre, such a fusion, such a visionary proteanism, are both relevant. The dreams are never cheap, but they seem likely to be the foundation of renewal across the spectrum of creative music-making. It is not the Tippett of the next millennium that matters, but metamorphoses, fresh reincarnations galore.

[3]Titles of ibid., chs. 2–4.

György Ligeti
[1923 -   ]

Although Ligeti's principal early influence was Bartók, by the mid 1950s, he was experimenting with electronic and tape composition and its concomitant "constructive" way of musical thinking. This exposure to electronic/tape music processes led directly to his two orchestral works that brought him widespread recognition: Apparitions (1958-59) and Atmosphères (1961), the latter (along with his Lux aeterna) finding an even larger audience some years later when it was used in the film 2001.

These two timbrally rich works explored and developed what Ligeti has referred to as "micropolyphony" and "super-saturated chromaticism," melding many layers of detailed, highly chromatic passages into densely textured, "static" yet often dramatic forms in which timbre can become a central focus. Other major works in his textural/polyphonic style include Requiem (1963-65), Lux aeterna (1966), and Lontano (1967).

In the late sixties and early seventies, Ligeti experimented with the use of microtones (String Quartet No. 2, Double Concerto, and Ramifications), quotational pastiches, and a pulsing minimalism (Three Pieces for Two Pianos). Through the eighties and nineties he has continued to write richly colored, densely layered pieces that are, in contrast to much of his earlier work, more heavily involved in rhythmic rather than timbral concerns, utilizing elaborate polymeters and reflecting his fascination with fractal mathematics and the music of Conlon Nancarrow.

The following interview is from György Ligeti: Eine Monographie, by Ove Nordwall (B. Schott's Soehne, 1971); translated into English by Sarah E. Soulsby in György Ligeti: in Conversation (Ernst Eulenberg, Ltd., 1983).

An Interview with Josef Häusler

Two days before the premiere of the orchestral work, *Lontano*—the recording had already been made—I had an appointment with György Ligeti to record a conversation with him for the Südwestfunk [South West German Radio]. I was actually thinking of nothing more than an introduction to *Lontano* in the form of an interview; nevertheless, we had not stipulated how the conversation should proceed, nor how long it should last, and since we were both improvising, the whole thing suddenly took a different direction. The fifteen to twenty minutes we had envisaged turned into nearly two hours of talk which, when it had been tidied up somewhat and musical examples added, yielded two Südwestfunk broadcasts.[1] They were called "From A*tmosphères* to *Lontano*." At first, obviously, it was not intended to publish them in print. As this possibility then arose, it proved necessary to edit the text in certain particulars, condensing it in various places, while endeavouring not to affect its character of an improvised conversation. The [original] publisher and the editor wish to thank György Ligeti not only for his permission to go into print, but also for taking part in this editing.

—Josef Häusler

* *Josef Häusler:* Mr. Ligeti, in a commentary to your orchestral work, *Lontano*, you wrote: "There is not just one single harmonic form process, but several simultaneous processes with different speeds which glimmer through, superimpose themselves on one another and produce an imaginary perspective through all sorts of refraction and reflection. It reveals itself gradually to the listener, as though he were going into a dark room from bright sunlight and little by little becoming aware of the colours and contours." I should be grateful if you would help me to perceive the colours and contours more precisely. Perhaps, to begin with, I could simply ask you a question: how is *Lontano* different from your earlier works, and what connects it to these works?
* *György Ligeti:* I should like to talk first about the question of similarity. *Lontano* and a few earlier works such as *Atmosphères*, *Apparitions*, or a work which came just before *Lontano*, the Cello Concerto—particularly the first movement of the Cello Concerto—the organ work *Volumina*, and the second movement from the Requiem—the *Kyrie* movement—these all have

[1] Broadcast by the Südwestfunk, Baden-Baden, on 19 and 26 July 1968

something in common, viz., the way in which the music appears. I do not mean by that the "musical form"; the musical form can be structured very differently, but I mean a kind of musical aura. It is music that gives the impression that it could stream on continuously, as if it had no beginning and no end; what we hear is actually a section of something that has eternally begun and that will continue to sound for ever. It is typical of all these pieces that there are hardly any caesuras and the music really does flow on. The formal characteristic of this music is that it seems static. The music appears to stand still, but that is merely an illusion: within this standing still, this static quality, there are gradual changes: I would think here of a surface of water in which an image is reflected; then this surface of water is gradually disturbed, and the image disappears, but very, very gradually. Subsequently the water calms down again, and we see a different image. That is, of course, merely a metaphor or association, but one can see metaphorical elements even in the titles of these works. Typical of this is *Atmosphères*, where the word "atmosphere" itself has a dual meaning: atmosphere in the literal sense of the word and also in the figurative sense. I would say that the music has a kind of metaphorical relationship to both senses of the word, in a similar way to the titles of the "Préludes" used by Debussy. In the score, Debussy put the titles not at the beginning but at the end of each piece, in brackets. This way of presenting titles—one can also find something similar in the realm of painting, with Paul Klee, who usually named his paintings and drawings later—is rather like mine: it's not an external thing, it belongs, as it were, to the conception of this kind of music. And to come back to *Atmosphères*: it has something atmospheric, that is to say, something floating, indeterminate, almost contourless, merging into itself, and on the other hand, something atmospheric in the figurative sense. I should like to hope, or believe that I could, that the work, even if it is not exactly expressive, nevertheless has a quite definite feeling or emotion about it, and that is precisely what is atmospheric or *ambience*-like. Yes, I don't think that one can say any more about it.

• *JH:* Let me return once more to your commentary on *Lontano*. You write there the lapidary sentence: "Polyphony is written, but harmony is heard." We have heard a passage from *Atmosphères* that represents, at least in part, a kind of 56-voice canon, and one could perhaps paraphrase your quotation by saying: "Polyphony is written, but tone-colour or plane of sound is heard." Before we come to talk about *Lontano*, just one little digression. This iridescence of the planes of sound, this dovetailing into each other, dissolving away from each other, the alternation of types of sound—from the sound of woodwind to the sound of brass, from the sound of brass to the sound of strings, and so on—may occasionally remind us of different kinds of noise-colours in electronics. Do electronics, or electronic sound concepts play a role in your music?

• *GL:* Certainly, an important role, and I've also dabbled in electronic music . . .

• *JH:* Yes, you created the work *Artikulation* in the studio of the Westdeutscher Rundfunk[2] in Cologne . . . .

• *GL:* Yes, and two other pieces which, however, are private, which I regard as finger exercises, as it were. I am often asked the question whether my orchestral works *Atmosphères* and *Apparitions* are not rather electronic music played by an orchestra. Many listeners who have heard the works only on tape, have asked me whether it was not just a question of manipulating tapes, and I have always answered, "No, nothing at all has been manipulated, there is nothing electronic in it at all, nor are there many unusual methods of playing the instruments. I do not want to say that there aren't any at all: there are certain methods of playing that are innovatory. . . ."

• *JH:* Perhaps you are thinking of the place where the piano's strings are rubbed with cloths and brushes?

• *GL:* Yes, or similar things, like having only air in the brass instruments: that happened at the end of *Apparitions;* or I think of quite definite, innovatory pizzicati that I tried out, mostly in *Apparitions,* or of certain sections in which the strings play a kind of harmonic but on parts of the string where there is no nodal point for a harmonic. Then you don't get the sound of a harmonic, but rather something noisy: I would say something between sound and noise.

• *JH:* It is therefore not a case of electronic manipulations; yet the conception of sound behind your *Atmosphères* is connected somehow with the concept of sound in electronic music—or would you consider that beside the point?

• *GL:* No, no, most certainly not. Not only is there a point of connection, but there are several of different kinds. First of all, my practical experience in the studio of the Westdeutscher Rundfunk where I learned a great deal from Stockhausen, Eimert and Koenig. All this naturally had an effect on my later instrumental music. For this reason, in *Apparitions* and *Atmosphères*—those were the first two instrumental pieces after my work in the electronic studio—there are certain sounds or sound transformations that would not have occurred otherwise. Perhaps I would still have composed them, but not in this form. So that was, as I said, the influence of working in the electronic studio. But I can turn the question round: I already had concepts of static planes of sound that gradually alter, before I had ever heard any electronic music . . .

[2]West German Radio - Cologne

391

- *JH:* . . . and did you also have these concepts before you came to Western Europe in 1956? Did they occur to you while you were still in Budapest?
- *GL:* Yes. I can tell you exactly: they date from 1950. Up to then, and even a little later, my compositions were largely influenced by Bartók and Stravinsky, and to a certain extent by Alban Berg. They were the three modern composers I knew well. Yes, and I knew Hindemith well, too, but was less influenced by him. Schoenberg and Webern, however, I scarcely knew at all. I would say, Schoenberg only a little and Webern not at all. For example, I wrote a string quartet in 1953 to 1954, *Métamorphoses nocturnes*, that was influenced not only by Bartók but also by Alban Berg's *Lyric Suite*. I only had the score, and hadn't actually heard any of Berg's works, but the score impressed me a great deal. Well, in 1950 I suddenly realised that I could no longer model my work on Bartók or Stravinsky. I was then twenty-seven years old, I had already composed a lot, and was dissatisfied with all of it. In addition, one has to know about the peculiar situation in Hungary, and in Eastern Europe altogether at the beginning of the '50s. We were totally isolated from all the musical developments in Western Europe. By chance, I happened to hear a few programmes broadcast at night by the Bayrischer Rundfunk,[3] the Südwestfunk,[4] the WDR[5] and the NDR;[6] but these were very curious impressions, since the German broadcasting stations, and all those in the West, suffered from a great deal of jamming: with a view to jamming not the music, but the news broadcasts. So it was with these programmes at night. Besides that, one never knew exactly when they were going to take place, as there were no radio magazines available. So at about 11 o'clock, one started excitedly trying to find something: between 11 and 12 o'clock there was always contemporary music. I heard, for example, pieces by Messiaen, Fortner, and also by Boulez, Stockhausen, Nono and many others, but usually only the very high notes—everything else disappeared under the crackle. This was hardly very informative. I would say that one learned about Western music more from hear-say. There was a time immediately after the war when one could get periodicals—*Melos*, for example—but one couldn't hear the music.

So I came to realise that it was of no interest whatsoever to continue composing in the manner of Bartók, even if I wrote music as advanced as, for example, Bartók in the string quartets of his middle period—although mine would of course be technically much more primitive. I didn't yet have this technical ability. But even works like that were composed only to

[3]Bavarian Radio—Munich
[4]South West Radio—Baden-Baden
[5]West Germany Radio—Cologne
[6]North German Radio—Hamburg and Hanover

be put away in a drawer. One could not perform that sort of thing. If someone like myself did not follow the political line of the day, then they were
forced to stick to simpler educational works and arrangements of folk-
songs. I did a lot in this field, which I didn't regard as a compromise. That
was the situation at the time in Hungary. Then there was an internal opposition, as it were, which consisted in concentrating on Stravinsky, on Alban
Berg, studying a few of Schoenberg's scores, which were available even
though one couldn't hear the music. Finally, and that was in 1950, I came
to realise that that wasn't satisfactory either: why should I, twenty or thirty
years after the event, continue in a style that already existed and had already been perfected? And then we had indirect information that totally
new ideas were in existence. I heard, although not until later, 1952/53,
that electronic music existed, serial music, that there was a person called
Cage in America and what he was doing. These were, I would say, snip-
pets of news relayed by someone who had heard it somewhere. Well, that
certainly made an impression on me. And at that time I had the first notions of static music, and in fact I was thinking of ceasing to work with
melody and harmony, and instead of trying to find a neutralized sound,
somewhere between music and noise. Ideas that I later realised in *Atmosphères* I had conceived in almost exactly the same way eleven years
previously, but I could not carry them out. The ideas were furthermore restricted because I could not get away from the notion of metrical rhythm;
in my first attempts in Budapest, the static planes of sound were still
squeezed into a conventional metrical scheme. I still use bars when I compose today, but that is only for practical purposes, so that the works can be
conducted. The bars are not bars in the traditional sense, but merely a
means of synchronizing the parts. The fact that I did eventually get away
from metre and bars, however, was really because of the immediate and
very great effect that Boulez and Stockhausen had on me—the music of
both of them, and then also my acquaintance with Stockhausen and my
first years in Cologne.

• *JH:* So then you carried out these ideas in the orchestral work *Apparitions?*

• *GL:* Yes, that was in '58/59. . . . I should like to add, apropos of *Apparitions*, that I have used the individual voices in the orchestra, especially
the strings, as though they were partials—they are sounds in themselves—
as though they were partials of an even more complex sound. Here there
is an analogy to the work in the electronic studio. On the other hand,
however, my interest in working in the electronic studio was aroused before I knew any electronic music because I already had similar ideas about
complex planes of sound. I would put it like this: I sought the opportunity
of learning about electronic music, of working with this medium and then

393

returning to instrumental music, because I wanted to apply not the sounds produced from electronic music, but rather the experience gained from working with electronic material. So there is in fact an indirect connection.

• *JH:* This path led you subsequently from *Apparitions* to *Atmosphères*. *Atmosphères* was followed by an organ work called *Volumina* in which you further developed the concepts which formed the basis of *Atmosphères*. Is that correct?

• *GL:* That is correct. I might say that *Volumina* is a very small tone-colour work, in which the tone-colours are primarily responsible for the organisation of the form. It also has the sustained and static form that was evident in *Atmosphères*, but with the limitations of a single instrument. I experimented in many ways to see what one can produce from this almost defunct instrument and I found that there is still a great deal to be discovered, which was not to be found even in quite advanced works, by, for example, Messiaen. Then there were many possibilities of sliding from one keyboard to the next. This technical feat has an immediate effect on the resulting sound. I should say that that was the last work in which the tone-colour transformations dominated to such an extent. I had come to a point at which I thought: I have worked out definite possibilities for myself now, and if I continue to copy them more and more, I shall have become a plagiarist of myself. And from 1962 I began to ask myself how can I develop my style, and therefore my direction organically, at the same time shifting the focal point of composition to other spheres?

• *JH:* *Atmosphères* could be described as purely a tone-colour work. *Volumina* for organ is, I think, a work in which colour and space are interrelated. You called one orchestral piece *Lontano*. The title alone suggests spatial aspects. "Lontano" means "far" or "distant": could you give me some sort of a catchphrase for this, which we could then illustrate with a piece of music?

• *GL:* For me, spatial associations play a major role in music, but the space is purely imaginary. There are for instance compositions by Cage and Stockhausen—I am thinking particularly of *Gruppen* and *Carré* by Stockhausen—in which actual space plays an essential, even a constructive role. I, on the other hand, had been trying to suggest space, or to generate space by association in my works. And in fact, that isn't anything new in itself. An illusion of space played an important part in romantic music, especially in Mahler. I can think of a passage at the end of the first movement of his Fifth Symphony. There is a trumpet-call, then suddenly silence, then the same trumpet-call can be heard, but transposed to a flute. Well, in terms of actual space, the flautist is sitting just as near or as far from the audience as the trumpeter. And yet, the sound of the flute, with the same musical outline as the trumpet had, seems to us in a purely imaginary fashion to be a trumpet-call from very far away.

• *JH:* Please tell me of a passage from *Lontano* in which we can hear particularly clearly the imaginary space that you were trying to convey.

• *GL:* In approximately the last third of the work we get, after a static, very soft plane of sound, formed by a major second and a minor third, a gradual passing into dim, deep regions. That in itself creates a strong spatial association. Now, this dark progress is suddenly lightened, as if the music had been illuminated from behind. . . . I constantly have light-associations which really do play a part in the work. . . . This progress, once it has begun, goes forwards: the violas, cellos and double-basses carry on the sequence that has started. All the other instruments, and then the cellos as well, take on a new gesture, something suddenly bright, often not perfectly delineated; it gets continually brighter and the music seems to shine, to be radiant. Dynamically, too, this is emphasized by a crescendo, and the pitch by a gradual ascent into higher and higher regions, until a single note, a D sharp, very high up, emerges and stands there, as if this musical light were at first diffuse, but slowly the diffuseness disappears and there is a single directed beam. I am expressing all this by the association of images. At the moment when the high D sharp is there, forming the concentrated "pencil" of this musical beam, suddenly there yawns an abyss, a huge distancing, a hole piercing through the music. It is a moment that has an irresistible association for me with the wonderful painting by Altdorfer, *The Battle of Alexander* in the Alte Pinakothek in Munich, in which the clouds—these blue clouds—part and behind them there is a beam of golden sunlight shining through. Well, this "shining through" [in the music] is suddenly interrupted; not entirely, since the high D sharp goes on sounding, but by means of a *subito pianissimo* it seems almost as though a light were turned down, is still there, then goes on fading away into the distance; a light too can die away, a musical light, I mean. And through this suddenly gaping distance and vast expanse can be heard the sound of horns. Well, the horn players are sitting in the normal orchestra pit: the orchestra is not far away; but they sound like something in the distance for various reasons of association. Firstly: after the *fortissimo-tutti* there is suddenly a *pianissimo* and the horns are muted. In addition, the very sound of horns has a "historical perspective." Horns coming in like that after a tutti awake in us involuntarily not a direct association perhaps, but an allusion, a reference to certain elements of late romantic music. I am thinking now particularly of Bruckner and Mahler, but also of Wagner. I can think of a passage in Bruckner's Eighth Symphony, in the coda of the slow movement, where with great tranquillity and gentleness the four horns suddenly play a passage that sounds almost like a quotation from Schubert, but seen through Bruckner's eyes. Well, there are many similar, not quotations, but allusions in *Lontano*. I would say that as well as spatial distance, there is also temporal distance; that is to say, we can grasp the work only within our tradition, within a certain musical education. If one were not acquainted with the whole of late Romanticism, the quality of being at a distance, or however I should express it, would not be manifest in this work. For this reason, the piece is double-edged: it is in a sense traditional but not literally as with Stravinsky, it does not treat exact quotations from late romantic music, but certain types of late romantic music are just touched upon. To come back to the spatial effect: the temporal distancing evokes also a spatial distancing. The horns can be heard from a distance and from long ago: almost, as it were, like the post-horn in Mahler's Third Symphony.

• *JH:* In speaking about the relationship between your orchestral work *Lontano* and the rest of your work, you used the word "tone-colour," mentioning *Atmosphères*, *Volumina* and *Apparitions* in that connection. It would certainly not be wrong to say, therefore, that *Lontano* is also a tone-colour work, although not in the exclusive sense that *Atmosphères* is.

• *GL:* In *Atmosphères*, to take an extreme example, the tone-colours were the musical elements pre-eminent in determining the form. In *Lontano* that is not so clearly the case. *Lontano* represents for me a further step in the development of my technique of composition and, indeed, of my concept of composition as it stood in *Atmosphères* and *Volumina*, and this step leads in a quite specific direction. In *Apparitions* and *Atmosphères* I got away from the preoccupation with harmony, or from working with intervals in general. I disrupted the intervals: that is to say, I inserted so many minor seconds that even the minor seconds, or the chromaticism, disappeared in the harmonic sense. It would seem as though I had returned in the more recent works, already from the Requiem and the Cello Concerto onwards and in the choral work *Lux aeterna* and even more clearly in *Lontano*, to an earlier stand-point that I had previously left, namely to working with clearly distinguished intervallic or harmonic configurations. Intervals, definite pitches, really do play an essential role here in the whole basis of the form and also in the image of all the music. The neutralized harmonies—or let us say, the eliminated harmonies, as in *Atmosphères* and *Volumina*—were very rapidly expended. Almost all these works have settled in particular peripheral areas in which one can go no further.

That is, one could go further, but not find anything new. There is a boundary, and then there is the desert; one is standing on this boundary, and if one goes on into the desert, one always finds the same thing: sand. And if you continue going further, you find more of the same thing: sand. If I were to go on composing pieces like *Atmosphères* and *Volumina* now, and working with totally neutralized harmonies, what would I find? Exactly the same thing, that is to say, I would copy myself. Well, I wanted to seek new frontiers. I have to ask myself, why are frontiers so important? Why take an extreme position? I could put it like this: creating something that already exists is not interesting for me. If something new has been tried out and a result has emerged from it, it is not worth making the same experiment again. That would be like a schoolboy repeating the same school chemistry experiment at home—it is nothing but pottering.

As well as searching for new domains, I have a strangely two-edged, or enigmatic relationship to tradition. On the one hand, I deny all musical tradition, and yet subliminally it continues to play a part. For example: *Volumina*, a truly radical work—radical even in the way in which it has been notated in a kind of new, apparently graphic notation, although it has, in fact, nothing to do with graphic notation—*Volumina* sounds different from all earlier organ works. Somewhere, however, under the surface, there remain vestiges of past writing for the organ. In some places you can sense certain baroque figurations, but they are very meandering; Liszt and Reger and the romantic sound of the organ are also there, playing a subliminal role.

• *JH:* Ulrich Dibelius in a book about new music said of you that you were forever striving to solve an equation with at least two unknown factors. What were the unknown factors in *Lontano*?

• *GL:* I could say that one unknown was the way that I was working with intervals and harmonies, that is, with complexes of intervals, in the otherwise neutralized harmonic space. And the other unknown factor would be the polyphony I composed. It is an extensively branching and yet strictly refined polyphony which, however, veers suddenly into something else. In *Atmosphères* it changes into tone-colour, in *Lontano* it has no longer changed exclusively into tone-colour, but into something in between. I don't have a name for it and I don't want to create a term for it. A kind of complex of tone-colour, movement, changing harmonic planes.

Let us talk first about the intervals or complexes of intervals. When in 1962 I came to the frontier district represented by *Volumina*—the total destruction of the intervals—I did not go any further, but began to look for another frontier. I asked myself, how can I work with intervals or with specific fixed pitches without returning to tonal music? That is to say, no chordal development, either in a tonal or an atonal sense. Can one work completely differently from the way in which one has previously worked with intervals or even harmonies that are really worn-out elements? I tried to do so. The first work that is indeed based on a clearly organized structure of intervals is the Requiem. In the Requiem specific connections between the intervals determine the form of the music, without the intervals or complexes of intervals entering into tonal relationships with each other.

I further developed this technique from the Requiem in the a cappella choral work *Lux aeterna,* and one end-product of this was *Lontano.* I believe that *Lontano* is the example that demonstrates most purely the crystallization of corner-stones or pillars that are specific intervals or single notes or harmonies. They provide a kind of contrast to the prevalent neutrality and tone-colour transformation, that is to say, on one level of the work there are tone-colour transformations, but there is another, harmonic level which, I would almost say, is behind it: that is also an aspect of *Lontano,* of being distant. At certain moments in the work there are single pitches or groups of intervals. To give you one example: at the very beginning I proceed from a certain note—an A flat. This A flat then plays a role in the work as a whole. If you then look for similar corner-stones later on, you find that all twelve notes emerge as pillars. That has nothing to do with twelve-note music—there is no note-row. It is merely a question of fitting all the twelve notes somewhere into the work: each of them as an element as yet unused. There are, of course, connections with dodecaphony, but it isn't dodecaphony in the usual sense. So, to return to the beginning of the work: we hear a single pitch that is clearly there, but gradually it becomes rather cloudy, rather hazy, because 'parasitic' pitches are joined to it: as well as A flat, we get G, then B flat, A and so on—all different pitches. And because of the fact that more and more adjacent pitches are played and because, besides that, the ensemble of strings is divided into many single instruments, the result is small deviations in intonation. For example, it is a known fact that a violinist going from C to C sharp and then to D, involuntarily makes the C sharp higher. The small deviations that result in this involuntary manner are here a constructive element in the composition. I haven't used any quarter-tones; of course, there may be some, but it was of no importance to me exactly how much the pitches deviate. So if I say the work is notated in equal temperament, but doesn't sound like it, I have indicated a general aspect of my musical conception, namely the relationship to the finished artefact. The music has something artificial about it: it is an illusion. There are many elements in it that don't manifest themselves, but remain subliminal. Thus the opening note of the work appears to be continuous, but this is not really the case, for the instruments change. The tone-colour of the work varies—that is the aspect of tone-colour transformation and it is gradually dissolved, almost as if I were throwing a salt crystal into water.

• *JH:* Would you describe the subsequent progress of the work to me?

• *GL:* In its intervals or harmonies, the work has the following structure: there are certain places in which a pitch or an interval or even several intervals—let us use the old-fashioned term "chords"—are clearly to be heard. Then in the middle of a chord the "parasitic" notes gradually sound; they are not ornamental in the sense of the passing notes or auxiliary notes of tonal music, but they do contain a slight allusion to them. The whole tradition of tonal music is present, but always hidden. Now this intervallic or harmonic plane gradually clouds over, and this cloudiness expands more and more, until finally the originally pellucid, clear harmonic structure dissolves into an opaque plane. In the middle of this opaque or neutral plane we then get signs of a new constellation of pitches which by degrees becomes more and more dominant. At first, the new constellation is barely audible. Gradually, however, the different parts gather together into the individual intervals which are later revealed in a bright light. That is to say, there is a harmonic transformation in a similar way to the tone-colour transformation in my earlier works. So I am of the opinion that this is not a return to traditional intervallic and harmonic music, but rather that harmony and intervals are treated as though they were tone-colours.

• *JH:* When I compare the orchestral work *Lontano* with *Atmosphères*, I have the impression that in *Lontano* the individual instrumental parts bear a far greater responsibility than in *Atmosphères*. Is this impression correct and is the second unknown factor connected with it, namely your work with polyphonic modes of composition?

• *GL:* Yes, definitely. In *Atmosphères* the individual instrumentalists sustain long notes for the most part, and are responsible for the dynamic alteration of these notes, but they do not have any function as soloists. *Lontano* is a work for a big orchestra, but one could say that it is for an orchestra composed of nothing but soloists. It is not a question of functioning as soloists in the sense of being virtuosi, but rather that each musician in this divided orchestra has a particular responsibility for the separate, expressive formation of his particular part. That is why I dedicated the work to the Südwestfunk Symphony Orchestra: the musicians in the orchestra are the true soloists of the work.

In several of my more recent works from the Requiem onwards, that is from the year 1963, I have a tendency to use the following device in my compositions: I propose something, expound something, begin something, and yet before it really exists, I take it back. Now, how does that happen, in a purely technical sense? In the following way: I set out as though a "theme" or a "great expansive melody" were now about to occur, and yet thinking in terms of themes is entirely alien to this music. There is only the rudimentary stage, suggesting that a theme is about to appear. So everything, before being quite expressed, is immediately withdrawn again. This brings me to the question of polyphony itself. Technically, *Lontano* is a completely and strictly structured polyphonic work: that is to say, there is a definite part-writing, there are vertical relationships between the parts and the individual instrumentalists play their parts as autonomous units. Through the complex overlapping and interweaving of the parts, however, the listener loses sight of them, although perhaps not entirely; that is to say, the traces of this polyphony remain audible. The polyphony in itself is not audible; I mean, polyphony like that of the Dutch school, or of Palestrina's or Bach's music is not to be found here. I would say that the polyphony is dissolved—like the harmony and the tone-colour—to such an extent that it does not manifest itself, and yet it is there, just beneath the threshold.

• *JH:* We spoke of polyphonic allusion, but you expressed it a little differently: "Polyphony is written, but harmony is heard." Why do you compose polyphony that cannot be heard?

• *GL:* That's a very valid question, and I could argue with myself about it. Why do I write such definite, detailed orchestral parts?

• *JH:* Yes, and one can extend the question even further. In *Atmosphères* where there are actually only planes of sound, the individual parts are written out in the minutest detail, without in fact being audible as individual parts in this detailed way.

• *GL:* Yes, it is apparently a contradiction. For me, too, it would be much simpler and, I might almost say, a more economical way of composing if I used a system of "generalized" notation such as that used by Penderecki. When a cluster is played by one group of instruments, let us say a high cluster in the violins, a small indication shows which instrument plays what note; this cluster is notated in a generalized manner and if there are then changes of pitch, the pattern of notation is changed, is shifted, that is, everyone playing *glissando*, etc. It is a very economical, practical and sufficient notation for the type of music that Penderecki composes. But for the kind of music that I compose, it is not adequate, for the following reason: I want to be able to steer the course of each separate part myself . . .

• *JH:* So you want to direct the internal fluctuation within a plane in an entirely conscious way . . .

• *GL:* . . . to steer and direct it entirely consciously. And that was my intention with the hidden polyphony as well. Within these planes there is a polyphony that has been developed in the composition and which appears in the score, but is not immediately audible; we hear not the polyphony itself, but its result. If I were to notate that in an undifferentiated way, the result would not be the same. As an example I should like to make this comparison: only a very small part of an iceberg is visible, the largest part being hidden under the water. But what the iceberg looks like, how it moves, how it is affected by various currents in the ocean, all these things are determined not only by the visible, but also by the invisible part. That

400

is why I call my method of composing and notating uneconomical, indeed somewhat prodigal. I specify many details that are not in themselves audible. But the fact that I have specified these details is essential for the general result—at least, that is what I hope. I think of a large architectural edifice in which many details are not visible. For the general result, for the formal quality of the structure as a whole, they nevertheless play an important role. Music is for me in the first instance something intuitive. Then, however, I begin to work conceptually, making concrete the original purely acoustic or musical vision. In finding a conceptual development that matches the musical vision, during which I prescribe rules for myself as to composition or form, something concrete emerges from the general vision, and that is the score. At the performance, however, there is a shift back to the original, general vision. So I do in the end hear the sound that I had had in my mind. In between the two, a rational product, so to say, has been manufactured. It is precisely this tension between the rational, constructed element on the one hand, the visionary on the other, that plays such an important role in composing for me.

• *JH:* You wrote in *Melos* in 1967: "The involuntary transposing of optical and tactile sensations into acoustic equivalents occurs very often with me. I almost always associate sounds with colour, form and consistency, just as, on the other hand, for every acoustic sensation I find form, colour and a material quality." This interrelationship of synaesthetic moments, this effect of crossing from one sense-impression to another sensual area, accordingly plays an important part in your work of composition, or perhaps rather in your musical intuition?

• *GL:* Yes, certainly, but here I must both complete the picture and limit it a little. Pronouncements like this, the way that I speak about music, could be misunderstood as being programmatic. So that I would then be composing a kind of programme music. But it is certainly not that. I could put it in this way: the relationships between different sense-impressions, tactile, olfactory, visual, acoustic, certainly play a major part. Whenever I listen to music, I see colours and shapes. But that does not signify that it is literary or illustrative music in the sense of programme music. If I say, for example, that *Lontano* is a work in which colours and space are very significant, these colours and this space exist only in the music. *Lontano*, distance, remoteness, as an aura of feeling that surrounds this music, is to be understood as a purely musical category. It has nothing to do with programme music as in Liszt, Berlioz or Strauss, for example. If I were to mention Debussy and Mahler, two composers whom I especially love, I would say that their music brings in its wake, as a comet in its train, a whole wide area of associations from every level of human experience. In this way, music or the artificial product, "a work of art," is truly bound for me

401

with every stratum of imagination and of actual life. But everything is
transposed into music! So I would say: Programme music without a programme, music that is developed extensively in its associations, yet pure
music. Everything that is direct and unambiguous is alien to me. I love allusions, equivocal utterances, things that have many interpretations, uncertainties, background meanings. And the various figurative associations in
my music are also ambiguous, as I see them, think them or feel them while
I imagine music.

George Rochberg

[1918 -   ]

*Rochberg has produced articulate and engaging works in a number
of different styles. Tonal and vigorously rhythmic, his early works
showed the influences of Bartók and Stravinsky. Coming under the
influence of Dallapiccola in Rome in 1950, he adopted a serialism
akin to that of the Second Viennese School.*

*Throughout the fifties, Rochberg honed and developed a terse se-
rial technique that extended beyond simple pitch manipulation. But
by the early sixties, he had grown disillusioned with serial writing
(his last serial piece was* Trio *for violin, cello, and piano, 1963) and
attempted to make his music more accessible and pluralistic in its
influences, dipping into many periods of Western music history and
employing direct musical quotations (his* Contra mortem et tempus,
1965, quotes from Boulez, Varèse, Berio, and Ives).

*By the mid seventies, Rochberg had embraced a neo-Romanticism
that attempted to fuse the present and the past, combining the tonal
with the atonal. In the following essay on his* Third String Quartet
*(1972), he discusses his problems with strict serialism and his deci-
sion to break from its clutches.*

Reprinted from Rochberg's *The Aesthetics of Survival: A Composer's
View of Twentieth-Century Music* (University of Michigan Press,
1984).

On the
Third String
Quartet

When I wrote my Third String Quartet I had no idea it would call forth the quantity and kinds of critical comment that followed its first performances and recording. Some critics rejected the work out of hand on the grounds that its combination of tonal and nontonal musics simply did not add up to being "contemporary." Some seemed fascinated but still puzzled by the phenomenon of structural fusion of past and present. The majority of writers, however, welcomed it even though they were uncertain whether the direction that the quartet pointed to could or would be followed up.

The acceptability of such a work hinges no doubt on whether one is able to reconcile a juxtaposition of musically opposite styles. In order to effect such a reconciliation, one has to be persuaded, first, that the idea of history as "progress" is no longer viable and, second, that the radical avant-garde of recent years has proved to be bankrupt. Both conditions lay behind the impulse that generated my quartet. Both were determining factors in my choice of ideas, levels of musical action, and the structure of the work itself. Far from seeing tonality and atonality as opposite "styles," I viewed them as significant aspects of an enlarged language of musical expression with branching subdivisions of what I like to call "dialects"—a particular way of stressing or inflecting parts of the whole spectrum of Western musical language. These dialects can be presented singly or in combination depending on what one wants to say and the particular size, shape, and character of the work one wants to say it in. In the quartet the dialects range widely from diatonic, key-centered tonality to forms of chromaticism which veer toward nineteenth-century or early-twentieth-century practices (but still structurally tonal) to a more atonally oriented chromaticism; from predictable to unpredictable periodicities of phrase structure; from simple to complex metric pulsation; and from continuous to noncontinuous gestural relationships between phrases, sections, and movements.

By embracing the earlier traditions of tonality and combining them with the more recently developed atonality, I found it possible to release my music from the overintense, expressionistic manner inherent in a purely serially organized, constant chromaticism, and from the inhibition of physical pulse and rhythm which has enervated so much recent music. With the

404

enlargement of this spectrum of possible means came an enlargement of perspective which potentially placed the entire past at my disposal. I was freed of the conventional perceptions which ascribe some goal-directed, teleological function to that past, insisting that each definable historical development supersedes the one that has just taken place either by incorporating or nullifying it.

In this view, the invention of classical twelve-tone methodology—and later total serialism—not only superseded everything that came before it but literally declared it null and void. Obviously, I rejected this view—though not without great discomfort and difficulty, because I had acquired it, along with a number of similar notions, as a seemingly inevitable condition of the twentieth-century culture in which I had grown up. The demanding effort to evolve and maintain a personal kind of transcendentalism still occupies me; but that effort has resulted in being able to compose whatever kind of music I feel deeply and intensely.

I am not aware that anyone has yet attempted a full-scale answer to the questions my quartet seems to have raised. Perhaps wisely—because I believe the issues involved are complex beyond imagining, and therefore certainly not susceptible to the kind of either/or, binary thinking so characteristic of the contemporary mind. To live with paradox and contradiction is not and has not been our cultural or intellectual way. I suspect that what my quartet suggests to others, and what I began to accept for myself at least fifteen years ago, is that we can no longer live with monolithic ideas about art and how it is produced. Nor can we take as artistic gospel the categorical imperatives laid down by cultural messiahs or their self-appointed apologists and followers of whatever persuasion.

On the contrary, the twentieth century has pointed—however reluctant we may be to accept it in all areas of life, social as well as political, cultural as well as intellectual—toward a difficult-to-define pluralism, a world of new mixtures and combinations of everything we have inherited from the past and whatever we individually or collectively value in the inventions of our own present, replete with juxtapositions of opposites (or seeming opposites) and contraries. In other words, not the narrow, pat, plus/minus, monoview of the rational-minded, but the web of living ideas which combine in strange and unexpected ways much as the stuff of biological matter does; not the self-conscious aesthetic or morality which excludes so much for the sake of "purity," but the sensed (if not quite yet articulate) notion that stretches to embrace everything possible to one's taste and experience, regardless of its time or place of origin. This not only makes it mandatory to see the "past" as continuously viable and alive in our "present" but also to be able to perceive large chunks of time as unities which create a vast physical-mental-spiritual web enfolding our individual lives, actions, and feelings.

I believe we are the filaments of a universal mind which transcends our individual egos and histories. The degree to which we partake of that universal mind is the degree to which we identify with the collective imagery, fate, wisdom, and tragedy of our still struggling species. By ourselves we are virtually nothing—but by opening ourselves to the transcendent collectivity of mankind and its experiences, we share in a totality which, however mysterious its sources, dimensions, and ultimate fate, sustains us.

Pluralism, as I understand it, does not mean a simplistic array of different things somehow stuck together in arbitrary fashion but a way of seeing new possibilities of relationships; of discovering and uncovering hidden connections and working with them structurally; of joining antipodes without boiling out their tensions; of resolving the natural tensions of contradictory terms on new symbiotic hierarchic levels—more than all of the above, a way of preserving the uncertainty of the artistic enterprise which itself demands that, out of the tensions and anxieties attendant upon it, we struggle for clarity and order, to gain not a permanent certainty (which is not possible anyhow) but a momentary insight into how it is possible to resolve the chaos of existence into a shape or form which takes on beauty, perhaps meaning, certainly strength. Art is a way of fighting the encroachment of the forces which diminish us. Through art we are all Don Quixotes battling Time and Death.

Granting pluralism, how is a composer to deal with it? From the inside out, i.e., from the internal psychic imagery which becomes the musical gesture to its artistic manifestation. Gesture, singly or in combination, successive or simultaneous, is the determining factor—not style, language, system, or method.

Given the very strong possibility that music is rooted in our biological structure—as are spoken language and mathematics—the gestures of music can only proceed authentically from one direction: from inside. That is where they get their energy, their power, their immediacy. The conscious effort to give voice to the vast range of these gestures becomes the act of composing, and inevitably demands not only freedom of choice but freedom of combination. If Beethoven, for example, had not felt this way, we would not have the late quartets—those glories of our civilization. There is surely no logic to a movement such as the "Heilegedankgesang" of Op. 132, with its combination of alternating Baroque chorale variations and eighteenth/nineteenth-century idealized dance which hides vestiges of the old courtly minuet; or to the insertion of a German folk dance in the more metaphysical surroundings of Op. 130 which Beethoven capped with the grandest fugue of them all. There's no rational way to understand Ives's placing a diatonic fugue in C major cheek by jowl with the layered musics of the other movements of his Fourth Symphony; or his juxtaposition and overlay of chromatic on diatonic, diatonic on chromatic, in his two gems, "The Unanswered Question" and "Central Park in the Dark." (Consider the juxtaposition of the intensely chromatic fugue and essentially pandiatonic last movement in Bartók's *Music for Strings, Percussion and Celesta*.)

The determination to write the Third Quartet the way I did (and other works similar in nature but cast differently, because of different gestural needs, balances, and projections) stems from my personal way of understanding composers like Beethoven, Bartók, and Ives, but is not limited to them. If, in the need to expand our sources—pluralism of gesture, language, and style—we lay ourselves open to the charge of eclecticism, we need not concern ourselves. Other and earlier forms of eclecticism may also be charged to medieval music or to early classical music or to Bach or to Mozart (who seemed thoroughly eclectic to his contemporaries), or to Stravinsky.

Some of the critics who have commented on my quartet have wondered out loud whether the work would "last." How can anyone tell? It is not important. Culture is not the additive product of a series of discrete, specific events or works. It is, like the biology that it rests on, a self-renewing, self-sustaining organism that proliferates, spreads, unites, subdivides, reunites, dies individually but lives collectively. The cultural mechanism for continuity (posterity; immortality) resides in human memory and the preservation of what is authentic and has, therefore, captured a piece of human wit or wisdom (as possible in music, as in painting, as in literature). The cultural mechanism for renewal resides in the courage to use human passion and energy in the direction of what is authentic again and again. The ring of authenticity is more important than the clang of originality. Whatever is authentic about the twentieth century will be preserved, and we need not worry about it. Given that certainty, we can safely leave it alone and get back to the business of writing music without falsely institutionalizing the means we use to produce it. But we must be sure that it *is* music; i.e., that we write what we believe in, write it consummately well and that we intend it at least for the delectation and edification of the human ear and heart—beyond that, if possible, for the purification of the mind.

To quote from my notes to the recording of the Third Quartet: "I am turning away from what I consider the cultural pathology of my own time toward what can only be called a *possibility* that music can be renewed by regaining contact with the tradition and means of the past, to re-emerge as a spiritual force with reactivated powers of melodic thought, rhythmic pulse, and large-scale structure."

407

Gunther Schuller

[1925 -   ]

A prolific composer, conductor, author, educator, and horn player, Schuller is perhaps best known for combining various popular American musics—particularly jazz—with the techniques of concert music. In the fifties and sixties, he did much to promote "third stream" music—an intersection of jazz styles and techniques and contemporary concert music practices—which was, for him, a natural drawing together of his interests of the forties and fifties, especially twelve-tone composition and modern jazz of that same period, most notably the work of Miles Davis, with whom he also recorded as a horn player.

Although Schuller's work as a composer has never defied the generally accepted decorum of the concert hall, his music has always attempted to challenge the listener chiefly by the combination of disparate and unusual instrumental groups and the cross-fertilization of various prevailing musical styles.

Schuller has written chamber music, orchestral works, choral works, operas, dance pieces, and film scores, and has arranged music by such composers as Charles Ives and Scott Joplin. Perhaps his most popular composition is his Seven Studies on Themes by Paul Klee (1957), an orchestral work that "repaints" seven of Klee's works with a rich and evocative instrumental palette.

Schuller is the author of two highly regarded jazz history volumes, books on horn technique and conducting, and numerous magazine and journal articles. He has conducted major orchestras in both the United States and Europe and has recorded works by many twentieth-century composers.

"Third Stream" originally published in The Saturday Review (1961); "Third Stream Revisited" originally published in a New England Conservatory brochure (1981). Both reprinted from Schuller's Musings (Oxford University Press, 1986).

Third Stream

About a year ago the term "Third Stream," describing a new genre of music located about halfway between jazz and classical music, attained official sanction by use in a headline of the *New York Times*. Since that day, almost everybody has had his say about this music and its practitioners, and, not surprisingly, much nonsense about it has found its way into print. I suppose this is inevitable. If we consider how much confusion and prejudice are attached to jazz and contemporary music as separate fields of musical activity, we can then imagine how existing misunderstandings are likely to be compounded when we speak of a fusion of these two forces.

I first used the term "Third Stream" in a lecture three or four years ago, in an attempt to describe a music that was beginning to evolve with growing consistency. For lack of a precise name, one was forced at the time to describe it either in a lengthy definition or in descriptive phrases comprising several sentences. I used the term as an adjective, not as a noun. I did not envision its use as a name, a slogan, or a catchword (one thinks back with horror to the indignities visited upon the modern jazz movement in the late forties by the banal commercialization of the catchword "Bop"); nor did this imply a sort of "canonization," as one critic facetiously put it; nor, least of all, did I intend the term as a commercial gimmick. Such a thought evidently comes most readily to some people's minds in a society in which commercial gimmickry is an accepted way of life. Ultimately, I don't care whether the term "Third Stream" survives. In the interim it is no more than a handy descriptive term. It should be obvious that a piece of Third Stream music is first of all *music*, and its quality cannot be determined solely by categorization. Basically I don't care what category music belongs to; I only care whether it is good or bad. As one fellow musician put it: "I like jazz, not because it's jazz, but because it's good music."

After a year of watching the confusion mount and the increasing commercial exploitation of the phrase "Third Stream" (often incorrectly used, to boot), and after reading numerous reviews revealing the writers' calloused misunderstanding of the music involved, I somehow feel obligated—since I may have indirectly instigated all this nonsense—finally to have *my* say about it, and in the process I hope to bring some clarity to the whole issue.

I am fully aware that, individually, jazz and classical music have long, separate traditions that many people want to keep separate and sacred. I also recognize the right of musicians in either field to focus their attention entirely on preserving the idiomatic purity of these traditions. It is precisely for these reasons that I thought it best to separate from these two traditions the new genre that attempts to fuse "the improvisational spontaneity and rhythmic vitality of jazz with the compositional procedures and techniques acquired in Western music during 700 years of musical development." I felt that by designating this music as a *separate, third* stream, the two other mainstreams could go their way unaffected by attempts at fusion. I had hoped that in this way the old prejudices, old worries about the purity of the two mainstreams that have greeted attempts to bring jazz and "classical" music together could, for once, be avoided. This, however, has not been the case. Musicians and critics in both fields have considered this Third Stream a frontal attack on their own traditions.

Characteristically, the jazz side has protested against the intruder more vigorously than its opposite partner. And since my music in this genre has by now been accused of everything from "opportunism" to "racial callousness," I had better make some points unequivocally clear. I can best clarify my intentions by some straightforward categorical statements: 1) I am not interested in *improving* jazz (jazz is a healthy young music, and I would not presume to be capable of improving it); 2) I am not interested in *replacing* jazz (a thought like this could only emanate from some confused believer in the basic inferiority of jazz); 3) I am not interested in "bringing jazz into classical music," nor in "making a lady out of jazz," in the immortal words of the erstwhile "symphonic jazz" proponents (Paul Whiteman, Ferde Grofé, et al., come to mind).

I am simply exercising my prerogative as a creative artist to draw upon those experiences in my life as a musician that have a vital meaning for me. It is inevitable that the creative individual will in some way reflect in his creative activity that which he loves, respects, and understands; my concern, therefore, is precisely to preserve as much of the essence of both elements as is possible.

Yet, with disturbing consistency, "jazz critics" keep appraising the Third Streamers solely on the basis of jazz. The producers of this music are also equally at fault. One recently issued recording describes itself as "Third Stream Jazz," and I suppose before long we will have some "Third Stream Classics"—whatever that might turn out to be. This is analogous to calling a nectarine a nectarine-plum. The standards of jazz, per se, are not applicable to Third Stream, any more than one can expect a nectarine to taste like a peach. A Third Stream work does not wish to be heard as jazz alone; it does not *necessarily* expect to "swing like Basie" (few can, even within the jazz field); it does not expect to seduce the listener with ready-made blue-noted formulas of "soul" and "funk"; and it certainly does not expect to generate easy acceptance among those whose musical criteria are determined only on the basis of whether one can snap one's fingers to the music. And, I might add, it is not an attempt to find a niche in the hearts of the American public by capitalizing on the brash, racy "jazziness" of some recent Broadway musicals.

In *my* understanding of the term, Third Stream music must be born out of respect for and full dedication to *both* the musics it attempts to fuse. (This is more than one can say for the pop song or rock 'n' roll commercializers of jazz, about whom, ironically, I have heard no serious complaints.) The lifting of external elements from one area into the other is happily a matter of the past. At its best Third Stream can be an extremely subtle music, defying the kind of easy categorization most people seem to need before they can make up their minds whether they should like something or not. As John Lewis once put it to me in a conversation: "It isn't so much what we see (and hear) in the music of each idiom; it is more what we do *not* see in the one that already exists in the other."

Certainly both musics can benefit from this kind of cross-fertilization, in the hands of gifted people. For example, the state of performance in classical music at the professional level today is, despite all we hear about our skilled instrumentalists, rather low. Most performances touch only the surface of a work, not its essence; and this is most true of the performance of contemporary music. If virtuosic perfection at least were achieved, one could—in a forgetful moment—be satisfied with that. But one cannot even claim this, since the leisurely attitude of the majority of classical players toward rhythmic accuracy is simply appalling, and would seem so to more people were it not so widespread as to be generally accepted. There is no question in my mind that the classical world can learn much about timing, rhythmic accuracy, and subtlety from jazz musicians, as jazz musicians can in dynamics, structure, and contrast from the classical musicians.

It is this kind of mutual fructifying that will, I believe, be one of the benefits of Third Stream. It seems, therefore, unfair for critics to blame a piece of Third Stream music because "the symphony orchestras can't swing." Of course they can't swing; even in their own music they barely manage. But perhaps they will learn; and, when they do, will the compositions involved then be intrinsically better? It is this kind of confusion of levels that I am deploring. It happens, needless to say, on both sides of the fence.

It is not a lame apology but rather a statement of fact to say that this movement is still in its beginnings. The performance problems are still enormous, and much musical adjustment will have to be made by both sides before the compositional ideals of the composers can be realized on the performance level. However, if a symphony orchestra can be made to swing just a little, and if a compositional structure that makes jazz musicians push beyond the thirty-two-bar song forms of conventional jazz can be achieved, are not these already important achievements in breaking the stalemate artificially enforced by people who wish tenaciously to keep the two idioms separate? (That there are not only musical problems involved here, but also deep-rooted racial issues, need hardly be emphasized.)

If historical confirmation is needed, it is easy to point to many precedents, which undoubtedly were met with as much scoffing as Third Stream has encountered. The next time someone invokes the old saw about oil and water not mixing, just tell him that the most sacred and rigorously organized music of all time, the Flemish contrapuntal masses, was more often than not based on what once had been semi-improvised lighthearted, often risqué secular troubadour ballads. Or tell him that the minuet, at first a simple and often crude popular dance, became a sophisticated classical form in the hands of Haydn and Mozart. Or if examples be needed from our own time, Bartók's music—originally compounded of Debussyan and Straussian elements—rose to its greatest heights *after* he was able to fuse his early style with the idiomatic inflections of Eastern European folk music. Many more examples exist.

It seems to me that the kind of fusion which Third Stream attempts is not only interesting but inevitable. We are undergoing a tremendous process of musical synthesis, in which the many radical innovations of the earliest decades of our century are being finally assimilated. Whenever I read one of the "it-can't-be-done" reviews, I think of Wagner's line in *Die Meistersinger,* addressing Beckmesser: "Wollt ihr nach Regeln messen, was nicht nach eurer Regeln Lauf, sucht davon erst die Regeln auf! Eu'r Urtheil, dünkt mich, wäre reifer, hörtet ihr besser zu." Freely translated: "Would you judge by conventional rules that which does not follow those rules? Your judgment, it seems to me, would be more mature if you listened more carefully."

It would seem that the Beckmessers of today are equally incapable of listening to music in terms of a total musical experience. When confronted with passages thoroughly fusing the worlds of jazz and classical music, they insist on hearing them in their separate categories, most likely because they can hear well only in one or the other. I am not by nature a polemicist or a crusader, and I would not, in any case crusade for Third Stream music. I simply would hope for critics (amateur and professional) who could appraise the music on *its* terms, not *theirs.*

Third Stream Revisited

Third stream is a way of composing, improvising, and performing that brings musics together rather than segregating them. It is a way of making music which holds that *all musics are created equal,* coexisting in a beautiful brotherhood/sisterhood of musics that complement and fructify each other. It is a global concept which allows the world's musics—written, improvised, handed-down, traditional, experimental—to come together, to learn from one another, to reflect human diversity and pluralism. It is the music of rapprochement, of *entente*—not of competition and confrontation. And it is the logical outcome of the American melting pot: *E pluribus unum.*

As originally articulated by Gunther Schuller, twenty-five years ago, Third Stream was a musical offspring born of the wedlock of two other primary "streams": classical and jazz. It was intended as a handy descriptive *adjective* for a music that already existed but which had no name. It was not intended as a *noun* and certainly not as a slogan, although that's how it came to be viewed once it made headlines in the *New York Times.*

That's when Third Stream's troubles began. How dare this mongrel upstart intrude on our sacred territories! How dare this half-breed contaminate our pure streams!

Admittedly Third Stream is anti-pedigree and anti-establishment—especially when establishment equates with entrenched, inflexible, self-preserving positions and closed minds. Attacks on its name by detractors notwithstanding, Third Stream is also the ultimate anti-label music, for its very essence is based on the concept of diversity and non-categorization. Third Stream is subject to both the benefits and the risks of cross-fertilization. It doesn't always work, but when it does it is something new, rare and beautiful.

And Third Stream is nothing if it is not new and creative; Third Stream is nothing if it dabbles and tinkers; Third Stream is nothing if it fails to amalgamate at the most authentic and fundamental levels. It is not intended to be a music of paste-overs and add-ons; it is not intended to be a music which superficially mixes a bit of this with a bit of that. When it does, it is *not* Third Stream; it is some other nameless kind of poor music.

Third Stream has not only survived; it has flourished and expanded its horizons. From its original idea to fuse classical and jazz concepts and techniques, it has broadened out—in ways that are an apt corollary to our expanded knowledge of non-Western cultures and the rapid shrinking of our globe—to embrace, at least potentially, all the world's ethnic, vernacular, and folk music. It is a non-traditional music which exemplifies cultural pluralism and personal freedom. It is for those who have something to say creatively/musically but who do not necessarily fit the predetermined molds into which our culture always wishes to press us. Third Stream, more than any other concept of music, allows those individuals who, by accident of birth or station, reflect a diversified cultural background, to express themselves in uniquely personal ways. It is in effect *the quintessential American music.*

Oh, yes, we almost forgot.

What Third Stream is not:

1) It is not jazz with strings.
2) It is not jazz played on "classical" instruments.
3) It is not classical music played by jazz players
4) It is not inserting a bit of Ravel or Schoenberg between be-bop changes—nor the reverse.
5) It is not jazz in fugal form.
6) It is not a fugue performed by jazz players.
7) It is not designed to do away with jazz or classical music; it is just another option amongst many for today's creative musicians.

And by definition there is no such thing as "Third Stream jazz."

Pauline Oliveros

[1932 -   ]

Pauline Oliveros studied composition with Robert Erickson from 1954 to 1960 and later became co-director of the San Francisco Tape Music Center, with Ramon Sender and Morton Subotnick. She held a professorship at the University of California, San Diego from 1967 to 1981, during which time she directed the UCSD Center for Music Experiment and organized a performing ensemble of women musicians and dancers.

Many of Oliveros's early compositions involved tape manipulation, and she has been particularly imaginative in using studio equipment in unique ways to design live performances. Later, increasingly interested in the theatrical aspects of ritual activity and informed by developments in the world of happenings and performance art, she created ritual scenarios within which performers interact with each other—and with audience members as well.

Other compositions explore ideas of gradual process—either specific textures, or an intangible "aura," imperceptibly changing over long time spans—as in her Aeolian Partitions and Doublebasses at Twenty Paces of the late sixties and early seventies.

In 1981 Oliveros left academia to devote all her time to freelance composing. She founded an ensemble called the Deep Listening Band in a small Hudson River community north of New York City, and many of her recent activities have involved collaborative performance activities—a number of them site-specific—with the other composer/performers of the DLB. She still retains her on-going concern for "sound," as the stuff of music, and the locus of ritual. The essay reprinted here speaks directly to that concern.

Originally published in Source: Music of the Avant Garde (1967); reprinted in Oliveros's Software for People: Writings 1963–1980 (Smith Publications/Printed Editions, 1982).

Some
Sound Observations

As I sit here trying to compose an article for *Source*, my mind adheres to the sounds of myself and my environment. In the distance a bulldozer is eating away a hillside while its motor is a cascade of harmonics defining the space between it and the Rock and Roll radio playing in the next room. Sounds of birds, insects, children's voices and the rustling of trees fleck this space.

As I penetrate the deep drone of the bulldozer with my ear, the mind opens and reveals the high pitched whine of my nervous system. It reaches out and joins the flight of an airplane drone, floats down the curve of Doppler effect.

Now, fifteen minutes since the beginning of this writing, the bulldozer has stopped for a while. The freeway one-half mile away, unmasked, sends its ever-shifting drone to join with the train whistle from Encinitas.

The bulldozer starts again moving the air like an audible crooked staircase before reaching its full power. As I lean on my wooden table, my arm receives sympathetic vibrations from the low frequencies of the bulldozer, but hearing seems to take place in my stomach. A jet passes over. Some of its sound moves through my jawbone and out the back of my neck. It is dragging the earth with it.

I would like to amplify my bowl of crackling, shaking jello. (Once in 1959 a bulldozer came through the side of my house while I was eating lunch. The driver looked at me, backed out, and continued to operate the bulldozer.)

I would like to amplify the sound of a bull dozing.

The bulldozer has stopped again. On the other side of the freeway, a dog repeats a high bark which curves downward. My dog has a tinkling collar. I would like to find a tree way.

Three days ago at UCD, I experienced a magnificent performance of Bob Ashley's *Wolfman*. My ears changed and adapted themselves to the sound pressure level. All the wax in my ears melted. After the performance, ordinary conversation at two feet away sounded very distant. Later, all ordinary sounds seemed heightened, much louder than usual. Today I can still feel *Wolfman* in my ears. MY EARS FEEL LIKE CAVES. Monday I am going to hear *Wolfman* again. It will be the fourth time I've heard *Wolfman*, and I can't wait to hear the feedback dripping from his jaws again.

**Some
Sound Observations**

My present bulldozer has started and stopped again. A faraway jet simulates a fifty foot tabla, accompanied by an infinite freeway tamboura.

I am tired of writing this article, but not of the opportunity it is giving me to listen and remember. My chair is creaking as restlessness grows. I wonder what God's chair sounds like? I would like to amplify it. I would like to amplify a spider spinning its web.

Loren Rush calls his new work "Theater of the Mind." Since last night, he is still playing and singing in the theater of my mind.

The bulldozer remains silent. A very low frequency is shaking my belly. (7 Hz at high intensity can make you sick or kill you.) It is an automobile becoming more apparent as it passes, now accented by a motorbike.

(Once in a half-waking state, my head was held hard against a wall by the sound of a model airplane motor. I thought some cosmic dentist was drilling for my mind's tooth.)

The breeze is rising and blowing my papers about the table. The rustling in the trees sounds like tape hiss until it mixes with the next plane overhead.

Recently, a young man described his experience working in proximity to jet engines. After overcoming fear of the sound, he began to find sounds to listen to, such as small tinklings within the engine.

Why can't sounds be visible? Would the feedback from ear to eye cause fatal oscillation? Can you remember the first sound you ever heard? What is the first sound you remember hearing?

Why shouldn't a music department in a university devote itself entirely to music since 1950? Without a substantial body of new literature and instrumentation, the symphony and opera will become defunct—dead horses in the 21st Century. Who cares.

I often think of the title of one of La Monte Young's pieces which I have not yet had the pleasure of hearing: *The Second Dream of the High Tension Wire.*

In the Schwann long-playing record catalog there are special sections for railroads, sound effects, sports cars, test records, and honky-tonk piano, but none for electronic music.

When a concert pianist is on tour, he usually finds a tuned Steinway grand piano to play. What kind of sound system does the electronic musician find?

When I stopped writing yesterday, I went on listening. I attended dinner in a Syrian restaurant and ate a concert with my *Wolfman* ears. The house lights dimmed to a singing SCR. Spots came up and the bassoon soloist walked on the stage, bowed to the applause, walked off again and told someone to turn off the heating fan which was playing a duet with the SCR. He returned, bowed again to the new round of applause. His taped accompaniment began. I heard trees rustling in the speakers.

417

**Pauline
Oliveros**

Loren Rush has synthesized a bassoon sound at the artificial intelligence center at Stanford. With John Chowning's programming, he can make it move in circles, ellipses, or figure-eights around two speakers. He can make the synthesized bassoon do a *glissando*. Loren has a lecture entitled "A Day in the Life of a Plastic Bassoon."

Next, a quiet trio played in the manner of Feldman, accepted, perfectly-cued car drones.

I listened to a Schubert Octet in the recording engineer's sound booth. The speakers added their characteristics to the orchestration. As we watched the audience, the engineer said, "Those people are not listening to the music as it was intended. They should be having dinner."

I am inside my house now. Outside, sounds are attenuated by the insulation. I hear a dripping faucet and the ticking of my cuckoo clock. They combine and are joined by the refrigerator. The planes from Palomar Airport dwindle in through the furnace openings.

I have listened to many refrigerators. There is often a flickering between the sixth and seventh harmonic. Once, while in the process of drinking *Ouzo* with David, Bob, and Orville, a refrigerator sent its harmonics out to surround my head with circles, ellipses, and figure-eights.

In 1963 I made a tape piece for dancer Elizabeth Harris. It was made from piano sounds. On the night of the first performance, I stood in the wings prepared to start the tape recorder. Suddenly, I heard the opening sounds of my piece, but the tape transport was not moving. The dance involved a mobile that was suspended from a strand of piano wire. When the mobile was lowered, it moved like a pendulum, causing the piano wire to vibrate.

In New York, Terry Riley led me fifteen blocks out of our way to hear a building ventilator. I wonder what microbes hear?

Sitting in a parking lot on my third day of article writing. I could listen to the stereophony of cars, starter gaggling, motor wigglings, door squeals, and "bllaps" forever. It's almost like Debussy, compared to Saturday's Wagnerian bulldozer.

The best part of Lincoln Center is the tunnel from the IRT to the Beaumont Theater. Walking toward the theater, my footsteps greeted me from the approaching wall; midway, they followed me from the opposite wall. I listened to this more than one hundred and fifty times—an Alice in Tunnelland—while moving from the saga of subway sound to Brechtian music drama.

"If the moon is ever visited, one feature of its environment will be known beforehand with certainty; the wastes will be noiseless except for vibration transmitted through the solid surface. Since there is no gaseous atmosphere, there can be no tread of footsteps heard, no rustle of clothing, and if an obstruction is dynamited, the debris will fly apart silently as in a dream."[1]

During the quiet evening of a summer vacation near the Feather River Canyon, Lynn, Bob, and I wanted to play music. We decided to read John Cage's *Atlas Eclipticalis* from the original score, which was shining brightly above. The canyon creatures joined us as we played, and we played until our awareness became imbedded in the canyon and summoned a ghostly, floating train, an apparition of metal meeting metal, reflected doubly, triply, endlessly from the canyon, from the mind, from the flickering passenger windows, the rumbling ties, OUR EARS FELT LIKE CAYONS. We didn't speak until morning.

One's ideas about music can change radically after listening to recorded works at fast forward or rewind on a tape recorder. Ramon Sender arranged Wagner's *Ring Cycle* by a series of re-recordings at fast forward to four successive clicks. "The auditory basis of obstacle detection by bats was independently recognized in 1932 by a Dutch zoologist, Sven Dijkgraaf, who made a careful study of these faint, audible clicks and noted how closely they were correlated with the echo-location of obstacles. This is an example of the need for care, patience, and appropriate conditions if one is to notice and enjoy some of the more fascinating facets of the natural world."[2]

According to Loren Rush, the reason for studying counterpoint is that you may have to teach it some day.

"Airborne sound waves are reflected back almost totally from the water, and underwater sound is equally well reflected back downward from the surface . . . once proper equipment was available for converting underwater sound to audible airborne sound . . . underwater listening became refined enough and common enough to reveal the immense variety of sounds used by marine animals."[3]

In most schools and universities the language laboratories are better equipped for sound processing and modifications than the music departments.

Human hearing is non-linear. Our ears are less sensitive to low and high frequencies approaching the limits of audibility. Our ears are most sensitive at about 3000 Hz where some people can hear collisions of air molecules.

A fast sweep of the audio range by a tone generator can produce a click.

[1] Edgar Villchur, *Reproduction of Sound*, AR Library, Vol. 2
[2] Donald R. Griffin, *Echos of Bats and Man*, Anchor Books, Doubleday and Co., Inc., Garden City, N.Y.
[3] Donald R. Griffin, *Echos of Bats and Man*

**Pauline
Oliveros**

"Some animals, notably insects, do not have ears in their heads but in such unlikely places as legs (some crickets) or the thorax, the 'middle' portions of the insect body to which the legs attach (some grasshoppers)."[4]

I stopped writing yesterday in order to go on listening. Monday's performance of *Wolfman* was somewhat marred because the sponsors failed to provide proper speakers and amplifiers. I heard Wolfman's ghost drooling feedback.

Many music departments are more concerned with analysis than communication.

When I was sixteen, my accordion teacher taught me to hear combination tones. The accordion is particularly able to produce them if you squeeze hard enough. From that time, I wished for a way to eliminate the fundamental tones so I could listen only to the combination tones. When I was thirty-two, I began to set signal generators beyond the range of hearing and to make electronic music from amplified combination tones. I felt like a witch capturing sounds from a nether realm.

In one electronic studio I was accused of black art, and the director disconnected line amplifiers to discourage my practices, declaring that signal generators are of no use above or below the audio range because you can't hear them. Since all active processing equipment contains amplifiers, I found that I could cascade two pieces of equipment and get enough gain for my combination tones to continue my work, plus the addition of various amplifier characteristics as orchestration. I worked there for two months, and, for recreation, would ride my bicycle to the town power plant where I would listen for hours to the source of my newly-found powers.

Saturday's bulldozer has gone away. The birds and insects share the air with waxing, waning plane and car drones. The insects are singing in the supersonic range. I hear their combination tones while the insects probably hear the radio frequency sounds created by motor drones, but not the fundamentals. If we could hear the micro-world, we would probably hear the brain functioning.

---

[4]Bergeijk, Pierce & David, *Waves and the Ear,* Anchor Books, Doubleday, Inc., Garden City, N.Y.

420

Steve Reich

[1936 -   ]

Steve Reich is universally acknowledged as one of the pioneers of a
major musical revolution which replaced traditional ideas of musical rhetoric, narrative, and development with models that focused
upon the power of repetition and gradual change. This revolution is
known by a number of different labels: minimalism, trance music,
pulse music, or (in Reich's own words) "music as gradual process."
His Come Out, a tape studio work of the 1960s in which a looped,
repeating fragment of recorded human speech is set contrapuntally
against itself in ever-shifting relationships, was one of his first works
of this style.

Reich's fascination with gradual process and steady rhythmic
pulse can be traced to his experience playing jazz drums and keyboards, his love for Bach and Stravinsky and, later, his study of religion and philosophy, his discovery of Medieval organum and African
drumming, and his experience with tape loops in electronic music
studios. Reich trained at Juilliard and Mills College (with Milhaud
and Berio), and he also studied African Balinese Gamelan and Hebrew scriptural cantillation.

In 1966 he founded Steve Reich and Musicians, a group devoted
exclusively to the performance of his music. He did not begin to
create works for traditional ensembles until the 1980s, most notably
the 1981-82 Tehillim ("Psalms") for a largely traditional western orchestra. Reich has recently begun to explore ways of applying his
techniques to aspects of music theater, as exemplified by The Cave,
a 1993 semi-staged chamber "opera" incorporating live musicians,
video images, sampled sound-loops, and visual collage (the latter
created by his wife Beryl Korot).

"Music as a Gradual Process—1968" is from Reich's book Writings
About Music (1974).

421

Music as a Gradual Process 1968

I do not mean the process of composition, but rather pieces of music that are, literally, processes.

The distinctive thing about musical processes is that they determine all the note-to-note (sound-to-sound) details and the over all form simultaneously. (Think of a round or infinite canon.)

I am interested in perceptible processes. I want to be able to hear the process happening throughout the sounding music.

To facilitate closely detailed listening a musical process should happen extremely gradually.

Performing and listening to a gradual musical process resembles:

> pulling back a swing, releasing it, and observing it gradually come to rest;
> turning over an hour glass and watching the sand slowly run through to the bottom;
> placing your feet in the sand by the ocean's edge and watching, feeling, and listening to the waves gradually bury them.

Though I may have the pleasure of discovering musical processes and composing the musical material to run through them, once the process is set up and loaded it runs by itself.

Material may suggest what sort of process it should be run through (content suggests form), and processes may suggest what sort of material should be run through them (form suggests content). If the shoe fits, wear it.

As to whether a musical process is realized through live human performance or through some electro-mechanical means is not finally the main issue. One of the most beautiful concerts I ever heard consisted of four composers playing their tapes in a dark hall. (A tape is interesting when it's an interesting tape.)

It is quite natural to think about musical processes if one is frequently working with electro-mechanical sound equipment. All music turns out to be ethnic music.

Musical processes can give one a direct contact with the impersonal and also a kind of complete control, and one doesn't always think of the impersonal and complete control as going together. By "a kind" of complete control I mean that by running this material through this process I completely control all that results, but also that I accept all that results without changes.

John Cage has used processes and has certainly accepted their results, but the processes he used were compositional ones that could not be heard when the piece was performed. The process of using the *I Ching* or imperfections in a sheet of paper to determine musical parameters can't be heard when listening to music composed that way. The compositional processes and the sounding music have no audible connection. Similarly in serial music, the series itself is seldom audible. (This is a basic difference between serial [basically European] music and serial [basically American] art, where the perceived series is usually the focal point of the work.)

What I'm interested in is a compositional process and a sounding music that are one and the same thing.

James Tenney said in conversation, "then the composer isn't privy to anything." I don't know any secrets of structure that you can't hear. We all listen to the process together since it's quite audible, and one of the reasons it's quite audible is, because it's happening extremely gradually.

The use of hidden structural devices in music never appealed to me. Even when all the cards are on the table and everyone hears what is gradually happening in a musical process, there are still enough mysteries to satisfy all. These mysteries are the impersonal, unintended, psycho-acoustic by-products of the intended process. These might include sub-melodies heard within repeated melodic patterns, stereophonic effects due to listener location, slight irregularities in performance, harmonics, difference tones, etc.

Listening to an extremely gradual musical process opens my ears to *it*, but *it* always extends farther than I can hear, and that makes it interesting to listen to that musical process again. That area of every gradual (completely controlled) musical process, where one hears the details of the sound moving out away from intentions, occurring for their own acoustic reasons, is *it*.

I begin to perceive these minute details when I can sustain close attention and a gradual process invites my sustained attention. By "gradual" I mean extremely gradual; a process happening so slowly and gradually that listening to it resembles watching a minute hand on a watch—you can perceive it moving after you stay with it a little while.

Several currently popular modal musics like Indian classical and drug oriented rock and roll may make us aware of minute sound details because in being modal (constant key center, hypnotically droning and repetitious) they naturally focus on these details rather than on key modulation, counterpoint and other peculiarly Western devices. Nevertheless, these modal musics remain more or less strict frameworks for improvisation. They are not processes.

The distinctive thing about musical processes is that they determine all the note-to-note details and the over all form simultaneously. One can't improvise in a musical process—the concepts are mutually exclusive.

While performing and listening to gradual musical processes one can participate in a particular liberating and impersonal kind of ritual. Focusing in on the musical process makes possible that shift of attention away from *he* and *she* and *you* and *me* outwards towards *it.*

T. J. Anderson

[1928 -   ]

Many African-American composers of "classical" music are confronted by a unique set of experiences—influences from two worlds,
so to speak. Thomas Jefferson Anderson has successfully balanced
both; his music speaks to, and draws from, the heritage of European
art music and the culture of black America. His principal compositions include the opera Soldier Boy and In Memoriam Malcolm X,
the latter commissioned by the Symphony of the New World. While
the second Viennese school and post-Webernian modernism may
motivate many of Anderson's works, blues, gospel music, traditional
African sources, and jazz have figured as equally important stimuli.

   This ability to reconcile supposed "opposites" has not only been a
recurring motive in Anderson's art, but in his life as well. His early
career as a jazz performer was balanced with mainstream academic
training, including studies with Darius Milhaud at Aspen and a
Ph.D. from the University of Iowa. Anderson was the first black
composer-in-residence of the Atlanta Symphony and was a resident
fellow at Morehouse College. He later moved to New England to assume a professorship and department chair at Tufts University.

   Anderson was active in the postwar rediscovery of Scott Joplin
and played an important role in the orchestration of Joplin's opera
Treemonisha. He served on the advisory board for Columbia Records' pioneering "Black Composers Series," supervised ragtime recordings for the Smithsonian Institution, and appeared as speaker
and panelist at numerous symposia. He is an articulate advocate for
the cause of new music in a multicultural society, as evidenced in
this interview with Elliott Schwartz.

This interview was conducted in 1996 expressly for the present volume.

425

An Interview with Elliott Schwartz

- *Question:* Tell me about your early musical training and the instruments you learned to play. Do you agree with Hindemith's dictum that composers should be fluent on as many instruments as possible?
- *Answer:* My first musical instructions were from my mother, a pianist. My father was a professor at Howard University and I attended elementary school in Washington, DC. There, I conducted a children's toy orchestra and studied violin with my father's colleague, Louis von Jones. I studied violin with Charles Keys while I was a junior high school student in Cincinnati. I also sang in an Episcopal church choir. High school in Coatesville, Pennsylvania was my first integrated school experience. I played trumpet and violin, sang in a chorus, and organized a jazz band. While in high school, I taught myself to play the saxophone by reading an instructional manual and cutting out the fingered positions on a broomstick. This experiment enabled me to pass an audition for baritone sax for the band at a nearby Veterans Administration hospital. Through the outstanding teaching of Edward C. Lewis, Jr. at West Virginia State College, I added bassoon, French and baritone horns. In graduate school at the University of Iowa, I occasionally played double bass in Fred King's band. My own teachings of instrumental music in elementary, junior high, high school and at college level proved to be invaluable lessons for me as well. It becomes obvious that my musical background reflects my total support for the Hindemith dictum.
- *Q:* What percentage of your early musical training was "white' repertory and/or performing technique? Were your first encounters with black music, by comparison, informal in nature?
- *A:* All of my early training (through junior high school) centered on classical literature. My teachers were all African Americans. In junior high school, I began to branch out into jazz and profited from a system described in Paul F. Berliner's book, *Thinking in Jazz*. This system was predominately improvisatory and the blues was its major structural form. My first encounters with music by black composers occurred in my home where my mother played the music of R. Nathaniel Dett, Scott Joplin, Eubie Blake, William Dawson, and William Grant Still. I was fortunate enough to become friends with the latter three. In an informal way, the cultural environment of the Howard Theater, night clubs, and black churches all served to expand my musical education.

426

An Interview with
Elliott Schwartz

Six teachers had a major impact on me as a composer: Edward C. Lewis, (West Virginia State College) orchestration; George Ceiga (Penn State University), inspiration; T. Scott Huston (Cincinnati Conservatory of Music), attention to details; Philip Bezanson University of Iowa), motion; Richard Hervig (University of Iowa), the importance of analysis; and Darius Milhaud (Aspen Music Festival), humility.

• *Q:* When did you first come into contact with important black composers of concert music, and during that first exposure which composers made the greatest impact?

• *A:* The first major black composers with whom I came in contact were Ulysses Kay, Hale Smith, George Walker, and Olly Wilson. I got to know them during and after graduate school. Through friendship with them I became more connected to the concert world and culture. As important as these contacts have been throughout my career, it was my association with the sculptor Richard Hunt that proved to be crucial in the crystallization of my ideas. As my patron he has been responsible for a number of my compositions. Through him, I met the writer Leon Forrest and the three of us became close friends and "spiritual brothers." Another source of inspiration has been my association with poets. My friendship circle includes M. B. Tolson, Pauline Hanson, Robert Hayden, Michael Harper, Philip Levine, Harryette Mullin, as well as two poets in the family: Pauline Kaldas and T. J. Anderson III. Yet, it is the composers who strike a chord in my aesthetic development. Ulysses Kay served as a mentor and explained the political aspects of being a composer. Hale Smith with his myriad background continues to serve as a sounding board for my musical ideas. I find his scores and the music of George Walker and Olly Wilson continually provocative. To this cultural mix, I would add the name Silvestre Revueltas. When I heard his 1938 composition *Sensemayá* while I was in residence with the Atlanta Symphony Orchestra in 1971 I began to see multicultural music in a much broader context. This work, which I find closer to the folk than Stravinsky's *Le Sacre du printemps,* could be called the "rite of spring" of the new world. With a European orchestra, the work brings together black Cuban and Mexican Indian cultures. As you can see by these remarks, I begin to have difficulty separating composers by race or ethnicity. George Gershwin could obviously be an African-American composer. The composer Robert Ward once told me that there was nothing Jewish about Mendelssohn's music, an observation which I totally support. When Yehudi Menuhin improvises Indian music, does he become Indian?

• Q: Your remarks—made during a panel discussion—on the difficulty of defining black music have been preserved in a volume entitled *Black Music in Our Culture.* Have your thoughts taken any new direction since then?

427

**T. J.
Anderson**

• *A:* My thoughts have not changed on the dialogue. The answers given at that time still appear relevant to me. In terms of recent consideration I mention the following observations. Symphony orchestras are currently interested in crossover audiences and have wooed Bobby McFerrin and Wynton Marsalis. While this move is superficially attractive, time does not permit me the privilege of discussing in detail the most important phenomena of the twentieth century: *integrated music.* If you examine the scores of Donal Fox, William Albright, Marga Richter, Donald Harris, George Russell, Thomas Oboe Lee, Donald Sur, Joan Tower, Alvin Singleton, Steve Reich, and Stephen Jaffe, you can only come to one conclusion. There is no international style. The influence of diversity propels concert music to the end of this millenium. White or black compositional expectations are a myth. They have been based on repeated clichés, cultural artifacts, cadential formulas, and musical shorthand that signify nothing. The music of the United States, like the music of Russia, Germany, Italy, France, England, and Japan, is pluralistic.

• *Q:* During your interview for *The Black American Composer Speaks* you note that (through the influence of various artists) you have "learned the value of *projection on different levels.*" (Italics are mine.) How does that particular phrase apply to your own work?

• *A:* In my early works I projected sound platforms by the use of dynamics. An example would be the composition *Squares, An Essay for Orchestra* (1965). This practice led me to the discovery of my orbiting technique. This technique as exemplified in *Intemezzi* has proven to be another means for accomplishing the same results. It might be noted that this work for three instruments can be performed as three solo pieces, therefore creating four performance possibilities. When Lukas Foss was conducting in Buffalo, he saw the score for *Squares* and told me that there are two types of composers. The first group solidifies an existing aesthetic (Bach, Haydn, Brahms, Stravinsky and Copland). The second group finds its own way through the extension of personality (Monteverdi, Beethoven, Scriabin, Sibelius, and Ives). He placed me in the second group. This evaluation fits in with the Thompson dissertation and the remarks by Nicolas Slonimsky (in *Baker's Biographical Dictionary of Musicians*) which classify me as "eclectic" and "quaquaversal."

• *Q:* During your long career you have held positions and/or extended residencies in Europe, Latin America, and North America. Even within North America, you have been an important figure at institutions based in New England and in the "Deep South," ranging from WASP universities to traditionally black colleges. Do you think there's been a difference in the nature of your work—and/or the reception it has received—at these different venues?

• *A:* It is true that my professional experience has been varied. The major difference that I found between white and historically black colleges was the lack of financial resources. This situation resulted in limited library holdings and a scarcity of permanent collections. Scores and recordings, lectures by visiting scholars, and concert performances of contemporary music were often unavailable in black colleges at the time I was teaching. In thinking about my students, I frequently found that white students relied on the printed word (books and scores as references) while many African-American students relied on creativity. In my role as a teacher I tried to broaden all of my students' horizons. Even now, many of my students continue to find me a mentor.

Your questions raise additional concerns about college teaching in America. In 1984, I chaired a study for the College Music Society, *Racial and Ethnic Directions in American Music*. This study showed that only two percent of full-time teachers are African American and that 81 percent of our schools have no African-American representation in music. When you can consider the fact that we are the dominant influence on our popular culture, the situation is obviously deplorable.

Living as colonized composers in America has been the destiny of African Americans. What African-American composer of concert music has received a MacArthur prize? I could mention that George Walker, age 73, became the first African-American composer to win the Pulitzer Prize. Why did it take so long? In books on American music, why is there a systematic exclusion of African-American composers? Are we separate and unequal, aliens in what should be a multicultural society? How many concertgoers have heard the music of Hale Smith? How often are commissions offered to black composers of concert music? I cannot escape being embroiled in a struggle.

Ben
Johnston

[1926 -   ]

*Probably most recognized for his work in just intonation (though he
also has worked in tempered and various microtonal tunings), Ben
Johnston is a part of the American iconoclast/visionary tradition,
which includes such musical figures as Ives, Partch, and Cage. He
has employed both serial and chance operations as well as his own
tuning-based compositional procedures, yet his music, while often
highly complex and intensely individual, usually remains in touch
with the vernacular.*

*The composer who probably exerted the greatest influence on
him was Harry Partch, with whom he studied in the early fifties and
whose music he has performed, championed, and written about. His
other important teachers include Milhaud and Cage.*

*Johnston's music may be divided into three somewhat overlapping
periods. During much of the fifties, he wrote a primarily equal-tem-
pered, neo-classical music that drew on his studies with Milhaud. In
the sixties, his focus turned to writing an often highly systemized microtonal music, expanding total serialism to tie pitch and rhythmic
ratios and allowing his tuning systems to influence many elements
of his compositions, including style and structure. In the seventies,
his music grew more emotionally rich and focused on the use of
"extended just intonation," which can yield a wonderfully rich tonal
palette.*

*Johnston taught at the University of Illinois from 1951 through
1983. Now retired from academia and living in North Carolina, he
pursues his own music full-time.*

The following essay was written in 1996 expressly for the present
volume.

Maximum
Clarity

Imagine looking at home movies when the person running the projector suddenly improves the focus. It is a pleasant but definite shock to see how much clearer the images are now even though we had accepted them before the adjustment. This is a very precise analogy to what happens when the players in a musical ensemble clean up the intonation. They do not have to compute this or even analyze the music to discover what it needs to bring it in tune. No, this is done "by ear": simply by listening for maximum clarity in the intervals that comprise the ensemble sound. Most players are scarcely aware even whether they have to raise or lower pitches in order to achieve good tuning: they make the adjustment quite directly as soon as they bring critical attention to playing in tune.

What is actually happening when such ensemble tuning is proceeding well is that the versions of the intervals which have the smallest numbers in the vibration ratios are being selected. This is what just intonation is, at its simplest. Of course, it can be more complex than that. There are usually several versions of an interval, all simple enough ratios to beguile the ear, so that one may select among them. The basis of this choice is usually what is called expressivity. It is what performers in the Indian tradition call "rasa," or emotional meaning. As one becomes more and more sensitive to this dimension of performance, one begins to characterize musical styles more successfully by means of particular expressivities produced by interval choice.

This degree of sophistication is by no means unusual among fine performance artists. When they are learning this from master teachers, they rely largely on imitation of other artists who already know how to do this sort of thing well. Very little, if any, intellectual explanation is given, and frequently the language used in making suggestions is geared more toward heightening emotional awareness than toward awakening the analytical mind. For instance, "Try to play that more warmly," or "This passage needs a sense of angst."

One of the easiest style characterizations to perceive is that of blues singing. Listen to a Gershwin song sung by a jazz vocalist and then contrast it with the same song sung by an opera singer. There are tangible intonation differences between the two. Technically, many of the blues intervals used by jazz singers involve relationships to the seventh partial of the overtone series, rather than the more "concert" sound of relationships to the fifth partial. Neither singer is at all likely to understand intellectually this difference, but by ear, the expression is quite distinct in the two unlike cases. By ear is how it is achieved and by ear is how it is appreciated. The criterion for the choice is an oral tradition: namely, the style.

When concert music draws on folk or ethnic traditions for its expressive content, various elements of performance style need to be adopted by the performer. The violin concerto of Max Bruch is a good example. These stylistic niceties are not written into the score, but a sensitive violinist learns them from oral tradition. Naturally, pitch idiosyncrasies are not the only such style traits: there are timbral and rhythmic nuances that are just as important. Jazz rhythm is not notated exactly as it is played. Play it exactly as notated and you will be accused of being "square."

There are even aspects of performance tradition that are attributable largely to the problems of the performer, which are created by compromises made by theorists, instrument designers, and even composers. When temperaments of various kinds were introduced during the sixteenth through the eighteenth centuries in Europe, they were theoretical constructs intended by theorists to make keyboard instruments feasible and to accommodate the design problems of instruments that were newly emerging as the main element in musical performance ensembles. Up to that era, art music in Europe had been predominantly vocal, and each part was performed by a single musician, with no massed unison as in a modern chorus or in the string section of a modern orchestra. In the earlier vocal style, vibrato was used only as a melodic ornament, exactly analogous to a trill or a mordant. Its use, like all ornaments, depended upon an oral, not a written, tradition. But the great difficulty of performing the pitches of these subtly comprised temperaments accurately, and the additional burden created by mass unison performance (which inevitably caused minute differences of tuning from player to player) made vibrato gradually adopted as a way of concealing these intonational imprecisions. In addition, there is a far more subtle but far more serious obscuring factor involving the practice of composers. The concept of consonance and dissonance, fundamental to Western music, strongly implies that consonance should be just-tuned, and in performance practice, this is what is normally attempted. But as notation developed, it preserved a visual distinction between an E flat and a D sharp, for instance, but none between the fifth of a dominant triad and the added sixth of a subdominant one. The former is the enharmonic equivalent or diesis, the latter the syntonic (or Didymic) comma. As composers accustomed themselves to temperaments, they began to disregard the differences of a syntonic comma. Thus there are passages in which the pitch will gradually go flat or sharp if all the consonances are carefully kept to just tuning. In more complex harmonic passages, it is impossible for all intervals to be consonant: somewhere in the context, an interval or several intervals will have to be tuned as dissonances. Vibrato helps conceal difficulties such as these.

It is a perfectly workable premise to base an artistic system upon a compromise such as this, as the successful existence of Western music demonstrates. However, there are consequences, some of which have yet to be squarely faced. Every aspect of an artwork is potentially symbolic, or to be more precise, the symbolic content of an artwork can be read to various depths. The symbolic meaning of a compromise like this is not a flattering commentary about a culture that imposes it upon every artwork *a priori*. It is rather like covering up emotional insecurities with superficial politeness, a not uncommon practice.

Plato said, "The soul is a harmony." Since the harmoniai were the modes of ancient Greek music, this formulation indicates a comparison not to a chord of musical tones but to a scale upon which melodies are formed. This view of the inner life is not only an ancient one: G. I. Gurdjieff called his school the Institute for the Harmonious Development of Man. In Gurdjieff's view, man does not have a soul unless he nurtures one in himself, and, in this process, beginning with merciless self-observation of all one's habits, attitudes, and weaknesses, leads into a gradual process of what could be accurately described as a bringing in tune of one's interior life and a unifying of what is exterior and what is interior. In his teaching, he laid great stress upon both music and movements as significant aids in this difficult effort. The emotional life, with its addiction to all kinds of negative states, is greatly in need of such tuning, so that it can become the means to further growth instead of the principal blockage preventing it.

Plato also viewed music as a producer or inducer of inner states, in sharp contrast to Aristotle, who viewed the effect of art as purgative. Plato's view accords, by the way, with that of Confucius. In this view, to expose oneself to art charged with violent and negative emotion is to tend to induce these feelings in oneself. This does not mean that such art is destructive, but rather that it brings one into contact with disharmony in need of resolution. If this resolution takes place in the art itself, the danger is lessened, but when the perceiver of the art is left to himself to resolve the conflicts induced by the art, there is tangible danger that he may not or cannot or even may choose not to make this effort. Such art arouses the tensions and leaves one with them.

As an art of time, music affects us on three time-scales: macro-time, which is the largest portion of an unfolding event; normal-time, which is countable, moment to moment; and micro-time, which is the proportions of relative speeds of sound vibrations. Events in macro-time are best understood by using intellect and memory. The whole area of form and development in music partakes of this nature. Normal-time events are rhythmic, affecting us through motor perceptions. The principal effect upon emotion is through micro-time events. It is here that the impact of tuning is manifest. With the reinforced vibrations that result when just tuning is achieved, there is an improvement not only in clarity and resonance but, concomitantly, a sharpening of emotional response to the sounds. This results in a much stronger attraction of the listener's attention and a consequent increase in what is retained in memory. In this way, the intelligibility of the large-scale form is more accessible to the listener.

Tonality can be defined as a system of pitches related to each other by a set of interval relations that can be followed by the ear. It implies harmonic relations, not simply melodic or motivic ones, which can be appreciated in terms of linear contour. In traditional Indian music, all the pitches are played in front of a drone, so that the rasa results from a fluctuation of just intervals against one single pitch level. In traditional Western music, melodies are accompanied by, or intersect in such a way as to constitute, a series of simultaneous pitch aggregates (chords) connected by common tones or by simple interval relation from a tone in one harmony to a tone in the next. When all the harmonic pitches are tuned in simple just ratios, harmonic intelligibility (actually, a series of mathematically simple relationships) is at a maximum. The typical listener is certainly not capable of performing an harmonic analysis by ear as he listens, but all listeners respond, with a fluctuation of feeling states, to this ongoing process. When the ear is defeated in its effort to follow the harmonic flux because of the complexity of the harmonic relationships, the sound can be described as atonal. In such a complex situation, the ear cannot easily refer all tones to a single central pitch, or tonic. There seems to be an ambiance in which any tone could be focal, or no particular tone.

In Indian musical tradition, the drone symbolizes the atman, the individual portion of God allotted to every human being, against which all else acquires its meaning in the process of experience. Our task is to bring our inner awareness into contact with atman, as is the practice of yoga, a word whose root means "to yoke." It is worth mentioning that the root meaning of religio, from which religion is derived, is "I reconnect." The tonic in Western music is our nearest equivalent to the drone, but it is not overtly and constantly present, so its function in bringing meaning to all other tonal events is mediated by the network of tonal relationships that make up the fabric of the music, and the tonic serves as both a point of departure (home) and also as a goal, even if not achieved.

The symbolism of atonality can be expressed, and is painfully expressive of our modern way of life. In such music, there is no pitch that can serve as a focus of organization. Indeed, on a micro-temporal level, there is no easily discernible organization. Thematic and motivic patterning is perceived on the same time-scale as rhythmic patterns. This absence of harmonic organizing factors, such as tonic pitches, chord roots and a logic of harmonic progressions, strongly recalls G. I. Gurdjieff's critique of "ordinary man," in whom, he says, there is no permanent entity which can say "I" for the whole psychic organism but, rather, an externally conditioned series of temporary and competing small "I"s, each of which is, so to speak, king for a day (in fact, only for a short moment) and none of which can really exert any will over the psychic flux. Atonal music has an "expressionist" angst that subordinates any emotional responses it may, in addition, evoke. This almost amounts to a description of what Gurdjieff called "negative emotions," which constitute the overwhelming majority of activities of the ordinary person's emotional life, preventing, by their monopolization of psychic energy, the experiencing of positive emotions. But like negative emotions, atonality is only a kind and a degree of complexity that defeats the efforts of our intelligence to analyze it. As the intensely moving music of Alban Berg demonstrates, the pushing of the effort to tonalize into such thickets of complexity awakens emotional responses. This is like the difficult and painful self-knowledge that Gurdjieff counsels modern man he must strive to acquire.

It is worth noting that Schoenberg did not like the term "atonal," preferring instead "pan-tonal." He did not view his harmonic usage as a means of achieving independence from all sense of tonal center, though he did indeed espouse "the emancipation of dissonance," which can even more illuminatingly be seen as a great extension of the boundaries of consonance. Even a casual reading of his *Harmonielehre* makes clear his view of the overtone series as a background source of the materials of our Western musical scale. That he not only accepted but openly espoused the use of twelve-tone equal temperament is well known, but it does not follow from this that he wished to jettison the whole phenomenon of tonality in music. This point of view can indeed be found among some of his followers, but by no means all of them.

The use of extended just intonation restores the strongest perceptual aid in perceiving the network of simple mathematical ratios that makes tonality possible. The term "extended" indicates the embracing of the great extensions made by Schoenberg and many other twentieth-century composers of harmonic and melodic interval language. The mathematics of just intonation brings the realm of micro-time into exact analogy with the way metrical rhythm has worked for centuries and makes even clearer why developments such as metrical modulation, with its numerous interrelated tempi, are so precisely germane to its use.

**Ben
Johnston**

Hard rock concerts place great emphasis upon a physical response to music. The insistent rhythm, the dominance of short, cyclically repetitive patterns, and amplified highly emotional voice stress a powerful body response. This is in sharp contrast with music that makes its primary appeal to emotion, not the physicalized emotions of body response, but the more subtle and longer-lasting emotions that have to do with our feeling responses to important events and relationships in our lives. On the lighter level, the majority of popular music is of this type, but lacks the seriousness of a Chopin, who certainly stressed emotional power and evocation. There is also an intellectual dimension to music, evident in such abstract designs as Bach's fugues or the serial compositions of Babbitt. Actually, much music lays some stress on all three of these kinds of stimulation to some extent. To the extent that these different aspects are well integrated, the music tends to acquire universality and greatness.

The harmonic innovations of the late nineteenth and early twentieth centuries have been characterized by Cowell as pushing the bounds of consonance to include higher partials of the overtone series. This is a particularly apt description of impressionist harmony and, therefore, of jazz, and it can be a meaningful description of numerous twentieth-century styles. It was thus a very natural and timely decision for Harry Partch to include the seventh and eleventh partials in his just-tuned scale, and subsequent use of the thirteenth, seventeenth and nineteenth partials is a part of this same expansion of consonance. It is not necessary to consider non-prime numbers similarly, as any of them can be produced by compounding simpler partials (e.g., the ninth is two superimposed fifths and the fifteenth is a compound of a fifth and a major third).

Just as superimposed meters involving numbers higher than five are markedly more difficult for performers to handle accurately, so prime numbered partials higher than five are harder to tune accurately. Add to this the unfamiliarity of these sounds to the vast majority not only of performers but of composers as well. The implication of these overtone sonorities in harmonic contexts is not an infallible guide, since these harmonic configurations are usually approximated by close relations which can be tuned with primes no greater than five. These are perfectly distinct and effective nuances of tuning. The true situation is that we have uncovered a huge variety of tuning nuances which need clarification and sorting. All of this is still further complicated by the ubiquitous use for keyboards of equal tempered twelve-tone-per-octave scales, or near approximations thereof. Such constructs as symmetrical scales are directly based on such tuning, which means that either the symmetry or the pure consonance of the tuning must be sacrificed.

The difference between these two compromises is actually profound. A symmetrical scale is a circular pattern, while its just intonation counterpart is a spiral one. The symbolic significance of circle and spiral are fundamentally different. This is exactly analogous to the difference between a repetition and a sequence. The sequence "travels," whereas the repetition is static. This is a very different meaning, exactly as different as the distinction between change and stasis. The various microtonal commas and dieses are the differences by which the spiral misses its starting point on its next cycle, unlike the circle, which meets its starting point again. The circle is two-dimensional, while the spiral is three-dimensional. It is the difference between a process that simply repeats itself and one which evolves.

Any equal temperament, of no matter what numerosity, is a closed finite system, while just intonation constitutes an infinite system which is forever open. It is of course just this infinite openness which creates the thorniest problems in making use of it. It is important to know the exact color of each interval and to sense clearly its rasa. Even the commas and dieses can find their way into the awareness of the performer, though it is difficult to be consciously aware of the displacements of spiral designs by these tiny intervals because of the time elapsed between individual coils of the spiral. A cumulative displacement of several coils becomes unmistakably perceptible, however. For instance the progression in a major key I vi ii V I, which is much used, if carefully tuned in just intonation will flat by twenty-two cents (circa) each repetition, so that five repetitions flat more than a semitone. There is even in temperament a sense of relaxing in this progression, as if tension were being released. How much stronger is this impression if actual flatting is occurring. Or try the romantic series of modulations by major thirds: C Major, E Major, G# Major, B# Major. In this case the pitch is flatting with each cycle by about forty cents, which is an easily perceptible amount. Even in equal temperament this progression builds considerable tension. How much more so when the pitch level changes each cycle by almost a quarter-tone. In both cases the pitch is flatting but in the first case the displacement results from an interaction of prime numbers three and five, while in the second case it is caused by a unilateral action of the prime number five. One cannot be so simplistic as to posit that flatting relaxes tension. The second example builds tension in spite of flatting. It is the rasa of the active intervals which determines emotional reaction to them.

The melodic dimension of music seems on first thought to be a linear patterning describable in one dimension. But it almost inevitably entails a hierarchical relating of pitches not only to tonic notes but also to implied chord roots. This is certainly the case in traditional tonal music and even in much non-traditional contemporary music. The tonalities involved may be much more complex than major and minor triads, but the process of tonality can still work in a way analogous to music of the European common practice period. In the music of Harry Partch otonal and utonal hexads are analogous to major and minor triads and can be found in progressions quite analogous to the progressions of traditional tonal music. The complexity is greater and so therefore are the possibilities. There is also in Partch a fondness for using pseudo-consonances as expressive distortions of more familiar chordal sounds. Thus a chord tuned E flat, F sharp, B flat serves, in *Barstow*, as a distorted minor triad. Similar examples abound, and heighten the slightly raunchy ambiance which Partch already delineates with his graffiti text and naturalistic speech usage. All this would be impossible without extended just intonation. The melodies of Partch are frequently those of ordinary speech, heightened no more than would be done by a skilled actor.

With pretuned instruments, like most of Partch's, one is held to a gamut of pitches which is strictly limited, sometimes severely so. The free soaring in an unlimited world of pitches organized into otonal and utonal hexachords linked by common tones or by simple interval relations from one sonority to the next is an idea one gets from his theories but much less clearly from his music. There is no doubt that the world he envisioned is there for the taking by anyone with the courage to leave pretuned instruments to a supporting role or else use them only in special circumstances in full recognition of the straitjacket they impose. For the ear to be one's guide, as it must be when pretuning is not used, there must be an unequivocally clear notation of intentions and a systematic that can genuinely rest upon tuning by ear. For this one must deal with intervals the sound of which the players either already know or can learn readily. The composer has to deal with these musical materials in such a way as to make possible finding all these unfamiliar relationships without artificial or preset means. This is quite analogous to dealing with extreme rhythmic complexity. Perhaps the future will give us the possibility to have instruments with digital intelligence which can help us to size up the situation in live performance and assist in realizing accurate decisions in adjusting the intonation of the pitch language of the music we are playing. So long as this leaves the performer in charge it will be a blessing. In the interim, computer realization of complex musical intentions leaves much to be desired. No one has yet designed a computer with emotional and intuitive abilities.

It has been demonstrated over and over that complexity generated by stochastic means is not distinguishable from complexity generated by serial complications or even by chance procedures. All that is necessary is to arrive at a degree of complexity which the human mind cannot easily unravel. But complexity that is truly intelligible, though pushing the limits of human ability, is quite another matter. This is one of the perennial preoccupations of twentieth century music, all shades of opinion and preference weighing in. If complexity is not to be pursued for its own sake, as a desideratum, one must decide what the reason for making art really is. Certainly our world grows more complex with each succeeding generation, and this is why such a theme shows up in our art. To deal with this issue truly well one must not only use intellect but also emotion and the intelligence of the body itself.

Cornelius Cardew

[1936 - 1981]

Almost single-handedly, Cornelius Cardew brought experimental music of the fifties and sixties—particularly the work of such Americans as Cage, Feldman, and Wolff—to light in England, and through his teaching at the Royal Academy of Music and his work with the improvisation ensemble AMM and the Scratch Orchestra, he became the mentor for a whole generation of British composers who sought to break away from their country's conservative concert music traditions.

As a composer, Cardew seems to have reinvented himself every few years. His two most noted works, both massive in scale, are Treatise *(1963-67) and* The Great Learning *(1968-70). The former, initially inspired by Wittgenstein's* Tractatus, *is a 193-page work for any number of musicians. As a purely visual statement,* Treatise's *combination of graphic notation and traditional musical symbols is stunningly beautiful. The Great Learning *is a seven-movement work (lasting almost seven hours), based on the writings of Confucius, for voices and instruments that brings together traditionally notated tonal and modal sections and graphically notated improvisatory sections.*

By the early 1970s, Cardew's interest in Marxism and Maoism led him to question and eventually repudiate most of his earlier compositions and begin composing a form of gebrauchsmusik. This was a direct outgrowth of his work with the Scratch Orchestra, a large, democratically run experimental music ensemble that he co-founded in 1969. Through his music and political actions of the seventies, Cardew strove to draw parallels between the development of music and man's struggle for a just and better world.

The following essay is from Cardew's book *Stockhausen Serves Imperialism* (1974).

On
Criticism

To begin I'd like to read a quotation from John Cage.

"A most salient feature of contemporary art is the fact that each artist works as he sees fit, and not in accordance with widely-agreed-upon procedures. Whether this state of affairs pleases or displeases us is not exactly clear from a consideration of modern clichés of thought.

"On the one hand we lament what we call the gulf between artist and society, between artist and artist, and we praise (very much like children who can only window shop for candy they cannot buy) the unanimity of opinion out of which arose a Gothic cathedral, an opera by Mozart, a Balinese combination of music and dance. We lament the absence among us of such generally convincing works, and we say it must be because we have no traditional ways of making things. We admire from a lonely distance that art which is not private in character but is characteristic of a group of people and the fact that they were in agreement. On the other hand, we admire an artist for his originality and independence of thought, and we are displeased when he is too obviously imitative of another artist's work. In admiring originality, we feel quite at home. It is the one quality of art we feel fairly capable of obtaining. Therefore we say such things as: Everyone not only has but should have his own way of doing things. Art is an individual matter. We go so far as to give credence to the opinion that a special kind of art arises from a special neurosis pattern of a particular artist. At this point we grow slightly pale and stagger out of our studios to knock at the door of some neighbourhood psychoanalyst. Or—we stay at home, cherish our differences, and increase our sense of loneliness and dissatisfaction with contemporary art. In the field of music, we express this dissatisfaction variously: we say; The music is interesting, but I don't understand it. Somehow it is not fulfilled. It doesn't have 'the long line.' We then go our separate paths: some of us back to work to write music that few find any use for, and others to spend their lives with the music of another time which, putting it bluntly and chronologically, does not belong to them."[1]

This is what John Cage wrote in 1948 at the age of 36. Substantially the same analysis could be made today, and substantially I agree with it. It is an expression of disillusion and frustration—the composer's bright dreams

[1] John Cage *Defense of Satie* (lecture delivered at Black Mountain College, 1948).

441

wither up and die for lack of audience—discontent with the state of music today as compared with the music of the past, which he says, revelling in his isolation, does not belong to us. Actually it does belong to us, to do with as we see fit. We must make the past serve the present. But I'll come back to this.

I believe I speak for the vast majority of music lovers when I say: let's face it, modern music (modern classical music as it is called) is not half as good as classical music (which includes baroque classical, classical classical and romantic classical music, etc.). What does "good" mean in that sentence? It means effective, wholesome, moving, satisfying, delightful, inspiring, stimulating and a whole lot of other adjectives that are just as widely understood and acknowledged and just as hard to pin down with any precision. These are the judgments of the music-loving public. By comparison with the effectiveness, wholesomeness, emotion, satisfaction, delight, inspiration, and stimulus that we (that is, classical music-lovers, and we are a class audience) derive from Beethoven, Brahms and the rest, modern music (with very few exceptions) is footling, unwholesome, sensational, frustrating, offensive, and depressing. Why is this? It is because the bourgeois/capitalist society that brought music out of church into the realm of bourgeois art, and reached undreamed-of power and imperial glory through the upheavals of the industrial revolution, and also undreamed-of power of artistic expression, is now in the last stages of decay, and modern music reflects that decay.

Because modern music is bad in this sense, decadent, it cannot submit itself to principled, objective criticism, it does not set up the criteria by which it would expose itself as nonsense.

I experienced this personally as a student at the Royal Academy of Music. The nearest we ever got to establishing a criterion was some remark like "it has a good shape." In fact, the handwriting, or the neatness of the layout of the score seemed to be a matter of more importance. There were some good sound practical considerations such as "Can it be heard?" "It looks interesting on paper, but what does it sound like?"

In retrospect I appreciate the technical criteria, dealing with the transformation of formal ideas into sound, even those to do with neat presentation, but the rest were so vague as to be useless. In fact I really can't remember what they were. I don't believe any criteria were applied.

The result was that when I came to occupy a teaching position myself at the Royal Academy of Music I instinctively took the line of "no criticism." Occasionally I might take issue with a technical point that seemed particularly crass, but generally as regards technical criticism I regarded it as secondary, and to apply secondary criteria while not applying the primary criteria would obviously result in misplaced emphasis.

On
Criticism

Also in retrospect I realise that I am not at all qualified to apply technical criteria because in my own period of training I had never mastered anything more than the rudiments. The rest had seemed irrelevant in view of my desire to break with the traditions of tonal music completely. The fact that I was able to pass exams and get diplomas despite my extremely limited compositional technique is due entirely to the fatally liberalistic attitude that permeates our education system.

Liberalism is just as oppressive as the religious dogma of the nineteenth century that it replaces. Liberalism is a tactic whereby the sting is taken out of the huge contradictions that run right through our cultural environment, so that we are tempted to pass them over and ignore them.

If a rebellious composer has to confront the situation that he cannot graduate from the Royal Academy of Music, then his rebellion may be broken if it is insubstantial in the first place, but if it is not then it will be immeasurably strengthened and his rebellion will be directed consciously against the establishment. This is a confrontation that the establishment is anxious to avoid, hence its tactic of liberalism.

"No criticism" in a teaching situation leads to psychologically insupportable emphasis on "self-criticism," resulting in introversion and lack of confidence. In 1969 Michael Parsons, Howard Skepton and I founded the Scratch Orchestra, a group of about fifty people devoted to experimental performance arts. Some were students, some office workers, some amateur musicians, some professional, and there were several composers. From the beginning our line was "no criticism."

The products of "no criticism at all" are weak and watery; the products of "no criticism except self-criticism" are intensely introverted. The tension built up until, after two years, the floodgates were opened and the members of the Scratch Orchestra poured out their discontent. This stage represents "collective self-criticism" and from it emerged criteria that we could apply.

This collective self-criticism was fruitful not in terms of output—this decreased sharply—but in terms of the seriousness and commitment of the members. The collective self-criticism was also painful, and so the criteria that came out of it are the product of struggle in a human situation, not an abstract scaffolding erected for aspiring composers to hang their beautiful ideas on. Perhaps they are not even criteria, just questions whereby a composer can externalise his self-criticism and actually do something about it.

Firstly: what does a composer think he's doing? Why and in what spirit does he sit down to compose? Is it to express his inmost soul? Or to communicate his thoughts? Or to entertain an audience? Or educate them? Or to get rich and famous? Or to serve the interests of the community and if so what community, what class?

443

Secondly: does the music fulfil the needs of the audience? This immediately opens up two areas of study. First the different audiences that exist, where they overlap and what their class character is. And second, what the needs of the different audiences are, what are their aspirations, what are their standards (which means what are their criteria for appreciating music), and are we content to accept these or must we progressively change them?

Thirdly: do the compositions adequately meet the demands of the musicians playing them? A composition should give the musicians involved a creative role in a collective context. If a composition doesn't create a stimulating situation for the musicians involved it is very unlikely that it will stimulate an audience except in a negative way.

Fourthly: what is the material of a composition? It's not just notes and rests, and it's not just a beautiful idea that originates in the unique mind of a genius. It's ideas derived from experience, from social relations, and what the composer does is to transform these ideas into configurations of sound that evoke a corresponding response in the listener.

Fifthly: what is the basis of a composer's economic survival in society? He can take employment in education, in the service of the state, teaching what he has learnt to other composers, or investigating the "nature of music" (whatever that may be). Or he can take employment in industry, writing film or background music, or commercial music of other kinds. Or he can attempt to win the support of an audience. Or a combination of these.

I must say, as a student at the Royal Academy of Music it would have been extremely useful if these matters had been brought up for consideration, never mind how reluctant I might have appeared at the time to take any notice.

Now I should like to talk about music criticism as a profession. Much propaganda is being done for the view that people are motivated by self-interest, the desire for money or fame or both. This is not true. The majority of people have a definite need to feel that they are serving the community in some way. We need the feeling that we are performing a useful function in society and not just living off society or other individuals in a parasitic way. Most music critics feel the same need.

Critics are an important link in the complex network that constitutes the relations of production of the musical profession. What can they do to serve the community?

A couple of months ago I noticed Andrew Porter saying something just at the end of a review of Wagner's *Ring* in Glasgow about Wagner's dream of the eventual end of capitalism as represented in *Götterdämmerung*. (This was in the *Financial Times*.) I must say, this inspired my curiosity. I

444

have never seen a Wagner opera, although I have seen Hollywood's *Magic Fire* based on his life. *Magic Fire* bears about as much relation to reality as a Tarzan story. I also know a piano duet version of the Prelude to Act III of *Tristan and Isolde*, and once played in the fifth desk of cellos in a non-professional performance of the same piece. As regards Wagner's life I know that he was exiled from Germany for his part in a people's uprising in 1849, the same year Karl Marx was exiled. This is the sum total of my knowledge about the most controversial composer of the nineteenth century. I can hear someone saying, "My lad, if you've reached the ripe age of 36 without having learnt anything about Wagner, you have only yourself to blame." Well, I think the reason is different. The reason is that virtually everything written and said about Wagner and his music is extremely boring and irrelevant to the present time, and reasonable musicians with a certain amount of work to do could not be expected to plough through it.

What does Wagner's music mean in relation to present-day society? If he had theories of Utopian socialism then it would be good to hear about them and criticise them. What is the historical basis of the myths that provide the material for the *Ring*? It would be wonderful to open a daily newspaper and find material of this kind, instead of yet another series of opinions and comments on performances, interpretations, readings of the score, etc. The music critic should indicate the cultural and political context of a work, and point out how the work relates to it and what relevance these matters have to society today.

With regard to the work of living composers the critic's task is exceptionally important. On the one hand he is the spokesman of the people. He must demand works that relate directly to the issues and struggles and preoccupations of the present, and lead the way forward to a better society, a truly socialist society. And on the other hand he must stringently criticise such works from the point of view of both form and content, with the aim of building up their strength. He should do this conscientiously and thoroughly, so that strong links will be forged between composers and critics, so that composers and critics can feel united in the performance of a common task in the service of the community, namely the production of good music for the benefit of the people.

"Good music"? According to what criteria is it "good"? And a basic criterion has already been implied, the criterion of the "people's benefit."

On the simplest level we can say any music is good that benefits the people, any music is bad that harms them, that tends in the long run to make their conditions of existence worse than they are now or the same as they are now. To make things stay the same is possibly the most grievous harm imaginable. This is the criterion of the people's benefit.

Then: by what criterion do people judge their conditions of existence to
be better or worse? (Basically this is the same criterion that composers and
critics apply to their work, because composers and critics are people too,
with a productive social role like other workers.) Good conditions of existence are: when your needs, physical and spiritual, are fulfilled, when you
are conscious of the way your work, your productive activity, contributes
to the society you live in, and when—through this consciousness and because your needs are not frustrated—you are able to expand and develop
your work so as to maximise its usefulness to society.

So the "people's good" is this: their basic needs are satisfied, and they
are conscious of their position in society; when these two conditions are
met, the people's creative energy is released, they can contribute to changing the world. Everything benefits the people that (a) satisfies their needs,
(b) raises their level of consciousness, and (c) (following from the others)
encourages them to develop the energy and ability and initiative to change
the world according to their collective needs. This is socialist construction.

Is capitalist society as we know it today orientated towards benefiting
the people? Let's apply the criteria. Does capitalism satisfy the people's
needs? No, it regards the people as consumers, and floods them with plastic bottles and white bread which bring vast profits to the manufacturers
but no benefit to the consumers, so that the majority of people remain in
conditions of hardship while the ruling class and its hangers-on live more
and more luxuriously and more and more wastefully. Does capitalism raise
the people's level of consciousness? No, the mass media feed lies to the
people (as, for instance, saying that the miners in their strike were holding
the nation up for ransom, whereas in fact they were not striking at the "nation" but at the government and the ruling class), it feeds them platitudes
under the guise of education, and crime and violence and sentimentality
under the guise of entertainment. No, the mass media not only don't raise
the level of consciousness of the people, they try to lower it, they aim to
deceive the people.

Obviously these two negatives—not satisfying the people's needs and
not raising their level of consciousness—do not produce a positive. In fact
under capitalism today people are not encouraged to develop the energy,
ability and initiative to change the world according to their collective
needs. There is no such thing as socialist construction under capitalism,
though Labour politcans will go on asserting that there is until they are
blue in the face. There can only be socialist construction in opposition to
capitalism.

I have been talking about politics. It's evident that the criterion of "the
people's good" is a political criterion. In music, the criterion "good music
is that which benefits the people" is a political criterion. "Raising the level

446

of consciousness of the people" is a political task. Everything that music can do towards raising the level of consciousness of the people is part of this political task, it subserves this political task. The artist cannot ignore politics. As Mao Tsetung says, "There is no such thing as art that is detached from or independent of politics." And I think I have also made clear what he means in the sentence, "Each class in every class society has its own political and artistic criteria, but all classes in all class societies put the political criterion first and the artistic criterion second." This is profoundly true, this point about the precedence of political criteria over artistic criteria. It can be seen to be true, objectively, in capitalist society and it will still be true in a socialist society. To deny this is to cast yourself adrift in the realm of fantasy and, if you are an artist, your work will still be judged according to the political criterion first and the artistic criterion second and it will be seen—notwithstanding any artistic merit it may have—to be misleading the people, not raising their level of consciousness, and hence supporting capitalism and serving to prolong its domination of the working and oppressed people.

Sofia Gubaidulina
[1931 -   ]

Inspired and informed by an eclectic mix of spirituality and mysticism, Gubaidulina's keenly honed yet emotional music, rich with religious and literary symbolism, revels in both highly complex and simple instrumental timbres, chromaticism juxtaposed with triadic writing, and evocative melodic gestures while at all times remaining deeply concerned with structure.

Trained in post-Stalinist Russia, Gubaidulina is part of what has been called the New Wave of Russian composers, which includes Alfred Schnittke and Edison Denisov, who rejected the constraints of socialist realism and embraced a broad spectrum of avant-garde styles and idioms, including the use of serial procedures and extended instrumental techniques.

Gubaidulina has written for a variety of instrumental and vocal forces and is especially fond of writing works that address the unique talents of specific performers. Among her noted works are Offertorium *(1980, revised 1982 and 1986),* a one-movement violin concerto, written for violinist Gidon Kremer, that traverses a great deal of musical territory (and musical history, including quotations from Bach's Royal Theme from The Musical Offering)—from eerie timbre and pitch constructs and tiny pointillistic gestures through broad expressive melody; the twelve-movement symphony Stimmen . . . Verstummen . . . *(1986);* Hour of the Soul *(1976, revised 1988) for mezzo-soprano, percussion and orchestra; and the seven-movement* Hommage à T. S. Eliot, *based on Eliot's* Four Quartets, *for soprano and an octet of winds and strings.*

The following interview was published in German in *Russische Avantgarde: Musik avantgarde im Osten Europas* (1992). It is published here for the first time in English.

An Interview with Dorothea Redepenning

- *Question:* In a BBC interview you once said that you have roots in four cultures: Tartar, Russian, German, and Jewish. Can you explain what these cultures mean to you?
- Answer: When I said that I have roots in four rather than two cultures, · that is what I meant: my mother is Russian and my father Tartar, which makes me a person of mixed blood. I spent my youth in the Tartar city of Kazan, which lies within a restricted area for Jews. That means that Jewish intellectuals, for example those musicians who had graduated from the conservatory in Leningrad (now St. Petersburg), were allowed to settle in Kazan. Kazan was the third largest city, after Moscow and Leningrad, in which they were permitted to live. These Jewish musicians belonged to the highest class of intelligentsia at that time. They simultaneously supported and inspired the Tartar culture in the city. So it happened that these people influenced me enormously during my youth, which is the time of education and spiritual development. These Jews dominated my childhood and were my first teachers. The German culture of Bach, Mozart, Haydn, and Beethoven was the first to inspire me. It was German literature, too, that first engaged me.
- *Q:* You became a public figure in the 1960s, roughly the same time as Alfred Schnittke and Edison Denisov. It has been said that you were all hated and oppressed. Is that right? Who criticized you? Why and in what way? Did that change at some point?
- *A:* This oppression did not manifest itself as criticism, but was realized quite simply through bans on performance. To illustrate this point I can give two examples of flagrant censorship. Some very good musicians from the state orchestra, the Soviet Union's best orchestra, were interested in music that was currently being composed and had decided to perform our works in their concert program. But before a performance could take place, it had to be approved by the director of the Philharmonic. When the leader of the ensemble, Pjotr Meshtshaninov, appeared before director Kusnezov, the director eliminated all our works from the list. He justified this by saying that we represented an incorrect ideological position and told the leader of the ensemble quite clearly that he had better show some maturity and had to understand that such works could not be performed under any circumstances. The second and even more flagrant example that I'd like to offer had nothing to do with the Philharmonic, but took place in

a much more humble setting. It concerned the composer association's concert hall, which is a small space with bad acoustics. Even there, if we were able to have our pieces performed at all, it was with great difficulty. Indeed, there was an artistic advisory board of very unimportant composers and even non-composers who eliminated our names. Although the programs had already been determined and the musicians had already learned the pieces, the music was not allowed to be heard. Such censorship affected not only my generation, but also younger composers like Victor Suslin and Vyacheslav Artyomov. Thus, our greatest problem was not criticism, but simple, indiscriminate bans on performance. As a consequence we were not only denied the opportunity to hear ourselves, but also the chance to receive honest evaluations.

• *Q:* You, Schnittke, and Denisov have been called the "Great Troyka," and when people talk about modern music of the Soviet Union, you three are always mentioned together. What connects you and what differentiates you from your colleagues?

• *A:* It seems to me that our common fate unites us. In the minds of our listeners and critics, we are grouped together according to the principle of contrast. We have three completely different philosophical outlooks. Let's consider Hegel's aesthetics and his definition of "classical and postclassical consciousness." What I really like about Hegel, although I'm not a great admirer of him in general, is what he says about these types of consciousness. According to Hegel, someone who looks for truth in the material itself possesses a classical consciousness. And when I think about Denisov, whose works place so much emphasis on the tonal material, the tonal fabric as it were, I think one can see him as a typical representative of this classical form of consciousness. From this perspective Alfred Schnittke seems—and I have often thought about this and am increasingly convinced that is so—to be a postclassical type. He transcends the limits of the materials to find the truth beyond these limits.

As I came to understand this, I began to think about myself and tried to look at myself objectively. I realized that I am a typical representative of the archaic form of consciousness. Hegel says that the idea of symbol is a central principle for this type of consciousness. For this type, the truth cannot be found in the material, nor beyond the limits of the material, but within the very substance of the subject itself, in which every idea is layered on top of another. Ideas are layered vertically, and thus cannot be separated, but merely clarified through symbols.

• *Q:* In some of your great pieces you work with quotations, with old material, like the Schütz quotation in *The Seven Last Words*, the theme from Bach's *Musical Offering* in *Offertorium*, or the passage of Gregorian music at the beginning of *Alleluia*. What do quotation and old music in general mean to you?

• *A:* This quotation, or the effort to use an already existing form as a point of reference is a basic characteristic of the twentieth century. We composers have found ourselves in a situation in which an enormous flow of information bombards us; in no other century has the composer been confronted with so many diverse kinds of information. I think that, in this way, one can explain the significance of figures like Charles Ives, Bernd Alois Zimmermann, Alfred Schnittke, and Luciano Berio in our century. Why this happens is a serious question and is worth thinking about. The fact is, all kinds of works attempt to reflect the abundance of information surrounding us. Yet the relationship to this familiar material is different for every composer. On the one hand it could be longing for a lost paradise. On the other hand it could be a relationship of opposition, an alienating, ironic relationship to a familiar text. Furthermore a quote can be used as a point of reference, a reference with a definite meaning, like a word.

I think the latter relationship is characteristic of me. In this way, I am fundamentally different from Alfred Schnittke and his grandiose conception of the polystylistic or stylistic pluralism. This pluralism requires the ability to transcend the individual parts of a culture and the corresponding capability for far-reaching cultural generalization. It is, so to speak, a view of the world from above and the ability to integrate this view into a meaningful conception. Schnittke has said that he conceives of history as a sphere. Positions that normally seem radically different from one another are pulled tightly together within the spherical conception. This is actually not only an historical and philosophical point, but a geographical one also. In other words, he creates a new historical time.

• *Q:* That leads us to another issue that I want to discuss with you, which is your relationship to time, to musical time. It is in this respect, in my opinion, that you differentiate yourself from other composers.

• *A:* The concept of time plays an essential role for me, if perhaps in a different way. To me, or at least this is how I put it, an artwork is a creation of essential time. This is a very important task, one crucial to the existence of mankind. Mankind as a whole creates "essential time," that is, the time that revives and cures the essence of the human spirit. This task is especially important to me when it is realized through art: sacred time.

• *Q:* In connection with that I'd like to ask what rhythm means to you.

• *A:* In the last decade I've concerned myself above all with problems of rhythm. I don't mean rhythm in a narrow sense of the word, but rather a kind of macro-rhythm, the rhythm of form. In recent years I've repeatedly given myself rhythmic challenges and I'm still trying to take a small step in this direction with each new piece. I believe that I can develop a technique this way, a real technique that works according to the demands of the material and the conditions of life.

- *Q:* You also use concepts like "harmonic," or "consonant" and "dissonant" rhythm.
- *A:* When I wrote the symphony *Stimmen . . .Verstummen,* I challenged myself rhythmically. The initial focus of this challenge was the culminating moment of silence—the break in the middle of the piece. I constructed this silence, a stillness of about forty seconds, so that the conductor's gestures actually give rhythm to the empty space. I set out to order the entire form of the piece according to rhythms laid down by the conductor during that silence. I wanted a rhythm based on the proportions of the "Golden Section," the so-called "Fibonacci Sequence." This is the well known second "Golden Sequence" that governs all the workings of nature. This rhythm is the primary focus of the symphony *Stimmen . . .Verstummen.* When the piece was played and I showed it to my friend Pyotr Meshtshaninov, he said, without prompting, that my piece seemed "consonant." I really liked his response, because I realized that the Fibonacci Sequence really does give the impression of consonance when it pervades the piece.

This raised a related question: what is rhythmic dissonance? This same theoretician, Pyotr Meshtshaninov, explained to me what the concept of dissonance might really mean. He showed me something I hadn't known before: there are an infinite number of golden sequences, and each one has quite a few derivative sequences. Now what does the "Golden Section" mean to such a sequence? It is the auspicious division of the whole into two unequal parts. At that division an organism comes to life, when the whole is divided into two equal parts, the result is crystalline rather than organic. A crystal is very beautiful, but is not a living organism. It is the Fibonacci sequence that defines the proportions upon which all of the nature is based. Yet this point can never really be reached. When we look at the sequence 1, 2, 3, 5, 8, 13, 21, etc., we see that with each pair of terms the degree of proportional inequality becomes increasingly less significant. The further along in the sequence, the more symmetrical this relationship becomes. However, an absolute symmetry is never possible. Now if we think about this sequence and its derivative sequences alone, we discover an increasing degree of asymmetry as the distance between each point of completion grows larger. The measure of perfection or symmetry depends on the distance of the derivatives to the ideal point, which is infinity in the Fibonacci sequence.

Through this numerical framework I can derive the definition of rhythmic dissonance. It is a very vague relationship that nonetheless conforms to certain laws. Looking at it this way, I realized that an instance of dissonance does not simply represent an arbitrary, chaotic relationship, but rather one that is far from resolution. That is my answer to the question of what consonant and dissonant rhythm mean.

- *Q:* The name Pyotr Meshtshaninov has been mentioned three times already. This theoretician, pianist, and conductor lives in Moscow and has developed an extremely interesting evolutionary music theory, in which all tonal systems, from early tetratonic and pentatonic to church tonalities, the major-minor system, free atonality, the twelve-tone system, and postserial systems, are considered equal. What does Pyotr Meshtshaninov's theory mean to your music?

- *A:* Meeting this notable musician was an important, decisive event for me. When Pyotr Meshtshaninov was sixteen, he followed in the footsteps of the inventor and engineer Yevgeni Mursin who had developed a music synthesizer in Moscow in the 1940s. This synthesizer, named ANS after the initials of Alexander Nicolayavitch Skryabin, was of course not very advanced, but it had an original design, unlike that of any later synthesizer. It provided the composers with a sound continuum that could be divided into the smallest parts. Pyotr Meshtshaninov understood that he was dealing with something very serious, with penetration of the tonal interval. And with typical rigor he also understood that one could not advance with this material arbitrarily and without rules. In the context of the new material's potential richness, division into a twelve-tone chromatic scale seemed coarse. On the other hand, the new and extremely rich material lacked the tonal order and consistent inner logic that existed in former centuries.

In those years and during this entire century there have always been composers who wanted to penetrate the tonal interval. And some also accomplished this—for example, Alois Hába and others who suggested the division of a half-step into two, three, or any number of parts. Pyotr Meshtshaninov studied all of these theories first. Yet none of these divisions conformed to the natural laws of the tone. So he created a foundation himself. His work led to the development of a theoretical construction that helps make the past, present, and future visible. If music history is roughly divided into linear, harmonic-homophonic, and the sonorous or "klangfarbenmelodie" periods, the latter representing our century, then he began in the middle. Thus, in this case, fifths and thirds provide the basis for interval relationships. The beginning, which corresponds to the linear period, was based on octaves and fifths. Most importantly, he developed a rule governing the transition or transformation from one state of musical materials into another.

It became clear to me that I could determine the exact state of my materials and position in history and what, in principle, my next step has to be. One can imagine the impression this theoretical construction made on me: this situation transformed me from a blind kitten into a seeing, intelligent human being! And now I can formulate a direct answer to your question. The most important element of this theory is that after I have understood my position, I can bypass myself and my own arbitrary will and can think instead about the music itself and the intrinsic requirements of the music material.

Alvin Lucier

[1931 -   ]

The "liberation of sound" (Edgard Varèse's ideal) took on new meaning after the pioneering example of John Cage. During the 1960s a
number of composers, influenced by Cage and further sensitized by
their experiences in tape music studios, entered into the exploration
of unique sound worlds of their own—creating a music of free-float-
ing, unplanned surface gestures, often activated by electroacoustic
means.

Alvin Lucier is among the most distinguished of such post-Cageian
composers. A native of New Hampshire, he was educated at Brandeis and Yale Universities, and then spent a period in Rome as a
Fulbright scholar. Lucier was a founding member of the Sonic Arts
Union, along with Robert Ashley, David Behrman, and Gordon
Mumma, and has frequently collaborated with such dance ensembles as the Merce Cunningham and Viola Farber companies. He currently teaches at Wesleyan University.

It is possible to approach Lucier's work (in the words of one critic)
as "sonic environment," or as sculptural multimedia installation,
often devised to explore the acoustic, symbolic, and ritualistic aspects of specific physical spaces. In his 1967 Vespers, for example,
performers use echo-location devices, such as those employed by
bats, to explore the dimensions and potential of their performance
site. In such works, Lucier reveals his keen interest in "sounds that
would never, in ordinary circumstances, reach our ears." Many of
Lucier's works create surface textures of slow change, involving repeated actions or gradually evolving "Minimalist" gestures, naturally
growing out of performance circumstances. One such piece is his
classic I Am Sitting in a Room, which is discussed in the following
interview.

Reprinted from Lucier's Chambers (Wesleyan University Press,
1980).

"I AM SITTING
IN A ROOM" (1969)

for voice and electromagnetic tape

Necessary Equipment:

1 microphone
2 tape recorders
amplifier
1 loudspeaker

Choose a room the musical qualities of which you would like to evoke.
Attach the microphone to the input of tape recorder #1.
To the output of tape recorder #2 attach the amplifier and loudspeaker.
Use the following text or any other text of any length:

> I am sitting in a room different from the one you are in now.

> I am recording the sound of my speaking voice and I am going to play it back into the room again and again until the resonant frequencies of the room reinforce themselves so that any semblance of my speech, with perhaps the exception of rhythm, is destroyed.

> What you will hear, then, are the natural resonant frequencies of the room articulated by speech.

> I regard this activity not so much as a demonstration of a physical fact, but more as a way to smooth out any irregularities my speech might have.

Record your voice on tape through the microphone attached to tape recorder #1.

Rewind the tape to its beginning, transfer it to tape recorder #2, play it back into the room through the loudspeaker and record a second generation of the original recorded statement through the microphone attached to tape recorder #1.

Rewind the second generation to its beginning and splice it onto the end of the original recorded statement on tape recorder #2.

456

"I Am Sitting
in a Room" (1969)

Play the second generation only back into the room through the loud-speaker and record a third generation of the original recorded statement through the microphone attached to tape recorder #1.

Continue this process through many generations.

All the generations spliced together in chronological order make a tape composition the length of which is determined by the length of the original statement and the number of generations recorded.

Make versions in which one recorded statement is recycled through many rooms.

Make versions using one or more speakers of different languages in different rooms.

Make versions in which, for each generation, the microphone is moved to different parts of the room or rooms.

Make versions that can be performed in real time.

• *Question:* What's your attitude toward a performance that consists of playing a tape?

• *Answer:* Well, all of us who have made pieces with electronics started with tape because it enables you to play with sounds in ways that no other medium does, but you soon get tired of that because live performances are more interesting than taped ones. Tape led us to discover things about sound that had hitherto been unknown and prepared us to go on and do more interesting things without it, but we always kept tape as a way to store sounds to bring into a live performance.

Now in *I am sitting in a room,* I didn't choose to use tape, I had to, because in order to recycle sounds into a space, I had to have them accessible in some form. Tape, then, wasn't a medium in which to compose sounds, it was a conveyor, a means to record them and play them back one after another in chronological order. Without tape I wouldn't have been able to do the piece.

• *Q:* When you worked on materials for the piece, there was never a moment until all those generations had been spliced together that the piece was complete.

• *A:* Yes, because the form is linear and cumulative; it changes from generation to generation until it reaches the point of diminishing returns. And it's funny because if I had consulted an engineer, he or she would probably have found a way to get the end result in one process, one fast process, or one generation. There are ways to by-pass erase heads on tape recorders or make large loops which could get the end result very quickly, but I was interested in the process, the step-by-step, slow process of the disintegration of the speech and the reinforcement of the resonant frequencies. Actually, when Mary and I visited the Polaroid Company in Cam-

Alvin
Lucier

bridge—Mary, as you know, did a visual analog to the tape by subjecting a Polaroid snapshot to a similar reproductive process—the art director, when he saw the end result, said, "I could do that in one step." He just didn't understand that what we found interesting was the gradual process itself. Often, people don't understand the process. They think that the same speech is dubbed from one recorder to another and each time the quality of the copy degenerates a little bit. But it's not that at all, it's playing the speech back into the space. The signal goes through the air again and again; it's not processed entirely electronically, it's also processed acoustically.

• Q: You've discarded one of the goals of electronic information storage. By reproducing the thing acoustically so many times, all the parameters that manufacturers strive to achieve in their tape recorders, such as linear frequency response, are bypassed.

• A: Actually, I used two Nagras in the original version. I recorded fifteen generations of the same text and you don't hear much distortion or disintegration of the tape matter. In fact, the machines did a marvelous job of maintaining it.

• Q: What I meant to say was that an engineer would probably say you've done a poor job of reproducing the sound. Of course what you had in mind from the start was to get out of the machines, to submit the material to a purposely non-neutral medium on its way to being re-recorded.

• A: Yes, the space acts as a filter; it filters out all of the frequencies except the resonant ones. It has to do with the architecture, the physical dimensions and acoustic characteristics of the space.

As you know, every musical sound has a particular wavelength; the higher the pitch, the shorter the wavelength. Actually, there's no such thing as "high" notes or "low" notes, we simply borrowed those terms from the visual world to describe something we didn't understand. A musical sound as it is produced on an instrument, in a column of air or a vibrating string, causes oscillations at a certain rate of speed. For example, the A that an orchestra tunes to vibrates at 440 times per second and can therefore be considered "faster" than the middle C on the piano that vibrates at about 262 times per second. But as those sounds move out into space they can be observed as various-sized wavelengths, so you can see how directly the dimensions of a room relate to musical sounds. If the dimensions of a room are in a simple relationship to a sound that is played in it, that sound will be reinforced, that is, it will be amplified by the reflections from the walls. If, however, the sound doesn't "fit" the room, so to speak, it will be reflected out of phase with itself and tend to filter itself out. So by playing sounds into a room over and over again, you reinforce some of them more and more each time and eliminate others. It's a form of amplification by

458

repetition. Thinking of sounds as measurable wavelengths, instead of as high or low musical notes, has changed my whole idea of music from a metaphor to a fact and, in a real way, has connected me to architecture.

My first impulse was to use various musical instruments playing a wide variety of sounds, but I tossed that idea out because it felt too "composerly." Instead I decided to use speech; it's common to just about everybody and is a marvelous sound source. It has a reasonable frequency spectrum, noise, stops and starts, different dynamic levels, complex shapes. It's ideal for testing the resonant characteristics of a space because it puts so much in all at one time. It's also extremely personal. And since I've been acting in George Manupelli's *Dr. Chicago* films, I've started paying attention to the characteristics of my speech which are original to my personality and don't sound like anybody else's; you know I'm a stutterer. So instead of trying to invent interesting speech patterns, I discovered that I have interesting speech patterns anyway; I don't have to invent them. Of course I have invented, when you think about it. A person who stutters or who has a lisp invents that or makes it up; it's not put on him from an external source. And while not everyone stutters, everyone has a certain amount of anxiety about speech. I've met many people who think they stutter. Bob Ashley, for instance, thinks he stutters. I wouldn't say so, but if he thinks he does, perhaps a lot of people think they do, and in that case, I feel that I'm in touch with people.

I am not as interested in the resonant characteristics of spaces in a scientific way as much as I am in opening that secret door to the sound situation that you experience in a room. For example, I made a preliminary version of *I am sitting in a room* in the Brandeis University Electronic Music Studio, a small, bright, somewhat antiseptic room in which I never enjoyed being very much. It was filled with electronic equipment, and one wall consisted of several large glass windows. The resonant frequencies got reinforced very quickly after the fifth or sixth generation, resulting in harsh, strident sounds. But the version I did at 454 High Street, in Middletown, took a longer time because it was a softer, friendlier room with a wall-to-wall carpet and drapes on the windows. When I first moved into the apartment I never dreamed that I would come to enjoy wall-to-wall carpeting, but I soon learned that if you do have it, people enjoy sitting on the floor. After some of the evenings we've had there, people have even gone to sleep on the floor, which they would never have felt like doing in the Brandeis Studio. Anyway, the carpet and drapes cut down on the production of the resonant frequencies so they took longer to achieve, but it gave us a more beautiful result. Didn't we get a different set of intervals in the Brandeis Studio than we got in this room? Do you remember what they were?

- *Q:* We got two sets of fifths in both of them but they were much more complex in this version.
- *A:* Did you notice that tunes seem to start? Every room has its own melody, hiding there until it is made audible. You know, I feel as though we're in the same situation as composers were when they first began perceiving overtones. Musicians were always aware of their effects, I think, but timbre was mysterious until someone could demonstrate their existence. Now we're just beginning to compose with architecture in mind, and I'm very pleased to be in on these first experiments.
- *Q:* Is it an extension of the idea of personal relevance that you chose the particular text you did?
- *A:* Well, the text that I wrote and used in the Middletown recording was personal to me, but was also meant for anyone else who wanted to use it. I guess I was suggesting that everyone's speech has irregularities. I also said in the finished score that other texts may be used. Perhaps that was a mistake because I don't want what goes into the space to be too poetic. I want it to be plain so that the space becomes audible without distractions; that's why I decided to describe the recording process so that the audience could more easily understand what's going on. I guess you could say that the score is built into the performance.
- *Q:* I'm interested in how far your idea about the piece extends into the mechanics of achieving it. In other words, if someone uses one of the other procedures you mentioned, a loop for example, can you accept that as really the same piece?
- *A:* Well, the piece is subject to many versions; I heard of a twenty-four-hour one made in a chapel in Oberlin, Ohio. Now I've been asked to make a version for the Pepsi Pavilion at Expo '70 in Osaka. The Pavilion is a large dome with interesting acoustics, and David Tudor and Gordon Mumma designed the sound system. It has loudspeakers deployed all over the space, arrays of microphones, and a flexible mixing console. I'm planning to use it to pick up and record the voices of the people walking through the Pavilion, and then to recycle them back into the space from many separate loudspeakers. But I must admit that I prefer the monophonic version; it more clearly reveals the features of the processes that I find fascinating. First of all, there is the superimposition of two very simple repetitive processes, tape recording and talking, but the mixture of these two ordinary activities in an acoustic space, with amplification by repetition, yields an extraordinary result, the evocation of the resonant frequencies of the space. Even though the form is repetitive as far as the recording and recycling procedure is concerned, the listener hears something quite different, and that is the climactic point at which the speech goes from intelligibility to unintelligibility, or from words to music. What's beautiful is

that this point is different for each listener; it's kind of a sliding fulcrum on a moveable time scale. The rate of transformation isn't constant either. For the first few generations it moves at a seemingly constant pace, then, in one or two generations, the movement speeds up, then slows down again. It seems to operate on its own set of rules. It's very mysterious.

When Mary did the visual part, she took a Polaroid snapshot of the chair that I sat in when I made the tape and subjected it to a copying process in which she copied the original, copied that copy, and so on. And because it was virtually impossible to align the copying camera and the pictures absolutely accurately, a slight error in size crept in, so that every time she made a copy, it made the image slightly enlarged. But of course the size of the picture stayed the same so the image began to move off the picture. There was a dark shadow behind the lamp which grew on each reproduction, until finally the fifty-second one is completely black; the shadow behind the lamp grew until it took up the whole image. Some dirt got on the reproductions too, and what you think you see at the end is a star map. And indeed, a friend of mine who was at one of the performances said the last slide looked just like "Job's Coffin," which is apparently a part of the stars.

Anthony Braxton

[1945 -   ]

One of the most critically praised and critically damned musicians to emerge in the past thirty years, Braxton is an enigmatic composer and performer. His concerns with music's nature as a primary life force and his vast, idiosyncratic system of theoretical procedures are detailed in his multi-volume writings about his own music—Tri-Ax-iom Writings—which codify an ornate and highly personal musical cosmology of a scope unlike anything else ever proposed by a jazz-based musician.

Braxton first came to the public's awareness in the 1960s, emerging from Chicago's hotbed of "free-jazz" activity as a composer and an alto saxophone and multi-reed player with an immediately iden-tifiable, sharply focused sound. This Chicago scene, personified as well by Roscoe Mitchell and Muhal Richard Abrams, gave life to a "free" music that was quite different—quirkier and displaying a more controlled emotionalism—from most "experiments" in "free" music that took place concurrently in New York City. This "Chicago sound," evident in Braxton's early recordings, offered up an often brittle and abstract chamber music that was sometimes jarring and confrontational, sometimes whimsical.

As Braxton's career has progressed, his music, realized by large orchestral forces, chamber groups, small combos, and soloists, has embraced the broadest spectrum of both jazz and European concert music influences. While his music has remained consistently engag-ing and, at times, edgy, his acceptance by the greater musical com-munity is no longer a point of contention.

The following interview is an edited excerpt from *Forces in Motion: Anthony Braxton and the Meta-reality of Creative Music* by Graham Lock (Quartet Books, Ltd., London, 1988; U.S. edition by Da Capo Press).

Bopbe

I've always respected the science in the music, though I haven't respected some of the related value systems: for instance, the concept of notation—I don't think notation is the problem, it's the concepts that surround notation. Bach, Beethoven, Mozart, all of the master Europeans who solidified Western art music were instrumentalists and improvisers as well as composers. Notation wasn't used then as a choking device to stop the blood, the dynamic, of the culture; it was later, when the technocrats made the process more important than the results, that we got the so-called crisis of Western art music, which is still with us. In fact, we can see the same mind-set entering the bebop continuum: now they're making bebop so "correct," it will be bopbe or something—it won't be the same music that Charlie Parker and John Coltrane played.

Inventing the Wheel
500 Times

• *Graham Lock:* The link between Bach and Charlie Parker being that each evolved a new musical language using improvisation as a major resource?

• *Anthony Braxton:* Yes. I'm interested in individuals who develop a *body* of music. In the sixties and seventies there was so much disrespect for composition: I felt that could not be correct, as everything that has been demonstrated in the last 1,000 years seems to have a relationship to preconceived variables as well as to spontaneity. I thought it a mistake to put down notation simply because of its misuse by the technocrats.

If you look at Bach, Mozart, Harry Partch, Fletcher Henderson, Duke Ellington—all of those people, though on the surface they seem very different, there's an awful lot in common there. I see similarities on every level. Bach . . . the first thing I have to deal with is the actual music, that's powerful music, it's . . . I don't want to say it's beautiful because that's one-dimensional and doesn't capture what I really feel about it. All I can say is, it's *real*; and that kind of music attracts me. There was a law, an order, about the music, and improvisation was used to establish the nature of that law system. It's the same for Duke Ellington's music, or any restructuralist who's trying to establish a body of work.

I'm interested in structure because the concept of structure can be transmitted on several different levels; the understanding being that there *are* things to be transmitted, to be forwarded. Without the concept of structure each generation would have to rediscover the same things, learn the same lessons: like, we'd have to invent the wheel 500 times. The significance of form is that information can be carried forward; a given form can make given variables come into play.

The concept of music science has to do with establishing the restructural dynamics of the time zone, establishing devices so people will later be able to participate—the concept of ritual. Of course, we're riddled with entertainment in the West, which is not my idea of the highest use of creativity: but form as ritual could serve as the basis to involve participation with meaning, to establish a context to be able to deal with what we call God or the higher forces. I think that is the proper role of creativity, and it's certainly in accordance with the dictates of African dynamics and with those of early Europe, before the technocrats came.

Going to See
the Chicken Fight

- *GL:* When we talked last year you told me one of your fascinations with structure was that given structures make certain things happen. Exactly what kind of things do you mean?
- *AB:* I'm saying that the reality of a given set of variables in the space sets into motion many different variables—*vibrational* variables. The problem with the nature of present-day Western expansionism has been that, in many cases, we've tapped into various areas of fundamentals but we've forgotten the primary information that made a given area what it is. We're working with a lot of areas of information whose spiritual function we don't really understand, so we're dealing only with the empirical function or with what happens when a given set of empirical operatives are put into the space. I'm saying that there's no real function without its meta-function and significance.

In *Tri-axium Writings 1* I talk about Indian music, the fact that they designed a music where, if a given scale is played, they'll tell you what that scale is for. When people die, there's a music for dying; when people are born, there's a music: different musics for different ceremonies. That's why I say the concept of ritual is the highest possible function, because the ritual is an affirmation of our existence. We've lost that since the onslaught of the European technocrat and instead we have whatever empirical logics are set into motion based on empirical criteria. OK, that's . . . interesting. I'm as grateful as everyone for the wonderful discoveries we have, whether it's frozen TV dinners or going to see the chicken fight (*laughs*). I mean, I'm constantly amazed at the wonder of Western culture (*laughs*).

But, in the process, I believe there are other variables which have been sacrificed in this time period, variables based on value systems; and, you know, the lack of some of these fundamentals has certainly made life in black America complex. Has made life for the creative woman (and the non-creative woman) complex. Has made life for the European mystic complex. Not to mention the so-called Third World.

I'd like to be part of some new realignment, although I have no illusions that my music or my thoughts are going to change anything, as far as the reality of present-day "influences." But I can still think about these matters and function in my music with respect to my beliefs.

Where Thinking
Is a Dirty Word

• *GL:* Last year we also talked about the relationship between structure and emotion, and the reasons why you don't discuss the emotional dimensions of the music in your notes. Your position is that emotion is brought to the music by the player, it's a subjective element that can't be composed— is that right?

• *AB:* Let me clarify that. Every member of the quartet, of course, has the possibility to take solos, extended improvisation; I try to get out of their way and make sure everybody has a chance to express themselves. That's part of what the family is; and inside that, each person brings their own emotions to the moment.

I didn't talk about emotion so much as a young man because of what I was dealing with then as a young African-American: everywhere I looked I was seeing a profound disrespect in how the music was written about. I reacted against that; I didn't want my music to be perceived as having no thought. I mean, only in jazz is thinking a dirty word! It's incredible, the value systems and political forces that surround and manipulate the music every day.

In this time period my work is perceived as being very cold and Braxton doesn't swing—that's only because those same forces are dictating and defining what feeling is. I don't think I'm the only one who suffers from this mind-set: the reality implications of the white improviser are not separate from the notion that white people can think great but they can't feel, while black people have all this feeling but no real thoughts. You know, the real experts on black people are white people. The experts on *elbows* are white people, the experts on *ankles* are white people. The experts on

Charlie Parker are white people. Well, that's fine, but it doesn't really express all of what's happening. (Let me also add this: if African-American and trans-African intellectuals are content to let the Europeans do all the defining, then it serves them right for us to be in the mess that we're in now.)

Emotional Zones—"I Never Meant Become an Android"

- *AB:* What more can I say about emotion? I mean, there's no one kind of emotion. If a given piece of music is written with particular dynamics, in terms of interpretation, I want it executed like it's written; but-when we get into the actual improvisation, there are other laws at work. What I've tried to do is design a music whose science would establish certain variables, and the improvisation will take care of itself. I don't *worry* so much about emotion, but that doesn't mean I have no respect for it. I'm interested in establishing contexts where we can fulfil ourselves and approach creativity on whatever level of emotion we can bring to it. So, the people in the quartet, I don't talk to them about what to play, I just establish a structural framework which will set into motion its own operatives. Improvisation in that context is improvisation in a controlled space or an understood space, a *perceived* space. And the structure will help define the nature of the thoughts which will take place in the music. As far as the emotion is concerned, we never know exactly what the emotions are going to be: our intentions are positive, though, just as my structural intentions are positive.
- *GL:* You've talked about music for different functions—music to heal, etc.: presumably there is also a music for sadness, a music for anger?
- *AB:* Yes, and my hope is, as I learn more about my work and as I'm able to work harder and evolve the music, that I might be able to create a music that would establish precise emotional zones—even further than that, let's say precise vibrational zones.
- *GL:* I want to ask you about something referred to in your 1984 *Cadence* interview, that at one time you had tried to exclude personality from your music. I assume you were really talking about ego.
- *AB:* There's more to it than that. I was actually trying to approach something else and that's been greatly misunderstood. I wanted, as a young man, for myself and for the people I played with not to think *only* about the dynamics that had been opened up by John Coltrane, the whole world of extended solos. Everybody was playing for five hours! I was looking for alternatives and I thought then in terms of not putting so much em-

phasis on your emotion at the expense of potential event-forming possibilities in the music. I kind of wanted to approach it from a Zen-like attitude—I was very influenced by John Cage in that period—but I found that that would not work for me.

I haven't changed my emotional relationship to the music in any real way. Even when I was trying to approach it from the other side, I never meant become an android, I just meant, you know, let's also look at the other responsibilities that take place in the space.

Freedom—
"Now I Can Kill You"

It's like, everybody wanted to use freedom as a context to *freak out*, and that was not what I was talking about. One of the problems with collective improvisation, as far as I'm concerned, is that people who use anarchy or collective improvisation will interpret that to mean "Now I can kill you"; and I'm saying, wait a minute! OK, it's true that in a free-thought zone, you can think of anything you want to think, but that was not the optimum state of what I had in mind when I said, let's have freedom. I thought any transformational understanding of so-called freedom would imply that you would be free to find those disciplines that suited you, free to understand your own value systems; but not that you would just freak out because "the teacher's not there." *The teacher is still there!*

It's one thing to talk about the post-Ayler cycle with respect to the events which took place in the first year, the second year . . . but if you look back at the last twenty years, what has freedom meant? For a great many people, so-called freedom music is more limiting than bebop, because in bebop you can play a ballad or change the tempo or the key. So-called freedom has not helped us as a family, as a collective, to understand responsibility better. Only the master musicians, the ones who really understood what they were doing and who did their homework, have been able to generate forward motion. So the notion of freedom that was being perpetrated in the sixties might not have been the healthiest notion. I say "healthiest notion" because I'm not opposed to the *state* of freedom; I believe that with correct information and an understanding of respect for humanity, human beings can rise to their potential. But fixed and open variables, with the fixed variables functioning from fundamental value systems—that's what freedom means to me.

467

Anthony
Braxton

Transformation
and Ritual

- *GL:* You've talked about transformational understanding, transformational culture. Could you explain more precisely the relationship between music and transformation?
- *AB:* Let me go back to how I see music. I've explained that for me the concept of form, in its optimum state, establishes some fundamental line about the workings of this experience, what we call physicality. I think the concept of form is also not separate from the forces it sets into motion.
- *GL:* You're talking about vibrational forces?
- *AB:* Yes, a hierarchy of vibrations which have to do with spiritual matters. Now, the degree you're talking about, the degree of transformation, there are several levels to that: *the vibrational function* would be that information transmitted to the individual based on self-realization and life experience—in the context of music, the vibrational function would have to do with what is set into motion in sound; *the living function* would have to do with establishing the scientific and spiritual inter-relationships of a given sound and how that would serve on a higher plane for the community; *the scientific function* would be calibrating the materials and understanding the order and inter-relationship and expansion of those materials in terms of how they express their laws, and the inter-relationship of that information to fundamentals; *the composite function* would be what that body of information would mean to humanity and how people would be able to use that information to live and, we hope, evolve; and *the ritual function* would be a ritualization of that information—the ritual function is the highest function that I will deal with in terms of establishing materials and establishing a meta-reality context for these materials.

Brian
Ferneyhough
[1943 -   ]

Brian Ferneyhough is widely regarded as the leading figure within the movement known as the "New Complexity," which focuses on polyrhythmic overlays and massive dense textures. He was born in Britain and trained at the Royal Academy of Music. He also studied with Ton de Leeuw in Amsterdam and Klaus Huber in Basel. Significantly, Ferneyhough first received widespread public attention not in England, which was late in coming to terms with this particular development, but on the European Continent at the Dutch Gaudeamus festival and the Royon festival in France. His teaching career began at the Freiburg academy, followed by residencies at the summer new-music institutes in Darmstadt, Florence, Siena, and Arezzo, and extended visiting professorships at the Stockholm Royal Conservatory and the University of Chicago. He currently teaches at the University of California, San Diego.

Ferneyhough's compositions may be approached as inquiries into the nature of performance, and as studies in multiple levels of continuity—"narratives" with many simultaneous time-lines and viewpoints. A number of his works reflect his insights into cultural models beyond music; for example, the 1981-86 grouping of seven pieces known collectively as Carceri d'Invenzione *was inspired by Piranesi etchings. The ferocious difficulty of Ferneyhough's music is legendary: the 1970* Casandra's Dream Song *for solo flute was considered unperformable for many years but, like the composer's other formerly "impossible" works, it is now being played with some frequency. The challenging nature of such music has, paradoxically, attracted a growing body of performers to his side.*

The following interview is reprinted from *Perspectives of New Music*, Volume 32, Number 1 (Winter 1994).

Composing a Viable (if Transitory) Self

Brian Ferneyhough
in Conversation with James Boros

- *James Boros:* I seem to recall your discussing the notion of musical complexity in terms of the dynamic transmission of information and its relationship to states of stability and instability.
- *Brian Ferneyhough:* Among other things, that's true. How to get a grip on the entire concept of "complexity" as applied to art has proven to be a major bone of contention. I have not been satisfied by what I have understood concerning the algorithmic definition, which measures complexity in terms of the number of algorithmic operations required to analyze-out a given state. For one thing, that's not how the brain works; for another, it's certainly not how most art seems to work. My own interests have gravitated towards how our perceptual ordering faculties react when attempting to make sense of borderline states—that is, situations in which an apparent disbalance between implied scale of observed system and actual apportionment of confirming or disconfirming subsystems conspires to create zones of instability in which linear modes of cataloguing incoming stimuli are suspended in favor of sudden leaps, fractures, or twists of focus. All music deals with this issue on one level or another; it's just that most stylistic conventions aim at large-scale equilibrium between containing frame and degree of permitted deviation of component details, whereas what I am aiming at is pretty much the reverse, in that what, in other music, might be seen as enhancing embellishment is constantly causing a high level of uncertainty about what the implied scale of the relationship "frame/detail" might be. The way it does that is partly by exhibiting high levels of self-referentiality and embedding procedures (encouraging "sliding" from one self-similar level to another), partly by having information presented in highly energized, coherent streams or vectors tending to offer concurrent, competing, and sometimes contradictory middle-ground "micro-narratives." It's not just a question of confusion, though: the sort of grid- or matrix-orientated formal techniques I usually use tend to bring about momentary clarifications where partial aspects of independently-moving patterns suddenly coincide, creating sudden, unexpected "windows." In fact, "complexity" in such cases is often increased by such un-

predictable nodes, since the sudden increase in perceived structural hierarchy makes passive, generalized reception difficult.

• *JB:* Steve McAdams once wrote: "A composition of sufficient, controlled complexity might . . . be perceptually infinite for a given listener." When I first read this, I immediately thought of your orchestral work *La Terre est un homme.*

• *BF:* I don't know in what context that statement was made, but, as it stands, it certainly corresponds pretty closely to my own thoughts on the matter. Of course, "complexity" is always relative to the implied position of the observer; even superficially quite simple phenomena can easily be "deconstructed" into unimaginably complex and, in detail, unpredictable flow patterns. The point about *La Terre . . .* is not that I am proposing something that, measured according to some absolute metaphysical scale, is quantitatively or qualitatively more complex than many another possible object of aesthetic appreciation, but rather that I am concerned with keeping the listener constantly *aware* of complexity as an inescapable given. In a good performance, at least, it's not possible to retreat to some globally undifferentiated impression: instead, the ear is constantly entrapped in some fine- or rough-trained strand of activity, or else engaged in the transition from one to another. That's why any given strand is highly detailed and defined according to its own internal frame of reference, as well as interlocking, on a higher level, with the activities and energies of other concurrent strands. This, together with the fact that I try not to prescribe more or less prioritized paths through the structure, would seem to correspond pretty much with the tenor of McAdams's statement.

• *JB:* In an earlier interview with Richard Toop, you recalled some very vivid dreams, and you described some parts of *La Terre . . .* that are "a very shadowy and distant reflection" of scores which you found yourself examining in those dreams. I've also had the strange experience of waking up in the morning with the solution to a musical problem fully formed in my head, handed to me, as it were, on a platter, all of which makes me wonder about the role played by time spent asleep in relation to the compositional process.

• *BF:* I wonder about it too, most often in terms of why solutions to particular problems come to me when just about to fall asleep, or at the end of a half-waking period during the night—under circumstances, that is, practically guaranteed to cause them to disappear again before I can write them down. Personally, a night's sleep seldom seems to bring me nearer the sought-after goal. On the other hand, it may be that I am simply not conscious of what is really going on. How does one tell? I have always needed much more sleep than the average person; maybe this has something to do with the pressures attached to the creative process. But these are such personal issues that I wouldn't even begin to draw general conclusions.

The most lasting effects of sleep on my composing have always been dreams—not the dreams in which actual sounds occur, but ones where I find myself leafing through a completed score. Some of these have been extremely disturbing (as when one seems to be furiously devouring a score, once lost, now found, about to be lost again); others have been lastingly encouraging, making me aware of riches within, even in "dry" periods. I've never actually set out to transcribe or recreate any of these scores *in toto*, but I've sometimes seen resemblances in areas of nuance and detail buried in otherwise quite different works long after the fact. Even allowing for the distorting effect of the suspension of the critical faculty in such situations, I find it amazing that the subconscious can come up with entire densely woven orchestral (or, in one case, orchestral and choral) scores in the space of a single brief dream. The score of mine which, I suppose, comes closest to the aesthetic of these images is *La Terre . . .* , but that took more than two years to compose.

• *JB:* I find it interesting that you have collected a voluminous quantity of "compositional reference materials" over the years. I have always ritualistically destroyed such things upon the completion of a work, perhaps as a way of purging myself. Other than creating clutter, what role does this material play in your life?

• *BF:* It's true that it does that! Certainly those materials are not there to be referred to by me in any systematic fashion. For one thing, they are in a completely unordered and slowly decaying state as the result of many moves and several accidents over the last twenty-five years, so that they have come to resemble a miniature Library of Babel, conceptually stimulating but referentially useless; for another, the specific steps that led to current positions are, for me, at best anecdotally interesting. Perhaps they represent a sort of repository of knowledge and belief, something like shell, constantly growing and equally swiftly outgrown? In any case, transmogrified documentation is part of tradition; it resembles somewhat in that respect our canon of fairy stories or folk myths. Maybe such traces are, to the individual, what prevailing communal paradigms represent to a society? In this way, rather than "creating clutter," they are there but not there, meaningful by dint of their functional absence.

When I first started composing, there were very few byproducts of this sort, or else they were not consciously preserved. It's probably only since the early seventies that rough workings have accumulated, particularly for larger works, like *Firecycle Beta* (1969–71), where layers or groups would be tested out in isolation before being inserted in the score. I've never really produced rough scores as such, owing to my habit of producing a definitive score parallel to the sketching process, so that it would be difficult, if not impossible, for someone other than myself to trace a path through the records that still exist. In any case, one should bear in mind that not all works naturally generate a lot of sketch material; there are some, too, where the level of definition of the sketches is too distant from the final result to be other than problematic as to attribution. In the case of Richard Toop's analyses I was quite surprised as to the things he came up with— things that I no longer remember doing, but am, on the basis of his evidence, prepared to admit that I really did!

Probably it is less old sketches which are sometimes of utility than old, mostly unperformed compositions. As one's style develops consistency of focus and a strong sense of direction it is inevitable that some aspects of one's initial potential wither and fall by the wayside, or at least remain fallow. Every few years I like to unearth some of those early scores and try to relocate the beginnings of paths not taken. It is always interesting and sometimes creatively enlightening. At the very least, it encourages me to view some of the efforts of present-day composition students with a healthy portion of humility!

Actually, it occurs to me now that there *is* one example of a sketch which *was* deliberately destroyed after a piece was written. At the outset of *Firecycle Beta* I composed a worked-out score page for full orchestra, complete in every detail. After acting as the quarry from which all other elements and relationships were ultimately derived, this was made inaccessible by burning. The actual page of origin was thus not incorporated as such into the final work, which in any case remained a torso not including many of the instruments which that generating page specified. Looking back on it, the deed does sometimes seem gratuitously demonstrative; on other occasions it still makes a valid statement as to the mutually consuming pyrrhic relationship between spontaneity and technical discipline.

• *JB:* The analyses by Toop which you describe above make extensive references to your sketches; however, I have yet to read an analysis of one of your works which is based only on what one hears, or what one sees in the score, without resort to sketch materials.

• *BF:* There is a problem common to most ventures of that sort, which, in the analysis course I have lately been teaching, I term "appropriateness." How does one ascertain with a reasonable degree of assurance what is a relevant way of approaching an unfamiliar work? Sometimes general stylistic attributes suffice to locate a piece and its concerns; at other times we can refer to the place the work occupies in the creative career of the composer, thus inferring something with respect to concerns and aesthetic priorities; on still other occasions the nature of the processes visibly/audibly at work permit a certain amount of legitimate extrapolative speculation.

There are also compositions, on the other hand, in which recognition and articulation of a particular problem or barrier affords an entry into a field of possible discourse in which work and reception are intertwined. I start from the assumption that "pure," value-free listening would require some sort of cultural amnesia which itself would act as a significant barrier to meaningful apprehension and reflection. Thus, one is never starting from a single fixed point, but always from a binary relation, whose poles are aural/visual stimulus and presumptive perceptual framework: the analyst just has to pick up some ball or other and run with it to see what happens. I am not by any means implying that analyses of the sort you describe are not possible; simply that they are always something in the nature of a poetic recreation whose ultimate degree of independence from its nominal object becomes itself an object of further reflective assessment.

The usefulness of the odd concrete analysis of values and operations actually employed by the composer is useful in a quite different way than one might initially assume, in that it provides a fairly stable point of departure for more informed associative flights. A "free" analytical discourse on and around a piece needs, in my view, to take account of the entire available work-process, by which I don't (necessarily) mean privileged access to the composer's workshop, but the chain from score image through various stages of the interpretational process right up until the act of reception itself. Anything less than that is not likely to be much more substantial than the averagely ephemeral newspaper review.

• *JB:* You've used the terms "object" and "process" in many different contexts. For example, I recall your contrasting your own music, and its concern with "the matter of the musical object and its processual manifestation," with that of Chris Dench, referring to his desire to create a flow of "nonobjects." Other composers, such as Stockhausen, Cage, and Steve Reich, have used "processes" in very different ways. How does your approach differ?

• *BF:* I have no axe to grind with terminology. An "object," for me, is simply a span of experience which is either sufficiently constant in itself, succeeds in defining its own outer boundaries with a reasonable degree of credibility, or balances out the conflicting demands of short-term memory and elapsed time so as to lock them into a unique perceptual frame and lend the impression of a certain "out-of-time-ness." A "process," by the same token, is a musical activity in which these levels are not coordinated in the same way, and whose complete identity is thus revealed only by accretion and degradation, whereby middle- and short-term memory are invoked to different degrees. Processes are interesting precisely because of

474

the immensely rich interplay between memory and predictive imagination they involve, but also because they extend the concept of "object" into more explicitly temporal domains. Process might even be said to be *the shadows of objects in time.*

- *BF:* The work which has recently occupied me, for violin and eight instruments, is entitled *Terrain:* it might, I suppose, be considered a distant reflection of some of Robert Smithson's "mental tectonics" imagery of the ruined inner world, even though the title is in fact taken from a poem by A. R. Ammons which also concerns itself with meditations on geological and other natural phenomena as manifested in the living world around us.
- *JB:* *Terrain's* ensemble of eight instruments is identical to that of *Octandre.* Is the work in any way a tribute to Varèse?
- *BF:* I suppose one could call it the payment of a long-standing debt. *Octandre* was always extremely important to me, for one because it was the first truly modern work I ever heard, for another because I, as a wind player, could immediately appreciate and relate to Varèse's sonic imagination in that medium. I wrote a lot of quite extended pieces for combinations of wind instruments in the very early sixties, some of whose textures are all too clearly derivative of Varèsian mannerisms, while unfortunately demonstrating little of his (in)formal acumen. So, once the idea of writing for concertante violin arose, I immediately focused on the vision of a violin/ensemble opposition towards which, apart from textural and processual distinctions, the color and weight of the *Octandre* combination would make a major contribution.

When you think about it, it's actually rather strange that this grouping never became a "standard" octet formation. It contains both a wealth of possible subensembles and an impressively cutting "bite" when employed as a single mass instrument. What proved most useful to me, actually, was the vast palette of registrally defined timbral nuances available: as well as more or less stable chordal states defined by absolute registral distribution, I was able to insert particular instruments in ways which would transform the entire perceived tessitura relationship of individual chordal components, thus allowing partial aspects of chords to be separated out and functionally distinguished by being heard as "high" or "low" irrespective of their actual registral location.

Actually, *Octandre* strikes me as being really rather relevant (again?) at the present time, for quite other reasons. Perhaps one of the few things that the brief flourishing of "postmodern" style collage has left behind has been an increased sensibilization to how the *edges* and *points of contact* of systems (in the wider sense of comportmental taxonomies) are usefully defined. It is interesting to observe young composers turning increasingly away from *collage* towards *montage* techniques, in which the formal ploys integral to certain types of stylistic and procedural homogeneity are objectified, isolated, dissected, and, ultimately, dynamically subverted by seemingly alien trajectories and rhetorical categories being extracted from them. It is perhaps one way of registering "decentered" deconstructivist formal innovation while resisting its implicitly high modernist residual vocabulary. In this sense, both *consistency* and *fracture* can be made to seem interestingly complementary, rather than simply staring resentfully at each other over an unbridgeable void.

Unlike some of the composer's later pieces, both of these principles are powerfully at work at point-blank range in *Octandre*. Just look, for instance, at how the "cut and paste" interchanges in the first movement set about demolishing the linear emphasis of the various harmonic strata so explicitly proposed in the opening measures, the way our sense of time passing skitters confusedly over the surface of that fast-but-immobile dyad at the beginning of the second movement, and the weird "time-machine" quality of the fugato which opens the last movement. None of these experiential fault lines would have functioned half as well if the harmonic framework had not been so obviously and coherently consistent in its setting up of transitional situations whose good graces are then so peremptorily overridden by extreme textural disjunction.

• *JB:* Your description of *Terrain* makes me think of *Mnemosyne*, which, to me, is a frighteningly bizarre landscape, a slowly solidifying temporal ooze. When listening to the piece, I experience a strong sense of persistent queasiness; it's as if I'm being repeatedly tossed into the air and forced to "hit the ground running," always at a different speed and angle, to continually adjust my mental frame of reference as best I can. The treatment of time in *Mnemosyne* also raises the old question of whether consciousness is merely "a spectator who experiences nothing but an 'action replay' of the whole drama." What are your feelings?

• *BF:* I see my own view of things as being more dynamic than that, with consciousness resembling more a novelist, so furiously writing the "supreme fiction" of perception that he has no time to stop and reread what he has written. It depends whether you accept the now somewhat discredited image of a little person inside your head riding herd over a flood of value-free, unordered incoming data. I reckon the process of constructing a viable (if transitory) self to be extremely conflictual and chaotic in nature, so that the sort of desperate struggle to stay afloat in the turbulent "delay wake" of listening which I envisage strikes me as a pretty adequate paradigm for the engenderment of self-awareness. If the question is suggesting that the "inner witness" makes sense of an experience after the event by replaying it in more or less unaltered form, then I cannot agree.

Composing a Viable
(if Transitory) Self

Whatever one actually experiences during a performance, the "piece" that one subsequently retains in the memory is usually a complete recomposition—edited, filtered, and reordered. That, in part, is why rehearing a composition is extremely important: you have the chance to actively map real-time and memory-time experiences onto one another. The shocking discrepancies that one sometimes encounters are further defining aspects of a notional topology of consciousness.

To get back to your comments regarding *Mnemosyne*: in a sense, the piece works as a mirror image of what I said about time flow in my music in general. It emphasizes what I term elsewhere the "tactility" of time, where one senses ruptures or unevennesses in the temporal flow almost as much a form of physical contact as the sonic events themselves. I composed the relationship between the rate of harmonic change and the density of surface figuration so as to encourage the mind to move "too fast" and, as a result, find itself constantly pulled up short by the slightly counterintuitive viscosity of information presentation. As the piece goes on, the linear dimension is progressively imprisoned, its impetus absorbed by an ever-tighter lattice of vertical reference pitches. The more insistent the presence of harmony as passive obstacle, the more the mind begins to focus in on one time in terms of momentary degrees of resistance rather than spaces within which it naturally unfolds. The more claustrophobic this situation becomes, the more temporal flow manifests itself as physical substance rather than a relational frame of reference within which materials are sequentially disposed. That's how I feel it, anyway.

- *JB:* Have you explored this approach in any other pieces?
- *BF:* Probably the first movement of my Third String Quartet (1987) would come the nearest, even though the means employed are scarcely comparable. The movement is composed of some twenty-three "types" of activity, some of which are relatively stable (such as, for instance, a particular nontransposing chord), others being much more fluid in their potential for variable realization (such as "glissando," which can be adapted to the specific needs of many contexts). The entry, duration, and density of type-superincumbence for the first two-thirds of the discourse were planned in advance, with the values being mirror-reversed for the final third. The essential difference was that not only was the order reversed, but the actual types themselves were exchanged with their opposite numbers at the other end of the chain; i.e. type 2 became type 22, type 3 was replaced by type 21, and so on.

The effect of this reversal was to thrust me into a situation where what had initially been a relatively "natural" flow of material (where the characteristics of each type had largely been reflected in their temporal extension) became a series of abrupt accommodations and stratagems, attempting to fit types into spaces and combinatorially specified roles which were often completely counterintuitive, having in no way been foreseen at the outset. I personally feel this "unease" of the materials at finding themselves in inappropriate or downright alien temporal environments quite audible and disturbing.

• *JB:* Your notion of a "viable (if transitory) self" brings to mind a comment by Antonin Artaud: "What is difficult is to find one's place and to re-establish communication with one's self." This difficulty arises each time I sit down to write music! For example, while working on the final section of my most recent work, which took some two years to complete, I found myself becoming increasingly uncertain as to who or what my "self" was, at that particular point in both "compositional" and "real" time, in relation to the "self" which began the piece. So much had changed!

• *BF:* There are many twentieth-century works which address (consciously or unconsciously) the temporality of the compositonal act as a perceptual transformation of the locus of self-awareness. The major composer who comes immediately to mind here is Bernd Alois Zimmermann. Not only did he seek to define self in almost theological terms as the zero point of intersection at the center of his "Time Sphere," in which all periods and styles are notionally reconciled; he also produced at least one work, *Die Soldaten,* in which frequent simultaneity of discrepant strands of dramatic action powerfully conspire to suggest dimensions of "temporal harmony" and "dissonance." If one listens to the entire opera one is immediately struck by the stylistic mutation that its language progressively undergoes. To me, this suggests a quite different sort of temporality, in which an entire era of compositional perception and technique passes in ever more intense and personal review—almost, on a much larger scale, like the famous Bergian "color crescendo." Apropos of such considerations, what about the impact made by the Prelude as it collides full tilt with the opening of the first scene? Since the Prelude seems to have been composed last of all, the effect of temporal reversal is like some apocalyptic time machine or centripetal mechanism attempting to thrust all those explosive energies back into the genie's bottle.

Interestingly enough, I have on occasions been forced to compose pieces *backwards*—perhaps one might speculate that the discourse's polarity had somehow been reversed?

• *JB:* How were your "forced" to compose them backwards?

• *BF:* Refining the precompositional processes involved in *Terrain,* it just happened that a useful level of definition was arrived at for the second half of the piece first. I'd sketched out the entire form (measure lengths, sectional paradigm switches, tempi and texture strategies, and so on) fairly rapidly, and it was the progressive growth of this momentum which brought supplementary ideas into play as I approached the end. So that's where I started. It was quite interesting to approach the opening violin solo from that perspective, rather than allowing everything that follows to emerge, as it were, from it. It's lucky for us that time is reversible, at least during the compositional act.

• *JB:* . . . Which brings us back to your response to my initial question, and to your tendency to eschew traditional, straightforward development in favor of "sudden leaps, fractures, or twists of focus." Why this need to, as you put it, "confuse the issue," to court the "counter-intuitive"?

• *BF:* I think I must have a pretty confused brain—or else a notably suspicious nature. Let's put it the other way round: I can see why someone might want to compose a "what you see is what you get" sort of music, in which the motivating issues involved have a very clear, immediate, and relatively stable relationship to material and operational identity. Some of it is as bracing, say, as a good crossword puzzle; some might even open the door to new perceptual vistas by virtue of its ability to tackle transformation in very small, constantly repeated steps. In the latter case, though, some sort of *anamorphosis* is almost inevitably at work—some distortion sensitizing our receptive antennae to discrepancies or fault lines in the correspondence of implied concept and realized manifestation. A lot of the later Feldman pieces typically work in this way, constantly defamiliarizing (by odd numbers of repetitions, extreme duration, or slight phase decoupling, for instance) things which have become so familiar a part of the weave as to be almost invisible. That, in itself, is a form of "twist of focus," don't you think? It's a temptation, I know, to consider the qualities you mention in your question as *attributes of a style* rather than characteristics of pretty much universal validity. It's true that my music happens to highlight insistently some of the more unstable and seemingly arbitrary facets of current compositional thinking: that necessarily follows from what happens to interest me, which is the expressive potential of ambiguous and volatile states. It would be a mistake, though, I feel, to assume that "continuity" on some level or other is not a prerequisite of my approach—no fracture or twist can be perceived *per se* unless it is a fracture or twist *of something,* at least one of whose constituent defining qualities or fundamental assumptions is understood as providing a referential constant. I make two assumptions of this sort at the very outset—firstly, that *unity and continuity of style* are necessary in order to define and unleash these structural dissonances and, secondly, that *analogical frames of reference* (categories of "seeing something *as*") are freely transferrable between articulative levels of whatever order of magnitude and formal scope. So, it's all very relative. Although I obviously see the area I'm working in as located at the center of where current sensibility is moving, in terms of how art

479

can make an active contribution to how we come to see the world as we do, I'd be the last person to suggest that foregrounding this aspect is the only strategy available. I hope not!

William Bolcom

[1938 -   ]

*Eclecticism—with its primary focus on stylistic cross-borrowing and
blurring of distinctions between "classical" and "popular," vernacular and learned, oral and written traditions—has become an important feature of new music since the late 1960s. William Bolcom, a
leader in this area of crossover art, has been blessed with an appro-
priately diverse background. His classical credentials include early
experiences as a young piano prodigy, "serious" compositional
training at the University of Washington and Mills College, and later
years of study in Paris with Darius Milhaud and Olivier Messiaen.
He has received grants from the Koussevitsky Foundation and
American Academy of Arts and Letters, Guggenheim Fellowships,
and the Pulitzer Prize for his 1988* New Etudes for Piano. *But his career also includes hands-on experience in creating works for musical theater (the shows* Dynamite Tonight *and* Greatshot, *and the set
of cabaret songs called* Black Max*), and a special fascination—as
composer and pianist—with ragtime. Bolcom and his wife, singer
Joan Morris, actively concertize and record a broad variety of parlor
songs, show tunes, Stephen Foster ballads, and Victoriana.*

*Bolcom's career is distinctive in that he has not attempted to keep
his different musical worlds separate. Every style or genre that has
moved him finds its way into his compositional palette. He has held
residencies at Yale, New York University, and the University of
Michigan.*

The following was written in 1990 and is reprinted from *Something
About the Music 2: Anthology of Critical Opinions*, edited by
Thomas P. Lewis (Pro/Am Music Resources, Inc., 1991).

481

From "Something About the Music"

To answer your question, "What does one mean by the *serious* music scene," this is, I assure you, not my own original term; in fact I hate it, as it implies that everyone not in it is not serious—popism, I suppose; it's almost racist. No, the term has a long history in the music business and is used by publisher, record company, concert agency, and opera house alike; "serious" refers to Bach, Beethoven, Brahms, the whole canon built around the opera, concert, and symphony institutions, modern music written for such forces. The real reason, in fact, why new music written for orchestra or concert or opera has not made an inroad with the general public is that people do not go to concerts in the percentage (nor to movies or theater or galleries) that they once did in the big cities exclusively (movies made it out to the hinterlands but not the others nearly so much), but watch TV mostly; so how are they supposed to tell Tower from Torke, Albright from Amram, if they haven't heard the concert or happened to listen to the piece on some college station or [New York's] WNYC or the like (which already means a committed listener to Art)?

Your other question: "shouldn't 'classical, serious' composers learn from the 'opposition' " is one my whole life has addressed. I feel claustrophobic about the limitation in audience and impact in the world my music perforce has because I write for the orchestra. I also rankle at the fact that the orchestra has not evolved to include the technological extensions and the incorporation of new instruments and instrumentalists on a constant basis, as it did in the past until the First World War (with the exception of the percussion section). This freezes it in time; the modern symphony orchestra is a Collegium Musicum designed for Tchaikovsky through Mahler as the central repertory. In my *Songs of Innocence and of Experience* I expanded the orchestra to include saxophones, many diverse percussion instruments, electrified violins, electric piano, guitar and bass; and hired people experienced in the styles of these instruments as they have developed. In Stuttgart it was funny to see the lifestyle collision of the opera-orchestra middle-aged portly German players and the young, badly-dressed louts brought in for the sax, electric guitar and electric bass parts! We put up a partition-board between the rockers and the strings, who couldn't restrain their vinegar-faces when the youngsters played. But it's just this kind of collision that delights me.

Blake said, "Damn braces! Bless relaxes," which can be read two ways, both true, if you gerundify every other word each time. It is one of the central koans of my life. The schism between pop and serious, or vernacular and aristocratic (just as bad) music, is so deep that neither side benefits from the other. Both industries are distinct; one is for profit, the other resolutely "non-profit," and their mutual dislike is always under the surface. Those like me who chafe at having to be in one camp or the other exclusively know how each side of the chasm has suffered. So I damn the brace that holds me from most of the audience; I deplore the sinking level of education most people here suffer under, and I realize that this limits the possible subtlety of musical language one could use if the desire is immediate consumption (which should be possible to any artist when the idea behind a work calls for this immediacy). Also, I bless the relax of watertight concepts in new music; I am delighted to see young composers frankly acknowledge and embrace their rock heritage (if such be the case), rather than try to suppress or deny it, as they did fifteen years ago. In the end, the only people who will transform our outmoded musical institutions (and that INCLUDES the dog-eat-dog hard-nosed criminal superstructure of the pop business in all its forms; Steely Dan once said about the pop-record business executives, "Some of these guys ought to be washing cars") will be the creative artists themselves, who will demand changes according to their strong and irresistible vision, whatever that may become.

I have often been berated for not being "original." I am said to possess no style of my own. In that I have not patented a type of interval treatment or poured the same stylistic brown sauce on all of my pieces, I plead guilty. But I do have faith in my total style; I am in love with the many genres of music and have learned that it is important to respect the genre you are contributing to if you want its expressive potential in your music. My use of it transforms the style into "something of mine," and there a careful musicological reading will find similar chicken-tracks musically in everything I've done. A similar case is the *oeuvre* of Kurt Weill; no matter whether for German, French, or English, or American audiences, he respected the style of each; it is now, forty years after his death, that we can begin to appreciate the similarities as well as the differences in each of his works in various styles (including the early Busoniesque avant-garde period). We now recognize any Picasso for a Picasso. I seem to belong to this genre (if not necessarily the quality—that is a matter of opinion), of the kind of inclusive artist that strives, as Blake did, for Exactitude.

My other reason for using so many genres of music is that I am fascinated with their interrelationships. At first shocking, a juxtaposition makes better sense with repeated hearings—if it is the right juxtaposition; not all will bear fruit. Over time I have learned to make juxtapositions smoother if

**William
Bolcom**

I like; in some way this depends on sensing that your recipient, the audience, has come to agree, because then the musical language is expanded, more can be expressed. (But some juxtapositions should keep their shock value; I still feel a shiver when the B-flat section of the last movement of Beethoven's Ninth comes on, and not all of that is pleasant, but I'm glad it's there.)

Other titles of interest

ALL AMERICAN MUSIC
Composition in the Late
Twentieth Century
John Rockwell
New preface by the author
294 pp.
80750-5 $14.95

CHARLES IVES REMEMBERED
An Oral History
Vivian Perlis
256 pp., 80 illus.
80576-6 $13.95

THE COMPANION TO
20th-CENTURY MUSIC
Norman Lebrecht
440 pp., 151 illus.
80734-3 $16.95

THE COMPLETE OPERAS OF
RICHARD STRAUSS
Charles Osborne
248 pp., 19 illus.
80459-X $13.95

THE DA CAPO CATALOG OF
CLASSICAL MUSIC
COMPOSITIONS
Jerzy Chwialkowski
1,412 pp.
80701-7   paperback $29.50
79666-X   hardcover $85.00

THE DA CAPO OPERA
MANUAL
Nicholas Ivor Martin
752 pp.
80807-2 $24.50

GENESIS OF A MUSIC
Harry Partch
517 pp., 40 photos, 28 diagrams
80106-X $17.95

IMPROVISATION
Its Nature and Practice in Music
Derek Bailey
172 pp., 12 photos
80528-6 $13.95

JOHN CAGE
An Anthology
Edited by Richard Kostelanetz
237 pp., 64 illus.
80435-2 $14.95

MUSIC BY PHILIP GLASS
Updated Edition
Philip Glass
Edited by Robert T. Jones
264 pp., 50 photos
80636-3 $13.95

NO COMMERCIAL POTENTIAL
The Saga of Frank Zappa
Updated Edition
David Walley
240 pp., 28 photos
80710-6 $13.95

THE PARIS DIARY &
THE NEW YORK DIARY,
1951–1961
Ned Rorem
New introduction by
Richard Howard
Preface to *The Paris Diary* by
Robert Phelps
431 pp., 29 illus.
80838-2 $16.95

Available at your bookstore

OR ORDER DIRECTLY FROM

DA CAPO PRESS

1-800-321-0050